Sales & Marketing
Resumes FOR
$100,000
CAREERS

Third Edition

Louise M. Kursmark

jist Works

America's Career Publisher®

Sales and Marketing Resumes for $100,000 Careers, Third Edition

© 2009 by Louise M. Kursmark

Published by JIST Works, an imprint of JIST Publishing
7321 Shadeland Station, Suite 200
Indianapolis, IN 46256
Phone: 800-648-JIST   Fax: 877-454-7839   E-mail: info@jist.com

Visit our Web site at **www.jist.com** for information on JIST, free job search tips, tables of contents, sample pages, and ordering instructions for our many products!

Quantity discounts are available for JIST books. Please call our Sales Department at 800-648-5478 or visit www.jist.com for a free catalog and more information.

Trade Product Manager: Lori Cates Hand
Interior Design: Aleata Halbig and Toi Davis
Page Layout: Toi Davis
Cover Design: Toi Davis
Proofreaders: Paula Lowell and Jeanne Clark
Indexer: Jeanne Clark

Printed in the United States of America
14 13 12 11 10 09   9 8 7 6 5 4 3 2 1

Library of Congress Cataloging-in-Publication Data

Kursmark, Louise.
  Sales and marketing resumes for $100,000 careers / Louise M. Kursmark. -- 3rd ed.
      p. cm.
  Includes index.
  ISBN 978-1-59357-669-1 (alk. paper)
 1. Résumés (Employment) 2. Sales personnel. 3. Marketing. I. Title.
  HF5383.K87 2009
  650.14'2--dc22
                              2009012619

ISBN: 978-1-59357-669-1

Contents

Introduction

Harold Hill. Willy Loman. The serpent in the Garden of Eden. The proverbial traveling salesman.

Through the ages, in folklore and fiction, salespeople have been viewed as fast-talking hucksters, sad-sack losers, evil incarnate, and philandering rogues. Thankfully, that perception has changed. Sales and marketing professionals are respected as serious professionals whose talents are fundamental to business growth and success.

If this describes you—if you are an accomplished sales, marketing, or business development professional who has made a positive difference for your customers and your organization—you might be eager to test the job search waters for an advanced or more lucrative position. Perhaps you've lost your job, been affected by corporate downsizing, seen your company merge with or be acquired by another, or desire a physical move because of personal circumstances.

For whatever reason, you've decided to write your resume and look for another job. And because you're reading this book, we can assume that you are or want to be among the best-compensated people in the country.

A career in sales offers you the unique opportunity to directly influence your own compensation through commissions and performance bonuses. Unlike many careers that require years of progressive experience to qualify for positions paying $100,000 or more, the nature of sales makes it quite feasible for an independent producer, in the right industry at the right time and with the right professional skills, to achieve this lofty income goal.

Premier salespeople, then, can earn six-figure incomes. So, too, can managers and executives in marketing, product management, marketing communications, and sales. But please don't assume that six-figure sales and marketing jobs are as common as ants at a picnic. If you currently hold such a position, you know what you did to get there and how hard you work. If you aspire to that level, be prepared to face some tough competition. To find the best jobs, you will have to mount a highly effective campaign to reach your goal. Your resume will be one of the weapons in your arsenal.

Although your resume is essential for your job search, it cannot in and of itself land you a job. What it *can* do is inspire interest, generate interviews, help structure those interviews, provide rationale for a hiring decision, and serve as an icebreaker in a variety of networking situations.

How does a resume for a $100,000 (or higher) position differ from one used for an entry-level or beginning management position? In both cases, the emphasis should be on demonstrating your potential value to an organization. The more experienced you are, the more material you have to work with, and the more detail you should include about your contributions in each of your positions. Senior-level sales and marketing people who pare down their experience in a well-intentioned effort to keep the resume to one page are making a serious mistake. At higher levels, everyone who will be reading your resume (such as executive recruiters, a company's top management, human resources recruiters, and so on) will want to know more about you—not only your success stories and the numbers that support your claims (although those are essential), but deeper insight into your management style, problem-solving approach, leadership skills, and ability to articulate and communicate a vision for the organization. A longer, more detailed, more thoughtful, and more strategy-focused resume will set you apart from the competition.

About This Book

This book is devoted to teaching and showing you how to create a powerful resume to help you achieve that six-figure sales or marketing position.

◆ **Part 1: Writing Your $100,000 Resume.** Part 1 gets right down to business, with three chapters devoted to creating your career target statement and then writing and polishing your resume.

◆ **Part 2: Sales and Marketing Resumes and Cover Letters.** Part 2 includes eight chapters of sample resumes, divided by function and level within the field of sales and marketing. As you read through these, it's a good idea to review resumes outside your own specific niche. Many resumes showcase careers that combine functions or that have crossed over from one function to another. The final chapter in part 2 includes a handful of cover letters, cross-referenced with the resumes they were written for, to give you a head start on this important companion to your resume.

◆ **Part 3: Job Search Strategies for Sales and Marketing Professionals.** When your resume is complete, you're ready to tackle part 3: putting your resume to work in your job search. In chapter 13, you will learn how to use your sales and marketing skills to advance your career. Chapter 14 discusses opinions and recommendations from recruiters and hiring managers, while Chapter 15 addresses organizational strategies to keep your search focused and on track.

The advice, suggestions, rationale, and recommendations in this book have been gleaned from my many years of experience as a resume writer and career coach. They are reinforced by the collected wisdom of other resume and career professionals and key insights from recruiters, human resource professionals, and hiring managers. The hundreds of sample resumes and cover letters in this book were written for real job seekers with quirky pasts and a wide range of sales and marketing accomplishments. (Of course, these samples have been fictionalized to protect clients' confidentiality.) The strategies, styles, language, career histories, and accomplishments included in the resumes helped these diverse job seekers achieve their goals. And they can help *you* reach new career heights.

Let's get started.

Writing Your $100,000 Resume

A resume is a complex document. It must convey a great deal of information in a concise format. The words you use, how you organize your material, and how you design and format the document can all have a tremendous impact (good or bad) on the effectiveness of your resume and thus your job search.

Part 1 walks you through the preparation and then the actual writing and design of your resume. By preplanning and taking a strategic approach, you won't be putting down words at random; each will have a reason and a purpose for appearing on the page. All aspects of your resume will work together to paint just the right picture of who you are and how you want to be perceived at this point in your career.

Chapter 1

Get Ready to Write Your Resume

Did you hear the one about the self-centered tenor? When warming up, all he sang was "mi, mi, mi, mi, mi."

As a job seeker marketing your talents to a variety of "buyers" (recruiters, human resources professionals, hiring managers, and so on), your mission is to appeal to the "me, me, me" of each of these audiences. Each has different, specific needs, yet all are consumed by one burning question: *What can you do for me?* Your resume is the first step in demonstrating that you offer solutions to their problems.

Of course, you have your own "me, me, me" agenda: your personal and career goals, needs, and preferences. Although these should be firmly fixed in your mind so that you make good career choices, you will not get a new position because of your needs and wants, but rather because of what you can bring to the organization. At the highest executive levels, in strategy development roles, in positions that require you to manage large numbers of people or a company's entire sales and marketing operation, the employer's needs are significant and the stakes are high. You will appeal to potential buyers if you focus on their needs rather than your own.

This chapter discusses my foundational philosophy of resumes. Then I help you get started by developing the cornerstone of your effective career strategy: the career target statement.

Three Absolutes for a Powerful Resume

You can (and probably will) read all kinds of advice about preferred page length, desirable font size, format, style, white space, organization, and structure with regard to resumes. I'll be sharing my own opinions on all these topics in the following chapters. But in preparing your resume, most of the decisions you'll make are subjective; they can be argued either way, with no answer being absolutely wrong or right. How, then, do you know what to do? To reduce resume writing to its essential core, I've developed three rules that, if you follow them, will yield a resume that captures the interest of employers because it respects their jobs as hiring authorities and responds to their business needs.

1. **Be clear and focused.** Don't leave readers wondering about the kind or level of position you're interested in. Instead of taking time to figure it out, or to speculate where your skills might be used within their organization, busy hiring authorities will quickly consign your resume to the trash. Don't muddy the waters with unrelated, irrelevant information or write your resume so generally and broadly that the reader is puzzled as to your professional interests. Make sure your skills, expertise, and potential are crystal clear and sharply focused.

2. **Be correct.** Carelessness can cost you a job offer—or a job. Make absolutely certain that all the facts in your resume are correct: dates of employment, contact information, company names, numbers, and results. An obvious error will send your resume immediately to the scrap heap; lies or distortions discovered during a reference check or even after hiring will cause you to lose the job.

3. **Prove it.** In a survey I took among my sales and marketing clients while writing this book, the factor they felt was *most instrumental* to their ability to generate interviews was the inclusion of *measurable accomplishments and sales results* in their resumes. This experience is borne out by the opinions of recruiters, human resources professionals, and hiring managers (details of this survey appear in chapter 14). When writing your resume, don't make unsubstantiated claims of greatness; back up your statements with evidence in the form of measurable, verifiable results that you've achieved for past employers.

With these three "absolutes" in mind, let's discuss how to get started on preparing your resume.

THE RESUME AS A SALES TOOL

Because you're in sales and marketing, you can appreciate the analogy of the resume as a marketing document designed to promote your features and benefits to potential buyers. The resume is not a fact sheet, owner's manual, prospectus, specification, or other dry compilation of vital statistics. Most sales professionals don't expect to generate much business just from sending out brochures; they realize that marketing materials might pique their prospects' interest, but you have to follow up written materials with a sales call. Similarly, on its own a resume cannot land you a new position; rather, it is designed to generate interviews, which are opportunities for you to sell your "product"—yourself—in person.

Part 3 explores putting your resume to work and using your sales skills to advance your career. Right now, let's focus on creating a resume that interests readers by appealing to their underlying motive: how you can help them.

The Basics

Your resume should be word-processed and printed on high-quality paper using a crisp laser or inkjet printer. Of course, you'll be transmitting many—if not most—of your resumes electronically, by e-mail or online application. In chapter 3 you'll find a complete discussion of how to adapt your resume for these purposes. But for now I'll talk about the traditional printed document that—despite the pervasive influence of the Internet and e-mail—remains an essential tool in your job search.

The appearance of your resume must be first-class. Careless or unprofessional word processing and formatting will be strike one against your candidacy. Remember, though, you're a sales professional, not a page designer. Compare your resume against the examples in this book, and don't be afraid to seek help if you need it. You can work with a professional resume writer, who can help you craft not only the appearance but the message and the overall strategy and structure of your resume. Another option is to engage a page designer, desktop publisher, virtual assistant, or secretarial service to dress up your draft into a sharp-looking presentation.

Whatever method you choose, you want to end up with a great-looking resume available to you in a Microsoft Word (.doc) file that you can print and e-mail.

Gather Your Resource Materials

Before beginning your resume, spend a little time organizing your work space and gathering the appropriate resource materials. Create "job search central," a spot where you can keep all your job search materials well-organized and at hand. Throughout your search you'll generate copious notes, copies of correspondence, job postings, news articles, and other related materials. You need a filing and organizing system that allows you to put your hands on the appropriate document at a moment's notice. For instance, when you receive a phone call in response to a letter you've sent, you'll sound professional and competent if you can immediately access the correspondence and speak intelligently to the circumstances of the position.

You should gather several resource materials before you start writing your resume. First, find copies of old versions of your resume. You might be surprised at the details included there that are relevant to your current search but that you might have forgotten over the passage of time. These older resumes will also help you recall details such as specific dates of employment, education, seminars attended, and so forth. Next, try to obtain copies of recent performance evaluations. These can be an excellent source for your specific achievements, particularly those that were noted by upper management and recognized as valuable to the organization.

Chapter 15 discusses creating a career portfolio to aid in future job searches. If you've been proactive in developing a file of materials that document your achievements, now's the time to pull it out and put its contents to work. Complimentary letters from supervisors, clients, coworkers, or other professional contacts are other good resources to gather and peruse before beginning to write your resume.

Allow Enough Time to Write Your Resume

You may be able to create your resume in a day or an afternoon, or you might devote several days to this task. It's important that you allow enough time for the process, beginning with serious introspection into your career goals; then writing, editing, and formatting; and finally sharing your draft with a few trusted people before you launch your search. (Details about all the steps in this process are covered in chapters 2 and 3.) Don't shortchange yourself by rushing through the resume-preparation task just to get something out there. Take the time to do it thoroughly, and you'll have a valuable document that will make every subsequent stage of your job search more positive and productive.

As a measure of comparison, it takes me an average of three to four hours to create a resume for a midlevel professional with 15 to 20 years of experience. For a senior executive, I spend an additional one to three hours. What's included in this time? Typically, I spend an hour consulting with my client; two to four hours planning, positioning, writing, editing, and formatting the resume; and an hour reviewing the document with my client and finalizing the print and electronic versions. As an experienced resume writer, I know the questions to ask, the types of accomplishments that will be meaningful, effective positioning strategies, and other information you might have to give more thought. I'm also a whiz at word processing and can zip through complex resume formatting that may cause you headaches and aggravation. Quite simply, to produce a high-quality resume, it's not possible to speed through the process on autopilot. Consider the time spent as an investment in your future. I'm certain it will pay off in a more effective job search.

Create a Career Target Statement

Remember the first absolute of resume writing: Be clear and focused. Before you plunge into writing your resume, take the time to develop a specific career target statement. Preparing this kind of statement helps you clarify the job elements that are most important to you and provides a central emphasis for your resume development and job search. Write it on a clean sheet of paper or in a separate word-processing document.

Here are two examples of career target statements:

I'm looking for a business-to-business sales position that involves a lot of consultative sales and gives me the opportunity to build relationships with my customers. I don't want a quick in-and-out sales job where I'm only worried about making quota this week. Ideally I'd like to sell to small, emerging companies so that I can grow with them. For stability, I'd also like to have a few solid Fortune 500–type accounts, and I prefer to have a defined geographic territory that involves limited overnight travel. Starting the job with an established account base would be nice, but I'm willing to prospect, provided that some leads are generated through the company's telemarketing and trade-show activities. I can sell both products and services and would prefer a fairly large product/service line so that I'm not limited to one solution for customer problems—I can look at their entire situation and recommend a variety of solutions to fit their needs and budget. I can work well independently, but ideally I'd like a manager who is a mentor and who helps me continuously improve my professional skills. A commission structure that rewards me for overachieving my established goals would be a great incentive. I'm highly motivated to earn a six-figure income, so I don't want my commissions to be capped.

I'm ready for a change. I've loved working for Key Products and have gained great experience in product management and marketing. But I'd like to work for a company that is smaller, nimbler, and growing more aggressively so that I can do more than recommend marketing strategies—I can put them into action and see the results. I'm creative and intuitive, and I want to be involved in every stage of marketing, from strategy development to implementation and assessment. Because I have both a traditional marketing background and experience in e-commerce initiatives, I'd be attractive to a technology company or any company that wants to beef up its website presence and sales performance. I've been well-groomed, and I'm ready to move up to a marketing leadership position. Ideally, I'd like to return to Boston or at least New England to be closer to my family and college friends.

Notice that these statements are not narrowly focused. They cover a variety of job circumstances and create a clear picture of the environment that is ideal for each of these candidates at this point in their careers.

As you prepare your own career target statement, give serious thought to what is most important to you in your next job to satisfy both personal and professional desires. The preferences you develop will be uniquely yours and will help you make good decisions about job offers you'll receive. For instance, if you and your spouse agree that it's a priority to remain close to extended family members in Cleveland, you should not accept a job offer in San Antonio, no matter how attractive it is. But it's unlikely that you'll find a job that matches every preference to a "t." You'll have to weigh all the factors to see which opportunity, in balance, best suits your needs. An acceptable compromise for you might be a position in Toledo or Detroit that will keep grandparents within reasonable driving distance.

Some or all of the following factors may be important to consider as you develop your picture of an ideal next position:

◆ Geographic location *Mpls / St Paul + Surrounding area*

◆ Distance from the airport *Not applicable*

◆ Proximity to family *Not applicable*

◆ Commute *No greater than 45 mins*

◆ Salary, commissions, bonuses, stock options
$150K Base + 5% commission + business + pension

◆ Benefits: health insurance, retirement plans, perks
health care must + 401K must

◆ Opportunity for advancement
Yes VP level

◆ Corporate environment (buttoned-down or freewheeling)
Buttoned |———————X——| Freewheeling

◆ Company growth plans
Growth plan established

◆ Corporate attitude toward change and innovation

Desires validated change, not to change to change. Innovation a must

◆ Senior management style

w/learning. mentoring, open. leadership by example

◆ Perceived compatibility with your management style

◆ Autonomy/schedule flexibility

Results driven with reasonable hour expectations

◆ Sales support

Catch'em you clean & fry. Mentor position

◆ Performance expectations

results expectations. Non-emotional performance opinions

◆ Opportunity to influence company plans, marketing initiatives, sales direction, and so on *High desire to have suggestion ability and influence*

◆ Company products or services

Products. Innovative & artistic

◆ Company size, reputation, industry

75+ million annual revenue. 150+ employees. Dependable reputation

◆ Opportunity for new challenges and learning

must. for promotion and new areas of learning

◆ Familiar environment offering chance for immediate contribution

Necessary

◆ Corporate policy on family leave, family activities, and priorities

2 weeks vacation. maternity leave

◆ Work demands (35 hours a week or 75?)

40-45/week

◆ Travel demands (how far and how often?)

2x/month domestic max. 4x/year international

◆ Advancement from your present position

VP level

◆ Education and training opportunities

◆ Responsibility to manage people (how many? too many?)

5 min & 10 max

◆ Compensation tied to performance; incentives

Commission/Bonus + attached

DO IT NOW: Write your career target statement.

Develop your own unique target statement, and keep it nearby as you work on the rest of your resume. You'll refer to it throughout the process to make sure you are creating a resume that will help you reach your goal.

Now, move forward to chapter 2 and start working on your resume.

Create a Powerful Resume

You've done the preparatory work. Armed with your career target statement and aware of employers' needs and concerns, you know where you're headed. Now it's time to jump into writing the resume that will help you reach that destination.

Resume information can be divided into five major sections:

◆ Contact information

◆ Objective and/or summary, profile, or qualifications brief

◆ Experience and accomplishments

◆ Education

◆ Miscellaneous additional information

The following sections discuss each piece of the resume puzzle in detail and guide you through the process of building your resume step by step.

Write Your Contact Information

Start at the top, with your name and contact information. Considering the vast range of communications methods used today, there is quite a bit of information that you might include. The goal is to provide quick, easy, and foolproof ways for potential employers to contact you.

Name

Your name should be prominent—although not so large that it distracts from the rest of the resume. Most business professionals use their full names (Kathryn T. Cox, not Kathi Cox), but if you are more comfortable with a nickname, feel free to use it—as long as it doesn't diminish the professional impression you want to convey.

If your name does not reveal your gender, consider using a small parenthetical after your name to give the reader a clue:

Lynn A. Webster (Mr.)

And if you have a foreign first name that appears difficult to pronounce, consider adding a friendlier nickname:

Genc "Jimmy" Gjerlani

Potential employers might feel uncomfortable calling you if they don't know whether you're a man or a woman or how to ask for you by name. And because the whole purpose of the job seeking exercise is to get people to call you, do what you can to make it easy for them.

Address and Phone Number

You should include a home address (a street address, not a post-office box number) and telephone number. And before you send out so much as one resume, be certain that your home telephone is answered with a brief, professional-sounding voice-mail or answering-machine message. (You can put the kids, dogs, and music back on after you land the job.) If you have children at home, consider spending a few dollars a month for a "distinctive-ring" service, available in most areas of the country from your telephone company. This service provides a separate telephone number connected through your home number. Reserve this number for your job search. Use it on your resume and all job search correspondence, and instruct family members not to answer the distinctive-ring calls.

Perhaps the easiest way around the phone dilemma is to use your mobile phone number as the primary or the only contact number you provide. Be certain you have voice mail. During your job search, be cautious about answering the phone if you're in a setting that's inappropriate for a business discussion (such as a crowded, noisy bar).

Include your work telephone number only if this is the sole means people can use to reach you during business hours, and only if you can take calls discreetly. You want to be careful about giving the appearance of spending vast chunks of your employer's time on a job search. It is not necessary to include a fax number.

E-mail

An e-mail address is a job search essential. One recruiter I surveyed for this book told me, "If a candidate does not have an e-mail address on the resume, we discard it." That seems extreme, but it points out the need for job seekers to be up-to-date with technology.

Be certain your e-mail address is professional. The best solution is to use your name:

JessicaSmith@gmail.com

adams.jim@aol.com

Not only is it professional, it helps recipients identify who the e-mail is from and, later, find your message in their list of past e-mails. Do not use your employer's e-mail address for your job search; this creates the impression that you will use your future employer's resources for your own benefit. And if you leave your job, you will immediately lose access to past and future e-mail messages.

Arranging Your Contact Information

Once you've compiled the necessary contact information, consider a variety of ways to arrange it for maximum impact. Here are seven examples. Also note that the resume samples in this book include an assortment of data points with varied arrangements. Be sure that this data does not overwhelm the resume but still makes it as easy as possible for potential employers to reach you.

David T. Callaway

7529 Pine Grove Road
Cincinnati, Ohio 45242

513-721-1212
dcallaway@gmail.com

David Callaway

7529 Pine Grove Road, Cincinnati, OH 45242
Home 513-721-1212   Mobile 513-300-1212
dcallaway@gmail.com

David T. Callaway

7529 Pine Grove Road, Cincinnati, Ohio 45242 ● dcallaway@gmail.com
Home 513-721-1212 ● Cell 513-300-1212

DAVID CALLAWAY

dcallaway@gmail.com

513-300-1212
7529 Pine Grove Road, Cincinnati, OH 45242

DAVID CALLAWAY

7529 Pine Grove Road, Cincinnati, OH 45242 — 513-721-1212
dcallaway@gmail.com — 24-hour Voice Mail 513-300-1212

DAVID T. CALLAWAY

7529 Pine Grove Road, Cincinnati, Ohio 45242
Home 513-721-1212   dcallaway@gmail.com   Cell 513-300-1212

David T. Callaway

7529 Pine Grove Road
Cincinnati, Ohio 45242
Home 513-721-1212
Cell 513-300-1212
dcallaway@gmail.com

DO IT NOW: Start writing your resume.

OK, it's time to get started. Begin your resume by creating a new document in your word-processing program and assigning a distinguishing name such as "Barb Smith Resume" or "KELLY Tim resume." (It's very important to use a descriptive filename when you e-mail your resume to companies, recruiters, and network contacts. You want them to know immediately what the file is.) Good margins to begin with are .75 inch top and bottom, 1 inch left and right. You can adjust these later if necessary. Don't worry about fonts or formatting at this point. In fact, don't spend any time trying to make your initial draft look right. First you'll work on writing the resume; then in chapter 3 you'll create a format to complement the content.

If you're writing your first draft by hand, start with a clean, crisp, lined pad. Use a pencil or be prepared to rewrite numerous times before your draft is complete.

What about using the resume templates that are available in some word-processing programs? These aids can help you produce a nice-looking resume, but their structure might be limiting, and trying to adjust the layout can be a frustrating experience. I suggest that you write your resume first in a plain, nontemplate document, and then copy and paste the text into the template if the format fits your content.

Start by writing your name and contact information at the top. Model your format on one of the suggestions here or elsewhere in the book that you find attractive. Put the data roughly in place; but again, don't worry about making this section appear perfect right now. Write it down, and then move on to the body of the resume.

Consider an Objective Statement

If you are in the position of reviewing resumes as a hiring manager, or if you perused several resume books before choosing this one, you are probably aware that objectives on modern resumes are like bank tellers in an age of ATMs: rare and a bit old-fashioned, yet sometimes helpful and even essential when your needs are more complex than a simple cash withdrawal. An objective statement that communicates your areas of expertise and experience level can indeed be helpful. An objective is particularly useful for individuals transitioning from one function or industry to another. (See resumes 11-1, 11-4, and 11-5.)

Using an objective has two main drawbacks. First, to be at all effective, an objective must be quite specific—and therefore narrow and limiting. Most job seekers are open to a variety of positions within their professional areas of interest. Listing a "product manager" objective may eliminate you from consideration for a marketing manager opening. Unless you want to tailor each resume to the specific job you're applying for, it's more beneficial not to use an objective.

Even more importantly, an objective is a very straightforward statement of what you want. There's nothing wrong with that—except that it doesn't respond to the most important concern of every hiring authority: *What can you do for me?* It's usually more beneficial, and certainly more employer-oriented, to use a summary, profile, qualifications brief, or other introductory material in place of an objective.

If you use an objective, make sure it communicates vital information and does not merely take up space on the page.

Here's an example of a wasted-space objective:

OBJECTIVE: *A challenging position in sales management that will capitalize on my proven skills and experience while offering opportunities for professional growth and advancement.*

Think about it—no one wants (or will admit they want) a dull position with the opportunity to tread water professionally. If you feel compelled to use an objective, be certain you *say something important*—something that will make readers want to learn more about your background and potential to help their organization. For instance:

OBJECTIVE: *Sales management position in the financial services industry in which my track record of leading sales teams to record performance levels can help an organization penetrate new markets.*

Before deciding whether to write an objective, review the next section, which discusses the use of a summary, profile, or qualifications brief.

Write a Summary, Profile, or Qualifications Brief

The career target statement you prepared in chapter 1 helped you develop a sharp picture of your ideal position. The next step is to show potential employers that you're qualified for it.

Leading off your resume with a summary or other central "positioning" statement allows you to sell the totality of your experience and skills—who you are and what you have to offer. Be as concise as you can, yet don't be afraid to sell yourself. You want to capture the reader's interest and entice him or her to read on—to discover more about you, absorb your experience and accomplishments, and get excited about your potential.

In advertising parlance, the profile is the "sizzle"; the experience and accomplishments are the "steak." Neither is complete without the other, and they must be complementary, or readers will be confused. (Imagine smelling steak and biting into a strawberry.)

The profile should support your career target; yet, unlike an objective, it should identify with the employer's needs *(here's what I can do for you)* rather than your wants. And it's very important that the profile communicate your professional focus. Anyone reading your profile should be able to say, immediately, "A-ha, a salesperson." "Oh, a marketing manager." "Hmmm… good background in product management." "Looks like a good candidate for our VP of Business Development position."

The summary or profile is comparable to a chapter summary in a textbook. In just a few brief paragraphs, the summary tells you the highlights of what you will read in that chapter. You don't get in-depth information, but you gain a general sense of the most important messages that are conveyed in the chapter. Similarly, your profile should reveal the most important information about you to the reader, who can capture that information in a 10-second read-through of the summary.

Here's how our marketing professional, whose career target is the second one presented in chapter 1 (see page 7), wrote a profile that appeals to employers' needs while also positioning her to reach her career goal. (This resume in its entirety is sample 7-3.)

MARKETING / MANAGEMENT PROFESSIONAL

Driving volume and share increases, expense reductions, customer satisfaction, and operational efficiency.

Innovative and intuitive marketing talent with proven leadership skills and a strong blend of expertise in classical marketing and new channels (electronic commerce, Internet / extranet marketing, global business integration). Effective manager and project leader skilled at developing collaborative working relationships with internal and customer teams. Record of leadership in sales force and marketing automation, sales, and strategic business planning.

Eager for new challenges in a dynamic business environment.

Nearly all the resumes in chapters 4 through 11 include a summary, profile, or qualifications brief. Skim through these to review a variety of approaches and to get a feel for how very different they can be, even for individuals in the same general profession of sales and marketing.

You'll note that these sections are long on specific, verifiable skills ("expertise in classical marketing," "history of establishing strong customer relationships," "proven ability to build market presence") and short on "fluff"—hyperbole, exaggerated claims of greatness, and adjectives that describe but don't measure. No matter how "excellent," "extraordinary," "dynamic," or "superb" you might be, you can communicate this more effectively through deeds (accomplishments) than superlatives.

Focusing on the facts doesn't mean your summary should be devoid of personality. In fact, including a personal branding statement or incorporating your personal brand attributes into the summary is great way to make your resume stand out.

A personal brand is defined as your "unique promise of value" and helps employers understand how you do what you do so well. You might position your branding statement below the headline or as the final element of your summary. You will find branding statements included in a number of the resumes in this book. To put together the information for your summary, refer to your career target statement and identify the primary qualifications for the position you want; then mine your background for evidence of your abilities in these key areas. Be prepared to back up any claims you make with solid, detailed evidence further down in the resume.

A Word About Keywords

Keywords are terms used to describe the essential attributes needed to perform a specific job. Including the right keywords in your resume is the only way your resume will be matched by a computer doing a keyword search, and in this day of electronic databases and applicant-tracking systems, keywords are very important.

There are no standard keywords; they differ from company to company, position to position, hiring manager to hiring manager. How, then, do you find the keywords that are right for your resume? Start by using your knowledge of the position, your profession, and the industry. Review online postings and want ads for comparable positions, and make a list of the terms that crop up most often. Imagine yourself as the hiring manager, and use your career target statement to create a list of primary qualifications.

Then, be certain you use these terms in your resume. There is no benefit to creating a separate keyword summary section on your resume (these words located anywhere in the resume will yield a match). Many of the resumes in chapters 4 through 11 include keywords in the summary, often in a multicolumn list format. Appropriate keywords are also used liberally throughout job descriptions and accomplishment statements.

DO IT NOW: Create your profile, summary, or qualifications brief.

Review sample formats and write the introduction to your resume: a profile, summary, or qualifications brief (and/or an objective if you choose to use one).

This is often the most difficult section of the resume to write, because it requires you to synthesize a lot of information, whittle it to its essential core, write concisely yet powerfully, and combine disparate elements into a cohesive style and format. If you're stuck, try using the profile section as a temporary holding place to store your jumbled thoughts and notes about your key strengths and career highlights. Every time you think of something that might go into the summary, toss it into that section as you continue to work on the rest of the resume. Then, when you return to the profile section after having written the rest of the resume, you'll have draft information to work with and can write a focused, powerful profile that clearly reflects your experience and accomplishments.

When you're done with the summary, carefully review it for three essential points:

1. Will the reader clearly understand the kind and level of job you're seeking?

2. Is the profile in tune with your career target?

3. Are all your success statements and attributes supported by specific accomplishments elsewhere in the resume?

(continued)

(continued)

Be certain that your sentence structure is parallel. If you include a bulleted list of qualifications, for instance, don't mix "Documented history of sales achievements" with "Leading teams to record performance" and "Expert communicator." Instead, be consistent in style: "Documented history of sales achievements"; "Record of leading top-performing teams"; "Expert communication skills."

Finally, ask yourself whether the profile presents a clear, accurate, and attractive picture of you and your professional strengths. Is it you, in a nutshell?

Describe Your Experience and Accomplishments

Now you've reached the "steak" of the resume: your specific work experience and what you did in each of those jobs.

Choose a Format

Decide which format you will use to present your experience and accomplishments. For most individuals, the traditional *chronological* presentation is the most effective. This style provides a logical method of delineating your career history and is the format that hiring authorities clearly prefer.

Of course, there are exceptions to every rule. The *functional* style is an effective way to combine diverse experience to create a cohesive record of achievements. This format can also be used to avoid repetition and create a more powerful resume for individuals who have a long history of positions with similar responsibilities. If you're considering creating a functional resume, see samples 4-5 and 9-1 for effective demonstrations of this style.

Sometimes a *combination* format—an extensive summary or highlights section, combined with a chronological job listing showing specific achievements—can be very effective. The resume for Sidney Mack (sample 10-16) is an example of a detailed three-page resume that begins with a summary and then uses most of page 1 for the Career Profile/Highlights of Accomplishments and Results sections. Without this functional grouping, the totality of Sidney's contributions would have been lost.

For good reason, however, nearly all the resumes in this book are in chronological format. Resume reviewers prefer this style hands-down because they feel it gives them the most accurate picture of a candidate's background. Functional resumes cause many hiring authorities to wonder what the candidate is trying to hide. If you choose to use a functional style, try to erase doubts by providing extensive detail on the places and dates of your employment, and be aware that executive recruiters in particular might find your resume objectionable.

Experience

Begin listing the various positions you have held. Each job listed on your resume should include dates of employment, company and title, and scope of responsibilities. The following sections deal with each aspect in detail.

Dates of Employment

In general, list years only (for example, 2005–2009), not months and never specific dates. There are, however, some exceptions to this guideline: If your total tenure on the job was less than a year, you might use dates such as "March–November 2008." If you very recently left a job, it's useful to include the month (2002–September 2009) to indicate the recent nature of your unemployment. And if you started a new position relatively recently, using the month may provide some longevity: "January 2008–Present" instead of simply "2008–Present."

Show your total tenure with a company, and then call out the specific time you held each position. For example:

MEGADIVERSIFIED CORP., Chicago, Illinois—1997–Present
Vice President Marketing—2004–Present
(details of responsibilities and achievements)
Regional Marketing Director—2000–2004
(details, etc.)
Field Marketing Manager—1997–2000
(details, etc.)

Occasionally you're better off *not* including total time of employment with one organization. Marla Amanpour's resume (sample 7-12) does an effective job of hiding work experience that began in the early 1970s—practically the dark ages to twentysomething resume reviewers. Instead, this candidate's recent and relevant experience and accomplishments are nicely highlighted; the vagueness of the earlier data implies that a few years have passed between college graduation and 1998, the first date shown. Of course, the candidate will be glad to supply exact dates and further detailed information when invited in for an interview. At that point, the resume has done its job of attracting interest in the product (you). It's your responsibility to overcome any stated and unstated objections during the interview process.

Company and Title

The company name and (usually) headquarters city are listed. You should note the location of your specific work site if it's different. You can also include the name of the parent company, particularly if it is impressive. Often it is helpful to add a brief line describing the company—its size and what it does—to give recruiters a more complete picture of your background and to put your responsibilities in perspective.

You should use exact job titles, but if you feel yours is misleading, consider adding a parenthetical clarification:

Klutz Tools, Inc.—Division of Tools "R" Us, Miami, Florida
($27M consumer division of $75M company that makes tools for the construction industry)
Retail Head (Regional Sales Manager), Salt Lake City, Utah

Position Description

Many job seekers make the mistake of giving too much emphasis (and space on their resume) to the duties of their job. Although it's important to establish context and give the reader a good understanding of what your jobs entailed, it's far more important to focus on your achievements—those contributions that are uniquely yours, as opposed to job duties common to anyone who holds the position.

Provide a concise picture of your areas of responsibility, the number of people you supervised, total sales dollars, and other factors. Once you've done that, you've established context and can move into the all-important accomplishments. Here's an example of a job responsibility description:

Develop strategy, oversee team and individual sales performance, and manage daily activities for $12 million, multiple-office district involved in sales of business information to midsized and Fortune 500 companies. Lead and mentor a diverse 16-member sales team, focusing on maximizing performance through training, motivation, inspiration, and effective supervision.

If you have not previously described exactly what the company does, include some indicators in your description of responsibilities:

> Managed sales initiatives for rapidly growing consumer division of $75 million plastics manufacturer.

Strive to use an active rather than passive voice in describing your responsibilities and accomplishments. "Responsible for" is passive; "directed," "managed," "guided," "led," "orchestrated," "spearheaded," and "launched" are all active. Thumb through the sample resumes in part 2 to gain ideas for new and varied ways to describe your activities.

Bear in mind that most people reading your resume will have a good understanding of basic sales and marketing functions. Particularly as you go further back in your career history, you don't need to spell out your daily duties when you can simply state "Managed $2M sales territory, cultivating major food and department store accounts" to give your reader enough information about the scope of your activities.

For hard-hitting impact, consider leading off each of your position descriptions with a strong "umbrella" statement that provides a capsule view of your overall achievements and contributions. Here's an example; you'll find other examples in chapters 4 through 11:

> **MARKETING MANAGER: FunFoods,** 2006–2008
>
> **Elevated FunFoods to market leader in its category and the most profitable brand in the company.** Developed and executed comprehensive marketing strategy that included sales and profit goals, advertising strategies, and brand positioning. Provided strategic direction to all support groups, including product development and advertising agency. Managed $30M annual marketing budget.

Go back through your career, listing each position you've held and summarizing the scope and responsibilities. In this first-draft stage, cover every position back to college or your first professional employment. You might decide later to eliminate or consolidate some of these positions for clarity or conciseness, or to disguise your age, but start by including everything.

Accomplishments

Now you're ready to tackle the most important part of your resume: your measurable achievements, accomplishments, and contributions to the business. These essential components offer powerful evidence of your ability to solve problems for a potential employer—because you solved similar problems for another company, or demonstrated an innovative sales approach, or consistently showed the ability to launch new products, or any number of other triumphs that are *proof* of your abilities.

When asked to rank the relative importance of 11 factors they consider when reviewing resumes for sales and marketing professionals, 81 percent of the human resources professionals, hiring managers, and executive recruiters surveyed for this book ranked "measurable accomplishments" as the #1 or #2 most important factor.

Include Numbers

Particularly in sales and marketing, numbers are the "proof of the pudding": measurable evidence of your contributions to company goals, growth, and success. Be sure to include as many numbers as possible in your accomplishment statements.

Note: Whereas traditional book format spells out numbers less than 100 and the word "percent," when creating resumes I prefer to use numerals and the % sign: 7, not seven; 43%, not 43 percent. Why? For two reasons: It saves space, and it makes the numbers much more visible. Because the numbers you've amassed during your career are one of the most important elements in your resume, it makes sense to have them stand out as much as possible.

To develop the numbers for your resume, begin by looking at straightforward measurements: Did you or a team you led exceed quotas or growth goals? A table or a graph can be an effective tool to show really strong numbers. See resume samples 6-1, 10-3, and 10-5, among others.

Another good perspective is to compare your performance to others in your industry, company, or region. Were you the #1 salesperson in your region? Did your team zoom up the ranks from last to fifth in the company? Did you outperform industry averages?

Sometimes it's most beneficial to talk about specific product sales rather than your entire line. Did you lead the field in new-product sales? Did you win sales competitions for a specific product line? Did you grow the market share of your company's top product? Look for ways you stood out, and back up your claims with specific numbers.

If you've held a position managing a sales or marketing team, you can claim credit for the success of your region as a whole, the results of individual members of your sales force, team responses to marketing challenges, or any other presentation of numbers that illustrates your ability to lead and motivate staffers under your supervision.

Marketing managers may cite details of the success of their marketing program based on established targets:

> Conceived strategy, developed implementation plan, and guided Superjuice marketing team in Fall campaign that delivered an incremental 8% market share nationwide (3% over goal and 5% above company average for beverage products).

As you look through the sample resumes, you'll note that in addition to numbers, they often include a brief explanation of *how* results were achieved. This level of detail allows a glimpse into your work style or problem-solving approach and is particularly important for people seeking executive-level positions.

Tell a Story

The best way to mine your background for your unique achievements is to think about how your efforts benefited the organization—and then keep digging until you come up with the numbers to support your story. The questions in the "Memory-Jogging Questions" section will get you started. As you recall your career history, take a clean sheet of paper or open a new word-processing document and write stories about your activities. This exercise will help you capture all the key elements of the accomplishment. At the same time, it is good preparation for interviews, when you will be asked to provide additional details about the achievements listed on your resume.

Let's look at an example of how this might work.

Reviewing her accomplishments as sales director for an educational publisher, Marijane tells the following story:

Well, we introduced a new product that year, a set of new social studies books, and we had to accelerate the production schedule. There was a big flap going on because Texas, which is of course a huge market, changed the social studies curriculum on really short notice, and all the schools had to buy new books. It's a mandated-curriculum state, where all the schools have to follow the same guidelines. Naturally we wanted to get in there first with our product, especially with the short time frame. We knew schools would be acting much more quickly than they normally do, and we wanted to be johnny-on-the-spot when they were ready to buy. So what I did was direct the design team in producing a really cute, interactive presentation and brochures to showcase our new books, and then I pulled in salespeople from other states and trained everyone really quickly. We blitzed the state—covered every school district in four weeks, which is about twice as fast as usual. And our results were phenomenal. We captured 47 percent of the Texas market, nearly double our usual penetration.

This is a great story. It's a dramatic situation, it shows how Marijane reacts to a crisis situation, and it quantifies her success in meeting this challenge with strong and specific results. There are several ways this story can be transformed into a meaningful accomplishment for Marijane's resume:

◆ **Doubled anticipated sales results** in a fast-paced, high-pressure sales challenge through effective leadership of sales team training and overall campaign.

◆ **Captured 47% of Texas market** (nearly double the company's average penetration rate) in a short time frame and under intense competitive pressure.

◆ Spearheaded preparation and execution of month-long sales blitz in response to an unexpected sales opportunity. Headed up collateral design, sales team recruiting and training, and campaign strategy. **RESULT:** Captured an incremental 23% market share, with excellent prognosis for long-term sales retention.

◆ **Capitalized on a key sales opportunity in a primary market** (state of Texas) and led sales team to successful penetration despite intense competitive pressure. Designed new interactive marketing presentation; bolstered sales team with recruits from other regions; trained all team members; and planned and monitored a month-long sales campaign that delivered **47%** of possible sales in the entire state.

The first two accomplishment descriptions are briefer and harder hitting; the second two provide more details about the extent of Marijane's activities. Any one of them would stimulate questions during an interview and would allow Marijane to expand on the briefly stated accomplishment with the complete details of her story.

How Can You Benefit the Company?

To pull some accomplishments from your own background, consider possible ways you can benefit a company:

◆ **Make money:** Meet or exceed sales goals, increase market share, increase account penetration, bring new products to market, conceive a highly effective marketing strategy, capture new markets, attract and retain customers, conceive a competitive advantage

◆ **Save money:** Decrease sales costs, reduce training costs, save travel time and expense, discover a new use for an existing product, maximize a technology investment, reduce staffing time and resultant expense

◆ **Improve efficiency:** Eliminate an unnecessary procedure, reduce tasks or the time it takes to do them, devise an efficient new procedure, solve a time-consuming problem, speed up customer service, automate a process

One of the easiest and most memorable methods of presenting this information is in the form of a "CAR" story: Challenge, Action, Results. (You might have seen this referred to as SAR, STAR, TAR, SCAR, CAB, or another acronym, but the concept is the same.) This approach will be helpful as you build your accomplishments, and again as you prepare for interviews.

The **Challenge** sets the scene:

I was a member of a team that was charged with developing some meaningful sales incentives for the launch of a new product. We didn't have an assigned team leader, and our first meeting was unproductive because we couldn't come to agreement on anything.

The **Action** tells what you did:

Before the next meeting, I circulated an e-mail suggesting a meeting structure and volunteering to serve as meeting facilitator to help us agree on fundamentals so we could complete our task. In the meeting I really worked on building a cooperative team spirit, and the meeting was very productive. I was unanimously elected team leader, and I led several intense brainstorming sessions that produced some really far-out ideas.

And, of course, don't forget the **Result**—the proof that your initiative helped the company:

Within three weeks, we had fine-tuned the ideas to realistic yet exciting incentives, and the new product met its initial sales goal faster than any other in company history. Not only that, our team effort really got us noticed, and most of us were promoted within the next year or so.

Just as in Marijane's example, this kind of story gives you several options for conversion into an accomplishment statement for your resume and prepares you to expound on the brief highlight during an interview.

Here are several suggested approaches for presenting your accomplishments:

◆ **Lead off with the benefit or result**, particularly if you can include a number. This approach is powerful and hard-hitting, and it definitely stirs interest.

◆ **Tell the story** and then finish with the results. This allows you to set the stage and provide context to the reader, who then may have a greater appreciation of the results.

◆ **Use the CAR format explicitly in your resume.** Check out resume samples 5-12 and 11-2 to see this approach in action.

Memory-Jogging Questions

As you review your career and recall your achievements, in addition to the general guidelines noted in the preceding section (make money, save money, improve efficiency), use the following questions to stir your memory and help capture your success stories:

◆ Was there a particular problem you were hired to solve? How did you address that challenge? What were the results?

◆ What did your managers commend you for? (If you have them, use prior performance evaluations as a great source of manager comments and a record of your measurable contributions to the business.)

◆ How was your performance evaluated? How did you know you were doing a good job?

◆ Did you receive any honors, awards, or recognition? What for?

◆ What was the highlight of that experience for you?

◆ Which of your skills were most used in that position?

◆ How was that job valuable to you?

◆ What problems/challenges did you face, and how did you solve them?

◆ How did your performance compare with that of others in similar positions?

DO IT NOW: Write about your experience and accomplishments.

Starting with your current or most recent job, summarize your responsibilities, providing scope and context; then write about your accomplishments.

As you write stories about your achievements, keep all the details stored in a separate document, and chisel down the story to create a sharply focused accomplishment statement.

The key to writing meaningful accomplishments is to keep in mind the employer's needs, concerns, and reason for interest in you. How can you help the organization? What benefits do you offer over another candidate? What have you done for companies in the past? How does your experience relate to the employer's current needs? To be certain you are capturing this truly essential viewpoint, keep digging further back into the specific accomplishment until you reach the bottom-line benefit. Here's an example of a dialogue between resume writer and client that may help as you interrogate yourself about your achievements:

Tell me some of the highlights of your Director of Sales job.

Well, one thing that was a real challenge, and which took up a ton of time, was cleaning up a big mess in the order-processing area.

What was the problem?

They had absolutely no system over there. Each order clerk would handle his or her own orders start to finish without creating any kind of central file—it was all kept separately on each clerk's individual workstation. So if someone was out, no one knew anything about his or her work, and that really annoyed customers when they called to check on their order. Plus we had a few less-than-great order takers. They weren't very efficient or organized, and lots of little details got lost.

So what did you do about it?

Well, I knew I couldn't just go in there with guns blazing and overhaul the department on my own. So first I created a new order-improvement team with the department manager, several of the clerks, and someone from the warehouse. We looked at the whole problem and came up with a centralized processing system so that any clerk could access the details of any order. Really, it was just a matter of using the technology we already had in place. We also set up a clear process for order

(continued)

management, and that helped a few of the poor performers. We fired one person and reassigned another to the warehouse and replaced them with much more qualified people.

And what was the result?

It took about six months, but we ended up with a very smooth-running department.

And...?

The customers were happier.

How did you know?

Complaints coming in to the manager were down, and our annual customer satisfaction survey showed an increase of 15 percent.

Were there any other benefits?

People in the department were happier.

How did you know?

They stayed longer. We had virtually no turnover in that department after the reorganization until the time I left two years later, except that the manager was promoted and one of the clerks moved up to the manager's job.

Was order-processing time improved?

Oh, yeah, we cut our average time from order to shipment from five days to three.

Having gathered this information, the resume writer can craft an achievement that appeals to the potential employer's concerns: save money, increase customer satisfaction, improve efficiency, save time. For example:

◆ Turned around underperforming order-processing department by driving a team initiative to identify inefficiencies and develop solutions. Within 6 months, improved customer satisfaction 15%, reduced order-processing time 40%, maximized the department's technology investment, provided staff-development opportunities, and virtually eliminated staff turnover.

The further back you go in your career, the less information you need to present. For lower-level jobs a decade or more ago, quite often a one-line responsibility summary and one significant accomplishment are enough to demonstrate a trend of contributing in every job you've held. Review the samples in this book to see how different accomplishments are presented. As much as possible, use numbers to support your achievements. Numbers make your feats believable and measurable and give the reader a basis of comparison.

After completing your accomplishment statements, take a moment to review your career target and see if the highlights you've selected do a good job of selling you for the position you want now. You can't include every detail of your career in just a few pages, so be certain you're presenting the achievements that are the strongest, most positive, and most relevant to your current career goal.

List Your Education

For most mid- to upper-level professionals, whose strongest qualifications are experience and accomplishments, education appears toward the end of the resume. If you have a "name-brand" education or other strong educational credential and you don't want it buried on page 2 of your resume, you might move this section up to just above the experience section. See resume samples 7-3 and 7-14 for effective page-1 placement of education. You'll note that in these samples the Education section is brief and to-the-point so as not to detract from the even more important experience and accomplishments. In sample 7-1, education takes up a more generous amount of space, but that's because this individual recently completed her MBA and is presenting this upfront as one of her strongest qualifications.

In listing education, provide the college you attended, degree earned, and major course(s) of study. Begin with your most advanced degree and work backwards. If you attended more than one school before graduating, it's not necessary to list earlier schools, although you might want to do so if the earlier school is highly prestigious or if you were involved in important activities. For instance, in resume 8-2 we chose to include leadership experiences from college because it added a dimension to Casey's qualifications.

If you earned your degree summa cum laude or with other academic distinction, it's OK to mention it, but don't make a big deal of events that occurred long ago. Avoid taking up valuable space on your resume with college activities, achievements, and honors unless they were truly stellar (such as a Rhodes Scholarship). Do not include high school information.

If you earned a bachelor's or master's degree in a field totally unrelated to sales and marketing or your target industries, consider listing only the degree— "Bachelor of Science"—without identifying the major.

Should you list your date of graduation? It's not at all necessary, and it's a good idea *not* to list dates if you are concerned about age discrimination. Although senior executives are certainly expected to be seasoned and mature, at all costs avoid appearing old. Dates in the 1960s and 1970s will label you as old (particularly if you interview with recruiters or HR people who were *born* in the 1970s or 1980s).

Omitting dates of graduation is also a good way to eliminate a few years of early experience, particularly if that experience does not support your current goals, without raising red flags in the reader's mind.

Perhaps you attended college but never completed a degree. If you intend to finish and are currently enrolled, you can use this kind of treatment:

UNIVERSITY OF CINCINNATI: Bachelor of Science in Business, anticipated May 2009

Some college is usually viewed more positively than *no* college. Let's say you dropped out after two years to go to work, or you have taken courses sporadically over the years. Here are a couple of options for handling this background on your resume:

UNIVERSITY OF CALIFORNIA AT SANTA BARBARA
Studies in Business and Economics (full-time 3 years)

COLORADO COLLEGE OF MINES
Completed 50% of requirements toward Bachelor of Science in Mechanical Engineering

Southern Connecticut State University, New Haven, Connecticut
Quinnipiac College, Hamden, Connecticut

◆ Coursework in Business, Marketing, and Economics, 1993–2000

Continuing professional development, especially sales and marketing training, is also of value, and you should include relevant courses, seminars, certificates, and licenses.

Observe the resume examples in chapters 4 through 11 for a variety of treatments of education. In most cases, the education is listed merely as a credential, an earned qualification that is important but significantly less so than the experience and accomplishments. In a few instances, no education section is included so as not to draw attention to the lack of formal education.

DO IT NOW: Summarize your education.

Complete this section of your resume draft. It should take only a few minutes.

Add Miscellaneous Categories and Information

What else should you include on your resume? Here are a few ideas to consider.

Computer Skills

As noted earlier, computer skills have become a basic business capability—so much so that it's really not necessary to mention them on your resume unless you have an extraordinary proficiency or are well-versed in specific software that is important in your industry.

Community Involvement

Volunteer activities, particularly those demonstrating leadership, can be mentioned if there is room. Unless this activity is truly stellar and highly relevant to your professional goals, you shouldn't include it at the expense of work-related accomplishments.

International Experience and Language Skills/ Willingness to Travel and Relocate

This information may be very important in today's global and mobile environment, but it doesn't usually warrant a separate heading and extensive space on your resume. Consider including it under a catchall "Additional Information" heading, along with any other miscellaneous data you think is important. If your goal is to work in an international environment, you should highlight these qualifications in your summary as well.

Hobbies and Interests

Usually these are not highly relevant and don't deserve space on your resume. Sometimes, however, an unusual interest or activity might make you memorable to hiring authorities. One of my clients wrote "Avid and knowledgeable New York Mets fan" on his resume and told me that every single interviewer commented on that and remembered him because of it. Use discretion in including this information, and don't include it at the expense of more important selling points.

Honors and Awards

There are several options for including these credentials: in a separate section, included with the relevant accomplishment/responsibility listing (see resume sample 4-3), or perhaps as a subsection of honors and awards within a specific job (see resume sample 4-8).

Military Background

Military background need not be included, but there is no reason to exclude it unless it occurred way back when (the 1970s, 1960s, or even 1950s) and it will make you seem too old. If you describe military experience, accomplishments, and honors that are relevant to your current career goals, be certain to translate military jargon to civilian language so that the reader has a clear idea of what you did and for what kind of organization.

Personal Information

It is inappropriate to include personal information (such as height, weight, marital status, date of birth, Social Security number, or number of children) on your resume. Never include a photograph of yourself.

References

References are not included as part of your resume, nor is it necessary to take up space with a "References upon request" notation. Develop a separate list of four to six professional references, using a style to match your resume, and have it ready to hand to an interviewer when asked during your meeting. Your references can also be an excellent networking contact; see chapter 13 for details.

DO IT NOW: Complete the final sections of your resume.

This should take only a few minutes.

Congratulations—you've completed the first draft of your resume! Now move on to chapter 3 to learn ways to polish it to perfection.

Polish Your Creation

The most time-consuming and thought-provoking work is behind you—but the job's not finished yet. Now it's time to format and polish your draft before sharing it with the world.

Before you're ready to tackle design and formatting, you might have a few questions about content that weren't addressed in the preceding chapter. The following section responds to typical questions and common problem situations that many job seekers face.

Deal with Problem Situations

Because we're all unique, it's inevitable that most job seekers will offer something other than a textbook career climb and perfect credentials. Perhaps you had a jog in your career path. How do you explain a lateral move? Did you take significant time off from work for child rearing or to assist elderly parents? Were you less than successful in your last position, for tangled business and personal reasons you don't want to make the focus of your next job interview? Whatever your situation, it's almost certain that any perceived negative looms larger in your mind than in a potential employer's. Still, it's important to be realistic about your background, how it will be perceived during a job search, and the most effective job search methods for you given your circumstances.

In Part 3 I discuss different avenues for finding a job; the advantages, benefits, and pitfalls of each; and how your personal circumstances dictate the best methods for you. For now, as you prepare your resume, strive to downplay any areas of perceived weakness—without being untruthful. It is never to your advantage to lie on your resume. Employers can check facts quite easily, and a discovered untruth or misstatement will eliminate you from contention. And even if you get the job, the employer may later discover the falsehood and fire you for it.

It's important to remember, however, that your resume is a marketing document in which you select and present the unique mix of information that will sell you to your next employer. You're not required to reveal every wrinkle in your background or bend over backwards to make sure a potential employer knows about your areas of weakness. Do not lie, but do approach these challenges with creativity and a focus on the employer's needs and interests rather than on any problems you perceive in your own background.

Whatever techniques you use to disguise certain situations on your resume, you must be prepared to answer questions about them from the very first phone screen. So be sure to practice your explanations so that they are concise, non-defensive, and as positive as possible.

Here are a few suggestions for handling common "problem" scenarios on your resume.

I'm Too Old

Most job seekers don't think they're too old; they think others will feel they're too old and discriminate against them. Age discrimination is a valid concern in our youthful culture. Even for senior executive positions, where maturity and experience are essential, the label "too old" can be a candidacy killer.

To avoid making your age obvious, try one or more of these techniques:

- ◆ Eliminate dates of college graduation.

- ◆ Avoid any dates in the 1960s, 1970s, and early 1980s.

- ◆ Truncate your experience by leaving off early jobs completely (disguising perhaps 5 to 15 years).

- ◆ Provide 10 to 20 years of experience, with dates, and then summarize prior experience under a subheading such as "Experience before 1990" or "Prior Professional Experience."

Many of the resume samples in this book use these techniques. When reviewing your resume, hiring authorities will assume that there is a gap but will not know precisely how large. The hope is that they will be so excited about your accomplishments and potential, they'll call you for an interview—at which time you can impress them with your expertise, energy, youthful outlook, and forward vision.

I Don't Have a College Degree

Unless you expect to complete your degree in the very near future, this is a situation you cannot remedy for your immediate job search. Don't obsess about this lack or assume that it will kill your chances in your job search. Lead with your strengths, and be confident about what you have to offer. Be aware that executive recruiters, who are striving to fill a "job order" that usually includes a college degree, will look less favorably on your resume. Therefore, limit your overtures to recruiters and concentrate more heavily in other avenues. (For more details on strategy, see part 3.)

To make lack of a college degree less obvious on your resume, consider these options:

◆ Eliminate the Education section altogether.

◆ Head up the section with "Professional Development" or another title that doesn't call attention to an education credential. Review samples in this book for ideas.

◆ See the "List Your Education" section in chapter 2 for ways to present a few years of college or current enrollment.

I Don't Have Experience in the Industry I'm Targeting

Again, lead with your strengths. Highlight your considerable and verifiable accomplishments, and try to bridge to the new industry through courses you've taken, special projects, personal interests, or other ways you can demonstrate that you do understand the industry. Executive recruiters should probably not be the primary avenue for your search because they prefer to recommend candidates with strong industry experience.

My Last Three Jobs Were Very Short-Term (a Year or Less)

Your concern is valid. Forty percent of the recruiters, hiring managers, and HR representatives surveyed for this book listed "job hopping" as a reason for *immediately* discarding a resume.

To present a more positive appearance:

◆ Consider eliminating one or more of your jobs, provided that doing so does not leave a gap that will provoke immediate questioning, thereby spotlighting the very thing you want to downplay.

◆ If circumstances beyond your control contributed to your short tenure, consider adding a brief explanation along the lines of "Merger with Megacorp eliminated all regional sales offices in fall 2008" or "Sales unit dissolved when software was discovered to be unready for market." Although I don't usually favor explaining or excusing in a resume, sometimes a brief statement like this can immediately overcome a negative reaction.

◆ Concentrate on finding job opportunities through networking, where a personal referral can get you in the door and you can then wow the interviewer with your capabilities and provide a rationale for the short tenure of your recent jobs.

And be as certain as you can be that your next position gives you several-year stability so that you don't face the same situation again in the near future.

I Wasn't Very Successful in My Last Sales/ Marketing Position

It's inadvisable to offer excuses and explanations, although you can subtly indicate reasons for lack of greater success:

◆ Try to find one or two success stories, and include them without a great deal of elaboration. For instance: "Only sales representative to secure multiple agreements for the company's primary sales strategy, a 3-month in-store trial." "Successfully maintained sales volume in a flat industry and market."

◆ If you were fired or left before you could deliver any results, point out what you did accomplish or learn: "Laid the groundwork for a successful career in real estate sales through intensive prospecting and community relationship-building." (Don't mention that you didn't sell a single piece of property.) "Developed regional marketing strategy to improve brand recognition and increase market share by 10 percentage points." (Why broadcast that your plan was rejected by the senior VP? The accomplishment you're claiming is the *development* of the plan, a valuable management skill.)

Sometimes the reasons for lack of success are beyond your control. Assess your experience, take accountability for what you did or didn't do, and use the experience and lessons learned as an opportunity to improve. Perhaps the position was not a good fit for you; that won't happen again if, using the career target statement you created, you are careful to find a position that meets your career needs for industry, environment, location, and so forth.

I Want to Relocate/I Don't Want to Relocate

If relocation is your desire (or at least an acceptable option), you can use a broad range of search strategies, including contacting recruiters nationwide, posting your resume on the Internet, and responding to a wide range of posted advertisements. You'll note that several of the resumes in this book end with a brief "Available for travel and relocation" or similar notation.

If you are targeting a specific city, it will be helpful if you give a strong indication of your intentions in your cover letter:

I plan to relocate to Bayonne within the next few months.

My wife's promotion to FedEx headquarters will bring us to Memphis in mid-March.

Also consider adding to the top of your resume and cover letter a local contact telephone number and/or address to give an impression of permanency and ease of contact. Here are two examples:

Jane McAllister
Current Address: 75 Second Avenue, New York, NY 10023—212-491-9004

El Paso Contact: 915-374-8766

Jane McAllister
Through 9/09: 75 Second Avenue, New York, NY 10023—212-491-9004

Beginning 10/09: 4523 Chisholm Trail, El Paso, TX 79924—915-374-8766

Look into getting a cell phone with the area code of your new location, and use only that number on your resume. You can even eliminate your physical address if you want, or use the address of a local friend or relative where employers can contact you.

If you strongly prefer to remain in your current location, broad-based search efforts will be less productive than if you were willing to relocate. Concentrate your efforts on local networking and local recruiters, but also scan national publications and Internet sites for positions in your city. If you choose to post your resume on the Internet, be sure you include a line such as "Geographic preference: Los Angeles" so that you don't get too many calls for jobs in Peoria.

I Was Demoted Following a Corporate Restructuring

With mergers and acquisitions being the norm today, reorganization due to restructuring is an explanation that is usually well accepted. Without lying, do what you can to put a positive spin on your move. Reassigned to inside sales?

> Selected to lead reorganization initiative to strengthen company's inside sales and customer support activities.

Demoted to managing a smaller sales area?

> Challenged to rebuild struggling region following total company realignment.

I Have Several Gaps in My Career History

If you are currently unemployed and have been unemployed for longer than nine months or so, it is important that you show some activity for this time period, such as pursuit of education, consulting projects, or professional association leadership activity. If the gaps occurred quite a while ago, you can eliminate dates from prior positions. Sometimes you can use a functional resume effectively to disguise gaps. If the gap occurred several years ago and your career history since then is strong, don't worry about it. It should have no impact on your job search.

Be Ready for the Big Question

It's important to realize that, whatever your perceived problem area, the topic will come up at some point during your interview, either directly or subtly. So, as noted earlier, be sure to rehearse concise, positive, natural-sounding responses to questions like "So, what have you been doing since you left XYZ in 2008?" or "Exactly how long were you at Smith & Jones?" Interviewers will not ask you how old you are, but they might request a college transcript or call your university to check on your date of graduation, so your age will not remain a mystery for long.

The point of disguising potentially harmful information in your resume is to give yourself a chance to meet and impress hiring authorities. Jobs are granted not through resumes but following a series of interviews. Your resume should do its job to get you in front of hiring authorities. From there, your interviewing skills become all-important.

Edit Your Draft

Now that you've compiled all this information, it's time to review what you've written, tighten the language, and make sure your resume contains only essential data. First, read it through once or twice and correct obvious errors or awkward phrasing.

Fix the Style Problems

Next, review your writing style and apply the following checklist to make sure your document uses proper resume language:

◆ **Tense:** When writing about the responsibilities of your current position, use present tense. For prior positions and for all completed accomplishments, use past tense.

◆ **Person:** Resumes are written in the first person but without the subject. For example, to describe your job in conversation, you might say, "I manage a team of 11 field sales reps and also oversee all operations in our regional office." To convert this to resume language, remove the subject ("I"): "Manage team of 11 field sales reps; concurrently, oversee all operations of regional office." Do not talk about yourself in the third person ("Manages team of..."); that style is outdated and awkward.

◆ **Crisp language:** To give your resume impact, pare down the language to essentials. Eliminate most articles (the, a, an, our) and helping verbs ("was selected for corporate task force" becomes "selected for..."). Then reread each statement to make sure you haven't included words that don't add meaning or impact. Compare the following statements:

  • "Motivated the store managers to do an excellent job in customer service. Made sure that this attitude carried down to their teams, with the result that half the stores in the district received awards for customer service."

  • "Motivated managers to instill store-wide focus on customer service; 50% of district's stores earned service awards."

  The second statement sends the same message using 61 percent fewer words and with more impact.

Then check your resume for overused words, phrases, and sentences, and eliminate or reword to avoid repetition, which is boring to the reader.

Select an Appropriate Font

Chances are, you prepared your resume using the Times New Roman font, which is the default font in many word-processing programs and therefore is the most commonly used. At this point, before you move on to fine-tuning your draft, consider trying out a few different typestyles. Compare several printouts and evaluate the following:

◆ Which is most pleasing to the eye?

◆ Which does a better job of drawing your eye to important parts of the resume?

◆ Which is most readable?

◆ Which looks cleanest and least "fussy"?

◆ Which feels most like "you"—and corresponds most closely with the personal brand you are attempting to convey in your resume?

There are no hard-and-fast font rules. What's important is that you like what you've produced, it's readable, and key facts are easy to distinguish. Throughout this book, you will see sample resumes and resume excerpts using many different fonts. They can be a good source of inspiration.

If you choose to a use a font that is nonstandard on most PCs, be sure to embed the font into your document so that people receiving it will view it as you designed it. If you don't embed the font, it will default to a common font such as Times New Roman, Arial, or Courier, depending on the settings of the receiving computer, and might totally mess up your careful formatting. To be as certain as possible that your resume won't create font incompatibilities, stick to one of the fonts that is standard on most systems:

- Arial
- **Arial Black** (use for headlines only)
- Book Antiqua
- Bookman Old Style
- Garamond
- Georgia
- Tahoma
- Times New Roman
- Trebuchet MS
- Verdana

As a final note, keep in mind that as long as it is readable and professional, a less-common font will be appealing to recruiters and human resources professionals, who review dozens or hundreds of resumes a day. A distinctive look will help set your resume apart.

Check the Length

Now, review your resume for length (which is usually too long in the first-draft stage). A reader can absorb only so much before reaching information overload. Although including all your key skills and significant accomplishments is of course a priority, don't let your readers' eyes glaze over at the sight of a dense, fact-filled, overly lengthy resume.

Break down overlong paragraphs. Consider resume sample 6-13 (Sheelah R. McIntyre), in which the details of key accomplishments are spelled out in several bulleted statements and the results are highlighted in a separate paragraph. If all this verbiage were presented in one paragraph, the reader might lose interest before reaching the all-important results.

Even if the items themselves are brief, avoid excessively lengthy lists. If the number of paragraphs or bullet points exceeds four or five, consider the following tactics to make your resume more reader-friendly:

- **Eliminate less-significant activities.** When cutting material, always look first at job duties before truncating your accomplishments.

- **Use sub-bullets to call out details.** Briefly describe an activity or achievement, and then list two, three, four, or more brief results using additional bullet points indented below.

- **Combine two or more bullet points into one consolidated statement.** Look for similarities among achievements to see whether you can create one overall accomplishment statement that will serve several purposes.

- **Create subheadings to make a visual break between groups of related achievements.** Resume samples 4-14 (Reesa Sobieski), 5-2 (Sonia Martindale), and 6-7 (Chris Mooney) are good examples. This is also an excellent tactic for distinguishing between separate areas of expertise (for example, sales, management, and training). Readers can choose to focus their attention on the specific area(s) of greatest interest to them. This format can also be extremely helpful if, for instance, you are interested in a sales management position but have no direct management experience according to your job titles. By including a subsection titled "Management Achievements," you can convey management qualifications through relevant activities and contributions.

Review Your Target Statement

Finally, review your career target statement and compare it to your resume draft to be certain you've presented strong qualifications for the job you want. And put yourself in the employers' shoes to see whether you've responded to their needs and interests and provided clear and compelling reasons for them to give you a call.

Design Your Resume for Maximum Impact

Resume development consists of two parts: writing and design. I think of these dual, equally important components as the one-two punch that is essential for a truly effective resume.

Appearance makes the first impression: Does your resume look professional? Are the key points easily visible? Is the material well organized? An attractive appearance will capture your readers' interest immediately. To keep that interest, your resume must be compelling, well-written, and relevant to their needs. Now that you have completed the draft copy, it's time to move on to organizing, arranging, and highlighting the material to create visual appeal and maximum impact.

Well designed does not have to mean fancy or complicated. A clean, easy-to-read layout with ample white space and logical organization appeals to busy hiring authorities, who need to grasp the essential information and rapidly make a "yes," "no," or "maybe" decision about the candidate.

Some General Rules

Give yourself the greatest possible chance to get to "yes." Skim through the resumes in this book and observe the organizational structure and formatting guidelines that were used effectively for real job seekers. You'll notice similarities among many of the resume styles:

◆ Major headings are in large or bold print for easy navigation through the resume.

◆ Job titles, generally more important than company names, are emphasized with bold print, underscoring, or other font enhancement.

◆ Accomplishments are clearly distinguishable from job responsibilities, either through a paragraph/bulleted-list format or through subheadings.

◆ Horizontal lines or other graphic elements frequently separate sections of the resume.

◆ The page has a pleasing balance—top to bottom, left to right.

◆ Formatting is consistent throughout.

◆ Font sizes are large enough to be readable but small enough to look professional.

◆ A variety of fonts are used, sometimes two different fonts in one resume.

◆ Bullet sizes and shapes complement the design.

◆ Indents are clean and tab settings are precise.

◆ Bold and italic type enhancements are used appropriately to emphasize words, phrases, or numbers.

◆ Dates are easily located but not overemphasized.

Many of the sample resumes in this book are two pages long; a few are three pages, whereas others fit comfortably on one page. Professionals with 15 to 20 years of experience will find it difficult to compress their background and achievements onto one page—and there's no reason why they should. If your resume is more than one page, just be certain that the most important facts— your strongest selling points—appear on page 1 so that they are not overlooked on a quick read-through.

For senior executives, two-page resumes are the rule, and a three-page resume is sometimes essential to communicate all key information. At that level, recruiters and top corporate executives will carefully scrutinize the details you provide in your resume. They need to know more than "how much" (the numbers you achieved); they need to know "how" and "why," because your vision, strategic skills, and leadership style will significantly affect the entire corporation.

Consider Exceptions to the Rules

As you thumb through the pages of sample resumes in chapters 4 through 11, you'll find examples that don't follow the general rules and guidelines espoused in this chapter and chapter 2. Why? Because people's lives and careers don't always follow the rules.

In each instance, when I was writing the resume, I made a careful evaluation of my client's goals, circumstances, history, strengths, and achievements and made judgment calls about the information, language, and tone. Perhaps I used a few tricks of the trade to get around perceived weaknesses in the individual's background.

For instance, in resume 7-4 (Daniel Montez), the description of Daniel's job responsibilities is more extensive than his accomplishments, and his two jobs with Computerkids are bundled rather than described separately. I did this for two reasons:

◆ First, his jobs were quite similar, and many activities were common to both.

◆ Second, his scope of responsibilities was quite extensive and covered a wide range of marketing functions.

I wanted to make sure that these capabilities were communicated. Bold type is used to highlight the most important details in the Key Accomplishments section.

In another example, Robert Axe, whose resume is sample 4-10, left off two very short-term sales jobs (before and after his position at Mahon Corporation). He was already concerned about looking like a job-hopper, and eliminating those jobs helped lend some stability to his background. In each case the reason for the short tenure was beyond his control, and he didn't want to take up valuable space on his resume, or waste valuable interview time, on lengthy explanations.

Sara L. McGuire, a VP of Sales for a seasonal merchandise distributor (see resume 10-25), was seeking a new position because a combination of factors had led to a steep decline in her firm's revenues (and, consequently, her income). Notice that no mention of this decline is made in her resume; instead, I focused on measurable and significant accomplishments—all of which are true and verifiable.

With your own resume, feel free to bend and even break the established resume-writing rules. Let yourself be guided by two principles:

◆ How can I most powerfully demonstrate that I can help a potential employer?

◆ What is the most effective approach for my unique circumstances?

Apply the Finishing Touches

After you've taken your best shot and developed a resume that effectively sells your qualifications and, at the same time, feels right to you, take four final steps before launching your job search:

◆ **Spell-check and proofread.** A typographical, grammatical, spelling, or punctuation error is the reason many hiring authorities give for immediately tossing a resume. And even if your resume isn't discarded, an error makes a bad first impression that will linger in the reader's mind.

Triple-check dates, phone numbers, spellings of names and cities—items that are usually not corrected by a computer spell-checker.

◆ **Get an outside opinion.** Show your resume to someone you trust, preferably a professional colleague who is knowledgeable about your industry. Listen carefully to judgments, recommendations, and suggestions for improvement. Whether or not you make any changes to your resume is up to you, but leave your ego at the door, and open your mind to the opinion of someone you respect and trust.

◆ **Get an inside opinion.** Show it to your spouse, significant other, or a close friend (not a business colleague). Immediately after this person finishes reading your resume, ask "What am I good at?" If the response isn't swift and accurate, go over your resume again to be certain you're communicating clearly and crisply. Ask whether the resume is a good representation of you. Take suggestions seriously; this person has your best interests at heart and can sometimes see strengths you've overlooked.

◆ **Proofread again.** It's during the revision process that errors tend to creep in, so look over your resume carefully one last time and do a final spell-check before you send it out into the world.

Choose Paper

If you are mailing your resume or taking it with you to interviews, print it on high-quality bond paper. There are many attractive colors and finishes. Choose a paper that prints well on your printer, mails without smudging (mail a test resume to yourself), presents a highly professional appearance, and is at least 24-pound weight. Choose 28-pound paper if you can find it, particularly if you are at the senior executive level. White, off-white, ivory, light tan, and various shades of gray are standard and highly acceptable paper colors. Be careful about using less-traditional colors such as ice blue or light mauve if you are in a conservative industry.

Because your resume will be copied repeatedly once it's in the hands of interested prospects, avoid dark papers or those with too many flecks. Designer papers can enhance your resume presentation, but be careful about going overboard and looking gimmicky rather than professional. Before choosing to use an unusual paper, be certain that it can be cleanly copied. Strive for an image of quality and professionalism.

You will most likely be e-mailing your resume most of the time, but when you have a networking meeting or an interview, always bring several top-quality printed resumes with you. And for those times when you choose to mail a hardcopy resume rather than e-mail it, it's important to strike the right note with the physical presentation of your resume.

You can mail your resume folded in thirds in a standard #10 business envelope that matches your stationery, or flat in a 9 × 12 white envelope available at office-supply stores. Whichever mailing method you choose, do not staple or clip together your resume pages. Stack your cover letter on top of your resume, fold (or not), and insert into the envelope facing outward, toward the flap.

Adapt Your Resume for an Electronic Job Search

Personal computers and the Internet have revolutionized multiple areas of daily life, not the least of which is individual career management. Although the need for an attractive paper resume has not yet been completely superseded, you need to create an electronic version of your resume for an integrated job search. In fact, you will probably transmit most of your resumes via e-mail.

You don't need to rewrite your resume for electronic transmission, but you do need to reformat it into the appropriate style according to the guidelines in the following section.

What About "Scannable" Resumes?

Most large companies and recruiting firms use electronic databases and computerized applicant-tracking systems to store candidate information. Previously, scanners and scanning software were used to read resumes into the system, and this required the production of "scannable" resumes that the scanners could read accurately. But now electronic resumes sent by e-mail are entered directly into the database and physical scanning is seldom required.

In the few instances where scanners are still used, the guidelines for submission will be spelled out in the job posting. Some requirements are more strict than others. The best advice I can give is to follow these instructions to the letter to ensure that your application is processed accurately into the database.

Electronic Resumes

There are three kinds of electronic resumes: those sent as a Word file attached to an e-mail, those formatted in plain text and pasted into an e-mail message or online application, and those converted to PDF format and attached to an e-mail.

E-mail Attachment

For the most part, it's best to send your resume as an attachment to your e-mail, with the cover letter making up the body of the e-mail. Microsoft Word is the standard word-processing software that the vast majority of businesses use. If you use a different program, you will probably run into file incompatibilities—your resume might be unreadable, or your careful formatting might appear as a mishmash when the recipient opens it. For this reason, I recommend using Microsoft Word.

ASCII Text Resume

A second kind of electronic resume you will need is a text version (also known as ASCII). The text resume is a plain, unformatted document that can be read by any computer system, regardless of the computer's native operating system, e-mail program, or word-processing program. You will use this when filling in online applications or posting your resume in online databases. If an ad or posting states "no attachments," you can paste your text resume into the body of an e-mail without worrying about formatting glitches.

To create an ASCII (text) resume, follow these simple steps:

1. Create a new version of your resume using the Save As feature of your word-processing program. Select "Text Only" or "ASCII" or "Plain Text" in the Save As option box.

2. Close the new file.

3. Reopen the file. You'll find that your word processing program has automatically reformatted your resume into Courier font, removed all formatting, and left-justified the text.

4. Review the resume and fix any glitches such as odd characters that may have been inserted to take the place of "curly" quotes, dashes, accents, or other nonstandard symbols.

5. If necessary, add extra blank lines to improve readability.

6. Consider adding horizontal dividers to break the resume into sections for improved skimmability. You can use an entire line of any standard typewriter symbol, such as *, -, (,), =, +, ^, or #.

PDF Format

PDF (Portable Document Format) is a very useful way to retain the visual integrity of documents created in just about any software. Thanks to Adobe Corporation's free sharing of its Acrobat Reader software, anyone on the Internet can download the software and open and read PDF files.

If your resume has a very sophisticated design or includes unusual fonts or graphics that are essential for getting your message across, PDF format is a good choice. It does have a serious disadvantage in that the file can't be read by many applicant-tracking systems, so your data might not make it into the database. As well, recruiters and human resources people strongly prefer the Microsoft Word format.

If you must create a PDF file because of the unusual visual nature of your resume, I recommend always including the ASCII text version as well.

DO IT NOW: Edit, format, proofread, and print your resume.

Spend the time and care that this important document deserves. Create multiple versions, as described in this chapter, so that you're well-armed and ready for action. But bear in mind that resume development is just the first step in the job search process. Some job seekers, overly concerned with making the resume "perfect," spend excessive time agonizing over revision after revision, striving for the ideal phrase or the flawless format to ensure a successful job search. Relax. Remember, your resume alone can't land you a new position. Do the job well, and then launch into action. This book tells you how; it offers sample resumes in chapters 4 through 11 and sample cover letters in chapter 12.

Examples of Electronic Resumes

The next pages show the same resume in two formats: traditional paper (Microsoft Word or PDF) and electronic (text).

Matthew Robertson

203-349-7090   27 Bridge Street, Durham, CT 06422   rob@verizon.net

Sales & Management Professional
Sales & Marketing • Account Management • Business Development

Accomplished professional with strong skills in business development, managerial team building, marketing, communication, organization, and leadership. Consistent record of achievement and results during 15 years in sales and sales management.

- Delivered sales growth in highly competitive industries, new markets, and established accounts.
- Repeatedly demonstrated strong relationship-management skills with both B2B and B2C customers; leveraged relationships to grow existing accounts and capture new business.
- Built, led, and motivated sales teams to high performance.

Experience and Achievements

Account Manager, DISPLAY-MATES, Meriden, CT   2007–Present

Rapidly learned new industry, new products, and new B2B sales strategies; delivered immediate and sustainable sales results for $2M company that provides sophisticated trade-show exhibits to corporations across the U.S. and internationally.

- Manage existing accounts and build new business via cold calling and prospect development.
- Assess needs, develop proposals, and deliver presentations at the executive level.
- **Sales Performance:**
  - Established 2 of the company's top 5 accounts, including first penetration of a $20B pharmaceutical company.
  - Landed first international account, a $50K multiyear contract with a company in Chile.
  - Doubled sales revenue in second year of employment.

Sales Manager, NUTMEG CADILLAC, INC., Hartford, CT   1994–2007

Achieved impressive sales growth, created winning marketing strategies, drove cost-reduction and profit-improvement initiatives, and contributed to company growth to $25M revenue.

- **Sales & Sales Management:** Managed and motivated sales team of 8 professionals: set sales goals, provided training and mentoring, and monitored performance.
  - Inherited an underperforming sales organization; quickly rebuilt and reenergized staff, and led new team to 100% gross-profit increase over 3 years.
- **Marketing & Advertising:** Performed marketing functions, including planning and executing all advertising promotions and campaigns. Controlled a $200K annual advertising budget.
  - Revamped advertising program to wring maximum performance from advertising dollars—successfully reduced budget while increasing sales revenues.
- **Operations Leadership:** Controlled and managed a revolving $2M vehicle inventory and $3M annual purchasing budget.
  - Established a subprime financing department and aggressive marketing program for after-sale services; resulted in generous revenue increases.

Education

B.S. Business Administration, 1994: Quinnipiac University, Hamden, CT

Figure 3.1: Sample resume in paper format.

```
MATTHEW ROBERTSON
27 Bridge Street, Durham, CT 06422
203-349-7090 * rob@verizon.net

===============================
SALES & MANAGEMENT PROFESSIONAL
Sales & Marketing * Account Management * Business Development
-----------------------------------
Accomplished professional with strong skills in business development,
managerial team building, marketing, communication, organization, and
leadership. Consistent record of achievement and results during 15 years in
sales and sales management.

* Delivered sales growth in highly competitive industries, new markets, and
established accounts.
* Repeatedly demonstrated strong relationship-management skills with both B2B
and B2C customers; leveraged relationships to grow existing accounts and
capture new business.
* Built, led, and motivated sales teams to high performance.

===============================
EXPERIENCE AND ACHIEVEMENTS

Account Manager, DISPLAY-MATES, Meriden, CT 2007—Present
-------------------------------
Rapidly learned new industry, new products, and new B2B sales strategies;
delivered immediate and sustainable sales results for $2M company that
provides sophisticated trade-show exhibits to corporations across the U.S.
and internationally.

* Manage existing accounts and build new business via cold calling and
prospect development.
* Assess needs, develop proposals, and deliver presentations at the executive
level.
* Sales Performance:
— Established 2 of the company's top 5 accounts, including first penetration
of a $20B pharmaceutical company.
— Landed first international account, a $50K multiyear contract with a
company in Chile.
— Doubled sales revenue in second year of employment.

Sales Manager, NUTMEG CADILLAC, INC., Hartford, CT 1994—2007
-------------------------------
Achieved impressive sales growth, created winning marketing strategies, drove
cost-reduction and profit-improvement initiatives, and contributed to company
growth to $25M revenue.

* Sales & Sales Management: Managed and motivated sales team of 8
professionals: set sales goals, provided training and mentoring, and
monitored performance.
— Inherited an underperforming sales organization; quickly rebuilt and
reenergized staff, and led new team to 100% gross-profit increase over 3
years.
* Marketing & Advertising: Performed marketing functions, including planning
and executing all advertising promotions and campaigns. Controlled a $200K
annual advertising budget.
— Revamped advertising program to wring maximum performance from advertising
dollars--successfully reduced budget while increasing sales revenues.
* Operations Leadership: Controlled and managed a revolving $2M vehicle
inventory and $3M annual purchasing budget.
— Established a subprime financing department and aggressive marketing
program for after-sale services; resulted in generous revenue increases.

===============================
EDUCATION
B.S. Business Administration, 1994: Quinnipiac University, Hamden, CT
```

Figure 3.2: Sample resume in electronic format.

PART 2

Sales and Marketing Resumes and Cover Letters

Working with individual clients for more than 20 years, I've had the privilege of writing resumes for thousands of motivated and accomplished people. Resume styles have changed a bit over the years, and advances in technology have had a huge impact on both resume development and job searching. But the challenge remains the same: to present the right information in the right way to communicate each individual's skills, value, and potential to contribute to the success of an organization.

Sales and marketing professionals have always been heavily represented among my clients. I attribute this to several factors. One, they know the value of a well-written and well-designed promotional piece. Two, they like being rewarded for performance and are quite open to searching for new, more lucrative opportunities. And three, I suspect I have a natural affinity for people in sales and marketing. I realize that the success of my business is directly related to my ability to sell my services, and as I've gotten quite good at that I've increased my understanding of the sales process and my appreciation of sales and marketing professionals.

In any event, when it came time to select resumes for inclusion in this book, I found strong contenders representing a wide array of sales-related functions, diverse industries, and broad levels of responsibility, from those seeking their first sales job to senior sales executives. Geographic diversity was evident, too, because I work with clients from around the country and around the world.

The samples in part 2 are all real resumes written for genuine clients. The majority are my work, but a few resumes were contributed by other professional resume writers. When looking for additional samples to round out this part of the book, I knew just where to go: to the handful of resume writers who share with me the most distinguished credential in our profession, that of Master Resume Writer (MRW), awarded by the Career Management Alliance (www.careermanagementalliance.com). I am grateful for the contributions of the following Master Resume Writers; you will find their contributions identified on each of their resumes.

Carol Altomare, MRW
World Class Resumes
Flemington, NJ
Phone: (908) 237-1883
E-mail: carol@worldclassresumes.com
Web site: www.worldclassresumes.com

Jewel Bracy DeMaio, MRW
A Perfect Resume.com Inc.
Elkins Park, PA
Phone: (215) 635-2979
E-mail: mail@aperfectresume.com
Web site: www.aperfectresume.com

Debbie Ellis, MRW
Phoenix Career Group
Houston, TX
Phone: (800) 876-5506
E-mail: info@phoenixcareergroup.com
Web site: www.PhoenixCareerGroup.com

Meg Guiseppi, MRW
Resumes Plus LLC
Andover, NJ
Phone: (973) 726-0757
E-mail: meg@resumesplusllc.com
Web site: www.
ExecutiveResumeBranding.com

Gayle Howard, MRW
Top Margin
Melbourne, Australia
Phone: 61397266694
E-mail: getinterviews@topmargin.com
Web site: www.topmargin.com

Abby Locke, MRW
Premier Writing Solutions, LLC
Washington, DC
Phone: (202) 635-2197
E-mail: alocke@premierwriting.com
Web site: www.premierwriting.com

Jan Melnik, MRW
Absolute Advantage
Durham, CT
Phone: (860) 349-0256
E-mail: CompSPJan@aol.com
Web site: www.janmelnik.com

Jacqui D. Barrett Poindexter, MRW
Career Trend
Kansas City, MO
Phone: (816) 584-1639
E-mail: jacqui@careertrend.net
Web site: www.careertrend.net

Marjorie Sussman, MRW
Edgewater, NJ
Phone: (201) 941-8237
E-mail: marjorie1130@aol.com

Ilona Vanderwoude, MRW
Career Branches
Riverdale, NY
Phone: (718) 884-2213
E-mail: ilona@CareerBranches.com
Web site: www.CareerBranches.com

In fictionalizing the resumes to preserve client confidentiality, I tried to remain true to the original material, but changing company names and disguising product-specific content naturally results in a more generic resume. There's quite a difference in implied significance between "Lever Brothers" and "XYZ Corp." In some cases, material that was too difficult to depersonalize was removed entirely. Still, the language, organization, formats, and general approaches represented should give you ample ideas for your own resume.

The resumes are annotated with comments about the client's job search process, a specific problem and how we overcame it, or other relevant information. I've also indicated which resumes have a companion cover letter in chapter 12 so that you can see the relationship between the resume and the approach and language used in the cover letter.

When working with clients, I always try to return to two primary considerations: the "me, me, me" priorities of *both* the client and the employer. As you review these resumes, keep in mind your specific career target. Filter all these samples through your own priorities, and don't be afraid to break any perceived rules or standards as you create a resume that will give you a competitive edge in your search for a six-figure sales and marketing position.

Chapter 4

Sales Resumes

The first section of resumes covers sales at the direct-producer level. The samples are roughly grouped in similar industries, but they range in experience level from novice to veteran.

MARTIN CRANLEY

7239 Little Miami Circle, Loveland, OH 45140
513-243-0904 ▪ mcranley@fuse.net

Pharmaceutical Sales Professional—Urology/Oncology Specialist

#1 in the Nation—District Rep of the Year—Consistent Growth in Competitive Territories

Proven ability to promote complex pharmaceuticals to physician specialists through consultative, needs-based selling. Recognized for "unmatched" product knowledge and for consistently delivering value in long-established physician relationships. Demonstrated complementary skills in territory planning and management, professional presentation, documentation, and follow-up.

"Another incredible year. No one would have believed you could have accomplished such a 2-year run in your area. You are a testimony to hard work and excellent planning." DM comments, 2008

Career Highlights

ASTRAZENECA PHARMACEUTICALS—1998 to Present

Oncology Sales Representative—Sales of oncology and urology products to office- and hospital-based specialists in territory encompassing Middletown (since 1998) and Xenia (since 2006).

☑ **Built one of the company's leading sales territories** on a foundation of exceptional physician relationships, needs-based selling, advanced product knowledge, and meticulous planning and preparation. Delivered consistent results during product and territory changes.

☑ **Sales Performance**
- #1 in the nation (total sales performance of 110+ peers), 2005; #7 in the nation, 2008.
- A leading performer in district that was #1 in the nation, 2003.
- District Representative of the Year, 2006, chosen based on sales results and leadership.
- Selected results: — 45% overall sales increase, 2008.
  — 66% product growth overall, 2007.
  — Double-digit growth for 18 consecutive months (Alatair), 2005–2006.
  — Drove Axil market share to 55% vs. national average of 25% (2004).
  — Repeatedly placed #1 or #2 in sales of Axil nationwide.
- Immediately penetrated newly added Xenia territory—urology sales +35% and oncology +6% in first year.

☑ **Additional Contributions**
- Developed thought leaders, including a nationally prominent bladder-cancer expert.
- As product coordinator for all products represented, shared expertise district-wide.
- Repeatedly accessed "no-see" physicians through resourceful approaches, persistence, and genuine rapport-building.
- Worked collaboratively to establish study sites and clinical trials.

GRANT PHARMA—1994 to 1998

Sales Representative, promoted to Oncology Specialty Representative after 2 years—Specialized in oncology line and introduced an innovative new therapy to specialists. Responsible for obtaining formulary approval for new drugs. Organized lecture programs.

☑ **Sales Performance:** #1 in sales, Southern Ohio Region, 1995, 1996, and 1997 for both specialty products—3 times higher than any other sales rep in the district.

Education

MS Management, 2001
BA Communications, 1993

MIAMI UNIVERSITY, Oxford, OH
XAVIER UNIVERSITY, Cincinnati, OH

Numbers and results are used liberally throughout this resume to drive home the fact that Martin is a top performer. The quote from his manager is a powerful third-party endorsement.

Paige Marinskaya

(561) 243-9988
paige@yahoo.com
25-B Atlantic Avenue, West Palm Beach, FL 33417

PHARMACEUTICAL SALES PROFESSIONAL	**Highly motivated top performer** with proven ability to develop client base and consistently achieve solid sales results.

- Skill at all levels of the sales process; particular strengths in closing the sale and building rapport with clients.
- Proven ability to establish a plan and carry through on objectives; extremely well organized.
- Strong work ethic, as demonstrated through a consistently high average daily call rate and effective communication and service to a large account base.

PROFESSIONAL EXPERIENCE

MEDI-MAGIC PHARMACEUTICALS, Paterson, New Jersey   2005–Present
Territory Sales Representative / Eastern Florida
Promote and market 9 pharmaceutical products, calling on primary care physicians, cardiologists, allergists, obstetricians/gynecologists, pharmacists and hospitals.

- Reestablished successful account relationships in a territory that had been vacant for more than a year.
- Maintained a high average call rate of 9 physicians per day.
- Established effective relationships with physicians, building rapport and maintaining consistent communication.
- Consistently met quota and growth objectives, particularly in growth of the company's top 3 products.
- Number 1 in district, number 5 in region in the sales of new Medi-Bene prescriptions since launch of product in February 2006.
- Promoted to Field Sales Trainer, November 2008.

GLOBAL INDUSTRIAL CHEMICALS, Miami, Florida   2004–2005
Sales Associate
Completed the Global training program for outside sales representatives.

- Curriculum included SPIN Selling, Negotiate to Win, and certification in Professional Selling Skills (PSS).

EDEN SPA & HEALTH CLUB, Miami and Coral Gables, Florida   2000–2004
Service Manager
Performed a wide variety of functions in high-volume, upscale health club.

- Demonstrated expertise in all aspects of hands-on client service and business development, including needs analysis, suggestive/strategic selling, and maximizing client potential.
- Managed 7-member team of personal trainers with emphasis on business development and workflow management.
- Accountable for all areas of facility management, including hiring and overseeing the productivity of maintenance staff.
- Instrumental in grand opening of the Coral Gables facility with regard to staff training and development, market penetration, public relations, and introduction of services to the general public.

EDUCATION

Bachelor of Arts, 1998 • UNIVERSITY OF MIAMI, Coral Gables, Florida

This was the second resume I prepared for Paige; the first, which included more details of her prior experience, helped her secure a pharmaceutical sales job. Now, with three years of directly related experience under her belt, she was looking to move to an industry leader with a better commission structure.

Paula S. Meadows

259-A Carriage Court, Fairfax, Virginia 22032

Phone (703) 791-0005 • Pager (703) 555-1010 • Email psmeadows@gmail.com

EXPERTISE: MEDICAL PRODUCTS SALES

Accomplished sales representative with experience in all phases of the sales process. History of developing new business for highly technical medical products and achieving sales growth.

Key Skills:

- Managing time and territory
- Setting and achieving sales objectives—both independently and in collaborative sales settings
- Introducing new projects
- Using outcome-based selling strategies to identify customer solutions
- Negotiating pricing with hospital administrators

PROFESSIONAL EXPERIENCE

CARDIO-CARE PRODUCTS, Chicago, Illinois   2003–Present

Sales Representative and Technical Consultant

Sell cardiac, cardiovascular, thoracic, and general surgery products in Virginia and Maryland. Major activities include introducing new products, attaining and expanding new and existing business, educating and training doctors and nurses on the clinical application, conducting in-services, attending surgeries, and writing and negotiating pricing contracts.

- **Sales Representative of the Year,** 2007.
- **Top Sales Award** (largest dollar volume), 2006.
- **Outstanding Sales Achievement Award,** 2004.
- Consistently one of the **highest sales volumes in organization.**

MEDICIA, Spokane, Washington   2001–2003

Sales Representative

Introduced and developed sales in Pennsylvania for two newly formed divisions of Medicia. Products included orthopedic implants and dental bone graft material.

- Attained **100% of quota** beginning first quarter 2001 through 2003.

PROVIDENT HOSPITAL, Philadelphia, Pennsylvania   1991–2001

Radiologic Technologist

Performed general and advanced radiology, diagnostic, orthopedic, vascular, and special procedures (angiography). Gained experience working in ER, OR, mammography, and vascular angiography suites. Served as Educational Coordinator for the department.

EDUCATION AND CERTIFICATION

UNIVERSITY OF PENNSYLVANIA, Philadelphia, Pennsylvania

- Completed Business, Language, Psychology, Writing, and Selling courses, 2000–2003.

POTTSTOWN COMMUNITY COLLEGE, Pottstown, Pennsylvania

- Associate Degree in Science, 1998.
- 2,200 hours clinical work in radiology at St. Elizabeth Hospital, Pottstown.

CERTIFICATION

- Board-Certified Radiology Technologist
- American Registry of Radiologic Technologists (ARRT)

Even with eight years of sales experience, Paula's patient-care experience is still relevant because she sells medical products in doctors' offices and hospitals.

Pamela Turner-Moore

29 Michigan Court
St. Louis, MO 63116

turner-moore@mac.com

Home (314) 869-2345
Office (314) 239-8910

Technical Sales: Medical / Pharmaceutical Industries

Proven performer with an effective combination of **sales ability** and **technical expertise** and a track record of impressive sales results in pharmaceutical, research, and hospital markets.

- Exceeded business development goals in launch of technical sales initiative in new market.

- Rapidly established market presence through creative prospective and sales strategies.

- Built on strong technical background and in-depth product knowledge to identify customer needs and concerns, recommend solutions, and become a trusted customer resource.

- Consistently demonstrated leadership, initiative, and strong communication skills.

Professional Experience

Sales Representative, West-Central Region: Strathmore Analytical, Inc., Pittsburgh, PA   2006–Present

Built the #1 territory in the company. Sell chromatography equipment to hospitals, research organizations, and pharmaceutical companies in 6-state Midwest region. Organize territory, establish prospecting targets, and implement effective sales strategies to capture both new and continuing business.

- Spearheaded the company's foray into a new market niche. Capitalized on industry knowledge to successfully penetrate lucrative pharmaceutical research market; achieved exponential sales growth.

- Achieved 246% of goal in 2008; only sales representative in the company to earn performance bonus every quarter of the last 3 years.

Quality Control Chemical Analyst: Quality Pharmaceuticals, Inc., St. Charles, MO   2003–2006

Performed and directed laboratory analysis of finished pharmaceutical products, assessing compliance with stringent quality standards for both market distribution and FDA approval. Utilized and maintained high-pressure liquid and gas chromatography systems (Waters, Hitachi, Kravos, and Hewlett-Packard equipment). Trained and monitored 30-member laboratory staff.

- Identified opportunities for improvements in safety procedures; recommended and implemented the changes, achieving measurable results.

Microbiology Laboratory Assistant: St. Charles General Hospital, St. Charles, MO   2002–2003

Evaluated bacteria for drug susceptibilities. Responded rapidly in emergency situations and advised clinicians of treatment possibilities.

Education

Bachelor of Arts in Biology: Washington University, St. Louis, MO   2002

Pamela's career path represents a fairly typical progression for the medical sales profession: a scientific/technical education followed by related experience, then transferring that experience to a sales position and moving up from there.

Edward Singh

510-949-0040 • eddiesingh@bay.rr.com
7892 Bridge Street, Oakland, CA 94611

QUALIFICATIONS	**Sales • Client Relationship Management • Deal Structuring & Negotiation**
Sales & Customer Focus	• Ten years in front-line customer contact positions with repeated success building relationships and creating win-win solutions. Includes 2 years of inside and direct sales to ophthalmologists, optometrists, and optical labs. • Assumed direct responsibility for the most challenging accounts in the company—restored relationships and grew sales 3% in one year. • Challenged to drive down inventory (competitive sales event)—made 50+ cold calls per day, sold $50K inventory in 3 months. • Promoted to handle escalated customer issues for Merrill Lynch.
Deal Making & Negotiation	• Put together creative solutions that deliver high ROI for company and customers. • Gained $12K incremental business in 5 weeks by offering a high-end lens at a low price based on positioning. Earned special recognition for creativity and results. • Successfully introduced a new product line by structuring a deal that paired complementary low-margin lenses with bulk sale of new product. Achieved exceptional client satisfaction and earned attractive margins for the new product.
Time, Territory, Program, & Account Management	• Manage a $3M book of business with 300 accounts—direct sales, customer support, order management, product introductions, deal structuring, and negotiation. • Created scheduled call cycles and executed plan so that every customer is contacted at least 6 times yearly. • As program coordinator, contacted hospitals and managed event details for Be Fit program that brought health screenings on-site for Merrill Lynch employees.
Quality, Accuracy, Product Knowledge	• As expert resource for designated programs, mastered complex details of 30 distinct investment plans at Merrill Lynch. Served as first-line client contact and manager/colleague resource. • Recognized for extraordinary quality and accuracy: 18 months of error-free transactions for Merrill Lynch.
Work Ethic	• In first year with Bay Optical, personally handled all order-picking as well as an active outbound sales function (30–50 cold calls daily). • Honored by Merrill Lynch's Reward and Recognition program for special effort in streamlining, updating, and improving usability of 401(k) plans and procedures.
CAREER HISTORY	***Direct Sales / Inside Sales / Account Management:*** Bay Optical, Oakland, CA • **TELESALES REPRESENTATIVE,** 2006–Present • **INSIDE SALES REPRESENTATIVE,** 2005–2006 ***Customer Service / Account Management:*** Merrill Lynch Investments, San Mateo, CA • **SERVICE DELIVERY SPECIALIST, PARTICIPANT SERVICES,** 2002–2005 • **CUSTOMER REPRESENTATIVE, PARTICIPANT SERVICES GROUP,** 1998–2002
EDUCATION	Bachelor of Arts, Communications, 1996 University of San Francisco

A functional format allows grouping of like activities and achievements, while employment is briefly but clearly spelled out at the end of the resume.

Diana Smithers

dsmithers@aol.com

(781) 948-7818
29 North Street, Stoneham, MA 02181

SALES / ACCOUNT MANAGEMENT
COMMERCIAL PRINTING / PRINTED PACKAGING INDUSTRIES

Consistently successful sales performance built on

- Demonstrated ability to build new business.
  - — Twice built successful territories from the ground up.
  - — More than doubled territory sales in first year on the job.
- Strong skills in customer relationship–building, effective listening, and needs discovery.
- Consultative, collaborative teamwork with customers, designers, printers, and others involved in the delivery of customer products and services.
- Proficiency and persistence in all stages of the sales cycle.
- Effective management of time and territory.

PROFESSIONAL EXPERIENCE

Bay State Packaging, Revere, MA, 2006–Present **Custom Corrugated / Preprinted Packaging**
Sales Representative

- Recruited to develop new and ongoing business, selling to industrial accounts (food, paper, packaging, and catalog companies) in southeastern Massachusetts / Rhode Island territory.
- Prospect for new business on a daily basis through cold calling and networking.
- Build relationships; entertain prospects and customers; conduct plant tours and presentations.
- Work collaboratively with engineering and manufacturing to design custom packaging solutions.
- Develop and present customized proposals.
- Ensure complete customer satisfaction through thorough follow-up both internally and externally.
  - — Increased territory sales 230% in first year.
  - — Proposed an innovative packaging solution that reduced customer costs while increasing volume and profitability of sales.
  - — Solved a quality problem for a prospect; success of this solution secured this fast-growing account, which currently averages $35K in monthly sales.

Powers Printed Packaging, East Boston, MA, 2005–2006 **Printed Packaging**
Sales Representative

- Recruited to build new Rhode Island / Connecticut territory. Built the business by establishing strong customer relationships based on a consultative, solution-focused sales approach.
- Worked with designers to develop custom packaging.
- Oversaw initial press runs, conducting careful quality checks to ensure customer satisfaction.
  - — Built territory from zero to $420K within one year.
  - — Identified and penetrated a new market niche for the company.

Greengrocer Marketing, Inc., Boston, MA, 2002–2005 **Printed Retail Packaging**
Sales Representative

- Developed business in 4-state New England region.
- Priced and presented quotations; delivered presentations with the use of mock-ups.
- Assisted marketing groups, design firms, and ad agencies with the design of graphics to conform with flexographic printing requirements. Worked with outside rotogravure and offset printers.
- Monitored and expedited the printing and production process, ensuring quality of prepress and finished work. Conducted press checks with customers.
  - — Built business from the ground up, developing 17 ongoing new accounts in 3 years.
  - — Secured a key client by identifying a performance problem in an existing product and recommending a workable and cost-effective solution.
  - — Leveraged a trade show contact to develop significant new business (first press run of more than 1 million impressions).

(continued)

Diana began her job search by e-mailing this resume to two executive recruiters who specialized in the packaging industry; both called her the same day to schedule interviews.

Diana Smithers   (781) 948-7818 • dsmithers@aol.com

PROFESSIONAL EXPERIENCE, continued

Elite Bag Company, Worcester, MA, 1992–2002   **High-Quality Printed Retail Bags**
Sales / Sales Service, 2000–2002

- Established and maintained effective communications with customers and field representatives both by phone and through frequent travel to customer sites nationwide.
- Served as resource and quality checker for in-house flexographic printing using photo-polymer printing plates and water-based inks.
- Participated in press checks at outside printing facilities providing rotogravure and offset printing.
  — Developed expertise in a wide range of sales and sales support functions—costing, quotations, order entry, scheduling, expediting, shipping, billing, stock level monitoring.
  — Established and maintained excellent customer relationships.

Director of Customer Service, 1995–2000

- Managed 10 employees providing order entry and customer service.
- Interacted extensively with customers and field representatives.
- Coordinated training for all new employees.
  — Instrumental in developing and implementing computerized order-entry process.
  — Improved the order-entry process by redesigning forms for use with computer applications.

Steadily promoted to positions of increased responsibility:
- Order Entry Supervisor, 1994–1995
- Assistant Supervisor, 1993–1994
- Clerk, 1992–1993

PROFESSIONAL DEVELOPMENT

- *Cold Calling for Cowards,* Hocutt and Associates
- *The Counselor Salesperson,* Wilson Learning Corp.
- *Value Added Selling,* Association of Independent Corrugated Converters
- *Dimensions of Professional Selling,* Jack Carew Positional Selling Systems
- *Supervisory Management,* Dun and Bradstreet
- *How to Supervise People,* National Seminars, Inc.
- *Management Skills for Women Supervisors,* Boston College
- *Keeping Your Customer,* Boston College
- *Superior Customer Service,* Sales Consultants, Inc.
- *Professional Telephone Skills,* Sales Consultants, Inc.

PROFESSIONAL MEMBERSHIPS

- Women in Packaging, Inc.—Boston Chapter
  Chair, Membership Board, 2006–Present
- Toastmasters International

Steven Evans

2525 Johnson Trail, Jacksonville, FL 32257
904-650-1527   SEvans@aol.com

Sales Professional

Expertise	**Industrial Sales / Paint & Coatings Industry**
Profile	Results-oriented sales professional with an effective combination of *technical abilities* (gained through hands-on experience in production positions), *selling and presenting skills,* and a *genuine commitment to customer service and satisfaction.*
Strengths	• Building effective customer relationships. • Establishing rapport and trust with prospects as the first step in new business development. • Managing time and territory through strong organizational, planning, and follow-through skills.

Professional Experience

M&M INDUSTRIAL PAINTS, Jacksonville, Florida—1990–Present
Industrial Coatings Sales Representative, 2003–Present

Sell specialty coatings to the product-finishing OEM market. Provide a high level of account service and problem-solving; recommend solutions to a variety of challenging manufacturing, durability, and performance problems.

Establish performance goals and prospect-development plans to gain new business. Organize territory calls to include a consistent number of cold calls weekly.

Key Accomplishments
• More than **tripled** territory sales (from $300K in 2003 to $930K in 2008).
• Consistently exceeded quota; **averaged 15% annual territory growth** (2003–2005) while undergoing two territory restructurings that relocated significant earned business to new territories.
• **Gained new, out-of-territory accounts** by specific recommendations from current customers.
• Through attentive customer service, **retained key account** for 2 years while lab struggled to solve a quality problem.
• Formally recognized by customer for 6 years of **"extraordinary" customer service.**
• Took on 2 accounts that were highly dissatisfied with both product and service; turned both around through equal emphasis on **customer service** and **product improvements** in response to their specific problems and needs.

Prior Experience: Production

Tinting Department, 1999–2003
Kinetic Dispersion Department, 1994–1999
Production and Warehouse, summers 1990–1994

Education and Training

FLAGLER COLLEGE, St. Augustine, Florida—B.S. in Business/Marketing: 90% completed

Professional Training
Dale Carnegie Training, 2000: Dale Carnegie Continuous Performance Award
Industrial Painting Processes, 2000: Society of Manufacturing Engineers

Computer Skills

Daily use of Microsoft Office to plan calls, organize information, and maintain a variety of business records.

Membership

Society of Manufacturing Engineers
Jacksonville Kiwanis Club

After 13 years with his company, Steven had moved from a production position into sales. The most recent six years in sales take up the bulk of his resume.

Derek Simms

dereksimms@aol.com

2954 Roman Way, Columbus, GA 31907
(706) 743-8765

PROFILE

Sales Professional with extensive background, expertise, and interest in the automotive industry.
A proven performer with the ability to

- Set and achieve aggressive sales goals.
- Build account loyalty and repeat and new business through superior service and relationship-building.
- Effectively manage a geographic territory with a diverse customer base (warehouses, jobbers, large automotive repair facilities, small shops).
- Proactively approach customer and business challenges, applying strong problem-solving skills, persistence, and resourcefulness to achieve positive results.

PROFESSIONAL EXPERIENCE

ALLIED AUTOMOTIVE, INC., Austin, Texas

1999–Present

Territory Sales Representative—Columbus, Georgia

Promote all divisions of the Allied product lines to both new and existing accounts in assigned territory. Key responsibilities include

Prospecting/New Business Development: Approach and build relationships with new or potential customers. Grow territory in total sales, number of accounts, and sales per account.

Account Maintenance: Consistently demonstrate responsiveness, strong customer focus, and ability to build good customer relationships. Serve as an ongoing customer resource and problem-solver. Maintain regular contact at all levels of customer organizations, including upper management.

Product Training: Organize and conduct training meetings and product seminars for customers. Maintain up-to-date knowledge of company's and competitors' evolving product lines. ASE-certified in Suspension and Steering, Brakes, and Heating and Air Conditioning.

Inventory Control: Monitor product distribution from manufacturer to end user. Anticipate and resolve problems to ensure smooth product flow.

Business/Organizational Functions: Effectively manage geographic territory for efficient and thorough account coverage. Prepare sales plans and reports.

Key Accomplishments

- Consistently **meet or exceed sales objectives** that require significant *new* as well as *retained* business every year.
- Successfully **expand sales** to existing customers through relationship-building and cross-selling; demonstrate thorough knowledge of our products and the automotive industry that gives credibility to product recommendations.
- Recognized for **effective account troubleshooting** and **strong sales presentation skills;** often called on to assist with major projects in other territories (new account changeover, sales presentations to key prospects, sales presentations at corporate sales meetings).
- In 2002, **successfully retained largest account** ($3 million annually) that was targeted by competitor. Customer decision was based on product quality and the sales and service relationship I have built with them over the years.

Honors and Awards

- **"A+ Leaders"** program, 2006 (awarded to top 10% of sales team for attitude and contributions).
- **District Manager of the Year,** 2005 (awarded to the top performer among all Eastern Region District Managers judged on sales, teamwork, and customer satisfaction).
- **"Attitude of the Year Award,"** 2004 (first runner up... #2 among all zone sales staff).
- **"Future Focus Award,"** 2001 (among top 10% of sales force selected to participate on product review/recommendation panel).

Having held the same position since 1999, Derek needed to show the diversity of his job duties to give some depth to his experience.

Derek Simms   dereksimms@aol.com ■ (706) 743-8765

PROFESSIONAL EXPERIENCE
continued

AUTO-PRO INDUSTRIES, INC., Daytona, Florida   1995–1999

Sales Representative—Columbus, Georgia

Managed assigned territory, calling on jobbers and installers to maintain existing accounts and build new business. Benefited from sales training and coaching provided by District Manager.

MATTHEWS AUTO PARTS, Columbus, Georgia   1991–1995

Assistant Store Manager, 1993–1995

Managed purchasing and inventory control, customer relations, sales, and shipping. Supervised and scheduled 7 employees.

Counter Sales, 1991–1993

Responsible for customer sales and service; served as customers' primary telephone contact.

- ■ **Top producer;** promoted to new store and subsequently to Assistant Manager.

EDUCATION

COLUMBUS STATE UNIVERSITY, Columbus, Georgia
Associate's Degree in Business

ADDITIONAL INFORMATION

Familiar with a variety of business software, including Word, Excel, and the Insight component of SAP. Skilled in Internet research and communications.

Casey Stanton

7509 Laredo Avenue, Austin, Texas 78741
512-555-8755—casey@gmail.com

Automotive Sales Professional

Highly motivated professional with a consistent track record of success in a competitive industry.

Possess an effective combination of interpersonal/sales/relationship-building skills and strong analytical and organizational abilities... resulting in thoroughly planned, well-executed marketing and sales strategies.

Build and maintain loyal customer relationships based on trust, communication, and a problem-solving approach that addresses issues immediately and strives for rapid resolution.

Key Areas of Expertise

- Sales and marketing of luxury automobiles
- Key account relationship-building and networking
- Customer service and quality assurance
- Technical seminar/meeting/sales presentations
- Marketing campaigns
- Product introductions
- Territory development
- Business analysis and planning

Experience & Achievements

➤ ELITE MOTOR COMPANY, Dallas, Texas   2004–2008
Sales Consultant

Sold Mercedes-Benz automobiles with an average price of $55K, top price of $135K. Successfully passed testing and earned certification on all elements of Mercedes-Benz features, functions, design, and product lines.

- Grew client base through positive, professional relationships with customers that led to **repeat business and numerous referrals.**
- Within 6 months, rose to **#5 of 9 sales representatives.**
- Contributed to the dealership's **consistently high (97%) CSI.**

➤ ACURA OF DALLAS, Dallas, Texas   2000–2004
Sales Representative

Developing clients from a solid referral base and effective marketing strategies, sold Acura automobiles with an average price of $33K.

- Consistently ranked among top performers; **#2 in 2002.**
- Contributed to strong dealership statistics: **#1 in sales volume** of 12 dealerships in 6 cities; **#1 in leasing** and **#18 in sales performance** of 298 dealerships nationwide.

➤ SUN COUNTRY MERCEDES, Phoenix, Arizona   1994–2000
Service Manager (1999–2000)

Selected by dealership owner for special assignment to improve the quality of service provided to our customers—a dealership priority in 2000. Brought a sales and service attitude to the department; reduced turnaround time and **improved Customer Satisfaction Index by 8%.**

Casey liked selling luxury automobiles and was good at it. When her husband was transferred to New Jersey, she sought a position in luxury auto sales and/or marketing at the corporate level. Her cover letter is sample 12-1.

Casey Stanton
512-555-8755—casey@gmail.com

➤ SUN COUNTRY MERCEDES, continued

Sales Manager (1997–1999), **Sales Representative** (1994–1997)

Developed a successful track record of sales achievements, consistently ranking with the top sales leaders. Promoted to Sales Manager with responsibility for sales staff, including all hiring, training, evaluations, and terminations.

- **"Gold Medal"** sales performer, 1994, 1995, and 1996.

➤ SANTO MEDICAL SYSTEMS, Phoenix, Arizona   1991–1994

Sales Engineer

Sold a full line of medical imaging products through client calls on hospitals, clinics, and private medical offices. Sales process required extensive coordination to achieve optimum equipment placement and the support of key technicians, followed by liaison with various leasing companies and ongoing training, service, and follow-up.

- Achieved top sales ranking by developing new accounts, maintaining excellent client rapport, and providing thorough after-sale support.
- **#1 in the Southwest Region** for top sales in several product lines.
- **#1 nationwide** for top sales of one product line.
- Increased sales territory from a ranking of 31st to 18th in first fiscal year; **improved to ranking of 14th** within 2 years.

➤ MEDI-CARE CORPORATION, Tucson, Arizona   1990–1991

Sales Representative: Hemodialysis Products

- Ranked #**3 out of 7** regional sales representatives in sales volume.
- Captured a large (500-bed) hospital's business through effective sales efforts and positive customer relations.

Education

UNIVERSITY OF MONTANA, Butte, Montana
   B.A., Sociology

UNIVERSITY OF ARIZONA, Tucson, Arizona
   Accounting and Management coursework toward MBA (3 years part time).

PROFESSIONAL DEVELOPMENT
   Seminars, workshops, and ongoing training to increase sales, communications, management, and automotive expertise.

ROBERT AXE

bobaxe@verizon.net
Mobile: 201-704-4409

235 Meadow Lane
Washington Township, NJ 07676

Home: 201-839-4490
Office: 201-348-2187

PROFILE

Accomplished sales professional adept at prospecting, strategic selling, business development, and territory management. Sales success built on strong customer service and deep expertise in sales and merchandising.

PROFESSIONAL EXPERIENCE

HEARTHGLOW, INC., Newark, NJ — 2007–Present
Account Executive

Develop and manage key corporate accounts for specialty maker of blown-glass oil candles. Perform multifaceted role—outside sales in 3 states plus inside/corporate sales for entire company, encompassing lead development and follow-up, trade-show marketing, and dealer training and support.

- Grew New England business 400% in 2008 through 3 major road trips.

- Took on added direct-sales responsibility for Pennsylvania and Delaware in 2007 after unsatisfactory performance of rep group; quickly reestablished solid company presence and on track to achieve sales above company average by year end.

- Represented Hearthglow at semiannual major Atlanta giftware shows. Teamed with reps on presentations to key accounts.

MAHON CORPORATION, Paterson, NJ — 2004–2007
Product Sales Manager—Industrial Wire

Managed Northern New Jersey sales territory for one of the largest industrial-wire manufacturers in the U.S. Generated sales, negotiated pricing, resolved customer problems, and built customer relationships.

- Increased sales volume 4% to existing accounts through excellent customer relationships.

- Rescued account representing more than $150K in annual business; worked closely with factory QC representatives to resolve quality concerns and restore customer confidence.

SALES TEAM ASSOCIATES, Washington Township, NJ — 1999–2004
Manufacturer's Representative

Marketed lines of gift items to gift stores; florists; floral wholesalers; and craft, garden, and chain stores in New York/New Jersey region. Acted as key company representative at Columbus and Atlanta trade shows.

- Increased territory volume 600% through development of new and existing accounts.

- Opened more than 150 new accounts and significantly increased volume in existing accounts.

- Established excellent customer service and follow-up.

EDUCATION

INDIANA UNIVERSITY, Bloomington, IN

Bachelor of Science, Marketing, 1999

Brief and to-the-point, this resume focuses on results.

Carla Schmidt

45 Hopkins Place, Baltimore, MD 21224
Home (410) 423-8910   Mobile (410) 208-4908

PROFILE   **Sales / Account Management / New Business Development**

Highlights

- Track record of sales leadership in diverse industries; solid command of a variety of sales strategies complemented by strong people-assessment and interaction skills.
- Strengths include developing and nurturing positive account relationships.
- Proven ability to motivate and lead an enthusiastic team effort that, balanced by solid planning and implementation skills, results in a high level of achievement.
- History of consistently rising to new challenges.

SALES AND LEADERSHIP EXPERIENCE

ACME TRANSPORTATION EQUIPMENT, Baltimore, MD, 2005–Present

Key Account Representative

Sales of transportation equipment (trailers, gear) to companies with large fleets and complex transportation needs—e.g., large retailers and frozen-food suppliers.

Analyze customer needs and recommend appropriate solutions. Establish rapport and develop positive, professional client relationships built on trust, problem-solving, and a demonstrated commitment to meet their needs.

Key Accomplishments

- Grew sales five-fold, from $10K–$12K monthly in 2005 to $55K–$60K currently.
- Increased customer base 62% through cold calling, diligent pursuit of leads, and effective networking.
- Took on additional assignment as interim Parts Manager, turning around a negative situation by anticipating customer needs and focusing on service.

JOHN HANCOCK INSURANCE COMPANY

Sales Representative, Baltimore, MD, 2003–2005

Insurance sales—all lines—to both corporate and individual clients.

Accepted permanent position upon graduation, following successful experience as a Telemarketing Representative while attending school.

Key Accomplishments

- Built customer base from zero to 100 established clients within a year.
- Named member of JH Achievers Club honoring top sales representatives.

Telemarketing Representative, College Park, MD, 2001–2003

Developed strong sales skills and the ability to rapidly assess people, achieving a steady income in an incentive-based, fast-paced, competitive environment. Handled all aspects of customer relations.

EDUCATION

UNIVERSITY OF MARYLAND—**Bachelor of Arts degree in English,** 2001

- Selected as facilitator for a pilot leadership program that has since been instituted as a permanent part of the curriculum.

COMMUNITY LEADERSHIP

Current: United Way of Baltimore

- Chaired 2006 Volunteer of the Year awards banquet.

College: Big Brothers/Big Sisters

- Worked with organization leadership to recommend and implement operational improvements.

A description of Acme Transportation's line of business was helpful in placing Carla's activities in the proper context. Her college job as a telemarketer led to full-time employment upon graduation, so we included this early evidence of her sales skills.

SARAH J. CONWAY

(203) 555-8745   271 Main Street, Branford, CT 06405   sarahconway@aol.com

SALES AND MANAGEMENT PROFESSIONAL

Seven-time President's Club Member — Top 5% in the Company

Consistently strong record of outperforming sales quotas, developing new business, building strong customer relationships, and effectively managing time and territory. Expert at recommending technology solutions to best fit customers' unique circumstances. Proficient and persistent in all stages of the sales cycle.

Energized by new challenges. Keen abilities in planning, goal setting, strategy implementation, and follow-up.

PROFESSIONAL EXPERIENCE

Printer Systems Ltd., New Haven, CT, 1993–Present

Maker of microprocessor-controlled ink-jet industrial printing equipment (average system $15K), laser-etching print systems (average system $40K), array printing systems, and related peripherals and supplies.

SENIOR SALES ENGINEER (2002–Present)—Charged with increasing sales in major national and global accounts (United Technologies, Echlin, Colt Industries) while also expanding local customer base. Focus on selling solutions to fit customers' unique technology needs; flexibly adapt sales tactics and presentations to match individual sales cycle, chain of command, decision-making process, and need for relationship-building.

Generate high sales volume: $1.2M annual sales quota, plus $1.4M additional equipment and $3M–$4M in supplies. Grow territory by an average of 20 new accounts annually through fundamental sales practices: telemarketing, prospecting, and networking.

- Exceeded sales quota by 130% annually for 2 consecutive years.
- Increased sales 50% in each of two key accounts. With one account, succeeded in reversing poor perception of the company through positive relationship-building and frequent product updates.
- Selected to mentor other members of the sales team, providing guidance and in-field sales coaching.

OEM SALES EXECUTIVE (2000–2002)—Marketed the company's products to systems integrators, machinery builders, and distribution networks over a 3-state territory. Primary focus was customer relationship-building to ensure integration of our product line into the turnkey packages they marketed to their clients.

- Met or exceeded all sales quotas and new account development goals.
- Gained expertise in working with the OEM sales channel.

SALES ENGINEER (1994–1999)—Managed Eastern Connecticut sales territory, selling primarily to small accounts. Maximized territory potential through aggressive and persistent performance of sales and prospecting functions. Developed strong customer relationships built on problem identification and solution selling.

Promoted new hardware and software to accommodate upgrade and service needs. Communicated problems and application queries to technical support; identified interfacing and internetworking needs; served as liaison between customer and home office. Wrote and delivered product presentations to customers and new sales employees.

- Delivered exceptional first-year sales performance (250% of sales goal); consistently and significantly exceeded sales quotas in each succeeding year.
- "Rookie of the Year" 1995; in top 5% of all company Sales Engineers every year thereafter.

CORPORATE INSIDE SALES REPRESENTATIVE (1993–1994)—Expedited incoming leads, communicated with sales engineers, and served as customer liaison. Rapidly learned product lines and demonstrated strong customer skills.

EDUCATION

Bachelor of Science in Business Administration / Marketing Major, 1993—Wesleyan University, Middletown, CT

The chronological format of this resume clearly shows Sarah's steady career progression. Bold print draws attention to her strong numbers and results.

Jeffrey B. Mendenhall

18 White Pine Lane • Madison, CT 06443
203.555.1212 (phone/fax) • 203.666.3434 (cell) • jeffbmenden@att.net

Profile

- Results-oriented **Sales Professional** with demonstrated success in cultivating opportunities that result in sustainable business and profitability. Proven experience in industrial sales discipline complemented by expertise in electrical insulation, transformer manufacturing, and power supply technologies.

- Uncompromised commitment to management and customer service excellence balanced by the highest degree of integrity in all relationships and transactions.

- Resourceful team player, responsive to changing business demands; strong strategic planning abilities; expert problem-solving skills complemented by the ability to quickly develop viable business solutions.

- PC expertise includes Microsoft Word, Excel, PowerPoint, and Outlook; ACT.

Professional Experience

GRAYBAR ELECTRIC, INC. • Newark, NJ   1990–Present
Sales Engineer

- Recruited to identify, develop, and expand business opportunities throughout the Northeast for a distributor specializing in transformer, power supply, solenoid relay, automotive electronic, wiring harness, and appliance manufacturer markets.

- Highly effective in rapidly building account rapport and cultivating key business development opportunities throughout the territory.

- Consistently achieve quota and pipeline development goals for product and service sales; flawlessly execute quotations and lead follow-up.

- Facilitate blanket order negotiations, successfully securing many strategic accounts.

- Manage local and international stocking through inventory-control programs.

- Utilize exceptional problem-solving skills, leveraging product sales while providing effective solutions to customers.

Key Accomplishments ...

- **Increased sales in southern New England territory twentyfold between 1990 and 2008.**

- Developed exceptional customer base throughout Connecticut, Rhode Island, New York, and northern New Jersey, comprising a balanced mix of Fortune 500 subsidiaries and privately held, multimillion-dollar companies.

- Exceeded a challenge to **successfully expand business** throughout 2 recessionary periods during a timeframe characterized by eroding manufacturing markets (moving offshore).

- Exemplary sales performance consistently recognized with numerous incentives and bonus awards, including

  – **2002 Top Sales Award;** Hilton Head trip
  – **1998 Top Sales Award;** Bermuda trip
  – **1996 Top Sales Award;** Puerto Vallarta, Mexico, trip

- Initiated and developed a PC database for target marketing of specific products. Result: enabled comprehensive selling and full integration between customer and staff.

(continued)

Resume contributed by Jan Melnik, MRW
Accomplishments are clearly identified with an attention-getting subheading, and notable achievements are further highlighted with bold type. Extensive civic involvement hints at strong relationships in the community.

Jeffrey B. Mendenhall

Professional Experience *(continued)*

UNITED TECHNOLOGIES CORP. • Ft. Wayne, IN / Philadelphia, PA / Cleveland, OH
Earlier career background includes 9 years of successful and progressive product-line management and sales engineering experience within UTC's Essex Group Magnet Wire and Insulation Division. Promoted to **Product Line Manager** (4 years) and **Sales Engineer** (8 years) after one year as **Sales Correspondent.**

Key Accomplishments ...

- Increased sales in eastern Pennsylvania and southern New Jersey **250% over 4 years;** developed and closed extensive business opportunities among OEM and aftermarket corporations.

- Led strategic marketing initiatives and established distributor relationships with manufacturing. Directed negotiations and established product line breadth and pricing, gross margin, and inventory allocation. Managed development of product catalogs, data sheets, and collateral advertising.

- Advanced product development through collaborative meetings with customers, sales representatives, engineers, management, and production staff.

Education	OHIO UNIVERSITY • Athens, OH • **BBA, Marketing** Extensive continuing education throughout career includes Executive Selling and Professional Selling programs with Anthony Robbins, General Electric, Loctite, and 3M.
Civic	• **Madison Zoning Board of Appeals—Member** (Elected: 2005–Present; 2000–2002) • **Madison Inland Wetlands Commission—Member** (Appointed: 1999–Present) • **State Central Committee—Communications Committee Chairman** (2005–Present) • **State Central Committee—Member** (2004–Present) • **Connecticut Commission on Aging—Secretary** (2003–Present) • **Madison Town Committee—Chairman** (1996–2004) • **Old Lyme Jaycees—Past President**

Reesa Sobieski

401-555-1212   27 Sea Hill Road, N. Kingstown, RI 02852   reesasobie@verizon.net

Sales / Territory Management
Expertise: Home Furnishings

Highly motivated sales professional with a track record of consistently successful territory and individual account management. Demonstrated accomplishments in

- Maintaining positive business relationships with diverse retailers.
- Overseeing long-term profitable sales growth with individual customers and throughout territory.
- Implementing new approaches in distribution and merchandising of home furnishings—specifically, successful start-up of independent sole-source retailers.
- Training customer sales staff in merchandising and sales strategies.
- Achieving ambitious sales goals through individually designed sales and merchandising programs.

Professional Experience

NU-AMERICAN FURNITURE, Burnsville, North Carolina—1996–Present

ACCOUNT REPRESENTATIVE / TERRITORY MANAGER (2000–Present): Market all of the company's product categories in a 3-state region (Massachusetts, Rhode Island, Connecticut) to superstores, chains, and individual retailers in both large urban and rural areas.

Product Categories: Bedroom, Dining Room, Occasional, Wall Units, Accents, Home Entertainment Centers, Fabric Upholstery, Leather Upholstery

Sales Performance:

- Consistently a growth leader and the dominant vendor in all accounts.
- Led territory sales growth from $579K in 2000 to $21M in 2008; tracking growth to $31M in 2009.
- Collaborate with accounts, establishing overall business objectives as well as specific merchandise and marketing plans to achieve joint sales goals.

Business Planning / Territory Management:

- Apply business and retail expertise to convert corporate sales goals to workable marketing strategies for territory as a whole and with each individual account.
- Regularly evaluate distribution and account activity to maximize exposure within each account.
- Uncover, analyze, and convert opportunities for new business within accounts and throughout the territory.

Nu-American Galleries:

- Most recently, fulfilled the company's primary distribution objective by completing a deal to bring 3 Nu-American Galleries to Massachusetts and 1 to Connecticut.
- Recruit current retailers for specialized stores through effective sales presentations and ongoing positive relationships.
- Qualify interested retailers and assist with all stages of floor planning, merchandising, advertising, staff training, eventual opening, and ongoing operations.

SUPERVISOR, CUSTOMER SERVICE (1996–2000): Supervised 13 customer service representatives who were the company's liaison with retailers for ordering, service, and problem resolution.

Education

UNIVERSITY OF NORTH CAROLINA, Chapel Hill, North Carolina—BS, Business Administration

Because most of Reesa's experience was in one position, we were able to create a resume that gives quite a bit of detail about her activities and accomplishments, yet fits nicely on one page.

Nicholas P. Alexander

Sales • Territory Management • Team Leadership

PROFILE	• Accomplished Sales and Management Professional with a strong record of developing new business, improving team and individual performance, and consistently achieving sales and operations goals in competitive environments.

• Effective negotiator skilled at directing discussions toward win-win outcomes.
• Recognized leader in establishing and communicating a strong customer service focus.
• First-rate presenter and good communicator from boardroom to warehouse.

PROFESSIONAL EXPERIENCE

2007–Present

Sales Manager — NU-TECH SYSTEMS, West Haven, CT

• Lead the marketing and sales initiatives for Web-based technology system targeted to large financial institutions, the educational market, and state regulatory agencies.
• Manage $3M, 5-state New England territory, working from 2 office locations.
• Accountable for business development, advertising (national and regional campaigns), project pricing, contract negotiations, client relations, and ongoing project management.
• As a key component of new business development, deliver PowerPoint-based boardroom presentations to executives, engineers, and top state regulators.

> **Captured $312K in new sales in 10 months while managing $2.7M in existing projects.**

2005–2007

Sales Consultant — NEW HAVEN MECHANICAL SYSTEMS, New Haven, CT

• Prospected and proposed preventative maintenance agreements for large mechanical systems; prepared competitive bids for new energy-management systems. Identified prospects through cold-calling and business analysis within eastern Connecticut territory.
• Negotiated all contracts, both new agreements and renewals of existing major accounts.

> **In first 3 months, negotiated $92K in new contracts, outperforming new-sales quota by 14%.**

2003–2005

District Manager — CINTAS UNIFORM SERVICES, Branford, CT

• Managed $2M district with more than 2,000 active accounts in a 285-mile radius. Worked directly with largest accounts to ensure excellent service and promote customer retention.
• Accountable for sales staff performance, business retention, and overall skill development.
• Negotiated new and extended contracts, resolving such issues as rate increases, payment schedules, and general service concerns.
• Developed and implemented a management strategy for monitoring 7 route representatives and 1 route supervisor.
• Established a strong track record of valuing employee contributions and input to the decision-making progress. Succeeded in motivating staff and improving customer service.

> **Increased district volume by $735K while decreasing losses 50% in fiscal year 2005.**

EDUCATION	UNIVERSITY OF CONNECTICUT	Bachelor of Arts, Economics, 2003
	PROFESSIONAL TRAINING	Sales Development Corporate Sales Training, 2004
		Karrass Effective Negotiating Seminar, 2005

ADDITIONAL QUALIFICATIONS

• Travel Experience: United States, Europe, Mediterranean, Canada, Mexico
• Language Proficiency (conversational): French and Spanish
• Computer Proficiency: Microsoft Excel, Word, PowerPoint, Access, Outlook

71 Riverwalk Park Lane, Hamden, CT 06492   (203) 555-4321 • nickal@yahoo.com

Contact information at the bottom leaves the focus on expertise at the top. The one key accomplishment for each position stands out nicely in this box format.

Thomas Silvers

mailing address	P.O. Box 4230, Washington, DC 20037
residence	8590 Promontory Way, Arlington, Virginia
telephone	(202) 555-7245
e-mail	tomsilvers@dc.rr.com

Profile

Experienced, results-driven sales professional with a track record of outperforming sales goals and delivering high levels of customer service.

Strengths

- Customer needs assessment and solution selling.
- Rapport- and relationship-building with both new prospects and existing clients.
- Account retention… through follow-up, delivery on promises, and exceptional attention to detail.
- New-business development… creative, well-organized, and persistently executed marketing strategies.
- In-depth knowledge of wireless communications, the company's products and services, and the Metropolitan D.C. business and retail market… commitment to continued professional development.
- Flexibility and team participation to meet the needs of the business.

Experience

2005–Present

WORLD WIRELESS COMPANY, Washington, D.C.
Business Specialist
Sell wireless telephone services to both business and retail customers, achieving consistent sales success through a strong focus on *learning and meeting customer needs* and *providing exceptional customer service*.

- Achieved 104% of sales quota, 2007; 110%, 2008; on track to finish 2009 at 127%.
- Consistently exceed goals for new account activations.
- Maintain existing business and capture renewals. Recognized for superior follow-up and responsiveness to customer inquiries and concerns.
- Prospect for new business through telemarketing, direct mail, and networking; manage this task effectively through good organization and follow-up.
- Effectively build customer relationships both by phone and in person.

2004–2005

DOWNTOWN DISTRICT HOMES, Washington, D.C.
Sales Associate
Laid the groundwork for a successful career in real estate sales through effective prospecting and networking.

2001–2005

ADDITIONAL EXPERIENCE
- **Financial Services Representative,** Bank of America, San Francisco, California
- **Registered Representative,** Smith & Henshaw Financial Services, Oakland, California
  Earned licensure: Disability and Life Insurance, NASD Series 6, Series 63

Education

1997

SAN FRANCISCO STATE UNIVERSITY, San Francisco, California
Bachelor of Science in Business Administration
- Minor: Political Science
- Internship: Representative Edward Wilson's office, Washington, D.C. (Summer 2000)

Tom marketed himself effectively through Internet resume posting and direct contact with telecommunications companies via their Web sites.

STEPHEN X. GORDON

4090 70th Street SW
Seattle, WA 98136

sgordon75@gmail.com

Home 206-447-1471
Mobile 206-561-7612

SALES ▪ KEY ACCOUNT MANAGEMENT ▪ BUSINESS DEVELOPMENT

Top-performing sales professional with record of *always* exceeding sales, profit, and market-share goals. Expert in consultative and solution selling with proven ability to identify and capitalize on sales opportunities. Strong planning, prospecting, cold-calling, presentation, and sales skills along with persistence and commitment to goal achievement. Excellent customer relationship skills. Notable efficiency, organizational skills, and ability to juggle multiple projects and priorities.

PROFESSIONAL EXPERIENCE

XYZ CORPORATION *(NYSE: XYZ)*   Seattle, WA, 2005–Present
$5B public corporation, a leading distributor of building products to dealers, retailers, builders, and industrial users

■ **Northwest Region Territory Manager—Industrial/Manufactured Housing**

Delivered exceptional sales and margin growth, managing key accounts and selling building materials to the industrial/manufactured housing market in Metro Seattle.

Create and execute sales/business plan for the territory, balancing new business development with account management and customer support. Work with a broad customer base (millwork houses, fixture/furniture/exhibit manufacturing facilities, cabinet manufacturers, concrete accessory and rebar customers), identifying needs and selling a diverse line of products/solutions.

- Achieved both sales and margin growth every year in a downward-trending economic cycle.

	Sales	Gross Margin
2005	$1.9M	$185K
2006	$3.1M	$384K
2007	$8.4M	$971K

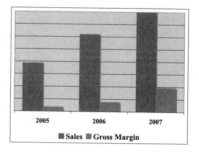

- #9 nationwide, #3 in Midwest for Gross Margin increase, 2007.
- Prospected and developed more than $1.2M in new accounts.
- Developed just-in-time programs that controlled costs and streamlined inventory for key accounts while driving sales growth and margin increase for XYZ.

NORTHWEST FOREST PRODUCTS *(NASDAQ: NWFP)*   Tacoma, WA, 2002–2005
The nation's leading manufacturer and distributor of wood and wood-alternative products; a $2.7B public company

■ **Account Manager**

Rapidly achieved impressive results in sales of structural panels, construction lumber, and composite products to industrial accounts in Washington–Oregon territory. Performed full range of sales, business development, and account management functions including margin accountability, product pricing, proposal development/presentation, order management, and A/R oversight.

	Sales	Margin
Quota	$1.09M	$83K (7.6%)
2003 Results	$1.60M	$145K (9.1%)
Performance to Plan	**147%**	**175%**

Eye-catching charts and tables ensure that stellar sales achievements are not overlooked.

NORTHWEST FOREST PRODUCTS, continued
- Aggressively promoted 2 new product lines, generating nearly **$700K** in new business:
  – **$500K** sales of TechTrim, a new polymer.
    Won internal SPIFF nationwide, selling more TechTrim than anyone else in the company.
  – **$180K** sales of Xpotential, a 100% recycled plastic product.
    Won internal SPIFF nationwide; set up 2 stocking dealers.

FASTENERS-R-US, INC. *(NYSE: FRU)*   Seattle, WA, 2001–2002
Major global distributor of wiring systems, networking products, and fasteners; $4.9B revenue

■ **Sales / New Business Development Representative**

Built and maintained business in Seattle region. Developed and qualified prospects; performed needs assessment; worked with technical team to create specifications; presented recommendations and closed sales. Built customer relationships, providing ongoing account management and maintenance.

- Selected as Sales Specialist for new product focus in digital and closed-circuit security systems Delivered immediate results and long-term contracts, including:
  – King County: **$12K** immediate business and authorization for test installation that resulted in commitment for all future CSU/DSU business.
  – Starbucks: Needs assessment, CCTV demo and test installation, and ultimate capture of **$175K** contract for 58 stores nationwide.
  – Sea-Tac Medical Center: **$130K** contract, networking system for new administration building.
- Identified need, defined solution, and led all aspects of specifying a new access-control system for Tacoma County. First-year revenue projected to be **$250K**, with no-bid follow-on sales for 10 years.

GEORGIA-PACIFIC   Portland, OR, 1994–2001
Second-largest manufacturer of forest products in the U.S.; $2.1B subsidiary of Koch Industries, Inc.

■ **Structural Panels Trader**

As product manager for structural panels, a wood-product commodity for the building industry, negotiated and sold products to target accounts in a $22 million, 8-state Western region. Qualified prospects and developed sales strategies for contractor, wholesale, and retail accounts.

- Grew sales **12%** in targeted key accounts.
- Increased gross margin by **32.5%**; maintained highest direct-sales profit of 15 traders in group.
- Played a key role in advancing group from last to **#3** in sales among 20+ groups nationwide.
- Worked closely with account managers to develop pricing based on market conditions.

■ **Account Manager,** 1996–1997 (40 accounts, 4-state territory)
  Inside Sales Representative, Salt Lake City, Utah, 1994–1996

EDUCATION / ADDITIONAL

B.S. in Management, 1994: University of Washington, Seattle, WA

Sales Training: Quality Sales Skills, Georgia-Pacific

Proficient in MS Word, WordPerfect, Excel, Access, PowerPoint.
Available for travel and relocation.

Barrett Smith

245 Seacrest Drive, Cohasset, MA 02025
781-459-2345 ➔ b.smith@hotmail.com

PROFILE

Energetic, highly focused **Sales and Marketing** professional who can effectively promote products, increase sales, work cooperatively with distributors and retailers, and contribute to business growth.

Key strengths are **people skills** (listening, determining needs, establishing cooperative working relationships), **product knowledge** (rapidly learned on the job), **speaking / presenting abilities** (to both in-house and outside groups), and high levels of **energy and enthusiasm.**

PROFESSIONAL EXPERIENCE

Ocean Spray Beverage Company, Plymouth, MA, January 2007–Present

SALES REPRESENTATIVE: BERRY-CRAN JUICES

Travel to sales regions throughout the Northeast to work with distributors, develop new accounts, and improve sales and merchandising of Berry-Cran juices. Accompany distributors on field visits; persuade retailers to add product line and allow more favorable product positioning. Frequently successful in overcoming retailer resistance to "one more product" through product sampling, persuasive skills, and genuine helpfulness.

Working in collaboration with the company's marketing agency, implement promotions including product samplings and radio station tie-ins. Lead kick-off meetings with new distributors to train on effective sales tactics and generate enthusiasm for the product.

Deliver presentations to groups of all sizes for large-scale product promotion—e.g., sell the merits of the product to school districts to encourage selection for school lunch programs.

Contribute to corporate marketing programs, including input on packaging design. Known for willingness to fill multiple roles and contribute in any area of the company's sales and marketing activities.

➔ **In 7 months, established 388 new accounts.**

➔ **Identified niche product need and developed proposal outlining product potential. Recommendation accepted by the company; new product line introduced July 2003.**

Growing Gardens, Hingham, MA, 2005–2007

INSIDE SALES REPRESENTATIVE

Sold landscaping materials to contractors and homeowners, focusing on best solutions for customers' needs. Represented the company at Home & Garden trade shows. Presented public seminars / demonstrations on effective product use.

➔ **Frequently requested by name to serve both retail and commercial customers.**

Walt Disney World, Orlando, FL, 2004–2005

CO-OP POSITION

In a fast-paced, customer-focused environment, gained exposure to one of the world's best-marketed and -managed organizations. Worked in a cooperative teamwork environment to ensure guest satisfaction.

➔ **One of 200 co-op staff selected from a field of 4,000 applicants.**

EDUCATION

Degree in Marketing / Management, magna cum laude (3.87 GPA)—2006
Bunker Hill Community College, Charlestown, MA

In this resume I tried to convey my client's energy, enthusiasm, and ability to come up with great sales and marketing ideas.

Tricia Santayana

259-A Canalview Place, New Orleans, LA 70130 • 504-555-0123 • tricias@yahoo.com

EXPERTISE

PROFILE

Sales—Account Management—Territory Management

Customer-focused sales professional with a strong track record of increasing sales, improving customer satisfaction, restoring customer relationships, and bringing a high level of organization and preparation to the sales process. A proven performer in both flat and growing territories. Eager for new challenges.

EXPERIENCE

"Tricia has taken over 2 separate territories where relations have been ruined. In these difficult situations, Tricia has flourished and restored rapport."
District Manager

"Great rapport with customers… Has customer focus in mind… Great sense of the big picture."
Coaching Feedback

H.J. HEINZ COMPANY   2005–Present

Territory Manager—New Orleans, LA (2007–Present)

Oversee sales, distribution, and customer service for $2.5 million territory. Manage 2 Retail Representatives and 5 part-time Service Representatives, ensuring execution of store-level plans.

Develop quarterly and period plans to achieve account-specific sales goals. Coordinate promotions with regional and national account programs. Identify in-store selling opportunities and plan display activity to meet all retail opportunities. Resolve customer questions and problems with a sharp focus on customer service and satisfaction.

- Promoted to rapid-growth territory based on outstanding performance in flat New Orleans market.
- Within 2 weeks, completely eliminated back-stock situation present in nearly every account. Brought accounts in line with annual projections and significantly improved customer satisfaction.

Territory Manager—Mobile, AL (April–December 2006)

- Exceeded sales goals (including several double-digit increases) in 3 of 4 quarters in a slow-growth territory.

Floating Territory Manager (2005–2006)

- Assigned to territories in transition. Reestablished positive customer relationships and restored order to stock and record-keeping.

MID-SOUTH BEVERAGE, Mobile, AL   2002–2005

Sales Representative

Managed and developed 37 accounts within the Greater Mobile area.

- Consistently met or exceeded sales goals.
- Continually ranked in the top 3 of 15 salespeople in the company for sales increases over the preceding year.
- Selected to manage high-volume "impact" accounts due to ability to build rapport and establish strong account relationships.
- Won incentive contests for sales of special promotion products.

EDUCATION

TUSKEGEE UNIVERSITY, Tuskegee, AL
BS Business / Finance

SALES TRAINING: D.E. Jones Sales Training (through Mid-South Beverage)
Ongoing H.J. Heinz sales and product training

This resume uses quotes to enhance and support Tricia's strong sales achievements.

Jennifer Styles

9 Mohawk Trail, Ledyard, CT 06339
860-345-2345 • jstyles@hotmail.com

Strengths • **Consultative Sales — Account Management — Relationship Building**
  • **Team Leadership and Motivation**
  • **Staff Training and Management**
  • **Operations Management and Process Improvement**

Professional Experience

2006–Present NATURE'S SECRET
Sales Representative

Manage sales territory covering 4 states (Connecticut, Rhode Island, western Massachusetts, and northern New York), performing account service, sales, and new-business development for vitamin and herbal supplement manufacturer.

- Opened new accounts in competitive niche market.
- Successfully rebuilt account relationships affected by the company's entry into mass markets.
- Achieved 103% of first-quarter sales goals.

1999–2006 ESTÉE LAUDER
Counter Manager • Macy's, SEASIDE MALL — 2004–2006

Managed staff and directed all sales and operational activities for busy retail cosmetics counter. Trained new employees and prepared staff scheduling. Recommended sales and promotional activities based on analysis of buying patterns and customer profiles; developed and coordinated event details. Also responsible for direct selling and client consultations.

- Achieved record sales for 2005: $960K, a 33% increase over prior year.
- Consistently met or exceeded monthly sales goals in highly competitive environment.
- Reorganized sales and operational activities, focusing on consistent and thorough application of the Estée Lauder selling system. Modeled correct sales techniques and motivated staff to improve consistency.
- Promoted a team concept so that all staff members felt essential to the total operation and shared in goal achievement.
- Implemented improved customer-tracking system, enabling staff to record and review customer preferences to improve customer service and increase sales.

Counter Manager • Macy's, WOODVALE MALL — 2003–2004

Promoted to management position and challenged to turn around a troubled operation. Completely reorganized all sales and operational activities; implemented and monitored correct application of company policies and standards. Augmented staff training.

- Doubled sales volume within one year.
- Successfully handled difficult personnel situations by instituting a teamwork concept, motivating staff to excel, and firmly adhering to standardized systems.
- Directed focus on customer service to increase customer loyalty and improve sales.

Consultant • G. Fox, FOREST PLAZA — 1999–2003

- Established loyal customer base through application of strong sales skills and outstanding customer service.
- Recognized as leader in a store-wide promotion to open new G. Fox charge accounts; opened more than 500 accounts during the promotion period.
- Consistently achieved highest total pre-sale orders during twice-yearly sale events.

Jennifer had made a successful transition from retail sales manager at a cosmetics counter to direct field sales. She wanted to move to a company that had products offering more growth opportunity.

Robert Anderson

513-791-8345   2933 Alydar Drive, Cincinnati, Ohio 45241   RobAnd33@aol.com

Top-Performing Sales Professional

#1 in the Nation—Stellar Customer & Account Service—Successful Product Introduction

High-energy professional with a talent for inspiring trust and building relationships—a natural communicator who connects easily with people from all walks of life. Experienced manager able to train, lead, and motivate teams to excel. Enthusiastic and personable. Motivated by new challenges.

- **Proven performer in challenging sales environments**—outperformed sales goals in every position and twice achieved #1 rank organization-wide.
- **Advocate of consultative/needs-based selling**—partnering with customers to find the best solutions.
- **Successful in penetrating new target accounts** by creating trust, building relationships, and customizing product/presentation to their needs.
- **Repeatedly demonstrated strong communication and presentation skills**—from sales training through rapport building and effective presentations at every level, including executive.
- **Rapidly learned large and complex product lines** and became a recognized product expert.

Experience and Achievements

CT OLSEN CORPORATION, Paterson, NJ   2006–2008
Midwest Market Supervisor, 2007–2008 / **Field Market Representative**, 2006–2007

Reversed market-share slide and led the nation in sales and profits.

Brought on board to solidify and grow regional sales for one of the top U.S. marketers of wines and spirits. Built excellent rapport and relationships with 25 broker representatives, enhancing their product knowledge, capturing new accounts, and leveraging brands and distribution network to build market share. Connected with customers—small retailers, on-premises establishments, and large corporate accounts—becoming a trusted friend and partner.

In newly created position, managed and directed sales, marketing, programming, and promotions for all company products throughout 5-state region—including broker relationships, key account calls, broker sales meetings, business review meetings, chain-account presentations, product pricing, and inventory management. Closely monitored competitors and set pricing to be competitive in a highly regulated industry with tight price-change restrictions.

- **Achieved remarkable sales and profit growth:** profits soared 46% in 2 years (#1 in the nation for growth as well as volume), and year-over-year case sales grew nearly 6%.
- **Jumped to quick success** in new position; quickly promoted from field rep to region manager.
- **Broke into a long-targeted account** (the largest chain account in the state) by slowly building relationships and then suggesting a creative seasonal marketing program that achieved 250% of goal.
- **Revitalized company's declining priority brand** through successful brand extensions. Conceived idea and championed to top management of the company. Gained approval for single-market test; participated in packaging, pricing, and positioning strategy. Launched new products and quickly achieved profitability—to the point that nationwide expansion is now in the works.
- **Negotiated brand placement** with Midwest Airlines nationwide.
- **Created first-ever sales manual** for broker sales force and then used it as a training tool during ride-along days and joint visits. Boosted sales by building familiarity with product line of 200+ items. Motivated reps to succeed.
- **Won "best in show"** award for booth display at a key trade show.

(continued)

A strong umbrella achievement statement opens each position, and additional accomplishments provide details and results.

513-791-8345 **Robert Anderson** RobAnd33@aol.com

AT&T, Columbus, OH 2005–2006
Account Manager

Turned around negative customer perception and rescued a multimillion-dollar account—cited by customer as the sole reason for renewing and doubling contract.

Assigned to manage remaining contract term for disgruntled customer. Served as primary point of customer contact, managing the processing and coordination of nationwide installation of voice and data services.

- **Applied customer-focused service** and problem-solving strategies to totally reverse customer dissatisfaction—to the point that they renewed contract for another year at double the price.
- **Quickly learned complex communications products,** services, technology systems, and installation issues.
- **Streamlined order processing** to speed up the installation process.

MODERN OFFICE SUPPLIES, Cincinnati, OH 2001–2005
Xerox Account Manager/Trainer

Increased territory sales 47% in 4 years—selling the highest-priced equipment in a competitive market.

Generated new business and managed existing accounts in industrial, commercial, and consumer markets for sales of Xerox business equipment. Employed cold-call, referral, and other prospecting techniques. Built exceptional relationships and a loyal customer base.

- **Specialized in consultative sales:** assessing customer needs and developing customized solutions.
- **Delivered effective sales presentations** that often involved technical product details.
- **Identified need, launched a customer training program,** and positioned this service as a key benefit.

Education/Honors/Activities/Computer Skills

BACHELOR OF ARTS, Magna Cum Laude, 2000: The Ohio State University, Columbus, OH
Major: Secondary Education/History; Minor: Social Studies

- GPA 3.8
- Dean's List

MANAGEMENT TRAINING: Xerox Leadership Seminar

COMPUTER SKILLS: Microsoft Word, Excel, PowerPoint

DAVID P. JOHNSON

555.555.5555 ▪ david.johnson@gmail.com
55 Circle Court ▪ Ashton, IL 55555

SENIOR SALES PROFESSIONAL

LIGHTING CERTIFIED (LC)

National Sales – Product Management – Business Development – Project Management

More than 15-year record in the lighting industry with background managing high-profile, Fortune 100 OEM and B2B accounts. Led sales teams of 50–60 people—up to 15 direct reports. Strengths in long-term relationship building, consultative sales strategies, and product migration.

THE 80% CONVERTER: Combining precision-targeting, in-depth needs analysis, and expert product knowledge to consistently convert 80% of prospects, increase margins, and exceed quota.

Thrived in industry's most challenging sales environment (A.B. Lighting) with highly complex go-to-market method selling to all cross-disciplinary project members:

> **Navigating complex, multi-year project cycles from concept to finalization.**
> **Negotiating with and selling to government organizations (including DOT) and municipalities.**
> **Driving margin growth while building legacy accounts up to $1M for premium brand.**

Proficient in Dodge Reports (marketing and sales research) and CRM software—Goldmine, Lotus Notes, and Pivotal. Advanced skills in Chief Architect and AutoCAD based photometric construction and design.

- Hold bachelor's degree in Economics -

EXPERIENCE & ACHIEVEMENTS

A.B. LIGHTING, Davenport, IL (telecommuted from home office)   2005 to 1/2009
(International leader in lighting solutions for industrial, emergency, and outdoor applications.)

Factory Sales Engineer—Lighting

Hired to manage high-growth southwest Illinois territory. Targeted specifiers, architects, landscape architects, consulting engineers, and interior lighting designers.

- **Maintained 80% conversion rate**—exceeding most peers, drawing on solid experience to accurately identify, target, and sell to realistic markets/customers.

- **Tripled number of specifiers approached,** previously unaware of A.B. Lighting brand.

- **Grew account from zero to $400K in 3 years, averaging 6% yearly sales increase while establishing legacy accounts:**

  - Realized margin of 5%–8% higher than peers on premium brands having minimum set margins.
  - Sold to and coordinated all stakeholders within process/project: engineer, contractor, distributor, and end user.
  - **Secured initial sales and established legacy accounts** with Certco, Owens Corning, and Rock Valley College Library (indoor lighting) and Sun Prairie, Beloit, and Evansville (street lighting), **delivering combined $1M+ in revenues.**

	2006	2007	2008
Revenue	$300K	$400K	$500K
Increase	*+5%*	*+8%*	*+5%*

(continued)

GETTERS INTERNATIONAL, INC., Provo, UT   2003 to 2005
(Global leader and pioneer in commercialization of getter, gas purification, and trace impurity analysis technology for industrial applications.)

Applications Engineer

Drove revenues, reengineered service processes, and added new third-tier, niche-market customers. Representative clients included Fortune 100s such as Osram Sylvania, Philips, and GE as well as OEM lamp manufacturers. Teamed with physicists and engineers to match product solutions to clients' high-speed manufacturing needs in ISO 9000/14000 environment. Developed sales and rollout plan for patented products throughout North America.

▪ **Delivered growth from $1.8M to $2.16M** (20% sales increase) during economic downturn.

▪ **Transformed service processes** to highlight technical product advantages, performance increases, and cost savings, resulting in successful acquisition and outsourcing of Osram Sylvania's getter/giver processes business.

▪ **Migrated first-tier clients from older to newer technology 6 months ahead of schedule:**

– Converted 2 of the "Big Three" lighting companies to new product and delivered $1M+ in annual sales from Philips ($200K+ increase from $800K).

INDEPENDENT MANUFACTURERS' REPRESENTATIVE   1995 to 2003
(Managed sales efforts for companies in refractory metals, industrial ceramics, and lighting industries.)

Sales Engineer / Product Consultant / Product Manager

Managed existing B2B and OEM accounts and acquired new business using multi-channel prospecting, telemarketing, and cold-calling strategies. Performed market research as basis for new product development recommendations to management. Served as corporate representative at seminars, conferences, and trade shows. Supervised up to 10 sales representatives.

▪ **Captured $2M in revenues** in 8-state Midwest territory by building sales of emerging, high-tech products for GTE Sylvania.

▪ **Rocketed territories from the ground up to $1M+ in annual sales** in 7-state Midwest region within 8 years with several product lines.

▪ **Shortened order lifecycle time from 2 weeks to 4 days** by implementing regional inventory plan.

EDUCATION & CERTIFICATION

Lighting Certified (LC), 2006
National Council on Qualifications for the Lighting Professions (NCQLP)

Bachelor of Science in Economics, concentration in HR, Labor, and General Business
UNIVERSITY OF ILLINOIS, Chicago, IL

AFFILIATIONS

▪ Treasurer, Illuminating Engineering Society of North America (IESNA), Ashton Section, since 2006

▪ Industry contributor to Wisconsin Focus on Energy lighting incentives program guidelines

▪ Member, Greater Ashton Chamber of Commerce

Chapter 5

Regional and National Account Management Resumes

A step above pure sales in both responsibility and compensation, account managers represent their company to key customers. Typically, these accounts correspond to valuable long-term relationships. Account managers work in partnership with their customers, applying their solutions (whether products or services) to solve their customers' problems.

Travis McCoy, Jr.

tmccoy@gmail.com

2345 Ashley Court
Dallas, TX 75229
214-853-2244

Marketing / Sales / Business Development Professional

Proven performer with consistently strong sales and marketing results achieved in a flat, highly competitive industry… Creative and strategic planner with solid implementation skills… Leader and consensus-builder energized by a collaborative teamwork environment… A history of contributions to corporate initiatives and organizational improvements… Fast-track advancement and 4-time selection to pioneer new positions.

Strengths:

- Strategic planning of marketing and sales activities.
- Industry, market, product and customer analysis.
- Project planning and execution.
- Preparation and delivery of effective sales and training presentations.
- Analysis of business processes, sales activities, training needs… recommendation and implementation of improvement solutions.
- Relationship- and consensus-building with both internal and external customers.

Professional Experience

CONSOLIDATED INDUSTRIES, INC., 2001–Present

Senior Account Manager   Dallas, TX (2008–Present)

Develop strategic promotional plans for high-volume, high-potential chain accounts (retail and wholesale) representing $128 million in business. In collaboration with clients' marketing and buying staff, create account-specific programs and promotions to grow share and volume.

Conduct quarterly business reviews. Maintain highly positive account relationships.

Communicate effectively with Consolidated sales and merchandising staff, training on program details, ensuring appropriate implementation and monitoring sales results.

- Improved Consolidated's market share by 2.8 points YTD, outperforming goal of 1.2.
- Captured $1 million in incremental sales volume YTD.

Corporate Assignment: Sales Force Study   New York, NY (2007–2008)

Selected for high-profile assignment to study, modify and develop sales processes and support systems for all levels of field and headquarters sales organizations for Consolidated Industries nationwide (the company's first-ever comprehensive analysis of its sales system).

As co-leader of the Field Sales Force assessment project, collaborated with outside consultants to study and evaluate existing business processes, systems and work activities of the 3,200-member field sales force and make recommendations to key decision-makers for improvement.

- Conducted focus groups, visioning sessions and meetings with external customers and various internal HQ departments. Presented findings and recommendations to Trade Marketing Directors, VP of Trade Marketing and the Senior VP of Sales.
- Created launch plan and coordinated the introduction of a new national sales planning tool. Sole liaison between field sales force, Information Systems and New York office.

Travis's impressive sales background was enhanced by a corporate-level team assignment that involved studying and improving the processes the field sales force was using.

Travis McCoy, Jr.   214-853-2244 ▪ tmccoy@gmail.com

Professional Experience

Supervisor, Sales Learning Centers   New York, NY (2006–2007)

Developed and delivered sales training and development programs, utilizing cross-functional field and headquarters working relationships to ensure appropriate programming.

- Planned, developed and supervised corporate training centers providing training to 100 field sales force members monthly. Evaluated use and impact of learning processes; created strategic training modules.
- Kept senior management abreast of the external learning environment and acted on opportunities for improvement.
- Implemented a "Train the Trainer" course involving outside consultants to improve the quality and impact of corporate training programs.

District Category Manager   Raleigh, NC (2004–2006)

Nominated to lead our distribution channels, including the field sales force, in transition into category management selling. Charged with developing an organizational strategy, carrying out the mission and measuring success both internally and externally.

- Succeeded in improving sales force performance and increasing customer satisfaction levels, proven through post-transition survey results.

Unit Sales Manager   Raleigh, NC (2003–2004)

Directed and grew a $35 million sales unit, managing a $4.5 million budget and leading a team of 5 Territory Sales Managers and 2 Merchandisers. Negotiated merchandising agreements.

- Developed strategic plans for individual accounts; oversaw implementation of programs and promotions to achieve sales goals; personally handled key accounts.

Special Account Representative   Birmingham, AL (2002–2003)

Recruited by Sales Director for newly created account management position. Developed game plans for 10 key accounts representing $22 million in sales. Actively participated in trade relations programs to improve relationships with key customers. Signed key account to exclusive agreement.

Territory Sales Manager   Jackson, MS (2001–2002)

Identified and capitalized on new business-building opportunities in 3 separate markets within geographic territory ($6 million sales revenue, $700 thousand promotions/merchandising budget). Top succession list candidate.

Education

Duke University, Durham, North Carolina—BA in Journalism/Advertising, 2001—Minor: Marketing

SONIA MARTINDALE

603-297-4598   22 Blueberry Trail, Dover, NH 03820   martindale@comcast.net

SALES, MARKETING & MANAGEMENT PROFESSIONAL
Revenue, Profit & Market Share Growth / Customer Penetration / Market Expansion

Accomplished sales/management professional with unbroken record of revenue and profit growth—
delivering consistently strong results in up and down economies, U.S. and international markets, established accounts, and new market niches. Consistently exceeded stretch goals and delivered top-notch customer service.

Consistently ranked in top 10% in sales performance, as both individual producer and sales manager.

EXPERIENCE AND ACHIEVEMENTS

<u>Standard Electronics</u>, New York, NY   2002–2008
A leading North American electronics distributor with 1,500 employees and 50 branches in the U.S. and Canada.

Outside Account Manager, Boston, MA, 2005–2008

Challenged to drive profitable sales growth within large national accounts based in the Boston area—representing the company's #3 account base in total sales billed.

- Grew sales volume **8.3%** during customer environment of downsizing and belt-tightening.
  — In 2007, ranked **#3** out of 112 peers company wide in percentage growth; **#11** in 2006.
  — One of only **20%** of peers to achieve account growth in 2007.
- Successfully maintained profit margins of **37%.**
- Specialized in delivering e-commerce solutions that slashed clients' procurement costs while strengthening long-term strategic relationships.
- Completed Six Sigma Green Belt training and led a corporate-wide process transformation for the order-entry area that saved more than **$2M** annually.

Branch Manager, Portland, ME, 2002–2005

Led dramatic turnaround of faltering branch office—developed sales strategy, provided focused leadership, and built a top-performing inside/outside sales team.

- Transformed stagnant branch to **#3** company wide.
- Grew total branch sales **41%** in 3 years—from **$1.2** million in 2002 to **$1.7** million in 2005.
- Delivered profit margins **4%** above healthy company average.
- Launched aggressive outside sales program to enhance the company's traditional inside sales approaches. As a result, developed significant new business with key clients and new markets:
  — Negotiated pricing agreement/e-commerce partnership with FedEx; grew account **15%.**
  — Targeted government agency business and grew that niche **90%** in 3 years.
- Initiated sales-call coaching and product training for all sales staff.

<u>Smith & Thomas</u>, Boston, MA   1999–2002
International manufacturer and distributor of electrical products for diverse industrial uses.

International Sales/Service Representative

Spearheaded initiative to grow sales in international markets. Worked with customers and strategic partners worldwide to develop integrated solutions, competitive pricing, and coordinated bid packages to boost revenue and global market presence.

- Grew top-line sales **12%** while profits soared from **18%** to **23%.**
- Increased international customer base by **10%.**
- Doubled sales in Israel and the Middle East.

EDUCATION

MBA, Marketing, 2001 ▪ **BS, Business Administration,** 1999
<u>Boston University</u>, Boston, MA

Sonia's resume shows strong career progression and quantified achievements in every role.

RODNEY S. MILLER

rodmiller@fuse.net

8029 Jamaica Way
Loveland, OH 45040
513-907-1234

PROFILE

Expertise

**Sales • Sales Management • Marketing • Marketing Communications
Direct and Distributor Sales
Metals and Plastics Industries**

Qualifications

SALES AND MARKETING	Consistently successful track record of increasing territory sales, both direct and distributor, through profiling, targeting, planning, and executing multifaceted sales and marketing programs.
CUSTOMER FOCUS	History of establishing strong customer relationships built on trust, exceptional service, and responsiveness.
SALES TRAINING	Proven ability to deliver product and sales process training in seminar settings and one-on-one.
MANAGEMENT	Experience leading a sales force with both direct and indirect supervisory authority. Skilled in managing large geographic territory (including international responsibilities), participating in strategic planning (both independently and with a team), writing reports, and communicating effectively both up and down the chain of command.
MOTIVATION	Strong vision and proven ability to achieve ambitious goals. Energized by large-scale challenges and the opportunity to make a difference to customers and the company.

PROFESSIONAL EXPERIENCE

INDUSTRIAL-IES, INC., Detroit, MI—*Manufacturer of supplies for metal stamping and plastic injection molding.*

2006–Present

Regional Sales Manager—Cincinnati, Ohio

Launched 3-state sales region (Ohio, Kentucky, Indiana) and developed a solid customer base in preparation for a planned manufacturing facility.

- **Increased sales from $600 thousand to $1.65 million in 2 years.**

Built territory through direct sales and strategic business alliances.

- **Charged with locating and recommending distributors.**
- **Developed relationship with Industrial Tooling & Machining Association; currently a member of Strategic Marketing Alliance Committee.**

Handle all phases of the company's regional trade show participation.

AUTO SUPPLIERS, INC., Detroit, MI—*Suppliers to the automotive and appliance industries.*

2004–2006

Regional Sales Manager—Worldwide

Managed the sales and marketing function for activities in 45 U.S. states and all international locations (primarily Canada, Mexico, and Europe). Oversaw 30 distributors and managed 25 sales representatives marketing our product lines along with products of other company divisions. Proposed, evaluated, and trained distributors.

- **Conducted region-wide distributor evaluations, identifying opportunities for improvement and initiating individualized training, monitoring, and motivational programs to ensure performance to goals.**

Set sales goals for distributors and representatives. Trained and worked with sales force, traveling to distributor sites for training and supervision.

- **Grew sales 288% in less than 2 years.**
- **Increased market share substantially.**

(continued)

An extensive qualifications summary highlights Rod's broad areas of expertise.

RODNEY S. MILLER

rodmiller@fuse.net ■ 513-907-1234

PROFESSIONAL EXPERIENCE

AUTO SUPPLIERS, INC., continued

1999–2004   **Outside Sales Representative—Illinois**

Sold diemaker supplies to manufacturers and tool and die shops in Illinois and Missouri. Provided sales training for distributors; monitored and evaluated their performance against sales goals.

- **Averaged 128% annual sales-to-goal in distributor sales; 132% in direct sales.**
- **Grew territory from $595 thousand to $2.3 million.**
- **Named Sales Representative of the Year three times.**

1996–1999   **Inside Sales Representative**

Coordinated product sales and assisted customers with a wide variety of product and service problems. Oversaw distribution systems (inventory and transportation).

- **Developed inventory control system that increased branch efficiency.**

EDUCATION

AA, Tool Engineering Technology, 1995
SANDUSKY TECHNICAL INSTITUTE, Sandusky, Ohio

ADDITIONAL INFORMATION

Recruited for freelance sales and marketing consulting project. Wrote in-depth sales and marketing plan for small software company, laying the groundwork for breakthrough growth.

Available to travel and relocate.

S. David Elkington

Technical/Industrial Sales, Marketing, and Application Engineering

Proven performer with verifiable accomplishments in technical/manufacturing consulting, sales, technical support, and product demonstration. Key areas of strength include the following:

TECHNICAL/CONSULTING ABILITIES

- Consulting experience in highly technical industrial equipment and energy systems/audits.
- Diverse engineering background and solid record of engineering accomplishments.
- Strong analytical and problem-solving skills, with a focus on workable solutions.

SALES/TRAINING/COMMUNICATION

- Skilled at communicating with people at all levels of responsibility, conveying technical information, establishing rapport, and building positive relationships.
- Demonstrated ability to increase sales through effective sales strategies complemented by a strong focus on customer satisfaction.

RESULTS-ORIENTED MANAGEMENT

- Effective time and territory manager who consistently meets project deadlines.
- Action-oriented; a track record of achieving ambitious goals through solid execution of well-planned strategies.

Professional Experience

2007–Present **INDUSTRIAL ROTARY PARTS, INC.,** Princeton, NJ
  Sales Engineer

Play an integral role in the company's sales/customer support function, working closely with the sales team and customers to analyze needs and develop custom solutions. On an ongoing basis, resolve field application problems and conduct technical research and analysis.

Develop and implement action plans that support business goals and objectives. Contribute to marketing and advertising initiatives, providing a dual technical/sales perspective. Maintain sharp focus on product quality and customer needs satisfaction as keys to business growth.

KEY ACCOMPLISHMENTS

- Spearheaded the effort to find a solution to a longstanding performance problem in one of the company's key products. Led the project team and motivated participation and support from Engineering, Marketing, and Manufacturing. Successfully improved performance to the level of our chief competitor, paving the way for significant sales growth through penetration of new markets.
- Implemented sales force automation that provides a more efficient and cost-effective method of developing customer contacts and service contracts.

2005–2007 **MID-LANTIC INDUSTRIAL CORPORATION,** Trenton, NJ
  Industrial Sales Manager, New Jersey and Delaware

Managed territory that included more than 600 customers in manufacturing, consulting, and educational fields, selling highly specialized industrial alignment equipment and services.

Specialized technical nature of equipment required a high level of customer support. Promoted strong customer relationships by encouraging customers to communicate problems and questions and by being readily available for training, problem-solving, and troubleshooting. Initiated contact with all customers at least monthly.

23 Pioneer Trail, Princeton, NJ 08543 • (609) 555-1818 • sdelk@hotmail.com

(continued)

The first resume I wrote for David helped him land the position at IRP; he used this updated version to apply to business schools.

S. David Elkington • (609) 555-1818 • sdelk@hotmail.com

continued   **MID-LANTIC INDUSTRIAL CORPORATION**

KEY ACCOMPLISHMENTS
- Increased equipment sales by 40% in two years. Ignited a stagnant territory with flat sales by thoroughly analyzing customers and sales activity, rebuilding customer relationships, and diligently following up on all leads generated through direct mail and trade-show participation.
- Instituted a strong focus on customer satisfaction; became known for providing a high level of service, solid training, and consistent follow-up.
- Implemented the company's first-ever tracking system, enabling better definition of history and goals.

2001–2005   **EDISON ELECTRIC,** Trenton, NJ
Program Engineer (2003–2005)

Performed quantitative and qualitative analysis on energy-management programs. Evaluated, upgraded, and adjusted new and existing programs to increase efficiency and determine cost effectiveness.

KEY ACCOMPLISHMENTS
- Calculated and forecasted new and existing program impacts for a 20-year period, utilizing engineering algorithms and forecasting software.
- Implemented engineering algorithms into EE's database tracking system to provide a more efficient and cost-effective manner for producing impact reports for New Jersey's Public Utilities Commission.

Consultant, Commercial and Industrial Energy Efficiency (2001–2003)

Conducted, analyzed, and presented more than 50 energy audits for industrial and commercial facilities. Analysis entailed the evaluation of HVAC equipment, motors, lighting, water heating, and other electrical-intensive processes.

KEY ACCOMPLISHMENTS
- Contributed to the development of the energy audit for EE's energy-management division. Wrote start-up procedures for the audit process, evaluated and purchased equipment, and performed pilot audits.

Education

Bachelor of Science—Mechanical Engineering, 2000
Worcester Polytechnic Institute, Worcester, MA

Achievements and Activities

Sales Training—Self-taught all aspects of sales techniques and territory management, 2003.

Engineer in Training—New Jersey Professional Engineers and Surveyors, 2000.

Casey V. Andrews

caseyvee@hotmail.com

259-A Morningside Drive, Kalamazoo, MI 49006
Home 616-243-0903 ▪ Mobile 616-208-3128

HIGH-TECH PRODUCT SALES SPECIALIST

High-Performance Sales Leader with more than 10 years of experience building new markets, spurring revenue growth, and improving competitive market positioning. Technically savvy and team-oriented, with the drive and determination to succeed in challenging start-up, expansion, and improvement assignments. Continuous record of driving change and improvement.

Career Highlights

- **Spearheaded entry into a new high-tech market segment**—built sales and marketing organization from the ground up, identified high-margin niche market, steered product development, and negotiated beneficial service alliances. *(Michigan Medi-Image Company)*
- **Rated #1 nationally in sales of high-tech capital equipment**—diligently pursued target accounts through lengthy sales cycle and closed millions of dollars of business in CT scanner sales. *(Meditron)*
- **Created worldwide service standard**—authored manual and earned role on global team dedicated to setting standards and protocols for service levels in critical healthcare environments. *(Meditron)*

Areas of Expertise

Strategic Sales & Marketing Planning	Product Development	Strategic Alliances & Partnerships
Capital Sales / Solution Selling	Account Management	Global Distribution Networks
Revenue Growth & Margin Protection	Technical Service & Support	Vendor Service Agreements
Product & Market Segment Launch	Executive Presentations	Team Building & Team Leadership

---

EXPERIENCE AND ACHIEVEMENTS

Michigan Medi-Image Company, Kalamazoo, MI   **2007–Present**

DIRECTOR, IMAGE-GUIDED PRODUCTS GROUP

Launched business segment to propel sales of technologically advanced CT scanner. From the ground up, built the Sales, Marketing, and Support Services organization and created a solid professional image for new high-tech segment of traditional medical products marketer.

As program director, set strategic direction and lead all facets of sales, marketing, business development, product support, and account services. Determine sales goals and formulate plans to capture business opportunities. Identify, secure, and implement strategic alliances and partnerships. Manage staff and budgets.

- **Created 5-year business plan** for flagship product, projecting $25M annual revenue in 5 years.
- **Increased sales 100%** during first year by identifying opportunity and refocusing efforts in high-potential, high-margin segment. Closed $2.4M sales and cultivated a solid pipeline of new business.
- **Achieved price realization of 89%**—17% above average for the imaging industry—through a creative sales-compensation plan that maximized margin incentives.
- **Drove product development,** teaming with OEM partner and internal engineering/manufacturing:
  - *Motorized transport system:* Opened new opportunities in the ICU market segment and upgraded revenue potential in the existing worldwide network of portable CT systems. Went from concept to prototype in 2 months.
  - *ICU patient scanning device:* Streamlined use of new scanner in ICUs and provided upgrade sales potential.
- **Negotiated the company's first vendor financing program** with Citicapital, enabling a total solutions package that opens C-level doors for all of MMI's medical sales teams.
- **Jump-started the CT field-service program** by negotiating national service agreements with equipment service groups across the U.S.
- **Developed interactive customer and sales-support CD-ROM** and traditional collateral material.

(continued)

The Career Highlights section at the top is a good way to showcase important experience and achievements that might otherwise be overlooked on page 2 of the resume.

Casey V. Andrews   caseyvee@hotmail.com ▪ Home 616-243-0903 ▪ Mobile 616-208-3128

Meditron Worldwide Medical Systems	1990–2007

CT PRODUCTS SALES SPECIALIST, Kalamazoo, MI   2003–2007

Led the nation in sales of Meditron's CT products. Developed and implemented strategies to drive long-term sales growth, spur immediate revenue, and penetrate competitive accounts. Consistently outperformed annual sales and margin goals, delivering millions of dollars of profitable revenue.

Efficiently managed all facets of collaborative product sales in a 3-state region. Teamed with Regional Managers and Account Managers to create overall sales plans for the product line. Developed sales forecasts and tracked open prospects. Provided ongoing field training to keep Account Managers current on product features and technical advantages. Developed and delivered custom solutions presentations to prospective clients. Collaborated with Account Managers to close orders in the territory.

- **#1 in CT sales nationally,** 2006; on target to repeat performance in 2007; #2 nationwide in 2005.
- **Named to Meditron's "President's Board,"** recognizing top performers in the country, 2006; first runner-up, 2005.
- **Maintained price integrity**—averaged sales price 2% above industry average in 2004, 2005, 2006.
- **Responded aggressively to corporate initiative** to drive sales on warranty service (profitable at 4X equipment sales)—sold extended warranty on 84% of orders in 2006.

REGIONAL TECHNICAL SPECIALIST, Chicago, IL   1995–2003

Served as expert technical resource for Meditron's entire line of CT and MRI products.

Fostered the sales process by providing product and implementation data to sales teams. Approved installation plans. Disseminated vital technical-information updates. Trained and mentored field engineers.

- **Independently developed and authored technical Planned Maintenance document** for Meditron's CT systems—adopted worldwide. Invited and participated on international Planned Maintenance development team with worldwide headquarters as a result of this effort.

CT ZONE TECHNICAL SPECIALIST, Chicago, IL   1993–1995
GROUP II SERVICE MANAGER, Philadelphia, PA   1992–1993
DISTRICT CT SPECIALIST, Philadelphia, PA   1991–1992
FIELD SERVICE ENGINEER, Chicago, IL   1990–1991

PROFESSIONAL PROFILE

EDUCATION   Electronic Technician Diploma, 1990—DeVry Institute of Technology, Chicago, IL
Undergraduate Studies—North Central College, Naperville, IL

SALES TRAINING   Principles of Sales Mastery, 2006—Paradigm Training, Inc.
Situation Sales Negotiation, 2006—BayGroup International
Strategic Account Management/Financial Skills Selling, 2005—Strategic Management Group
Strategic Selling, 2004—Miller Heiman, Inc.

TECHNICAL EXPERTISE   Exceptionally computer-literate and highly proficient with a wide variety of hardware and software packages, including web-based and graphics programs (Adobe Acrobat, Photoshop, Illustrator) and advanced use of the entire Microsoft Office suite. Solid understanding of networking and data management. Experience with Lotus and similar mail clients. Expert PowerPoint and presentation skills.

Tammy Eisen
23 Dogwood Drive, Nashua, NH 03060 ❑ 603-764-6030 ❑ teisen@gmail.com

SALES PROFESSIONAL: TECHNOLOGY PRODUCTS & SERVICES

- ☑ Ten years of progressively responsible experience, repeated promotions, and measurable sales accomplishments.
- ☑ Creative problem-solver and troubleshooter whose strong technical background contributes to effective sales. Extensive knowledge of computer hardware and networking systems.
- ☑ Effective time manager with outstanding communication and relationship-building skills and a genuine commitment to customer service.
- ☑ Team player and facilitator with proven ability to work cooperatively with diverse individuals and lead productive team efforts.

PROFESSIONAL EXPERIENCE

NETWORK COMMUNICATIONS, Nashua, NH   2000–Present
Senior Account Manager (2005–Present)
Sell computer network communications equipment to more than 350 accounts, covering New Hampshire and Vermont. Develop new business through cold-calling and prospecting. Recommend product configurations, negotiate pricing, and shepherd sales from initial call to installation. Utilize strong time- and account-management skills to handle a large customer base and provide a high level of ongoing service and support.

- ☑ **Instrumental in growth of company** from $2 million in 2000 to $14 million currently.
- ☑ **Added 47 new accounts** during 2007–2008.
- ☑ **Consistently exceeded sales quotas:** 142%–2008; 102%–2007; 300%–2006.
- ☑ **Sales Representative of the Month:** July, November, December 2008; May, June 2006.
- ☑ Achieved the **largest gross margin deal** for the quarter on two occasions.
- ☑ **Based on sales accomplishments,** became the only sales representative in the company to acquire the support of a Customer Service Representative to handle administrative details and allow increased time for prospecting calls and customer contact. Interviewed and trained newly hired CSR.

Sales Representative / Networking Consultant (2004–2005)
Prospected and sold to new and existing accounts in the Southern New Hampshire area. Evaluated customer sites and needs to make recommendations for networking design. Functioned as "Team Manager" with customer, applications engineers, and manufacturers of existing system elements to ensure smooth integration of newly upgraded system.

- ☑ **Sales Representative of the Month:** February, March, May, June, July 2005.

Manager, Used / Refurbished Equipment (2002–2004)
Managed the company's activities in purchase, repair, and resale of computer networking and communications equipment. Maintained daily contact with brokers across the country, seeking out equipment and negotiating purchases and sales. Tracked costs and established profitable sale prices.

- ☑ **Created a database** for efficient tracking of equipment purchases and sales.

Applications Engineer (2000–2002)
Designed and installed data / telephone communications applications based on analysis of customer needs and equipment capabilities. Assisted sales representatives in pre-sales recommendations.

EDUCATION

NEW HAMPSHIRE TECHNICAL COLLEGE, Manchester, NH, 2001–2003—Major: Data Communications
INTERNSHIP: Customer Service Representative, DATA COMMUNICATIONS CORP., Manchester, NH

SPECIALIZED TRAINING:

LAN / WAN Data Communications	Voice and Data Integration
Digital / Analog Data Communications	Bridgers, Routers, and Gateways
T1 / T3 and Fractional T1 Communications	Troubleshooting and Problem Resolution
Numerous Sales Seminars	

Bold type is used to stress Tammy's strong and consistent achievements. Note the Specialized Training section. For individuals in technical fields, it's often helpful to mention specific products and technologies in which you have expertise.

Samuel P. Erving

235 Rear Morse Avenue
Greensboro, NC 27401

Home 336-287-2222
Office 336-903-3363
serving@mac.com

Expertise

Consultative, Relationship-Based Industrial / Technical Sales and Account Management

Key Qualifications

- Keen analytical problem-solving skills… a solution-focused approach to complex challenges.
- A genuine talent for building relationships, communicating across all levels of the organization, and acting as a liaison with customers, vendors, and other members of the sales team.
- Knowledge of manufacturing processes, product applications, and engineering approaches.
- Strengths in goal-setting, planning, and organization.

Professional Experience

Account Executive: Industrial Machinery Co., Greensboro, NC, 2003–Present

Manage local, national, and international accounts, providing consultative sales services to match customer needs with industrial equipment solutions. Work closely with customer Engineering and Manufacturing professionals in a solution-focused team environment.

Serve as Project Coordinator for complex equipment sales, overseeing all functions—specifying, quoting, purchasing, managing project installation, serving as vendor and customer liaison.

——Recent Sales Results

- Built territory from $200K to $1.2M in sales, with 100–150 primarily long-term accounts.
- #2 in sales, #3 in gross profit, among all company sales representatives in 7 offices, 2008.
- Consistent top performer in Greensboro office. In 2007, personally delivered 65% of total sales.
- Greensboro team achieved largest growth in sales and profits company-wide, 2007.

——Representative Accomplishments

- To capture a key sale ($900K) in 2007, teamed with another sales professional, worked closely with client, and successfully persuaded vendor to commit to project with a tight time frame. Succeeded against a direct manufacturer competitor.
- For a national client, solved a significant packaging problem by recommending an equipment modification. Customer has become a significant source of ongoing business.
- Conceived, planned, and facilitated an extremely well-received program for the company's annual sales meeting: interactive Q&A forum with top sales performers.

Sales Representative: R. Giles & Company, Durham and Greensboro, NC, 2000–2003

Recruited as first Greensboro-based commissioned salesperson. Recommended and sold casters, wheels, and conveyor belting to manufacturing clients.
- Developed account base from zero to approximately 200 active customers.

Buyer, Purchasing Department: Industrial Mixing Manufacturers, Durham, NC, 1997–2000

Purchased parts and equipment for maintenance and manufacturing of industrial mixing equipment. Managed buying relationships with 400 vendors.
- Developed strong knowledge base for industrial suppliers and resources in North Carolina.
- Gained insight into the perspectives and priorities of both Purchasing and Sales.

Customer Service/Inside Sales: Samples Manufacturing Co., Durham, NC, 1996–1997

Education

Bachelor of Arts degree, 1995: North Carolina Central University, Durham, NC

Professional Development: Courses in Salesmanship, Educational Psychology, Speed Reading, Insurance, and Risk Management

We broke Sam's accomplishments into two parts to avoid "information overload" from an overabundance of bullet points.

Stella A. Eisenhauer

23 Bluebird Terrace
Greenfield, MA 01301
(413) 555-8590
stellaeisen@usa.net

Expertise

Industrial Capital Equipment Sales — Marketing — Project Management

Successful 20-year career with consistent history of strong sales accomplishments.
Proven abilities include

- Creating new business and developing new markets.
- Partnering with clients... building strong relationships... persisting over a long sales cycle.
- Managing project details and collaborating with engineering firms for successful large-scale installations.
- Researching the marketplace for new and rewarding sales opportunities and market niches.
- Developing and delivering persuasive presentations.
- Effectively communicating with internal and external team members — sharing plans and progress, solving problems, building consensus, and collaboratively achieving goals.
- Negotiating large and small contracts.
- Organizing plans, activities, processes, and systems to achieve results.

Professional Experience

Industrial Experts, Inc., Greenfield, MA — 2007–2009

Sales Manager

Directed sales and marketing activities to develop new markets and provide consistently high levels of service to existing accounts. Company manufactures and sells pressure vessels for industrial uses — capital equipment ranging from $50K to more than $1M, involving long sales cycles and consultative sales/sales engineering relationships. Key clients are producers/distributors of bulk liquid products, including petroleum-based products and chemicals.

Managed partnership programs with Dupont and Shell Oil. Identified and pursued new partnership opportunities. Monitored and managed sales process from purchase order to delivery, installation, and operation.

- **Leveraged expertise** in large on-site installations to expand into **profitable new market.**
- **Successfully managed** complex logistical shipping project for installation in Saudi Arabia.

Press-Co, Inc., Springfield, MA — 2006–2007

Sales/Purchasing Manager

Developed new business, maintained existing accounts, and negotiated contracts for manufacturer of pressure vessels and tanks.

Managed field project teams. Created production schedules with Microsoft Project. Developed design requirements in conjunction with ASME, API, and AWA. Oversaw installation and use of AutoCAD system.

Selected, retained, and served as primary liaison with engineering subcontractors and attorneys.

- **Delivered substantial new and expanded business** — $500K Northeast Steel contract and increase in General Foods project from $50K to $1.1M.

Applied Manufacturing, Enfield, CT — 1997–2006

Sales Manager

Recruited to lead the sales and marketing initiative for a newly formed company manufacturing tanks and pressure vessels for the beverage, food, pharmaceutical, and pulp and paper industries. Additionally, served as project manager for large capital equipment installations, overseeing profit and loss, engineering functions, in-field erection, manufacturing start-up, and troubleshooting. Contributed to the creation of in-house systems for estimating, purchasing, and subcontractor management.

Accomplishments continued on page 2

(continued)

Stella's entire career had been spent in industrial sales within one highly specialized industry. To position her more effectively for other industries, we did not include her specific industry expertise in the top portion of the resume

101

Stella A. Eisenhauer

Applied Manufacturing

Sales Manager, continued

- As the company's sole sales professional, personally **grew total company sales from $600K in 1997 to $5M in 2006.**
- **Identified new market opportunities;** developed and implemented marketing plans targeting different industries.
- **Persisted over long sales cycle to develop key accounts**—pursued Ocean Spray Beverages for 6 years before capturing several million dollars in new business.
- Developed **excellent relationships with large engineering firms** (such as Standard Engineering) during customer projects lasting from several months to 2 years.

Stanley & James Manufacturing Company, Albany, NY — 1990–1997

Regional Sales Representative: Tanks and Vessels, 1994–1997

Managed sales and account maintenance with breweries, wineries, and juice producers in 9 Northeast states.

Product Manager and Sales Manager: Formed Heads, 1991–1994

Identified market niche and spearheaded national launch of new formed heads product line.

While retaining direct sales responsibilities, additionally handled all estimating, production evaluation, quality assurance, engineering, advertising, inside/outside sales, purchase negotiation, order processing, and transportation for formed heads product line.

- Built from the ground up to **$1.4M in business in 3 years.**

Estimator, 1990–1991

Education

Bay Path College, Longmeadow, MA

- Associate in Science degree, Business

Professional Development

- Business Law: Westfield State College, Westfield, MA
- Organization and Business Management: Western New England College, Springfield, MA

Professional Affiliation

Professional Brewers Association of America

Philip Mandolay

75 Pompano Drive
Tallahassee, FL 32306

philman@aol.com

Home 850-238-4567
Mobile 850-607-6789

SALES / MANAGEMENT / ACCOUNT MANAGEMENT
MANAGED CARE / MEDICAL INDUSTRY

- New Account & Territory Development
- Physician & Hospital Relations
- Operational Management

- Contract Negotiations
- Consultative/Solution Selling
- Program Management

EXPERIENCE & ACHIEVEMENTS

TALLAHASSEE HEALTH PLAN, Tallahassee, Florida (Division of Miami Health Plan)   2003–Present
Provider Services Manager (2008–Present)
Senior Provider Recruiter (2003–2008)

Selected to establish new provider services network in the Tallahassee area. As the company's sole local representative for provider services, charged with recruiting and securing contracts with health care providers to create a viable network for Tallahassee Health Plan to gain state approval as a Medicaid network provider.

- Generated initial interest through cold-calling physicians and hospitals, both general practitioners and specialists in all medical and ancillary areas.

- Successfully sold Tallahassee Health Plan to physicians, overcoming the obstacle of being a new managed care provider in competition with large, established providers such as Blue Cross/Blue Shield and HMO Florida.

- Contributed to the RFP process; responsible for all documentation of providers. Became the first of 5 competing companies to receive state approval for implementation.

- Established the company as the preferred provider in the area, favored by physicians because its sole focus is on Medicaid patients and is not diluted with attention to other client groups. Successfully sold this focus as a benefit to providers.

- Achieved 13% market penetration in the Tallahassee area, in a market where 50% of potential clients were already enrolled. Other plans that were new to the market have achieved less than 5% penetration.

- Need for recruiting outreach has been eliminated because, through successful marketing and provision of services, the company is now approached by health care providers wanting to be part of the network.

Serve as primary coordinator of provider services. Manage all communication and relationships with providers, both individuals and facilities.

- Negotiate contract agreements with physicians and hospitals.

- Set up and maintain the provider directory that presents provider options to Medicaid patients.

- Problem-solve with care providers, resolving administrative and other difficulties. Maintain frequent, open communication through on-site visits and consistent and thorough follow-up to problems, approaching problems with the philosophy of handling small issues before they become large ones. Recognized by providers as a resource for diverse health care and business issues.

- Achieve consistently high service-satisfaction ratings as determined through provider surveys.

(continued)

Since Philip's position had two distinct areas of responsibility, each with significant activities and accomplishments, it was helpful to organize and present this information in two sections.

Philip Mandolay
philman@aol.com

Home 850-238-4567
Mobile 850-607-6789

TALLAHASSEE HEALTH PLAN (continued)
Lead a variety of management and operations initiatives.

- In response to company growth, recruited additional representative whose primary duties consist of making outside service visits to less-critical providers. Trained new rep and supervised her activities.

- Established a Providers Council whose goal is to gain feedback on current operations as well as proposed changes to the system. Recruited representatives selected from the most influential providers. Coordinate all activities of the council, including scheduling and leading quarterly meetings.

- Until the establishment of a corporate Credentialing department, handled all details and documentation relating to credentialing and approval of physicians by the company medical director and Quality Improvement committee.

COLUMBIA HEALTH CARE CORP., Miami, Florida   2001–2003
Recruiter/Coordinator

- Coordinated services to providers in Dade County. Built positive provider relationships and served as a problem-solver and liaison to other areas of the company.

- Conducted facility audits to ensure conformance with safe medical practices.

GOLDEN MEDICAL, Miami, Florida   1999–2001
Physician Liaison

- Recruited and interviewed physicians on a national level for placement on U.S. armed-forces installations around the country. Reviewed and verified physician credentials. Recommended candidates to on-base medical directors and selection committees.

- Trained and assisted new recruiters.

- Position involved travel up to 80% of the time.

Coordinator of Recruiting Services

- Developed and implemented quality-control system for physician credentials.

- Created "in house" direct-mail advertising system; coordinated advertising.

NATIONWIDE EMERGENCY SERVICES, Coral Gables, Florida   1998–1999
Associate Director of Operations

- Maintained staffing for 10 emergency rooms throughout the Southeast. Recruited, negotiated wages, and placed physicians in contracted emergency rooms.

- Coordinated replacement and emergency staffing through a personally developed network of physicians, ensuring adequate coverage at all times.

EDUCATION

FLORIDA STATE UNIVERSITY, Tallahassee, Florida
Post-graduate coursework in Health Services Administration

UNIVERSITY OF MIAMI, Coral Gables, Florida
Bachelor of Science in Business Administration (1998)
Major: Marketing; Minor: Speech

Patrick Stevenson

254-710-3435   75 Ramon Drive, Waco, Texas 76798   stevenson@hotmail.com

QUALIFICATIONS SUMMARY
- Highly motivated and accomplished sales/marketing professional with demonstrated expertise in all facets of account development, cultivation, and management.
- Excellent analytical skills; able to rapidly assess competitive markets, implement effective strategic sales and marketing plans, and build, direct, and motivate highly successful sales organizations; especially effective negotiation skills.
- Expert relationship-building abilities and keen business acumen.
- IBM/Mac computer proficiency: Microsoft Word, WordPerfect, Lotus 1-2-3.

PROFESSIONAL EXPERIENCE
HOME & AWAY, INC. • Atlanta, Georgia   2005–Present
Market Sales Manager/Texas (06–Present)
- Promoted to manage key Buildarama and Home Warehouse accounts within the state of Texas for one of the fastest-growing companies in the nation.
- Grew account volume **10%** in 2006, **12%** in 2007, **9%** in 2008, and tracking **14%** growth for 2009.
- Instrumental in representing Home & Away to opening of Buildarama's first Texas store; established premier in-store presence, successfully positioning against competition.
- Highly effective in developing/maintaining key relationships through expert rapport-building, tenacity, and consistently successful sell-in of products and displays.

Territory Sales Manager (05–06)
- Managed the gamut of sales responsibilities for 24 major accounts in northeast Texas.
- Consistently achieved sales performance ranking of **#2** out of 15.

TELEPHONE ADVERTISING SPECIALTIES • Fort Worth, Texas   2004–2005
Telephone Account Executive
- Managed sales, service, and design of Yellow Pages advertising programs.
- Achieved **200+%** of sales quota, with net gain in sales of **9.8%** (against goal of **4.8%**).
- Conducted needs analyses, partnering with clients to better understand and sell in to their businesses; exceeded sales quota net growth of last campaign in the face of drastic rate reductions.

K-MART CORPORATION • Waco, Texas   2003–2004
Operations Assistant Manager/Management Trainee
- Promoted to manage efficient phase-out of closing store, overseeing all store operations; trained new staff and provided leadership/motivation of associates through closure.
- Successfully maximized profitability via innovative promotions and sell-through of existing inventory; minimized costs while maintaining superior customer service.
- Established relationship with professional consultants retained to implement liquidation.

BOARDROOM CONSULTING GROUP • Waco, Texas   2003
Assistant to the Vice President (Marketing Internship)
- Research/sales management support to insurance and management consulting firm.

EDUCATION
BAYLOR UNIVERSITY • Waco, Texas
- Bachelor of Science, School of Management (2003)
- Dual Major: Marketing & Philosophy—Cum Laude Graduate (GPA: 3.62)

Resume contributed by Jan Melnik, MRW
A qualifications summary was an effective way to present Patrick's extensive qualifications in fairly short, easy-to-read bullet points.

Kenneth Baker

75 Countryside Lane, Fort Wayne, IN 46845
Home 219-555-9988 • Office 219-349-0505
Mobile 219-304-1290 • kenbaker@juno.com

SALES AND MANAGEMENT PROFESSIONAL
Key Account Management—Global Account Management—Solution Selling

Track record of delivering significant and sustained revenue and profit improvements—building territories—managing key accounts—developing strong client relationships—collaborating with field sales teams—ensuring customer satisfaction.

Successful experience managing sales, customer service, and operations staff. Talent for building team spirit, introducing new systems, and motivating staff to high levels of group and individual performance.

PROFESSIONAL EXPERIENCE

GLOBAL EXPRESS CORP., Fort Wayne, Indiana, 2003–Present
Worldwide express and package services

➤ **Key Accounts Manager/International Accounts Manager,** 2005–Present

Challenged to maintain current accounts and grow the business with key and international accounts headquartered in 12-state Midwest region. Travel frequently to customer sites around the country for sales visits and account support.

Visit client HQ at least quarterly to maintain relationship and probe for additional business needs. Focus on "solution selling," serving as a business resource, and providing value-added services to clients.

Communicate with operational areas to resolve customer issues and problems and gather appropriate data for account service presentations. Team-build with field sales and service staff to provide a high level of customer service and support.

Closely tailor business proposals to client needs; effectively negotiate account contracts and rate increases.

Remain alert to new business opportunities through a variety of resources, including business publications and networking.

- **Recognized for outstanding performance (#1 among 29 peers in the U.S.)** based on revenue, budget, business growth, and achievement of management objectives.
    Key Account Manager of the Year, 2008
    Key Account Manager of the Quarter, 2008 and 2 quarters of 2007
    International Account Manager of the Quarter, 2005 and 2006

➤ **Local Account Representative,** 2003–2005

Developed new business and provided service and support to existing accounts.

TRANS-WORLD DELIVERY COMPANY, New York, New York, 1996–2003
International express, air freight, and remail company

➤ **Region Manager,** Indianapolis, Indiana, 1999–2003

Directed the company's sales activities and new-account development in a 3-state region, servicing both local and national accounts. Hired, trained, and supervised sales, operations, and customer service staff.

- **Opened new markets** in Cincinnati, Fort Wayne, Cleveland, and Detroit.

- **Grew weekly revenues from $13K to $78K while driving profits to #1 of 8** regions in district.

- **Captured business from competitors** and successfully sold premium-priced services by promising—and delivering—superior customer service.

- **Instituted a strong customer service focus among staff.** Created procedures for sales follow-up activities by both inside and outside reps.

Because Ken feels strongly that his military experience is a significant element of his background, we included it but omitted dates that might age him. The resume elaborates on the duties of his current position, with very short, to-the-point, and attention-grabbing accomplishments.

Kenneth Baker

Home 219-555-9988 • Office 219-349-0505
Mobile 219-304-1290 • kenbaker@juno.com

PROFESSIONAL EXPERIENCE

TRANS-WORLD DELIVERY COMPANY, continued

➤ **Product Development Manager, International Delivery Service,** Bay City, Michigan, 1998–1999

Launched marketing and sales initiatives to introduce new product (international mail).

- **Increased revenues more than tenfold**—from less than $1K to more than $10K per week.

➤ **Account Executive,** Bay City, Michigan, 1997–1998

Developed new business through prospecting and direct sales solicitation.

- **Increased territory sales 220%** in one year.

➤ **Terminal Manager,** Detroit, Michigan, 1996–1997

Managed terminal operations and local sales.

- **Substantially increased account base and revenue** while reducing labor costs.

FREIGHT EXPRESS, Toledo, Ohio, 1995–1996

➤ **Account Executive,** Columbus, Ohio

Launched the sales operation for new less-than-truckload motor carrier.

- **Built revenues from start-up to $12K per week.**

ERIE MOTOR EXPRESS, Toledo, Ohio, 1990–1995

➤ **Terminal Manager**

Managed sales, operations, and customer service for interstate motor carrier.

- **Increased revenues 250%** ($4K to $10K) per week while maintaining the highest profit among 11 terminals in the region.

EDUCATION / PROFESSIONAL TRAINING

Denison University, Granville, Ohio

- Bachelor of Science degree in History; minors in English and Psychology

Xerox Professional Sales Skills II
Dale Carnegie Professional Development

MILITARY

Commissioned Officer, U.S. Army, 4 years

- Combat platoon leader—staff officer—basic-training company commander

REBECCA LEE

2940 Arroyo Street
Houston, TX 77021

713-987-2091
rlee@aol.com

SOLUTION SELLING — ACCOUNT MANAGEMENT — CUSTOMER RELATIONSHIP BUILDING

Driving revenue growth and market-share increases by consistently delivering value, performance, and dependability... building loyal, long-term customer relationships... developing creative solutions to customer and market challenges. Strong negotiation, consensus-building, and team-leadership skills. Unquestioned integrity and dedication to win-win solutions.

EXPERIENCE AND ACCOMPLISHMENTS

Continental Air Lines, Houston, TX   1985–2008

Senior Account Manager (2003–2008) — **Account Manager** (1997–2003)

Managed $300M territory, servicing Fortune 500 accounts such as Dell Computer, Midland Oil, and Shell as well as large regional travel-agency accounts. Used solution-selling approach to drive continuous market-share increases in a challenging and competitive environment. Built strong customer relationships based on performance and trust.

Presented to and negotiated at all levels, from purchasing and travel managers to senior executives. Overcame objections and devised creative strategies to retain business in an environment of severe cost competition and travel alternatives.

- ▶ Averaged 5% annual increase in market share.
- ▶ Recognized for top performance among 150 account managers nationally.

Representative account-management achievements:

CHALLENGE	▶	Eliminate drive-market opportunities, increase productivity, lower cost, and consolidate travel services for a major national corporation.
ACTIONS	▶	Developed and presented quarterly reviews with a consultative approach to finding win-win solutions. Analyzed savings opportunities and implemented a corporate sales agreement. Actively managed the relationship to maximize productivity and increase discount opportunities. Initiated a team-selling approach to effectively consolidate the company's travel programs for added savings.
RESULTS	▶	Increased market share 12%, delivered client savings of $1.3M, and grew total account revenue 41%.

CHALLENGE	▶	Address 20% decline in corporate travel that, combined with airline commission reductions, threatened a key travel-agency account relationship.
ACTIONS	▶	Through consultative selling, negotiated an incentive agreement that rewarded share increases and maximized revenue opportunities.
RESULTS	▶	Performing 4.6% above goal, customer earned additional incentive revenue of $375,000 while Continental increased market share and maintained customer loyalty.

The Challenge-Actions-Results format shows both strategic thinking and performance outcomes—and it's a real attention-getter, too.

REBECCA LEE
Page 2

713-987-2091
rlee@aol.com

Continental Air Lines   **continued**

Regional Automation Manager (1995–1997)

Sold automation services to corporate accounts and travel agencies with $1M–$10M in airline sales annually. Trained accounts on new features and functionality to increase productivity; drove traffic to Continental and boosted customer relationships.

 ▶ Negotiated contracts for new business and retained customers through performance-based sales incentives.

Reservations Sales Supervisor (1985–1995)

Managed the performance of reservations and ticketing agents in a fast-paced call-center environment.

 ▶ Created a team-selling atmosphere that featured open communication and active participation.

Additional Experience   **High School Softball, Volleyball, & Golf Coach**

EDUCATION

Baylor University, Waco, TX

 ▶ M.Ed.
 ▶ B.A. History

Professional Training

 ▶ Continental Air Lines Supervisory and Management Training
 ▶ PAR Sales Training (needs-based solution sales)
 ▶ Microsoft Word, Excel, PowerPoint

Daniel Savarin

savarin_dan@itt.net
Home 626-349-1010 ♦ Mobile 626-390-3404
2523 Cactus Flower Drive, Pasadena, CA 91103

Sales and Account Management Professional

Strengths

Building customer relationships

Selling value and benefits

Providing extraordinary levels of client service and support

Managing extended sales cycles… ensuring contract renewal

Contributing to corporate initiatives that focus on customer service and support, continuous improvement, and operational effectiveness

Professional Experience

SENIOR ACCOUNT MANAGER—Golden State Health Care, Pasadena, CA—2003–2009

Sales and Account Service

Managed account base of major corporate clients representing $80 million in annual revenue, with multiple product lines customized for each client. Accountable for financial performance and account renewals as well as ongoing customer service… served as the company's principal contact with these key clients.

Account profile: local and national… 500+ employers… large corporations and school districts… primary client contact with benefit managers, benefit committees, school board treasurers, and union leaders.

Key Activities

♦ Developed and implemented marketing and sales plans.

♦ Researched and wrote industry and market updates including competitive analysis and price comparisons.

♦ Served as a permanent member of many customer health/benefit committees.

♦ Developed sales presentations and proposals based on the unique selling environment of the individual client.

♦ Delivered employee presentations at customer sites during annual open enrollment periods… throughout the year, attended Q&A sessions, supplied printed materials, and assisted at health and benefit fairs.

Results

♦ Averaged 97% customer retention rate over 5 years… attributable to strong account relationships developed through very high level of customer service, responsiveness, and follow-through.

♦ Secured contracts based on value, benefits, service, and customer satisfaction rather than price.

♦ Negotiated annual renewal contracts with 8- to 10-month sales process.

♦ Successfully converted several accounts to multiyear contracts.

Team Activities

Directly involved in key corporate initiatives:

♦ "We Care" Customer Initiative—supporting corporate mission of "exceeding customer needs"—assembled data from customer surveys and created reports for presentation to senior management.

♦ "Top 50" Program—to involve top management in customer interactions.

♦ Continuous-improvement teams—focusing on employer services and improvements to the annual enrollment process.

♦ Led the team responsible for revamping the company's marketing/sales tools (universal sales presentation, renewal analysis, color brochures, etc.).

Management

Served as acting sales manager for 8 direct reports during manager's maternity leaves. Participated in planning and development initiatives for the sales team, directed daily activities, and helped field representatives close sales.

Subheads are used to distinguish among three areas of responsibility to highlight team and management activities as well as sales results.

Daniel Savarin

savarin_dan@itt.net
Home 626-349-1010 ♦ Mobile 626-390-3404

Professional Experience—continued

ACCOUNT MANAGER—Grayson Benefit Group, San Diego, CA—1999–2003

Provided a high level of account service to employer benefit administrators.

- ♦ Recommended and sold additional products and services to existing clients.
- ♦ Compiled and presented competitive information to support contract renewal negotiations.
- ♦ Led employee question-and-answer meetings.
- ♦ Participated on numerous internal organization development teams with the goal of continuous operational improvement.

SALES REPRESENTATIVE—Standard National Life Insurance Company, San Diego, CA—1997–1999

Focused on working with small business owners to set up employee benefit programs, tailoring plans to fit employer needs.

- ♦ Developed and presented proposals; closed the sale; provided ongoing account service.
- ♦ Prospected and cold-called to develop new business.

Education

Bachelor of Science in Business Administration, University of California–San Diego, 1997

Professional Training

- ♦ Getting to Yes: Negotiation Skills Workshop
- ♦ Tom Peters: Lessons in Leadership Seminar
- ♦ Strategic Selling Workshop
- ♦ Dimensions of Professional Selling
- ♦ Zenger Miller: Frontline Leadership Program
- ♦ Effective Business Writing Workshop

Dale Simmons

7529 Rocky Road, Denver, CO 80208 > 303-349-2727 > dsimmons@aol.com

SALES / NEW-BUSINESS DEVELOPMENT / NATIONAL ACCOUNT MANAGEMENT

STRENGTHS

> **National corporate account development** *(Coca-Cola, Procter & Gamble, McDonald's, Kraft).*
> **Sales presentations and supportive analysis.**
> **Solid understanding of corporate marketing strategies and assessment methods.**
> **Relationship building** with individuals at all levels of the organization.
> **Territory management;** proven ability to juggle multiple assignments and achieve high performance levels in both local and national territories.

HIGHLIGHTS

> Independently developed and maintained $3M of new business contracts (in an $8M company).
> Successfully marketed the unique services of an industry pioneer; negotiated and closed large contracts with national accounts that had never before utilized this type of service.
> Recognized for significant and consistent contributions to the success of the company.

PROFESSIONAL EXPERIENCE

INFO-MASTERS, INC., Champaign, Illinois—*Market-research firm* 2003–2009

National Director of Business Development (2006–2009)—Solicited, negotiated, contracted, serviced, and maintained national accounts. Concurrently, completed field assignments on-site at national accounts' regional offices in a 6-state Western region.

Conducted national and specific market research analysis. Applied marketing and sales expertise to assist clients in developing effective marketing programs in response to research data. Negotiated new and renewal contracts, dealing with senior management at national companies. Wrote corporate marketing materials for national use.

> **Selected for new position to meet corporate goal of growing large base of national accounts.** Successfully laid the groundwork for key new accounts *(including McDonald's Corporation, a company that had previously shunned all marketing overtures).* Developed and pursued leads through research, direct mail, cold-calling, and networking, and began the relationship-building process that is the first step in this industry's lengthy sales cycle.
> **"Corporate Contributor of the Year,"** 2008.

National Accounts Manager (2004–2006)—Directed marketing programs on-site at key national accounts, including Coca-Cola, Kraft, and Procter & Gamble.

> **Developed and renegotiated continuance contracts with large national clients,** including successful renegotiation/renewal of major Coca-Cola contract (annually 2004–2006).
> **Independently developed Kraft business;** overcame corporate reluctance to pursue this account based on predicted failure.
> **"Corporate Contributor of the Year,"** 2006.

Account Executive—Northwest Region (2003–2004)—Developed business and provided account service in a 10-state region.

> **Challenged to grow business in a stagnant region** with the lowest billing in the company. Successfully developed relationships and built business to more than twice its former size.
> **"Rookie of the Year,"** 2004.

EDUCATION

MBA studies, 2003–2004; BS Marketing & Management, 2003 UNIVERSITY OF COLORADO, Colorado Springs

Top customers are identified by their well-recognized names. Dale's success will be important to a company trying to penetrate these Fortune 100 companies.

KATHLEEN STANSFIELD

257 Lakeview Drive, Apt. 15-B
Chicago, IL 60623
312-498-8888 ■ stansfield@aol.com

PROFILE

CONSULTATIVE SALES PROFESSIONAL with a track record of delivering exceptional sales results, creating innovative sales and marketing programs, and developing strong and ongoing client relationships. Demonstrated accomplishments in

Sales and Management	**New-Business Development**
Solution-Focused Account Service	**Territory Expansion and Maintenance**
Public Speaking and Executive Presentations	**Fortune 500 National Account Management**

PROFESSIONAL EXPERIENCE

Medi-Test Clinical Laboratories, New York, New York, 2002–Present

REGIONAL MANAGER, NATIONAL ACCOUNTS, 2004–Present
SENIOR ACCOUNT EXECUTIVE, 2002–2004

Market corporate health service programs to national accounts (Fortune 100–500 companies) in a 7-state region. Prospect and present proposals at the VP or Director level; build strong client relationships through consultative, solution-focused sales approach.

Maintain high level of customer service to $4 million account base.

Frequently a featured speaker for professional meetings and corporate seminars; build visibility and corporate image through 15–20 well-received presentations annually.

- 8-year track record of outperforming sales goals—#1 in the country for sales consistency:

2002	2003	2004	2005	2006	2007	2008
143%	**226%**	**172%**	**189%**	**179%**	**162%**	**130%**

- Maintained closing ratio of better than 1 in 2.
- Devised and implemented a random-selection program that benefited clients while providing a competitive advantage for Medi-Test. Subsequently, program has been implemented by other account executives nationwide with very positive results.
- Created an "all-in-one" kit that increased customers' ease and convenience in using our service. Captured several large accounts directly as a result of this kit.

Windy City Business Partners, Chicago, Illinois, 2001–2002

ASSOCIATE ACCOUNT MANAGER

Created and delivered motivation / performance improvement programs for corporate clients, working in a consultative sales mode to assess client needs and provide custom-tailored solutions. Established and maintained strong client relationships; built business through persistent prospecting and account development.

- Achieved $1.5 million in sales in one year with a major automotive aftermarket client.
- Served as in-house account manager / project head for 7 major client programs.

Lakeside Bank & Trust, Belleville, Illinois, 1999–2001

RESIDENTIAL LENDING OFFICER

Established and maintained relationships with primary customers (real estate professionals) to develop steady stream of mortgage business.

- Maintained more than $1 million in loan originations per month.
- Created territory analysis and strategic marketing plan for 24 "A" and 16 "B" accounts.

(continued)

Kathleen's numbers were so good, it made sense to call attention to them in chart format. In the companion cover letter (sample 12-2), these same numbers are presented in a different way (showing the seven year average) for added impact without being repetitious.

KATHLEEN STANSFIELD

312-498-8888 ■ stansfield@aol.com

PROFESSIONAL EXPERIENCE

Illinois Financial Services, Belleville, Illinois, 1997–1999

SENIOR MARKETING MANAGER

Developed, coordinated, and managed marketing programs in support of new and existing financial services to targeted national and regional referral sources. Program elements included consumer and trade advertising, direct mail, sales promotion, trade show participation, and national sales meetings.

- Received two "Awards of Excellence" at industry marketing conventions, 1998 and 1999.

Megamanufacturer Company, Rockford, Illinois, 1996–1997

PROMOTION MANAGER, MEGA ADVERTISING

Working within Megamanufacturer's in-house advertising agency, served as Account Manager for "Supercola" beverage products.

- Created and implemented marketing plan that included a monthly promotion to 6,000 nationwide retail stores with dual objectives of dealer participation and consumer draw. Managed promotion budget that ranged from $250,000 to $2.2 million monthly. Directed and supervised copywriters, art group, and print production.
- Secured product placements in feature-length films from major motion-picture studios.

Stop-N-Go Stores, Rockford, Illinois, 1992–1996

REGIONAL MANAGER, 1994–1996

Maintained profit center responsibility for 9 Northeastern states. Developed marketing and margin analysis; created volume-building promotions; managed 3 District Managers; oversaw inventory / expense control.

- First-year territory sales increased 42% and then accelerated by 58% and 30% the following 2 years (national average 8%).
- Reduced store failures 23% through intensified programming.

DISTRICT MANAGER, 1993–1994
STORE SUPERVISOR, 1992–1993

Corporate Travel Specialists, Chicago, Illinois, 1990–1992

TRAVEL DIRECTOR

Developed, presented, and coordinated customized travel programs for corporate clients that included General Motors, Procter & Gamble, and Citibank. Spent 80% of time out of country, accompanying corporate trips as on-site trip director and troubleshooter.

EDUCATION

B.S., University of Illinois at Urbana-Champaign, 1990

ADDITIONAL INFORMATION

Conversationally proficient in Spanish and Italian.

Available to travel and relocate.

Rachel K. Stein

941-243-8901   25-A Cove Road, Sarasota, FL 34243   rkstein@juno.com

---

SALES / MARKETING / ACCOUNT MANAGEMENT

Aggressive, persistent, hardworking, highly motivated sales / marketing professional who thrives on meeting new challenges and strives for continuous personal improvement and professional growth.

➤ Strong track record of successful sales in competitive arenas built through excellent customer relationships, new-account development, and substantial increases in market share and penetration.

➤ Proven ability to analyze trends and sales results, determine appropriate merchandising mix, and create product displays to maximize sales opportunities.

PROFESSIONAL EXPERIENCE

B&B BAUBLES & BEADS, New York, NY   2004–Present
Jewelry—watches—hair accessories—gifts—children's jewelry.
Account Executive

Sell and service a $4 million territory covering major accounts (large retailers) in South / Southeast. Analyze performance data and make buying recommendations and, for some accounts, independent buying decisions. Develop and maintain strong relationships with buyers, management, and merchandising and sales staff at all accounts. Coordinate, modify, and personalize retail fixtures and point-of-sale collateral to maximize sales.

➤ Achieved 26% increase in net shipments for Spring 2008 to achieve highest bonus level.
➤ Increased net shipments at largest account, JC Penney, by 34% for Spring 2007.
➤ Gained 11% increase for Shiveley's Jewelry business during 2006.
➤ Improved penetration in the Megamart Hair Accessories account to 25% in the department.

CONSOLIDATED DEPARTMENT STORES, Atlanta, GA   1991–2004
Corporate buying and management—career goals achieved through consistent promotions.
Buyer—Ladies' Fashion Accessories—MEGAMART (2000–2004)

Accountable for sales and profitability of $12 million multifaceted accessory business for 42-store chain. Developed and implemented sales and marketing strategies and financial plans.

➤ Increased volume by $1.1 million in 2003, an 18% increase over previous fall season.
➤ Capitalized on hair accessories trend, expanding the department and increasing total sales by $649K from 2000 to 2002; achieved best performance for Consolidated in 2001 with a 38% increase.
➤ Regularly visited 4 key markets to negotiate space and prepare floor and fixture plans for seasonal shops.

Buyer—Handbags and Small Leather Goods—MEGAMART (1996–2000)

Responsible for sales and profitability of an $8 million business.

➤ Increased small leather goods by $375K from 1995 to 2000.
➤ Successfully introduced innovative electronic card concept and sold 10,000 units in 1999.
➤ Actively participated on the Consolidated Handbag Committee, traveling to European markets and the Orient to develop products for all divisions.

Buyer—Men's Furnishings (1994–1996)—STONE'S (presently Megamart)
Department Manager—Ladies' Ready-to-Wear (1992–1994)—STONE'S
Assistant Buyer—Budget Sportswear (1991–1992)—STONE'S

EDUCATION AND TRAINING

B.A. in Psychology, 1991: Florida A&M University, Tallahassee, FL
Ongoing Professional Development:
   Retail Negotiation—Management Training—Time Management—Planning and Organization

Having made a successful transition from retail buying to sales and account management, Rachel was ready for new challenges. She planned to look for a position with a larger company, preferably a household name in the fashion industry.

Matthew Seles

9 Old Liberty Street, Unit 12C
Philadelphia, PA 19103

215 / 891-6372
mseles@yahoo.com

EXPERTISE Sales and Sales Management
Regional / National / Key Account Management
New-Business Development

Consistent top producer in territory and national sales positions within the food and beverage industry. Verifiable accomplishments in the following key areas:

- Opening, building, and developing new food service sales territories
- Revitalizing territory sales and increasing profitability
- Marketing to institutional food service distributors, restaurant and convenience store chains, and retailers in local, regional, and national accounts
- Introducing new products and new programs; shepherding through start-up to established status
- Selecting, training, developing, and managing both direct and broker sales forces
- Delivering effective sales presentations; creating and presenting sales training programs
- Developing strong professional customer relationships

A proven performer ready for a new challenge.

PROFESSIONAL EXPERIENCE

BETTER BEVERAGES, INC., Vancouver, WA

2004–Present

Brought beverage expertise to specialty marketer of coffee products. Contributed knowledge of sales channels, marketing strategies, and product trends to help company develop new products, capture new accounts, and increase distribution and sales.

▶ **Regional Sales Manager,** Philadelphia, PA

Directly marketed coffee products and services to regional and national institutional accounts.

Provided sales leadership to branches throughout the East and Midwest by accompanying representatives on sales calls, demonstrating effective techniques for marketing and selling coffee, and stimulating new-branch sales in allied products and food products. Acquired new accounts and increased penetration in existing accounts.

Key Accomplishments

- Introduced new coffee products to **Wendy's** at the national headquarters level; succeeded in gaining approval for test marketing and subsequent product roll-out at regional locations.
- Captured all cappuccino business and solidified coffee business for **Sunoco** convenience-store locations.
- To increase sales through product knowledge, educated chains on merchandising, advertising, promoting, and pricing specialty coffee beverages.
- Developed **private-label coffee programs** for national office coffee company.
- Instrumental in the development of a **new coffee product;** contributed product and industry expertise and sales / marketing perspective to R&D, product marketing strategy, POS materials, and pricing decisions. Product successfully introduced in convenience store market.

STARBREW COFFEE, San Francisco, CA

1998–2004

Recognized for strong ability to open, build, develop, and manage highly successful and profitable sales territories. Consistently challenged with higher levels of sales management and responsibility based on superior performance.

▶ **Regional Sales Manager, Food Service Division,** Philadelphia, PA, 2000–2004

Developed and maintained accounts in a 10-state region, with primary focus on full-line food service distributors, secondary on convenience-store chains, national and regional restaurant chains, vending and office coffee distributors. Created, designed, and developed private-label coffee programs, packaging, and POS materials for customers.

The level of detail in this resume matches Matt's style and preference. He quickly landed a new position that provided new challenges and met his personal goal of significantly reducing his business travel.

Matthew Seles   215 / 891-6372 ► mseles@yahoo.com

PROFESSIONAL EXPERIENCE, continued

STARBREW COFFEE

► **Regional Sales Manager, Food Service Division,** continued

Established ambitious sales quotas; developed and monitored budgets; created and implemented sales, marketing, and pricing plans to increase productivity, sales, and profitability of the territory.

Trained broker sales force and direct sales staff on product positioning, sales techniques, new-account development, and territory maintenance and planning. Organized, planned, designed, and worked national, regional, state, and local trade shows.

Key Accomplishments

- Increased gross sales **tenfold** (from $1.5 million to $15 million) in 4 years.
- Increased sales **405%** in allied products (tea, iced cappuccino, flavored coffee); finished first in allied sales in the entire Food Service Division.
- Named **Salesperson of the Year,** 2001, 2002, 2003.

► **District Sales Manager, Food Service Division,** Pennsylvania / New Jersey / Delaware, 1998–2000

- Increased territory sales from **$675 thousand to $1.9 million.**
- Named **Sales Representative of the Year** (Food Service Division), 1998; **Manufacturer Sales Representative of the Year** (National Coffee Organization), 1999 and 2000.
- Closed key account with the largest hot cocoa food service distributor in the U.S.
- Sold complete beverage programs to the most food service distributors in a single year for the Food Service Division.

MIDWAY FOOD SERVICE, Lancaster, Pennsylvania   1996–1998

Consistently outperformed sales targets in both territory and national sales positions. Developed strong skills in advising and training product users to achieve increased product usage.

► **National Account Manager,** 1997–1998

- Achieved **100%** of all sales objectives in $4 million sales territory.

► **Territory Manager,** 1996–1997

- Sold full line of food and beverage products to institutional customers in Eastern Pennsylvania market. Increased territory sales by **30% within 4 months** (a branch record).

EDUCATION AND PROFESSIONAL DEVELOPMENT

Consistently attend seminars on sales techniques and sales management strategies.

TEMPLE UNIVERSITY, Philadelphia, Pennsylvania
Completed 95% of coursework for Bachelor's degree in Business Administration / Sales Management.

PROFESSIONAL AFFILIATIONS

National Coffee Organization   National Association of Convenience Stores
National Automatic Merchandiser Association   American Marketing Association

ARNE SWEDENBORG

2795 Planters Court, Alpharetta, GA 30004
404-297-4440 • aswede@aol.com

EXECUTIVE SUMMARY

Experienced sales professional with a record of outstanding results in highly competitive markets. Consistently develop new business and expand established accounts through a customer-driven, solution-oriented focus and a total commitment to building long-term partnerships. Especially adept at explaining complex technical solutions to nontechnical people.

Areas of expertise include *direct sales, broker/distributor management, sales training,* and *team building.* Exceptional interpersonal and leadership skills with a management style that brings out the best in people.

PROFESSIONAL EXPERIENCE

K-PACK CORPORATION, Kansas City, Missouri   2008–Present
Consultative thermoform packaging manufacturer and contract manufacturer

Senior Account Manager, Custom Products

Manage 12-state Southeast U.S. territory and key national accounts, serving in a consultative sales role to develop custom packaging solutions. Maintain full P&L responsibility for business results. Challenged to develop substantial new business in diverse industries (health care, automotive aftermarket, office supply, electrical, consumer products). Customers include Fortune 100 companies such as Coca-Cola, American Home Products, and Hewlett-Packard.

- Developed business that will deliver $1.3 million in new sales revenue by year-end 2009 (representing a 65% increase in territory volume).

- Leading a successful initiative to expand the company's markets into the food processing / food service arenas.

- Gained approved vendor status with key accounts, including Colgate-Palmolive, Pfizer, and General Electric.

ACME PACKAGING COMPANY, Houston, Texas   2004–2008
National manufacturer of thermoform packaging

Senior Account Manager, Plastics Packaging Division

Held total P&L responsibility for sales forecasting, budgeting, pricing, and new-business development for a 7-state southern territory. Directed all sales activities with customers in food service, copackaging, medical/pharmaceutical, and consumer products industries. Managed key national accounts. Based in Atlanta, Georgia; reported directly to Divisional Vice President.

- Expanded sales volume from $250,000 to $3.5 million in 2½ years.

- Created a new product application for a key national account that generated $1.7 million in annual sales.

- Consistently earned corporate incentives for exceeding sales objectives.

- Established and maintained key account relationships with national customers including Coca-Cola, Procter & Gamble, GTE, Emerson Electric, and Texas Instruments.

The boxed Executive Summary clearly distinguishes this important information. Arne wanted to explore opportunities outside his industry, so we did not include industry-specific information in the summary.

ARNE SWEDENBORG • Page 2   404-297-4440 • aswede@aol.com

PROFESSIONAL EXPERIENCE, continued

REDI-PACK, INC., Tampa, Florida   1997–2004
Regional manufacturer of thermoform packaging

Regional Sales Manager

Managed a 15-state territory based in Atlanta. Held key national account responsibility for Fortune 500 customers such as GE, Campbell Soup Company, Pepsi, and GTE. Established and maintained relationships at all levels, from purchasing agents through CEOs. Trained, supervised, and motivated a team of 3 to consistently provide high-quality customer service and sales support.

- Built sales from $600,000 to more than $4 million in 6 years.
- Positioned the company as a recognized leader of packaging applications in the processed foods industry.
- Served on a corporate task force that successfully reengineered the inside sales and customer service departments.
- National Sales Manager of the Year, 2003.

BEAUTY BASICS CORPORATION, New York, New York   1994–1997
Manufacturer of cosmetics distributed through better department stores nationwide

Area Manager

Directed the activities of 120 sales professionals in 10 cosmetic departments in retail department stores.

- Increased sales volume 70% by designing and implementing a comprehensive promotional and merchandising plan.
- Boosted net profit 36% by establishing better expense-control procedures.
- Consistently achieved top store performance, ranking in top 5% of 800+ stores nationally. Led a team effort that propelled one site to #1 in the U.S.
- Honored as Supervisor of the Year, 1995.

JOHNSON & JOHNSON, New Brunswick, New Jersey   1993–1994

Sales Representative

Developed product knowledge through rotating assignments at 5 J&J sites across the country.

EDUCATION

UNIVERSITY OF GEORGIA: BS/BA, Marketing Management, 1992

ONGOING PROFESSIONAL DEVELOPMENT: Sales seminars by Carew, Earl Nightingale, and Dun & Bradstreet; Xerox Professional Selling Skills I and II; Xerox Effective Listening Skills I and II.

COMPUTER SKILLS

Proficient with Windows-based applications: Microsoft Word, Excel, PowerPoint, Access, Outlook.

Chapter 6

Sales Management Resumes

In sales management resumes, it's important to show both the ability to sell and the ability to achieve results through others. Most sales managers begin with a successful career in sales and then advance to training, leading, and motivating a sales team. Their success stories are often of group accomplishments and region-wide or national sales results.

Shaun L. Madden

781-639-9876 ▪ slmadden@aol.com

47 Mulberry Street
Wellesley, MA 02481

Sales & Marketing Executive
Regional, National, & International — Project, Product, & Team Management

Track record of delivering consistent revenue streams and outperforming sales goals:

2008	2007	2006	2005	2004
170%	**197%**	**134%**	**143%**	**189%**

Energetic, creative, proven performer committed to continued excellence. Proven strengths include

- Maximizing revenue and profit in a predictable and repeatable fashion.
- Training/developing sales professionals... communicating the *science* of the art of selling.
- Creating and implementing sales and marketing strategies for existing and new products.
- Contributing sales expertise to product development, corporate planning, and cross-functional initiatives.
- Driving highly effective sales organizations... communicating vision, methodology, and goals.

Professional Experience

GIANT SOFTWARE COMPANY, San Jose, California   2001–Present

➤ **District Manager, Northeast Region**   1/08–Present

Direct the sales activities for the industry segment, selling Giant software products (business communications solutions) to 300 corporate accounts, each having 5,000 or more employees. Manage a 6-state region that delivers $47+ million in annual revenue (largest volume of all sales districts worldwide).

Manage sales team (currently 7 sales professionals) to consistently high performance levels. Create and nurture a well-balanced, diverse, focused team through motivation, leadership, training, and establishment of sales process as the foundation for business success.

Collaborate with technical team leader, providing direction for a total of 25 sales and technical professionals who work cooperatively to recommend the most appropriate business solutions to fit customers' complex communication and information needs (such as messaging, Internet / intranet, knowledge management, and rapid application development).

- Delivered the highest percentage performance against plan (**197%**) among all Giant locations worldwide, 2007.
- In 2008, *all* team members performed above **125%** of plan... 75% attained at least **150%.**
- Maintained **zero** negative attrition while hiring talented people, growing existing talent, and grooming several for promotion.
- Delivered highly consistent and predictable sales results, meeting or exceeding targets *each quarter*.
- Manager of the Year, 2008; singled out among 650 U.S. managers for contributions to the business.

➤ **U.S. Sales Initiative—Project Leader**   3/08–Present

Assumed corporate staff assignment while retaining all responsibilities as District Manager.

Charged with spearheading the transformation to sales process methodology throughout entire U.S. sales organization—strategizing, planning, and implementing processes and programs to achieve a fundamental change in the way the company approaches the sales challenge.

- Transformed a highly unpredictable revenue stream into the business' *most predictable*. In 1 year, reduced variance of forecast from **20%** annually to within **3%**... in first quarter 2009, achieved variance of only **0.3%** on revenue for *entire U.S. sales operation*.

Serve as consultant to senior management on issues relating to sales force productivity, automation, and process improvement.

The numbers that Shaun's teams put together are pretty hard to beat. This data, in table format, immediately captures the reader's attention. Shaun's cover letter is sample 12-3.

Professional Experience

GIANT SOFTWARE COMPANY (continued)

➤ **Acting Manager, Northeast Region**   10/07–12/07

Managed 4-member direct sales team selling Giant enterprise products.

- Outperformed sales target, achieving **172%** of plan.
- Doubled revenue forecast for the quarter.

➤ **Product Sales Manager**   2/07–10/07

Developed sales strategy and sold Giant products in a 4-state territory.

- Achieved **165%** of sales objectives.
- Created sales strategy for 20-member sales team that resulted in team performance at **106%** of plan.

➤ **Territory Sales Representative**   2004–2007

Effectively managed 4-state sales territory while maintaining consistently high levels of sales performance and customer satisfaction.

- **Doubled** number of accounts in first year; grew business consistently from first day on the job until the last.
- Outperformed sales goals in each measured period.
- Rookie of the Year, 2004; Salesperson of the Year, 2005.
- Personally sold in excess of **$1 million** every year.

➤ **Global Product Marketing Manager: Mailcom**   2001–2004

Created worldwide marketing and sales strategy for launch of industry-first product line (Mailcom communication, mail management, and message-switching technology).

- Captured **$10 million** in sales and **75%** market share within 3 years—the company's most successful worldwide market introduction.

Directed 10-member cross-functional project team that delivered cutting-edge technology product on budget, with planned functionality, 30 days ahead of schedule.

- Achieved profitability in first year.

XANADU ADVERTISING & MARKETING, INC., Pawtucket, Rhode Island   1999–2000

➤ **Director, Business Development**

- Achieved new-business revenues of more than **$2.5 million** through acquisition of new accounts and close focus on customer satisfaction.
- Secured national accounts for the first time in the company's history.

Education

PROVIDENCE COLLEGE, Providence, Rhode Island
Bachelor of Business Administration, 1998 / Major in Management

PROFESSIONAL TRAINING
Solution Selling, 2001–Present (Student and Coach)
Effective Negotiating (Chester Karrass), 2003

Sybil Masterson

502-349-3401   3525 Derby Drive, Louisville, KY 40255   smasterson@yahoo.com

Sales • Sales Management • Key Account Management

- Successful 20-year sales and management career distinguished by rapid advancement with industry-leading business information provider and consistent delivery of strong sales results as both producer and manager.
- Exceptional ability to deliver effective sales and product presentations to diverse decision makers, including top executives of Fortune 500 companies.
- Proven talent for motivating and inspiring sales teams to immediate and long-range performance gains.

Professional Experience

1990–Present   DATA SALES CORPORATION, New York, NY

District Manager, Louisville   2006–Present

Develop strategy, oversee team and individual sales performance, and manage daily activities for $12 million, multiple-office district involved in sales of business information to midsized and Fortune 500 companies. Lead and mentor a diverse 16-member sales team, focusing on maximizing performance through training, motivation, inspiration, and effective supervision.

- Grew sales an average of 9.3% annually, outperforming the company's district average of 6%.
- Reduced operating expenses 30% upon assuming management responsibility for 2 additional branches (Lexington and Indianapolis) in 2007.
- Maximized sales initiatives within the company's most profitable segments by training and coaching the sales team in effective business development and penetration strategies.
- Personally developed a Fortune 500 client from minor account status to $600 thousand annually by proposing in-depth integration of business information with new SAP platform.

District Manager, Minneapolis/St. Paul   2005–2006

Managed sales for $6.3 million district with 11 sales associates and 3-member support staff.

- Delivered 20% increase in new business.

Director of Customer Support, Minneapolis/St. Paul   2003–2005

Provided training, direction, and leadership to 100 sales representatives focused on the development of specialized solutions for customers such as 3M Corporation and Lucent Technologies.

- Oversaw development of several custom products that were subsequently reconfigured and rolled out nationwide.

District Manager, Information Resources

Minneapolis/St. Paul	35 associates, $1.5 million budget	2003
Hartford	20 associates, $1.2 million budget	1999–2002

Oversaw operations and staff in the collection and management of information—the company's stock in trade, with stringent data management requirements.

National Trainer, Miami   1998–1999

Provided comprehensive training to business analysts and front-line managers, focusing on selling skills and other business functions critical to their success.

Divisional Manager, Tallahassee	1995–1998
Business Analyst, Atlanta	1991–1995
Account Representative, Atlanta	1990–1991

Education

ST. SEBASTIAN COLLEGE, Atlanta, GA: B.A. in Communications / Minor in Business Administration, 1990

Sybil's original resume focused on job activities and lacked quantifiable accomplishments. The new version makes her a very competitive candidate.

Philip T. Allison

2525 Fifth Street NW • Renton, WA 98058
(425) 555-8765 • ptallison@hotmail.com

Sales Management • Operations Management • Operational Startup and Expansion
Expertise: Automotive Leasing and Financing

▶ **STRENGTHS**

- **Creative leadership:** conceiving and articulating vision; communicating new initiatives; providing overall program direction
- **Sales and sales management:** a 13-year track record of consistently successful individual and team sales
- **Planning and goal setting** for practical implementation
- **Selecting, training, motivating, and mentoring** individuals to high levels of professional achievement; bringing together diverse individuals to form a cohesive team
- **Contributing to the creation of products and services** that meet defined needs and assist in niche marketing efforts

---

Professional Experience

AUTO-INFO SERVICES, Bedford, Massachusetts   1/2009–Present

District Manager: Northwest

Challenged to open new Northwest territory for leading provider of automotive leasing software. Drawing upon extensive automotive leasing expertise, market state-of-the-art application to auto dealers, banks, and other financial institutions. Supervise sales assistant.

- Within a few months, effectively penetrated new territory and captured major accounts.

FIRST FEDERAL BANK, Renton, Washington   2005–2008

Assistant Vice President / Director of Sales

Directed the sales effort and overall strategy of the Automotive Division, which generated roughly $1 billion in loan revenue annually. Directed a staff of 8 Area Sales Managers; supervised an additional 15–20 support staff. Managed all department operational responsibilities, including staff supervision and evaluation, budgeting, and establishing and implementing action plans tied to the achievement of long-term goals.

Designed, implemented, and supported the bank's product offerings, including lease and loan contracts, specialized financing products, and innovative alternative income sources.

Developed overall market strategy and trained representatives in sales techniques that built upon customer relationships and service. Scheduled or personally delivered regular, extensive training covering all stages of the sales process and ongoing customer and industry education.

Led exploration and research to support expansion into new geographic regions.

▶ **KEY ACCOMPLISHMENTS**

- **Increased lease unit production 50% and dollar production 85%.**
- Contributed to the establishment of a tiered, risk-based pricing system. Played a key role in determining the bank's product offerings; identified ways to maximize fee income while maintaining a competitive posture in the marketplace.
- Led major initiative to evaluate division's overall portfolio; as a consequence, restructured loan policies and established a more secure foundation for bank loans. Within one quarter, more than regained the volume of business that had been achieved with less stringent loan policies.
- Spearheaded a program to maximize profitability on all returned lease vehicles.
- Developed and implemented critical reports and updates to measure effectiveness in all areas (credit, sales, and operations) as well as to track and analyze customers and competitors.

(continued)

Philip's sales/management job with First Federal was affected by a merger that absorbed the leasing division. He parlayed his leasing experience into a direct-sales position with a software company marketing to auto leasing customers. Adding this position to his resume, he planned to continue his search for a higher-level sales or operations management opportunity.

Philip T. Allison

BUY-CAR AUTO LEASING, Seattle, Washington   1999–2005
Director of Leasing
Held total responsibility for all aspects of leasing cars, trucks, and vans at 5 locations in the Greater
Seattle area, with 3 distinct areas of focus: Consumer Lease, Fleet Operations, and Renewal Team. In
addition to supervising a staff of 12 customer service representatives and 15–20 lease consultants,
managed all budgeting, forecasting, planning, and goal-setting for the leasing department. Led product
development and support initiatives.

▶ **CONSUMER LEASE**

- Hired, trained, motivated, and supervised the day-to-day activities of 2–3 lease consultants per
  location, each generating 8–12 new vehicle deliveries per month with average gross profit per unit
  of $1,100.
- Trained all consultants on the concepts and benefits of leasing. Ensured that consultants
  maintained in-depth knowledge of quoting and delivering through a variety of finance
  sources.

▶ **FLEET OPERATIONS**

- Provided leadership and direction toward the goal of maximizing the return from the huge
  and virtually untapped leasing market.
- Hired, motivated, and supervised 4 Area Managers; trained managers in all aspects of
  corporate fleet programs, dealer programs, and consumer lease products.

▶ **RENEWAL TEAM**

- Directed a team of 4 highly experienced lease consultants providing lease-renewal services.
- Achieved consistent growth in renewals (900 in 2004; 1,225 in 2005).

SMITH AUTOMOTIVE GROUP, Tacoma, Washington   1995–1999
General Sales Manager (1996–1999)

Hired, trained, scheduled, and supervised 4 sales managers and up to 40 staff. Optimized inventory to
ensure maximum dealer profits as well as guaranteeing the best selection and value for the customer.

- Averaged 250 to 300 new and used units per month—an 18% increase over the previous
  management team.

Sales Manager (1995–1996)

- Maintained a consistent gross average profit of $1,350 per sale and consistently achieved an
  excellent customer satisfaction rating.
- Negotiated and closed deals for the entire sales staff.

Sales Representative (1995)

- Recognized for maintaining excellent customer relations through consistent follow-through.

Education
SEATTLE PACIFIC UNIVERSITY, Seattle, Washington
   BS, Psychology, 1995

Taylor Jorgenson

2525 Pelican Pathway, Tampa, FL 33614
Home: (813) 554-9943 • Office: (813) 421-0070
tjorgenson@tampa.rr.com

Sales Management Executive

Delivering impressive revenue gains, profit growth, and market-share increases through strategic sales leadership within high-technology companies.

Consistent record of career achievement in sales and management with high-tech companies and emerging technologies. Strong ability to develop, train, lead, and motivate sales teams to top performance. Record of identifying and seizing opportunities to achieve objectives in highly competitive markets. Experienced in applying CRM and ERP e-business solutions to sales and operations functions across the organization. Innovative and resourceful, with excellent understanding of today's business conditions and ability to develop alliances to promote corporate objectives.

Experience and Accomplishments

BroadNet, Inc. — Tampa, FL   2007–Present

A leading supplier of test equipment and network-management systems designed to ensure the optimal performance and utilization of optical broadband communication networks. $325 million annual revenues.

REGIONAL VICE PRESIDENT (SOUTHEAST REGION) — Create sales strategy and lead combined direct/distributor sales force selling to public network operators, network equipment manufacturers, component vendors, and enterprise network operators. Hold full P&L responsibility for regional performance.

- Led region to top performance in the nation, generating 47% of the total U.S. revenue in the first half of 2008.

- On track to achieve 100% of a $37 million quota in 2009.

- Strengthened performance of sales team through effective leadership, goal-setting, and creation of appropriately motivating incentive and commission structures.

- Focused sales strategy on solution selling to strategic accounts. Developed training programs for account managers targeting strategic accounts across 12 business units.

Electronic Devices, Inc. — Clearwater, FL   1990–2007

Reseller of electronic test and measurement equipment and telecommunications equipment. In sales leadership roles, contributed to growth of company from 40 employees to 375, and $7 million revenue to $385 million.

NATIONAL SALES MANAGER (2004–2007) — Drove sales, rentals, and leases of high-tech equipment through national sales force. Directed staff of 80. Formulated strategic marketing plans; established goals; recruited, motivated, and managed high-performing sales force.

- Achieved aggressive growth of 20% per year in sales revenue.

- Secured critical distribution channels and initiated partnerships to consistently meet sales goals and market share.

- Designed, developed, and deployed new commission incentive program; increased sales by $2.6 million in first year. Overall, tripled annual sales from $7 million to $21 million.

(continued)

The tagline directly below the headline summarizes areas of achievement that relate specifically to accomplishments detailed in the Experience and Accomplishments section.

NATIONAL SALES MANAGER (continued)

- Instituted "Quality and Excellence" program for clients and staff; key clients included 3Com, Cisco Systems, EMC, Sprint, Dell Computer, IBM, Nortel, and Qualcom.

- Responsible for the asset-management process of a $42 million inventory.

- Championed organizational development and training programs.

- With committee members, analyzed business needs and recommended implementation of SAP ERP software.

REGIONAL SALES MANAGER: FLORIDA (1997–2004) — Coordinated business development throughout industrial, commercial, aerospace, and military markets. Directed fulfillment, administrative, public relations, and marketing activities. Tasked assignments, determined realistic goals, and set priorities to meet deadlines. Provided product training and direction on territory-management techniques.

- Managed #1 office in the U.S. in total sales volume for 7 years.

- Achieved over 100% of quota each year while maintaining 35% gross margins on sales; won Regional Manager's Award for greatest business volume ever concluded in a single month.

- Delivered clear, effective, leading-edge presentations.

- Successfully negotiated numerous major corporate contracts.

SENIOR ACCOUNT MANAGER (1990–1997) — Utilized excellent networking and communications abilities to consistently build strong client relationships. Generated customized marketing and presentational strategies to maximize account-development opportunities with largest customers.

- Achieved over 100% of quota each year; won recognition as #1 sales performer in the U.S.

- In competition with 30 other representatives, won 3 national sales contests based on total revenue and new accounts.

BioTools, Inc. — Tampa, FL   1987–1990
World leader in biomedical instrumentation.

SALES REPRESENTATIVE / SERVICE TECHNICIAN

Education

Northeastern University, Boston, MA
BACHELOR OF SCIENCE IN BUSINESS MANAGEMENT

Interests and Activities

Golf / Waterskiing / Tennis

References and additional information available on request.

Patrick T. Miller

4320 Primrose Lane, Ft. Worth, TX 76110
ptmiller@aol.com • 817-555-1124

PROFILE

Creative, competitive, and experienced sales/marketing professional with strong background in medical sales management and a track record of consistent sales accomplishments.

- Known for partnering with clients to learn their needs, recommend solutions, and build relationships.
- Committed to goal-setting, planning, and follow-through to achieve results.
- Possess proven communication skills, leadership abilities, and a bottom-line orientation.
- Perform well under pressure and against deadlines, both independently and with a team.

Key areas of expertise: Medical sales… advertising… marketing… supervision… troubleshooting… training… promotions… employee motivation… inventory control… presentations… P&L… financial management… vendor relations… prospecting… business start-ups… creative problem-solving

PROFESSIONAL EXPERIENCE

NATIONAL HOSPITAL SERVICES, Baltimore, Maryland · 2005–Present

District Manager — Dallas District (2007–Present) — Sales, operational, and P&L responsibility

SALES
- Call on hospital and care facility material managers, CFOs, and central supply supervisors as well as physicians, selling hospital-supply leasing services and special-care products.
- In top 5 of 43 representatives selling DPAP products to pulmonologists, neurologists, directors of sleep labs, and home care companies.
- Achieved strong sales that made the NHS Pro-DPAP our district's number-one growth product.

MANAGEMENT
- Turned around struggling operation, achieving profitability within 8 months and remaining profitable ever since. Replaced entire staff, reaching stability within 4 months.
- Led district to 2008 revenue of 149% to budget and operating income of 393% to plan.

Account Manager (2005–2007)
- Brought on board to launch the Dallas District Office. Through aggressive sales, grew at new-district rate that was the third fastest in the company's history (since 1939).
- Established a strong customer base of 60 accounts.
- Developed quarterly and monthly plans; submitted weekly reports.
- Sales management responsibilities included budget-to-plan, 10% growth, days outstanding, and 25% margin on net income.

MEDI-SERV, INC., Dallas, Texas · 2002–2005

Territory Manager
- Built close client relationships with 75 hospitals and 20 home-care companies.
- Increased market share 30% through aggressive cold-calling and follow-up.
- Prepared and delivered in-service presentations to end users and decision makers.
- Transformed a $25,000 loss into profit of $15,000 in 6 months by controlling P&L.

MORE MUSIC, Fort Worth, Texas — 15-store regional chain of music retailers · 1997–2002

Senior Purchasing Agent
- Administered and controlled annual purchasing budget of $3 million. Supervised 6 purchasing agents.
- Increased revenue 30% by initiating sale of food, clothing, and accessories.
- Slashed annual losses $90,000 by instituting new "bad debt" procedures.

EDUCATION

BA Communications, 2000 • Texas Christian University, Fort Worth, Texas
- Earned 100% of college tuition and expenses through employment and entrepreneurial ventures.

Patrick's "Key areas of expertise" can be viewed as a keyword summary, which is helpful for matching traits that are used to search resume databases.

Adrian H. May

294 Village Drive
Englewood, NJ 07053

Home 201-349-0904
Office 212-769-2378
mayday@optonline.net

Sales and management professional with in-depth knowledge of the health care industry, specifically managed-care plans and programs. Proven leadership skills in developing staff, implementing programs, managing teams and projects, and initiating process improvements.

A key contributor to the success of one of the nation's most highly regarded managed health care companies; a consistent top performer in a fast-paced, challenging environment.

STRENGTHS

- **Organization and time management:** flexibility in the face of changing priorities.
- **Team leadership and participation:** proven ability to contribute to cross-functional initiatives and maintain a focus on established goals.
- **Staff coaching and development:** in both formal training and daily supervision.
- **Communication and presentation skills:** both internally and externally; demonstrated ability to represent customers' viewpoint and to communicate value.
- **Strong desire to grow professionally and personally.**

Professional Experience

MAJOR MEDICAL CARE OF THE NORTHEAST, New York, NY   2000–Present

Sales Manager, Account Management (2005–Present)

Manage a team of professionals generating new business and providing service to existing accounts. Direct departmental processes and methods of service delivery, staying alert for opportunities to increase levels of service. Lead or participate in interdepartmental and cross-functional process-improvement initiatives.

Develop sales strategies to assist account managers in servicing and retaining accounts. Participate in customer meetings and presentations to communicate the values and benefits of Major Medical programs. Assist account managers in closing renewal business. Maintain focus on consultative selling and a high level of customer service.

Prepare and manage $1.1 million department budget. Establish department sales forecasts and sales team goals.

Represent the sales department and customer viewpoints throughout the organization; contribute customer perspective to proposed plan changes and new-product development. Stay up to date on relevant legislation.

Work with staff to create individual development plans. Conduct performance evaluations.

KEY ACCOMPLISHMENTS

- Averaged greater than 96% account retention over 5 years during periods of significant account growth (in both members and revenues). Consistently met or exceeded individual account membership goals.
- Provided support and assistance in the strategic planning and account negotiation process for key renewals. This included managing the implementation process for taking large accounts to sole-source status, including customizing benefit plans, transitioning patients in ongoing treatment, and educating new members. Retained accounts included NYNEX, New York City Schools, Citibank, and Northeast Digital.
- Developed process for Top 50 Account Reviews.
- Successfully managed departmental operations during territory realignments. Encouraged mentoring relationships among staff to ensure ongoing training and development of less experienced staff.
- Developed employer survey instrument for use in evaluating staff members.

TRAINING EXPERIENCE

Develop, direct, and lead training programs to sales staff and throughout the company. Recent experience includes

- Objections Training and Role-Plays.
- Improving Sales Effectiveness: Increasing product knowledge, competitive knowledge, and productivity.
- Sales Tracking System: Assisted in training field representatives on new software.

This resume is detailed but well organized. It condenses a lot of information into relatively short, easily digestible paragraphs and bullet points. Accomplishments are well highlighted.

Adrian H. May   Home 201-349-0904 • Office 212-769-2378 • mayday@optonline.net

Sales Manager, Account Management (continued)

PROJECT MANAGEMENT EXPERIENCE

As a member of Major Medical's management team, lead and participate in a variety of special projects and team initiatives in addition to fulfilling primary job responsibilities. Representative examples:

- Sales Incentive Program: Led the project to design a new program.
- Strategic Business Units: Led the project to coordinate sales between business units.
- Sales Tracking System: Designed, developed, and implemented an automated database providing better management of account information.
- Employer Utilization Report: Participated in report redesign to better meet customer expectations.
- Customer Advisory Panel: Assisted in coordinating panel meetings and establishing group objectives.
- Corporate Issues Group: Worked with Executive and Senior Management to identify corporate issues to assist during planning process for future direction of the company.
- Professional Environment Team: Chaired a team to enhance sales environment.

Senior Account Manager (2002–2005) — **Account Manager** (2000–2002)

Consistently met or exceeded sales goals during growth of company from $93 million to $300 million in revenues. Contributed to company initiatives through participation on a variety of teams, committees, and special projects.

- Consistently exceeded aggressive quarterly membership goals.
- Provided a high level of service to high-profile customers; managed nearly half of the company's top 50 employer groups.
- Averaged 98% account retention over 5 years.

Education

NEW YORK UNIVERSITY, New York, New York
> B.S. Business Administration, 2001

Ongoing Professional Development

SALES

> NYU School of Business: Sales Management and Marketing Strategies
> Strategic Selling
> AMA: Sales Management for the Newly Appointed Sales Manager
> Sales Trainers: Dimensions of Professional Selling
> HMO Underwriting and Pricing
> Negotiations Training
> Objections/Media Training

MANAGEMENT AND LEADERSHIP

> Business Writing
> Leading Effective Meetings
> Project Management
> Zenger Miller: Team Building
> Peter Senge: Building a Learning Organization
> Leading Organizational Change
> Union Training
> Management Principles

Professional Licenses

New York Department of Insurance: Life, Health, AD&D

Professional Affiliation

Northeast Association of Health Insurance Providers

Chris Mooney

235 Michigan Drive #4-C
Bay City, Michigan 48708
cmooney@aol.com
517-654-0987

PROFILE

Highly motivated sales management professional with a strong track record of successful sales and account development. Proven ability to select, train and motivate sales staff to achieve ambitious goals.

Strategic planner skilled at both short- and long-range goal setting (big-picture orientation). Proven ability to focus on what is truly important.

Creative marketer with a flair for designing innovative ways to go to market.

Effective communicator with excellent relationship-building skills.

PROFESSIONAL EXPERIENCE

INTERNATIONAL OFFICE EQUIPMENT, LTD., Bay City, Michigan   2005–Present
Sales Manager • Bay City Division (Headquarters) (2008–Present)
Direct 12-member sales team generating $28 million in sales of furniture, office products and supplies.
- Exceeded sales targets every month, averaging 107% of goal.

Sales Manager • Kalamazoo Branch Office (2005–2008)
Led 9-member sales force in sales to commercial accounts of all sizes.

Sales Management
- Instrumental in invigorating an organization with flat sales for the previous 5 years. Increased sales 340% in 2 years ($2.5 million to $8.5 million).
- Office recognized for largest sales increase in past 2 years among 50 branch offices and 23 distribution centers nationwide.
- Pioneered innovative and highly successful recruiting program on college campuses.
- Expanded sales to existing client base and established new accounts, including 3 with annual sales of $1 million-plus.

Staff Development
- Selected, hired, trained, coached and managed highly motivated individuals and gave them the tools and training necessary to succeed.
- Directed sales staff in forecasting and setting sales goals. Focused on the individual skills and needs of each account executive, executing an individual strategy for each.
- Encouraged sales through creative incentives while relying primarily on staff professionalism and self-motivation.

Customer Relations
- Promoted positive ongoing customer relationships and served as a problem-solver and resource to customers.
- Communicated to sales staff a focus on customer service and communication.

PREMIER OFFICE SUPPLIES, Kalamazoo, Michigan   1995–2005
Account Executive
- Ranked #5 among 60 account executives selling office products/supplies to commercial accounts.
- Consistently achieved annual sales increases in the 15%–20% range.
- Developed territory from ground up and expanded annual sales from zero to $2 million.
- Developed accounts through unique presentation to each prospect and commitment to service and follow-up.
- Successfully regained 4 large accounts that had been lost to competitors due to pricing issues.

EDUCATION

UNIVERSITY OF MICHIGAN, Ann Arbor, Michigan — Bachelor of Business Administration, 1992

Subtitles call attention to different aspects of Chris's expertise.

S. Gil Montgomery

20 Terrapin Circle, Raleigh, NC 27612
919-249-2020   monty@verizon.net

Senior Sales Manager

Demonstrated success in achieving corporate profit and increasing sales through enthusiastic, intuitive, and innovative direction of sales staff.

KEY STRENGTHS:

- **Astute hiring**
- **Providing sales staff with tools for success**
- **Devising meaningful planning and reporting tools**
- **Motivating sales staff to achieve and maintain top performance**

Professional Experience

PROFESSIONAL BUILDERS SUPPLY CORPORATION, Phoenix, AZ   1991–2009
REGIONAL SALES MANAGER, SOUTHEAST REGION (2004–2009)

Managed $14 million region, the company's second-largest in dollar volume and profit ($4 million). Prepared annual sales and expense forecast for $900 thousand annual budget.

- **Exceeded profit and sales plan 2005, 2006, 2007, 2008.**
- **First Regional Manager to formulate and implement quarterly report (State of the Region) analyzing market trends and designing sales strategies. This report is now standard in the department.**

Successfully developed, directed, motivated, and evaluated sales team of 7 representatives and 1 technical assistant. Interviewed, hired, and trained staff.

- **Improved team sales volume and profit annually, increasing sales by 37.5% from 2004–2008.**
- **Produced the #1 Sales Representative (nationally), 2005 and 2007.**

Implemented sales and marketing strategies through network of distributors, contractors, and architects.

- **Increased specifications by 25% from 2005–2008.**

Led negotiations with various trades in Raleigh, Atlanta, Miami, and Charlotte.

- **Reduced settlements by average of 10% in 2007.**

ASSISTANT REGIONAL SALES MANAGER (1998–2004)

Assisted Regional Manager with budgeting and performance evaluations. Interviewed and assisted in hiring sales representatives; contributed to performance evaluation process. Trained and motivated sales staff while monitoring their achievement of sales plan goals and devising sales and marketing strategies.

- **Produced 2 National Sales Representatives of the Year and 2 sales representatives promoted to management.**
- **Formulated and implemented National Builder Incentive program.**
- **Conceived and constructed new product display.**

(continued)

Each separate area of responsibility is highlighted by one or more quantifiable accomplishments, noted in bold. This is a good way to avoid overly long groupings of either job duties or achievements.

S. Gil Montgomery   919-249-2020   monty@verizon.net

PRODUCT PROMOTION MANAGER (1995–1998)

Trained representatives on product features and benefits. Conducted architectural presentations and building code seminars.
- **Generated national specification for new product.**

SALES REPRESENTATIVE (1991–1995)

Met sales plan through a solid sales effort focused on promoting the features and benefits of PBS products.
- **Named Salesman of the Year, 1991; Ceiling Salesman of the Year, 1995.**

SEARS ROEBUCK   1988–1991
DIVISION MANAGER (1988–1991)

Managed complete operation of various departments, supervising both full- and part-time sales staff.

DIVISION MANAGER TRAINEE (1988)

Education and Training

SHAW UNIVERSITY, Raleigh, North Carolina
BA IN COMMUNICATIONS, 1988

PROFESSIONAL TRAINING AND SEMINARS:
- **American Management Association**
- **Professional Selling Skills**
- **Professional Selling Skills/Coaching**

Volunteer Leadership

RALEIGH-DURHAM BUILDERS SOCIETY, Raleigh, North Carolina
PROGRAM CHAIRMAN, 2005–Present

Rita M. Kaplan

7599 Old Viking Way
Cincinnati, OH 43241

513-781-9040
ritakaplan@aol.com

Sales Management

Sales leader who propelled revenue growth of $1.25 million and increased direct operating income 520% in only 11 months.

- Increased revenue by 253%, gross profit by $425K.
- Maintained among the highest profit margins in the company's history: 26% in a down market.
- Led sales center to a national ranking of 11 out of 380+, despite inheriting an $84K loss to start the fiscal year.

Natural leader with expert ability to develop high-quality management and sales teams, communicate business goals, and motivate staff to exemplary performance.

- Improved sales profits ninefold with limited resources.
- Promoted multiple salespeople to general management positions.

Innovative problem-solver and effective communicator adept at delivering superior customer service and developing new business.

- Increased customer satisfaction by 25%.
- Spearheaded effort to reduce existing legal cases; 5 reduced to 0.
- Significantly increased customer traffic through strategic marketing campaigns.

Professional Experience

PREFABULOUS HOMES CORPORATION, Winston-Salem, NC   2005–2009
$1 billion corporation, the largest retailer of manufactured homes in America

Sales Manager, Cincinnati, OH, 2007–2009

Rapidly turned around an unprofitable multimillion-dollar manufactured housing dealership, creating and executing the sales strategies to transform business from a below-average performer to #11 among nearly 400 dealerships nationwide.

- Restored profitability within months; in less than one year, led the business to a top national ranking.
- Introduced innovative selling techniques and retrained entire sales staff. Rapid results from new methods galvanized sales team and led to consistent growth in both revenue and profits.
- Moved quickly to address myriad operational issues that hindered growth.
- Received national award for outstanding sales results. Earned President's Circle status every year.

Sales Representative, Oxford, OH, 2005–2007

Successfully marketed land and home packages in the manufactured housing industry. Managed sales process from prospecting to closing, and then scheduled the construction of homes, hired and coordinated contractors, scheduled service, and ensured customer satisfaction. Gained extensive experience in finance, insurance, prospecting, cold-calling, and all aspects of marketing.

(continued)

In this resume, the college graduation year is omitted because it was just four years ago, and this top performer didn't want to limit her chances for a senior sales management position because of the perception that she was too young.

Rita M. Kaplan

513-781-9040

ritakaplan@aol.com

Sales Representative, continued

- Contributed significantly to sales center's national ranking and leap from 29th place to 4th out of 400.
- #1 in branch sales of insurance, including physical damage, extended warranty, and credit life.
- Conceived a creative marketing strategy targeting an easily converted niche prospect group; built this business to 25% of sales.

EXCEL COMMUNICATIONS, Oxford, OH   2002–2005

Area Coordinator / Senior Managing Representative

Profitably marketed a unique business opportunity in the telecommunications business.

- Successfully promoted the business and recruited an extensive network of 200+ representatives.
- Developed and delivered effective training programs; created call scripts; coached inexperienced representatives to become successful producers.
- Honed public speaking skills through regular "opportunity meetings" held to recruit new reps.

HIGHLIGHTS OF ADDITIONAL EXPERIENCE

- **Consultant** to start-up network marketing company. Designed, tested, and launched a highly successful cold-market recruiting system.
- **#1 Sales Representative, Midwest Region,** in direct sales for Vector Marketing Corporation.

Education

BACHELOR OF SCIENCE IN MANAGEMENT, Miami University, Oxford, OH

SALES CERTIFICATION, Prefabulous Homes, 2005

ONGOING SALES AND MANAGEMENT TRAINING through Prefabulous Homes, 2005–2009

JAMES GRINWALD

38 Avenue Grand
San Clemente, CA 92672
949.555.1212
grinwaldj@yahoo.com

PROFILE

Seasoned sales leader offering more than 25 years of revenue performance on domestic and multinational scales.

True value is the ability to strategically identify opportunities, capture new revenue, build brand, and strengthen the bottom line.

Diverse industry background, with revenue success in every position held. Excellent in start-up, growth, and turnaround environments.

Finesse for building and directing sales teams that deliver in highly competitive markets.

Strategic Sales & Marketing
Strategic Business Operations
New Business Development
Brand Development
Relationship / Consultative Sales
Key Client Relationship Management
Product Development & Launch
Competitive Positioning
Major Account Management
Major Project Management

EXPERIENCE & ACHIEVEMENTS

OPTICAL USA   **San Clemente, CA**

National Sales Manager, Motorsports Division (2006 to Present): Doubled revenue performance in the domestic sales division by revitalizing stagnant products and pitching those products to new customers. Provided strategic managerial oversight and actively trained more than 250 distributor sales representatives. Held senior responsibility for opportunity identification, customer relationship management, and major account management.

- Improved division sales in 2006 by 14%, 2007 by 35%, 2008 by 11%, chiefly through recommending, developing, and releasing new products.
  - Leveraged an existing lens pattern for a new goggle that aligned well with the competitive market. Used a universal replacement component that benefited retailers and consumers.
  - Conceptualized innovative graphic designs that led the industry and subsequently inspired similar goggle graphics across the marketplace.
- Captured $180K in new revenue directly through retail after executing a lengthy sales process and successfully pitching the division's brand even though the retailer carried several competing brands.
- Pursued and secured private-label sales relationships with three partners, essential in enhancing profitability beyond the Optical USA brand.
- Strategically managed and grew distributor relationships, evaluating their performance region by region and identifying opportunities to seek deeper market penetration.
- Expanded grassroots marketing initiatives to garner significant trade publication attention through new product press releases as well as editorials.

RACING AMERICA   **Corona, CA**

Brand Manager (2005 to 2006): Strategically guided sales, marketing, product development, and graphic identity. Led an 8-member sales team.

- Maximized profit margin by establishing two international licenses with manufacturers who paid Racing America royalties and assumed all responsibility for inventory and shipping.
- Reined in more than $250K in overspending in operations, advertising, and staff salaries.
  - Instituted controls so all expenditures required written approval, to accurately track expenses and eliminate overspending.
  - Reduced permanent staff, some of whom were underutilized, and recruited contractors for apparel design and advertising projects during peak periods.

(continued)

Resume contributed by Jewel Bracy DeMaio, MRW
James made a successful transition from a career as a landscape architect to a top-performing sales manager. His entrepreneurial landscape company is included because it demonstrates his longstanding business-building abilities.

JAMES GRINWALD

Page 2

949.555.1212
grinwaldj@yahoo.com

ARCHWAY OPTICAL   **San Clemente, CA**

National Sales & Marketing Manager, Motorsports Division (1999 to 2005): Structured and launched the Motorsports Division and repeatedly exceeded sales projections. Instrumentally guided product line development, marketing, and sales. Built the sales infrastructure, recruited the sales team, and personally cultivated direct sales relationships with retailers and distributors domestically and globally. Recruited professional and amateur athletes to market the brand; negotiated their salaries and contract terms.

- Identified and capitalized on cobranding opportunities with noncompeting products, essential for further penetrating the ideal market segment.
  - Partnered with a motorcoach company to advertise on their vehicle that traveled nationwide to professional sports events. This pioneering type of partnership became common industry practice.
  - Cobranded with an apparel company and leveraged its 80-member sales team to target the retail market.
- Designed and launched a comprehensive sales training program to equip the sales force with effective strategies for approaching retailers specifically in motorsports.

CITY OF IRVINE   **Irvine, CA**

Landscape Program Construction Specialist (1983 to 1999): Coordinated $10 million annually in landscape construction and maintenance projects that involved landscape construction design, development, and rehabilitation across 500 acres. Directed a team of city and contracted construction and maintenance staff.

- Conceptualized and launched a landscape lifecycle program that identified major components to retrofit on a prescribed schedule, to facilitate procurement of grants and capital improvement funding.

- Introduced a pricing program that required contractors to bid for repair projects based on defined criteria, essential to controlling costs for work beyond the regular maintenance contracts.

- Developed a landscape installation standards manual to promote project quality and consistency on both new and retrofit projects.

- Captured a $100K savings by recommending and installing a computerized central irrigation system that significantly reduced water usage and expense.

SOUTHERN LANDSCAPING, INC.   **Irvine, CA**

Owner (1984 to 2004): Strategically directed the launch of this venture and managed operations and new business development to achieve more than $200K in annual revenue at peak. Aggressively sought large contracts with businesses, homeowner associations, and local governments. Introduced high-profit niche services to customers and contractors. Instituted a labor measurement program to control labor expenses and maximize productivity.

Stuart R. Mossbacher

295 Dominion Trail, Charlotte, NC 28234

704-349-6789 ♦ stu_mossbacher@yahoo.com

PROFILE

Sales and marketing professional with proven ability to increase market share, outperform competition, and increase profits.

Key accomplishments in

- ♦ Leading successful sales organizations at the international, national, and regional level; managing new and established product lines.
- ♦ Identifying, prioritizing, and pursuing new business opportunities.
- ♦ Conducting marketing research and devising effective sales strategies.
- ♦ Structuring business deals and negotiating contracts.
- ♦ Developing sales staffs; building and leading teams.
- ♦ Delivering profitable results under pressure and against deadlines.

EXPERIENCE

TYLER RESEARCH AND DEVELOPMENT CO., Charlotte, NC   2006–2009

Director of Sales and Marketing

Selected to direct, manage, and expand the international sales business for Tyler's Biologic Research Company, a subsidiary of Tyler R&D. Recruited and signed new organizations internationally to market and sell the company's products. Achieved add-on operating income through existing accounts with product line extensions.

- ♦ Led the sales effort for the company's only income-generating business, achieving a 28% net income.
- ♦ Increased sales of dormant business from 7 figures to well over 8 figures in just under 3 years.
- ♦ Directed a team of sales and marketing professionals with international responsibilities.

FOOD-PAC PRODUCTS, Charlotte, NC   2000–2005

National Chain Account Manager (2003–2005)

Led the growth and expansion of national chain accounts as well as the institutional food service business for Food-Pac Products, a subsidiary of Bigfood USA. Held total sales responsibility for accounts valued at $9.5 million (16% of total company sales).

- ♦ Increased sales 60% in 2 years in the company's largest chain account (annual sales $7.3 million).
- ♦ Team leader of 10–15 field sales agents.
- ♦ Net income of business represented 18% of the company's total.

Product Manager (2002–2003)

Held responsibility for day-to-day management of the total Food-Pac product line. Interfaced with sales, operations, purchasing, quality control, product development, customer service and upper management.

- ♦ Developed marketing plans in support of $60 million in annual sales.
- ♦ Performed cost and profit analysis for all private-label business nationwide.
- ♦ Designed all private-label packaging.

(continued)

The technique of using years (rather than months and years) does a good job of hiding what was more than a year of unemployment for Stuart after he left Food-Pac. The bullet-point accomplishments are short and very easy to absorb.

Stuart R. Mossbacher   704-349-6789 ♦ stu_mossbacher@yahoo.com

FOOD-PAC PRODUCTS (continued)
Regional Sales Manager (2000–2002)
Accountable for the management, growth and profitability of distributor business.
- ♦ Grew the distributor business $4 million (14%) in one year.
- ♦ Total business of $32 million represented 65% of total sales.
- ♦ Organized and coordinated all regional and national trade shows.
- ♦ Team leader of 10–15 sales agents.

SAMSON SCIENTIFIC INSTRUMENTS, Charlotte, NC   1998–2000
National Sales Manager
Managed a start-up division for this small, high-quality equipment manufacturer.
Developed and implemented the division's marketing plans.
- ♦ Achieved $1.2 million in start-up sales volume in less than 14 months.

EDUCATION

Bachelor of Business Administration
ELON COLLEGE, Burlington, NC
- ♦ **Financed 100% of college education and expenses working full time.**

Additional studies and seminars in Marketing and Total Quality Management.

COMMUNITY ACTIVITIES

Active involvement in Habitat for Humanity and church finance board.

Douglas B. Renton

949-450-2390 — dougrenton@aol.com
235 Lemon Grove Drive, Irvine, CA 92620

SALES AND MANAGEMENT PROFESSIONAL

Track Record Successful leadership of sales teams and district / divisional operations. Effective use of *analytical, management,* and *motivational* skills to drive key initiatives and deliver results.

Expertise
- Sales, merchandising, and retailing
- Financial management, cost containment, and profit improvement
- Strategic planning and effective implementation

Strengths Rising to new challenges. Leading staff to high levels of individual and team performance. Achieving results by *eliminating roadblocks, maximizing resources, and supplying motivation.*

PROFESSIONAL EXPERIENCE

2004–
Present MASTER MERCHANDISERS, Chicago, Illinois
The country's 2nd-largest national retail merchandising operation.

Director of Retail Operations — Western Division (11-state region), 2007–Present
Director of Retail Operations — California, 2005–2007

Manage district operations and direct the activities of 6 District Managers, 2 District Sales Managers, 10 Key Account Managers, and their sales and merchandising staffs (400 total). Direct team revenue, strategy, and profitability.

Provide retail solutions for the grocery business. Implement merchandising programs for major retailers and manufacturers, including Kmart, Safeway, Ralston-Purina, and Megamanufacturer. Deliver ongoing / contract merchandising services as well as project management and implementation for product roll-outs and integrated merchandising programs.

As sales / merchandising liaison between retailers, wholesalers, and manufacturers, strive to create win-win environments. Sell the company's merchandising expertise as a tool for maximizing product sales and profitability.

Develop sales team for increased responsibility through training, motivation, and assignment of new challenges.

Highlights
- **Managed division to a 100% turnaround in profitability,** from a $500K *loss* in 2007 to a $550K *profit* in 2008. Achieved results through cost-cutting, implementation of sales incentives, and sales team training, motivation, and accountability.

- Created "Lightning" program and sold key client on pilot. Successfully managed Western Division team to 2-week implementation of 3 BigBox toothpaste SKUs at 2,700 grocery stores. Results exceeded client targets for distribution and sales. Within 2 weeks, toothpaste had acquired 17.6% market share **(best results in the U.S.).**

- Coached and developed a team of 200 people and achieved the financial plan in a turnaround situation following district reorganization and absorption of under-performing division. Reorganized the division 4 times to meet corporate initiatives.

- Implemented a team of Retail Sales Specialists to meet the needs of commission clients. Team generated in excess of **$200K in additional revenue** in 2007 and 2008.

- Improved store call frequency from **85% to 99%** monthly.

- Finished **#1 in Western Division** in profitability and **#2 in the U.S.** in 2006 and 2007.

(continued)

This resume effectively positions Doug for a senior-level position. The summary is succinct, easy to skim, and potent. Notable achievements (especially numbers) are highlighted in bold.

Douglas B. Renton

MASTER MERCHANDISERS, continued

District Manager — Washington / Idaho, 2004–2005

Directed sales and account management activities of 10-member sales team and 2 key account managers. Focused on contract sales to grocery stores and collaborative services to meet the needs of retailers, wholesalers, and manufacturers.

Hired, trained, and managed sales force to cover 425 grocery stores throughout territory. Trained sales team in effective sales strategies; accompanied sales staff on account calls; represented the company at food shows, a key source of client and prospect contact.

Highlights

- Effectively managed and motivated sales force by focusing on training in key success factors: time management, sales strategies, and meeting customer needs and expectations.

- Sold full-service coverage to key clients, achieving significant sales results ($60K annually with Jellystone Jelly, $42K annually with Tasti-Bake).

- Demonstrated success through a variety of measurements: increased case sales, ACV and Nielsen independent ratings of product distribution levels, and store audits.

- Ranked **#1 in client satisfaction,** as measured by client survey results, in the Western Division in 2005.

1996–2004   NATIONS GROCERS, Los Angeles, California

Drug / General Merchandise Manager, 2002–2004

Chosen to develop and implement an inventory-control plan with the goal of increasing revenue in categories with potentially high profit margins. Retrained employees and restructured operations.

- Successfully increased revenue for store that had been struggling to achieve profitability.

Grocery Manager, 2001–2002

Accountable for sales and profit objectives and for controlling wage budget. Prepared store sales plans; analyzed and approved employee scheduling; assisted manager in all store operating capacities.

Drug / General Merchandise Co-Manager, 1999–2001

Selected to open two Nations Grocers Millennium Stores. Directed all activities, from purchasing and display of merchandise to budgeting and overall supervision of new stores. Hired and trained staff of 300 for each store.

- Ranked **#1 in gross profit** in 1999 and 2000 in Los Angeles marketing area.

Grocery Co-Manager, 1996–1999

EDUCATION

UNIVERSITY OF CALIFORNIA AT LOS ANGELES
B.S., Communications — 1999
A.S., Retail Management — 1995

Sheelah R. McIntyre

212-494-9664 • srm@hotmail.com
79 Webster Street, New York, NY 10014

Sales • Marketing • Sales Management

STRENGTHS

- Strategic planning of sales and marketing activities.
- Envisioning and implementing change and improvement within a variety of sales structures (salaried and commissioned staff, distributors, brokers).
- Rapid assessment: strong ability to analyze results and quickly revise and refocus tactics as necessary to ensure progress toward goals.
- Interaction and relationship-building with key accounts and sales force.
- Communication: speaking, writing, creating, and delivering effective presentations.
- Consistent success achieving sales goals through effective leadership of a sales force.
- Energized by ambitious goals: creative, self-motivated, enthusiastic, profit-oriented.

Education

MBA, 2004: VANDERBILT UNIVERSITY, Nashville, TN
BS Marketing, 1999: UNIVERSITY OF ILLINOIS AT URBANA-CHAMPAIGN, Urbana, IL

Professional Experience

BEAUTY CONCEPTS INT'L. (Division Giant Consumer Goods, Inc.), New York, NY   2008–Present

Regional Sales Manager

Direct operations for 7-state Northeast region, managing and motivating 2 vastly different sales forces: direct sales representatives, who sell Beauty Concepts hair-care products directly to salons; and distributors, who market GCG products to chain stores. Develop and implement marketing strategies. Prepare and monitor all sales and expense operating budgets and forecasts. Formulate and deliver effective sales and business presentations throughout the region.

KEY ACCOMPLISHMENTS

▶ Spearheaded the complete restructuring of the employee sales force, from commission-based to a salary-and-benefits structure.

- Led the retraining effort with the sales force; this involved a complete turnaround from quick-visit, product-focused sales to consultative selling and assisting salon owners with long-range marketing and business planning.
- Concentrated the refocused sales effort on the top 40% of accounts. Sales to the remaining 60%, primarily small salons, were outsourced to a high-quality telemarketing firm.
- Piloted the sales force restructuring in the Northeast region; program is currently being implemented in half of the company's remaining districts.

RESULTS: Sales increased 26% in first year and 20%–25% (projected) in second year.

▶ Increased the focus on distributor sales, a previously neglected segment of the sales effort.

- Established effective relationships with selected key distributors to achieve a broader distribution of the company's products.
- Implemented merchandising service at larger chain accounts to ensure that products were well stocked and properly displayed.

RESULTS: Achieved sales growth of 85% in 2008, 40% (projected) for 2009.

(continued)

Note page-1 placement of strong educational credentials—but briefly, so as to leave plenty of room for experience. Projects are spelled out in great detail, with results highlighted with a bold subheading.

Sheelah R. McIntyre   212-494-9664 • srm@hotmail.com

Professional Experience, continued

MESSERSCHMIDT COMPANY, Cincinnati, OH   2006–2008

Regional Sales Manager

Accountable for 15 key brokerage networks and the accounts they represented in a 7-state area. Motivated a brokerage sales force, relying on communication and relationship-building to achieve widespread and consistent promotion of the company's products. Developed promotional strategies and supervised their implementation by regional brokers. Crafted and delivered financial/sales presentations to new customers. Prepared and monitored sales forecasts.

KEY ACCOMPLISHMENTS
- Acquired a key account that yielded $2 million in annual sales.
- Achieved 15% increase in sales from existing accounts.
- Developed effective strategies for motivating an independent brokerage sales force.
- Maintained direct relationships with customers through joint visits with sales brokers.

HALLMARK CARDS, Kansas City, MO   2002–2006

National Account Manager (2005–2006)

Held direct responsibility for $8 million Winn-Dixie account. Developed and planned implementation of all sales strategies.
- Achieved sales increase of 6.5%, nearly double the industry average.

Store Planning Supervisor (2004–2005)

Traveled extensively to work with field sales representatives and retailers, negotiating and planning greeting card departments with the goal of maximizing profitability while minimizing fixture investment to the company. Supervised 4 Senior Designers and CADD Production Assistants.
- Analyzed existing department sales history and demographic profiles to develop account-specific product mix. Delivered sales presentations based on these findings.
- Generated merchandising standards for the organization in conjunction with other departments.

Territory Sales Manager, Springfield, IL, and Nashville, TN (2002–2004)

Developed 2 Midwest territories, marketing to supermarkets, mass merchants, deep discounters, and retail drug chains. Supervised as many as 30 merchandisers.
- In both locations, restored profitability to a floundering operation. Focused on strengthening the merchandising representation to ensure clean, organized, and well-stocked departments.
- In each territory, achieved sales increases in excess of 13% while the company average was 7%. Consistently exceeded the company's sales and profit goals.
- Developed strong, loyal client relationships.
- Promoted from $8 million Iowa City territory to Nashville, a $24 million territory with major retailers, including Winn-Dixie.

CORCORAN FOOD BROKERS, Springfield, IL   1998–2002

Customer Service/Inside Sales Supervisor

Established a 7-person customer service department. Implemented sales contests and incentive awards for the inside sales department. Instrumental in the implementation of a new computer system.

Community Activities

Literacy Volunteer, 2000–Present—Springfield, Nashville, Kansas City, New York
Big Sisters Association volunteer, 2008–Present

Samantha Meyers

22 Rocky Ledge Lane, Bangor, Maine 04401
550-423-2323   sammy@aol.com

PROFILE

- ❑ Experienced sales/sales management professional with a strong track record of accomplishments in both direct sales and territory leadership.
- ❑ Strong abilities in developing and motivating staff, improving morale, and maintaining a stable work force in a normally high-turnover operation.
- ❑ Proven success in enhancing profitability by increasing sales and devising systems for efficient distribution.
- ❑ Committed to customer satisfaction.

PROFESSIONAL EXPERIENCE

2001–Present   SPORTS PUBLISHERS, INC., Rahway, New Jersey

Northern New England Zone Manager (2007–Present)

Oversee distribution and in-store merchandising of 7 sports publications in a 3-state area. Manage 18 distributors with an average circulation of 5,500 copies.

- ☑ Expanded into Northern New Hampshire, adding 2 new routes and 450 copies a day.
- ☑ Saved $7,500 annually by consolidating routes.
- ☑ Tightly controlled receivables, consistently maintaining average of 97%.
- ☑ Received "Special Recognition" (employee of the year) award for 2008 performance.

Maine Zone Manager (2003–2007)

Managed distribution and merchandising throughout Maine. Supervised 3 District Managers who oversaw 43 independent contractors responsible for daily and weekly paper delivery.

- ☑ Implemented major distribution route restructuring to reduce expenses while improving customer service. Analyzed distribution system; devised new, more efficient structure; worked with District Managers to implement and monitor the new system, which resulted in annual savings of $76,000.
- ☑ Consistently maintained receivables at 95% with no write-offs during tenure.
- ☑ Managed distribution operation during periods of significant growth.

District Sales Manager (2001–2003)

Directed distribution, service, merchandising, and collections in Central Maine. Coordinated/supervised network of 15 independent agents providing daily newspaper delivery to chains and large and small outlets.

- ☑ Consistently met monthly home delivery service goal of fewer than two complaints per thousand deliveries.
- ☑ Named corporate Employee of the Year (2002).
- ☑ Received General Manager's Awards (2001, 2002, 2003).

(continued)

Formatting enhancements and short paragraphs make this resume highly skimmable. The reader can pick up a lot of information quickly.

Samantha Meyers   550-423-2323   sammy@aol.com

PROFESSIONAL EXPERIENCE, continued

1995–2001   MOM'S HOMEMADE COOKIES, New York, New York
                   Division Sales Manager, Nashua, New Hampshire (1999–2001)

Managed sales and business operations for Northern New England
Division, selling to 16 distributors, 14 chains, and 55 vending companies.
Hired, trained, and supervised all sales personnel.

- ☑ Trained 7 sales representatives, 4 of whom were subsequently
  promoted to management positions.
- ☑ Met all sales volume goals; total sales were more than $38 million in
  2001.
- ☑ Supervised growth of division from 15 employees to 22.

Assistant Division Manager, Nashua, New Hampshire (1998–1999)

Assisted Division Manager in implementing work plans and developing sales
programs in accordance with company guidelines. Trained new sales
representatives.

- ☑ Developed management skills through the hands-on application of
  thorough training.
- ☑ Chosen as instructor of Professional Selling Skills course presented to
  all sales employees in New England (Boston, July 1998).
- ☑ Completed "Managing for Motivation" seminar (1999).

Merchandising Manager, Boston, Massachusetts (1997–1998)

Management training position providing exposure to chain account
management. Called on chain-store clients and participated in chain
presentations.

Area Sales Representative, Boston, Massachusetts (1996–1997)

Called on various chains, vending companies, distributors, and retail
accounts. Developed skills in establishing customer relationships and
completing the sales process.

Sales Representative, Worcester, Massachusetts (1995–1996)

Responsible for sales, product display, and advertising for accounts within
established territory. Developed account and territory management skills.

EDUCATION   Bachelor of Science in Business Administration, 1995
                   UNIVERSITY OF NEW HAMPSHIRE

KATHERINE OBERLIN

95 Island Avenue ◆ Hicksville, NY 11801 ◆ (516) 572-7501 ◆ koberlin@comcast.net

SALES EXECUTIVE
Sales Leadership / Staff Management / Consultative Sales / Business Transformation

High-energy change agent with expertise in facilitating business transformation...
... and skill in turning vision into practice

Strategic, forward-thinking sales executive with a stellar record of success in leading initiatives to improve business operations and drive revenue growth. Respected, influential leader and proven change agent with expertise in identifying business needs and delivering innovative solutions. High-energy manager; a recognized team advocate who is effective in leading sales organizations to achieve outstanding results.

Key Deliverables:

⊳ Providing vision and leadership to sales organizations, driving initiatives to build stronger, more effective teams while advancing business goals.
⊳ Promoting successful partner-based sales environments, growing sales by maximizing value to clients.
⊳ Developing and implementing strategic plans to drive revenue growth and promote market expansion.
⊳ Cultivating and maintaining C-level alliances to support sales goals and gain buy-in for programs.
⊳ Creating positive work environments that promote and sustain performance excellence.

PROFESSIONAL EXPERIENCE

POWER TECHNOLOGIES   1993 to present

Earned fast-track promotions, driving strategic initiatives to improve sales and sales force effectiveness during period of monumental change within Power Technologies.

Sales Vice President, Enterprise Business Services (2006 to present)

Lead $300 million sales organization while directing 25-member sales team in delivering comprehensive IT networking solutions to company's largest corporate clients in NY metro region.

- New to position, retooled sales team around strategic, solution-based sales methodology, driving transformation from vendor status to trusted business partner. Worked with team to promote collaborations with clients to understand business needs and develop on-target solutions.

- Taking on region's most challenging accounts, revitalized relationships to turn around performance, leading team to achieve 100% of goals in first year.

- Repeated performance in 2nd year of tenure after exchanging 6 solid accounts for 8 troubled accounts. Made immediate impact, taking accounts to 9% growth on $300 million base.

- Led sales center to top-ranking customer satisfaction ratings in region despite account challenges. Improved overall team results by assessing individual performance and delegating work to capitalize on individual strengths.

Director, Sales Readiness, Merger & Integration Team (2006)

Drove sales organization's strategy as part of team chartered to ensure smooth transition following merger with Global Telecom, keeping revenue commitments whole. Mapped out and implemented go-forward plan for integrated sales team.

- Served as point-person for resolution of all sales-related issues, overseeing command center designed to provide resources to ensure smooth transition following merger. Successfully coordinated all details to open fully staffed command center that was ready to handle issues as of day 1 of integration.

- Created guidelines and tools for sales team to ensure seamless integration that remained virtually transparent to customers.

- As a testament to success, gained very positive feedback from customers during and after merger.

(continued)

Resume contributed by Carol Altomare, MRW
A powerful branding statement highlights this resume and is backed up by numerous sales accomplishments.

Key Account Director, Business Sales (2003 to 2006)

Led 7-member team in servicing company's largest global accounts while establishing new standards for performance excellence.

- Served on team that built and introduced new client-centric sales model that emphasized strategic partnerships and solution-based sales. Developed standards and assessments to identify top talent and lay the foundation for development of world-class sales service center.

- Developed and implemented strategic account plans, leveraging knowledge of technology and emerging trends to promote business growth. Transformed client relationships, engaging clients early in process to drive sales.

- Led team to consistently exceed goals, frequently outpacing competitors. Among many successes, won multimillion-dollar network conversion contract with prominent global financial services client.

- Re-tooled account support, billing clean-up, service management, and issue resolution, effecting substantial improvements to achieve and maintain the highest standards of customer satisfaction.

Division Manager, Executive Relationship Programs (2001 to 2003)

In high-visibility position, ran key executive relationship programs in support of sales objectives.

- Led large-scale Client Executive Program designed to leverage executive talent within organization to forge strategic high-level relationships with clients to drive revenue growth. Promoted program, conducted interviews, identified matches, and tracked scorecard results to ensure success of program.

- Orchestrated partner program that drew on expertise of influential C-level clients to provide insight and advisement to internal leadership team in key areas. Among successes:

  ▷ Spurred by 9/11 crisis, hosted 2-day roundtable discussion that brought together industry leaders to put together slate of security recommendations that were subsequently implemented throughout organization.

  ▷ Established trade agreements with key clients, leveraging relationships to win favorable terms for purchases.

Division Manager, Business Services (2001)

As revenue accelerator project leader, established and manned "war room" designed to assist sales teams in closing strategic sales opportunities by streamlining processes and removing roadblocks.

- Provided high-level support to help close deals worth more than $1 billion in annual revenue. Intervened to simplify processes, engage stakeholders, and remove roadblocks to accelerate deals.

- Identified best practices and developed formalized procedures to guide future sales transactions.

District Manager/Chief of Staff, Business Services (1999 to 2001)

Provided direct support to president of 2 business segments worth more than $30 billion.

- In key role, provided high-level support in the areas of strategy development, business model transformation, revenue growth, and expense reduction.

District Manager, Business Services (1996 to 1999)

Led team in the development and negotiation of complex voice and data offers, providing support to all company business services clients in market with more than $500 million of revenue potential.

Middle Markets Account Manager, Business Network Sales (1993 to 1996)

EARLIER EXPERIENCE

Account Executive, Business Services Division, Sprint, 1992
Sales Representative, IBM, 1991

EDUCATION

BS, Manhattan College, Riverdale, NY, 1991

Stephen Molinari

smolinari@juno.com
307-209-8765 Mobile • 307-781-2380 Office
279 Crosswoods Lane, Laramie, Wyoming 82071

Areas of Expertise

Sales / Sales Management: Consistently strong track record of sales team leadership and individual performance.

Direct Mail Advertising: Expert knowledge of electronic media (radio—television—on-hold advertising), newspaper, and demographically targeted advertising.

Business / Marketing Consulting: Strengths in developing comprehensive marketing/advertising strategies to help customers achieve business goals.

Sales Training: Proven ability to develop sales training *systems* and implement in multiple markets; a knack for instilling confidence and motivation while teaching sales planning, strategy, and organization.

Professional Experience

WESTERN DIRECT MARKETING, Laramie, Wyoming   2000–Present
Publisher of Reach *Magazine,* In Touch *Magazine, and Val•Pak — 3 distinct direct-mail advertising vehicles.*

Sales Manager—2008–Present

Direct sales and marketing for $5.6 million Laramie market. Lead a 12-member sales team with a strong focus on consultative selling—learning each customer's business and recommending comprehensive sales/marketing/advertising strategies to help them achieve well-defined goals.

Management

- As member of the company's management team, participate in planning, goal-setting, policy development, and overall operational management.

Sales Management / Training

- **Created and piloted the company's first formal sales training program,** which incorporates an industry-specific, multiproduct sales system; currently beginning roll-out of the program in the company's 5 other markets.
- **Led sales team to outstanding performance:** projecting $1 million over goal for 2009. Provide thorough training along with support, motivation, and leadership that has resulted in high levels of individual performance.
- Developed and implemented annual and quarterly action plans and individual sales tracking systems to allow representatives to set goals and evaluate progress throughout the selling cycle. Monitor results in quarterly performance reviews.
- Monitored profitability of each sale to assist representatives in determining compensation (based on profitability).

Sales / Marketing

- Initiated creative revisions to publications that increased usefulness of the material for both advertisers and readers.
- Developed effective cross-retailer promotions.
- Continue to serve as account representative for several key accounts; on target to exceed sales goals for 2009.

Operations

- Manage 12 sales representatives and support and production staff. Recruit, hire, train, supervise, and evaluate performance against clearly stated objectives.
- Determine compensation packages; monitor commission and bonus payments.
- Initiated customer service practices (satisfaction survey, focus group, consumer profile studies); oversee administration and follow-up.

(continued)

Beyond pure sales management, Stephen has experience in general management and operations functions. The subheadings make it easy to pick up this information in a quick skim.

Stephen Molinari

307-209-8765 Mobile • 307-781-2380 Office • smolinari@juno.com

WESTERN DIRECT MARKETING, continued

Team Leader — 2007–2008

While continuing to outperform individual sales goals, took on added responsibility of training, leading, and motivating a team of account executives. Developed promotions and sales contests; accompanied staff on sales calls; coached on presentation skills.

- **Led top sales team in 2007 and 2008;** subsequently promoted to Sales Manager position overseeing all 3 teams.

Key Account Executive — 2004–2008

Consistently exceeded sales and profit goals through new business development and effective management of key accounts.

- Developed national accounts; expanded successful local efforts by placing demographically targeted advertising in markets across the country.
- Created a turnkey direct-mail program that was instrumental in the growth of a start-up company from local to international status.
- Prepared and set up several client photography shoots; designed storyboards.
- *Special Assignment:* Lent to Cheyenne market to stimulate sales for *Reach Magazine* and Val•Pak. Developed $200K in new sales each year for 2 consecutive years; created and communicated comprehensive systems for identifying and selling to new clients. Trained and managed performance of 3 sales representatives. Responsible for growth and profitability of target market.

Senior Sales Associate — 2000–2004

Prospected for new business; developed and delivered sales presentations; negotiated contracts; designed print advertising.

- Successfully developed a strong account base and maintained relationships through follow-up, persistence, and genuine commitment to helping customers' businesses grow through effective advertising.
- Conducted regional training programs with a focus on cross-promotional sales and nontraditional revenue sources.

KWYO RADIO, Cheyenne, Wyoming
1998–2000

Account Executive

- Originated radio programming for individual clients.
- Surpassed monthly advertising goals by prospecting unique businesses for radio.
- Produced and performed creative radio productions.
- Assisted in the development of quarterly direct-response mail combining radio and print advertising.
- Developed promotional ideas to generate profits for both station and clients.

Education

B.S. Mass Communications, 1998 — University of Washington, Seattle, Washington
Area of concentration: Media Management

Awards

- Achievement Club Winner — surpassing all goals (2002–2008)
- Millionaire's Club (2007–2008)
- Val•Pak Chairman Club Member (2007 and 2008) — for sales over $1 million — 1 of 10 people nationwide, in 300–400 franchises, to achieve this level
- Highest Average Sale Club (2006–2007)

Christopher Curtis

295 Vancouver Drive, Portland, Oregon 97219
503-792-1895   chriscurtis@gmail.com

BROADCAST INDUSTRY SALES MANAGER

Consistent 15-year record of delivering market share improvements, identifying and capturing new revenue sources, and managing productive teams during transition. Key strengths include

- **Innovation:** Creative thinker with a track record of pioneering approaches to sales, promotion, and sponsorship underwriting.
- **Sales Team Leadership:** Consistently strong record in recruiting, training, developing, motivating, and mentoring sales teams and individuals to top performance and professional advancement.
- **Relationship-Building Skills:** Commitment to working cooperatively with sponsors and advertising agencies for mutual growth.
- **Win-Win Negotiations:** Thorough grasp of the sales process and a determination to find solutions to customer needs.

PROFESSIONAL EXPERIENCE

KPOR-TV, Portland, Oregon (NBC Affiliate)   July 2008–Present
General Sales Manager

Challenged to reverse 3 years of declining market share, restructure the sales department, and improve account relationships, with a need for quick turnaround.
- Achieved the first quarterly market share increase in 2 years.
- Overhauled the station's inventory management program.
- Instituted a highly effective sales training program for experienced and new sales team members.
- Hired, trained, and developed 6 new sales staff; significantly improved quality, productivity, and morale of the sales team.
- Restored confidence in the advertising community through personal visits to local and national accounts and advertising agencies with subsequent delivery on promised improvements.

KNEW-TV, San Francisco, California (CBS Affiliate)   2006–2008
Local Sales Manager

Brought on board to ensure consistency and leadership during ABC-to-CBS network affiliation transition.
- Conceived and implemented successful marketing strategy to sell sponsorships of station's interactive telephone system.
- Consistently met budget and exceeded revenue projections.

KBAY-TV, San Francisco, California   2001–2006
Director of Local Sales

Increased sales revenue 20% annually over a 5-year period.
- Devised innovative concepts to package the station's entire inventory to improve overall results.
- Increased revenue 500% in 4 years from nontraditional sources through creative advertising, sponsorship, and promotions in the areas of event, sports, and children's marketing.
- Focused sales efforts on developing advertisers new to the medium; in 2005, achieved more than $500,000 in revenue from sponsors who had never before advertised on television.
- Created the position of Retail Marketing Specialist to pursue cooperative advertising tie-ins and sales promotions with regional decision-makers of national companies.
- Promoted staff development and education with regular guest speakers, presentations, and training programs.

(continued)

Chris received an excellent reception to this resume from hiring managers. He quickly obtained a new general sales manager's job in the broadcast industry when an ownership and management change at KPOR-TV caused him to lose his job there after only a year.

Christopher Curtis

503-792-1895   chriscurtis@gmail.com

PROFESSIONAL EXPERIENCE, continued

WBLT-TV, Baltimore, Maryland   2000–2001
General Sales Manager
- Led station to two monthly revenue records in first year.
- Developed local sales effort emphasizing merchandising and promotional strategies to add new accounts and increase share of business from existing accounts.

WBOS-TV, Boston, Massachusetts   1995–2000
National Sales Manager 1998–2000
- Increased national sales 33% in first full year; only station in the market to post revenue increase.
- Sold anchor sponsorships on "Sports Talk," a locally produced, statewide-syndicated talk show.
- Prospected and developed more than 50 local contacts to maximize share of national business budgets.

Account Executive 1995–1998
- Leading generator of new accounts and revenue, 1997 and 1998.
- Successfully met the challenge of marketing a start-up station in first position in broadcast sales.

MODERN OFFICE SYSTEMS, Newton, Massachusetts   1993–1995
Account Manager
- Increased sales of copying and duplicating systems in downtown Boston territory by more than 100% in first year, 75% in second year.

EDUCATION

Boston University Graduate School of Journalism, Boston, Massachusetts
- Television News, 1995

University of Massachusetts, Amherst, Massachusetts
- BA Economics, 1989

PROFESSIONAL MEMBERSHIPS

Portland Advertising Club (current)
San Francisco Advertising Club (prior)

American Marketing Association (current)
- Board of Directors, San Francisco Chapter (prior)

IRINA PETROV

Permanent e-mail address: irinapetrov@hotmail.com

Through September 2009: Malaskaya 37/15, Moscow, Russia — Telephone (095) 555-23-45

SALES AND MANAGEMENT PROFESSIONAL

Publishing / Advertising / Special Projects

- Track record of exceptional sales, marketing, and management contributions, including launching new initiatives and maintaining market presence during severe economic downturn.

- Strengths include marketing strategy development, account management, ad agency relationship management, media buying, and effective leadership of sales and special project teams.

- Multilingual, with strong communication and presentation skills and international experience.

- Highly motivated top performer eager for new challenges upon emigration to Los Angeles in September 2009.

PROFESSIONAL EXPERIENCE

2005–Present   INTERNATIONAL PUBLISHING GROUP LTD.
International publishing house represented in the Russian market by Trend, Ladies' Day, Beauty Basics, House & Home, International Living, Male Beauty

Trend Magazine / Russian Edition
Joined *Trend* upon its launch on the Russian market.

❏ Advertising Director (October 2007–Present)

Create and implement advertising and marketing strategies for Russian *Trend* and special regional projects. Manage and motivate 5-person advertising sales team.

Manage communication and interaction with large Russian advertising agencies and major international agencies (BBDO, Ogilvy & Mather, DDB Needham, Optimum Media, and others).

Communicate multilingually (Russian, English, French, German) both orally and in written correspondence.

- Assumed leadership position during period of economic crisis in Russia and effectively managed sales team to consistently excellent performance.
  - Exceeded established goals for advertising volume and revenue by 20%–40% each issue.
  - Re-signed advertising agreements with all major clients for FY 08.
  - Motivated sales team through performance incentives and portfolio assignment rewards.

- Attracted numerous elite French, Italian, and global brands, including Guerlain, Givenchy, Chaumet, Cartier, L'Oreal, and Procter & Gamble.

- Selected to develop and implement the magazine's first regional supplement.

❏ Senior Advertising Sales Manager (February–September 2007)

- Sold average of 80% of all advertising for each issue; exceeded targets by 20%–40% monthly.

- Expanded advertising client base to international companies including Pfizer, L'Oreal, Hoechst, Avon, Reebok, Nike, and Champion.

(continued)

Irina's strong sales accomplishments and evident leadership skills should translate well to an American company. Her cover letter (sample 12-4) explains her emigration plans and time frame.

Irina Petrov

irinapetrov@hotmail.com

PROFESSIONAL EXPERIENCE

Continued   INTERNATIONAL PUBLISHING GROUP / *TREND* MAGAZINE, Russian Edition

❏ **Junior Advertising Sales Manager** (2005–2007)

Directed the sales team for a groundbreaking special project: *Trend 850,* an 850-page special edition of the magazine honoring the 850th anniversary of the city of Moscow.

- Developed advertising strategies to strengthen competitive advantage of each advertiser. Encouraged creative contributions, beyond traditional branded advertising messages, to stimulate multiple-page participation.

- With sales team, set a Russian record for number of advertising pages sold: 600. Personally sold more than 200 pages.

2004–2005   CATHERINE ENTERPRISES

LIVING MAGAZINE — *Russia's first glossy lifestyle magazine*

❏ **Senior Advertising Sales Manager**

2003–2004   PROVINCIAL INVESTMENTS LTD. — *Joint stock company*

❏ **Foreign Trade Department**

EDUCATION AND PROFESSIONAL DEVELOPMENT

Moscow Pedagogical State University

- **Diploma (5-year program; Master's Degree equivalent),** 2004
  Major: Foreign Languages (French and German)

Strategic Training International (STI)

- **Selling Skills,** 2006

Russian University of International Relations

- Completed courses in **Business, French, Economics,** and **Marketing** presented by the Chamber of Commerce in Geneva, 2003–2004

LANGUAGES

- Russian — native language

- English, French — write, read, and speak fluently

- German — read, write, and understand

Marketing, Brand Management, Product Management, and Business Development Resumes

Marketing is more of a big-picture profession than sales, so these resumes must show strategic contributions to the overall success of the company's brands, products, or services. In some cases the individual evolved into a marketing role after an early career in sales. Therefore, although the sales achievements are important, they must not overshadow the marketing activities and accomplishments, which often are more subtle than a direct increase in sales revenue.

ROXANNE LOWE

249 Marlborough Street
Boston, MA 02116

rolowe@gmail.com

Home: 617-823-4949
Mobile: 617-300-4004

MARKETING

PRODUCT MANAGEMENT ▸ PRODUCT DEVELOPMENT ▸ PACKAGING

Track record of revenue growth, profit enhancement, and successful product-line management during 9 years in progressively challenging marketing-management roles. Strong foundation in market research and technology paired with creativity and the ability to innovate. Talent for leading and inspiring teams to top performance.

- ▸ **Set new business directions** by recognizing and seizing market opportunities.
- ▸ **Improved performance in all products and brands managed;** grew revenues, cut costs, developed unique retailer programs and packages, and improved brand image.
- ▸ **Effectively prioritized multiple projects** to align results with business objectives.

EDUCATION

2009   **MBA** — Concentration: Marketing Management   Babson College, Wellesley, MA

- ▸ **Key Projects:**
  - —**Case Study / Marketing Strategy for Delta Airlines,** identifying marketing opportunities in a down-trending travel environment. Pinpointed competitive issues, market advantages, and financial strengths. *(Project Leader)*
  - —**Balanced Scorecard Study:** Analysis of corporate culture and practical application of balanced-scorecard system to the 4 business perspectives. *(Capstone Class Project)*
- ▸ **Graduate Research Assistant / Teaching Assistant:**
  - —Taught Marketing Research to undergraduate business students, bringing real-world perspective to theoretical class learning.

2007   **BS** — Computer Information Systems   Suffolk University, Boston, MA

1997   **BSBA** — Concentration: Management   Boston College, Chestnut Hill, MA

EXPERIENCE

CORE CORPORATION, INC., Woburn, MA   2003–2007
($180M public company manufacturing and marketing consumer comfort products. Marquee brand is HappyFeet; key accounts include Walmart, Federated, and other national retailers.)

SENIOR MARKETING MANAGER, 2005–2007

Drove marketing strategy and programs for 3 product lines totaling $150M sales. Held P&L accountability and coordinated the efforts of design, product development, manufacturing, and other departments to deliver products for seasonal deadlines. Managed $2M marketing budget. Also directed the development of sales brochures and marketing materials, developed and gave sales-force presentations on seasonal product lines, and managed national sales meetings for upper management and national sales organization.

Increased sales and profitability in all 3 brand segments:

- ▸ **Value Brands:**
  - —Boosted profit margins from **25%** to **39%** through continuous improvement efforts that removed cost from every point of production — sourcing, production, packaging, distribution.
  - —Grew Walmart program from **$3M** to **$7M** by identifying and capitalizing on sales trends and market opportunities.
- ▸ **HappyFeet™:**
  - —Identified growth opportunity and then created and launched Premier Collection with high-end retailers. Increased brand-segment sales **60%** — **$5.8M** to **$9.3M**.

After taking time off to complete her MBA, Roxanne positioned herself to return to a marketing and product management role in the consumer packaged goods industry.

Roxanne Lowe
rolowe@gmail.com   Page 2   Home: 617-823-4949
                                                                 Mobile: 617-300-4004

▶ **HappyFeet™,** continued
  —Initiated licensing partnership and developed proposal that included entry into nontraditional markets and projected **100%** increase in men's product line.
  —Spearheaded redesign of product displays to accommodate **20%** more product without increasing costs.

▶ **CoreComfort™:** Challenged to redesign product packaging to improve visual appeal and create distinct brand image. Worked with designers on new packaging and with manufacturing on technology-based line restage; spurred **31%** increase in product sales.

▶ **Additional Business Contributions:**
  —Developed new packaging that increased inventory flexibility and saved **$95K** in first year of implementation.
  —Managed the company's market-research function, critical to product-line development, and increased understanding of industry dynamics, competition, and target customers.
  —Stepped in as interim Visual Manager for 8 months and managed a complete packaging restage from concept through implementation. Worked with outside agencies on the development of new packaging line, displays, and advertising.

PRODUCT MANAGER, 2003–2005

Recruited to join newly strengthened marketing team tasked with improving performance of both private-label and branded products.

  ▶ Contributed to record sales performance, 2004: **$148M, 9%** growth over prior year.
  ▶ Developed POP sales program that increased retail space by more than **200%.**
  ▶ Spearheaded a packaging restage that generated **$8.1M** in incremental sales, reduced packaging costs **15%,** and improved packaging image and brand identification.

LOWELL FIBERS, Lowell, MA   1998–2003
$50M apparel and materials manufacturer.

ASSISTANT PRODUCT MANAGER, 2000–2003

Promoted to manage more than $11M in private-label and branded products for accounts such as JC Penney and Sears, with responsibility for pricing, promotions, advertising, forecasting, and product/packaging development. Performed yearly budgeting/planning activities for private-label and branded product lines.

  ▶ Spurred **40%** year-over-year sales increase for product lines under management.
  ▶ Instrumental in developing new markets for an existing single-market product line that has become the company's signature product and currently generates **55%** of total revenue.
  ▶ Aggressively pursued a key catalog retailer (Lands' End), spearheading product development and product-mix selection, and pricing and working collaboratively with Lands' End buyers to develop what became one of its best-selling catalog promotions ever. This was the first step in a key business relationship that culminated in Lowell's being selected as the primary supplier for a major new Lands' End line (today an **$18M** account).

MARKETING ASSISTANT, 1998–2000

Recruited out of college based on strengths in statistics, mathematics, and analysis.

  ▶ Created a forecasting system that, for the first time, included sales history, inventory turns, and planned account expansion. Increased forecasting efficiency and improved on-time/complete shipping from **89%** to more than **95%.**

AFFILIATION

American Marketing Association
Board Member (professional chapter)—Event Chair (student chapter)

Brian J. McDonald

2523 Country Club Heights, Detroit, MI 48219
(313) 555-2312 (res) • (313) 555-2254 (ofc)
brianmac@comcast.net

Professional Summary

- **Well-rounded senior marketing manager with extensive background in consumer packaged goods,** demonstrated during 14 years of progressively responsible experience in Fortune 200 companies. Track record of consistently achieving dynamic business results. Functional experience includes 8 years of Marketing and 6 years of Sales. Broad industry experience in Health & Beauty Aids, Foods, and Household Products. Skill set complemented by participation in the evolution from a multinational to a global business.

- Demonstrated expertise in effective relationship management complemented by strategic planning skills to produce outstanding business results despite competing against a world-class competitor. Breadth of management experience and marketing/sales acumen attests to ability to fully utilize resources. A pragmatic planner who can creatively anticipate the future while effectively executing present responsibilities. Turnaround expertise with ability to effect positive change and results in a lean organization. Skilled in motivating and developing professional staff.

Professional Experience

2003–Present   ATLAS SHAVING PRODUCTS, Division Worldwide Products Corp. • Detroit, MI

Over the past few years, Atlas' business in the U.S. has been completely overhauled and successfully turned around from survival mode to aggressive growth. As compared with 2003, Atlas' dollar sales have doubled, market share has grown nearly 40%, and profits have multiplied many times over. More importantly, Atlas' business is well positioned to continue this growth in 2009 and beyond.

Senior Marketing Manager *(6/08–Present)*
Atlas Men's and Women's Refillable Systems
Selected to manage expanded responsibilities for 9 lines representing 70%+ of U.S. business. Develop strategic and tactical marketing plans; 2 direct reports.
- Engineered strategic shift in marketing communication plans. Currently spearheading initiatives to accelerate execution.

Senior Product Manager, Men's Systems *(5/06–6/08)*
Managed Atlas' lead business segment (7 lines constituting 40% of U.S. business).
- Grew lead brand by 17% in 2008 and increased profits by more than 40%. In 2007, achieved growth in lead brand of 17% and increased profitability by more than 500%.
- Moved "Atlas Plus" market share from a distant #3 position to competitive #2.
- Spearheaded global strategic alliance with another leading consumer products company.
- Elevated Atlas' collegiate intramural event, held on 600 college campuses, to next level by attracting such outside sponsors as ESPN, Ford, and Procter & Gamble.

Senior Product Manager, Disposables *(6/05–5/06)*
Managed Disposables businesses and worked on next global new-product introduction.
- Maintained double-digit growth on the company's leading disposable brand.
- Orchestrated promotion with fast-food chain, resulting in largest sampling initiative ever.

Resume contributed by Jan Melnik, MRW
The brief paragraph describing Atlas's turnaround and growth prospects provides a powerful context for Brian's contributions to that success story.

Brian J. McDonald   (313) 555-2312 (res) • (313) 555-2254 (ofc) • brianmac@comcast.net

---

Professional Experience   *(continued)*

Senior Product Manager, Men's Systems *(5/04–6/05)*
Promoted to manage Men's Systems businesses and co-manage cross-functional team for the development/global introduction of a new product. P&L responsibility, advertising, new-product development, forecasting, and management of 2 direct reports.
- Successfully introduced "Atlas Plus" in the U.S.; co-managed global launch.
- Increased sales of Atlas' lead brand more than 25% versus 2004, representing first profitable year in the U.S.
- Managed creative process and production of new commercial during manager's extended overseas assignment; reported directly to Division President.
- Managed all sports marketing activities; developed fully integrated promotion plan.

Marketing Manager, Special Projects *(10/03–5/04)*
Hired by Director of Product Management for North America to spearhead several category initiatives, including Category Management, Strategic Planning, Packaging Graphics/ Structural Overhaul, and Sports Marketing.
- Identified opportunity to develop Category Management program and launched first phase of ongoing program.
- Managed comprehensive overhaul of packaging, resulting in a global change to company trademark, new graphics for 30 SKUs, and structural packaging changes.
- Managed sports marketing activities for Major League Baseball co-sponsorships.

1999–2003   PROCTER & GAMBLE • Cincinnati, OH
Regional Business Manager *(2/01–10/03)*
Recruited to upgrade Regional Marketing activities within North Central Region Sales organization and manage sales of $125 million. Managed trade spending and strategic and account-specific planning, and monitored 11 Division Sales Managers.
- Achieved largest gross sales increase among Snacks Business Managers for 2002; winner of 2 major sales incentive programs.

Product Manager, Pringles *(1/00–2/01)*
Directed all activities on Pringles businesses ($15 million marketing budget). P&L responsibility, advertising, promotion, market research, forecasting; 2 direct reports.
- Doubled brands' profitability by increasing promotion efficiencies.
- Leveraged company portfolio to create fully integrated sampling promotion involving 3 companies. High degree of success resulted in repeat of promotion for 3 years.

Assistant Product Manager, Tide *(2/99–1/00)*

1998–1999   THE J. CLEAN COMPANY • Oakland, CA
Brand Assistant, New Detergent Products

Education   UNIVERSITY OF MICHIGAN • Ann Arbor, MI
- **MBA, Marketing** *(1998)*
- Marketing internship with Pepsi-Cola Company

NORTHWESTERN UNIVERSITY • Evanston, IL
- **Bachelor of Science, Finance** *(1995)*

ALECIA A. MOORE

425 Rittenhouse Lane, Atlanta, GA 30309
404-392-2323 • aamoore@verizon.net

MARKETING / MANAGEMENT PROFESSIONAL

Driving volume and share increases, expense reductions, customer satisfaction, and operational efficiency.

Innovative and intuitive marketing talent with proven leadership skills and a strong blend of expertise in classical marketing and new channels (electronic commerce, Internet / extranet marketing, global business integration). Effective manager and project leader skilled at developing collaborative working relationships with internal and customer teams. Record of leadership in sales force and marketing automation, sales, and strategic business planning. Eager for new challenges in a dynamic business environment.

EDUCATION

Master of Business Administration—International Marketing, Boston College, 1999

Bachelor of Science—Marketing / Finance, University of Georgia, 1995

Managing in the Global Business Environment, Dartmouth / Tuck Executive Education Program, 2003

PROFESSIONAL EXPERIENCE

KEY PRODUCTS COMPANY, Atlanta, GA (2000–present)

Global Sales Marketing Manager (December 2008–present)

Manage the corporate initiative to deliver key business and marketing information to 11 global customers representing 37% of Key's total worldwide sales. Lead and direct an 18-person team (located around the globe) challenged to identify opportunities and develop systems for global, multichannel integration of marketing, sales, and business activities.

- Identified a need for new information-access technology systems (electronic shipment tracking and data analysis via intranet interface) that are currently in development and scheduled for online implementation in November 2009.
- Contributed to the creation of a retailer extranet interface to provide more complete and timely access to information.
- Created a process to incorporate customer point-of-sale data, integrate consumer measures and research, and deliver information to support business analysis, tracking, and management in both standard and ad-hoc formats.

Information Sales Marketing Manager (2006–2008)

Managed $3.5M budget for purchasing data, $1.4M budget for the delivery tool, and 15-person multifunctional team to support the analysis and business-tracking needs of the U.S. field sales organization. Worked collaboratively with business team leaders to identify opportunities where data technology could contribute to the achievement of business goals.

Presented initiatives and analytical solutions to a wide range of national and regional retailers and to e-commerce retailers from the CIO level to buyers.

- Captured $4.3M in direct savings and $3.6M in indirect (staff hours) savings through automation and delivery of standard analysis reports.
- Increased total volume 22% and customer satisfaction 20% through industry-leading market development and penetration programs for key retailers. Consulted with retailers and Key Products customer teams. Conducted traditional and focus-group research to evaluate Internet shopping behavior. Developed business strategies and co-marketing programs integrating traditional, e-commerce, and Internet marketing approaches.
- Conducted Internet pricing study that supported the creation of loyal customer programs. Directed additional research assessing low-income and ethnic buying trends.

Accomplishments continue on page 2.

A downsizing initiative with a lucrative buyout gave Alecia the time and financial security to pursue a job search in her native New England. Her strong educational credentials are placed up front in a brief format.

ALECIA A. MOORE

404-392-2323 • aamoore@verizon.net

PROFESSIONAL EXPERIENCE

<u>KEY PRODUCTS COMPANY</u>

Information Sales Marketing Manager (continued)

- Instituted consumer data analysis and category management standard reports that contributed to 27% volume growth in managed categories.
- Spearheaded the creation of a standardized, automated efficient assortment process that delivered 35% growth in market share. Assessed internal and external needs, from executive level to sales force; designed formats, delivered support, and deployed the software.
- Designed and delivered a real-time performance information system, available electronically to Key business teams, for precise analysis and up-to-the-minute customer service. User-friendly system design resulted in a $120K reduction in technical support costs and a $2M annual reduction in meeting expenses.
- Leveraged expertise in consumer data to choose from among data vendors, design new applications, and develop training programs to aid in application, understanding, and analysis. Effectively negotiated vendor agreements for purchase and content of data.

Golden Key Sales Award, 2007.

Account Executive, New England (2004–2006)

Developed and coordinated strategic plans to deliver market share and volume, merchandising, distribution, and pricing for all beverage brands in major grocery accounts representing sales of more than $37M.

- Achieved volume growth of 19% in 2005 and 23% in 2006 in a flat channel and market.
- Spearheaded efficient assortment and category-management marketing programs that delivered 38% increase in share of shelf, 20% increase in share of distribution, and 21% growth in volume.
- Developed and implemented a plan that successfully eliminated "diverting" at customer locations and increased direct shipments 30%.
- Completed extensive training in valuing diversity, creating high-performance work teams, and facilitating work groups.

Golden Key Sales Awards, 2004, 2005, 2006.

Market Field Representative, Boston-Providence (July–December 2003)

Planned and delivered merchandising, distribution, and pricing programs for beverage brands in major grocery accounts representing more than $6.4M in sales. Managed a unit of career sales representatives and developmental candidates.

- Developed and delivered a training program for new employees.
- Led management team training in sales technology and business planning.

Sales Representative, Northern Massachusetts / New Hampshire (2000–2003)

Coordinated retail priorities for 10 sales representatives for a major grocery account with sales of $80M.

COMMUNITY ACTIVITIES

Big Brothers/Big Sisters volunteer (2008–present)

American Cancer Society volunteer (2005–present)

Daniel Montez

77 Mustang Trail, Round Rock, TX 78680 ♦ 512-345-0123 ♦ danmontez@austin.rr.com

MARKETING PROFESSIONAL

Track Record: Consistent and measurable contributions in the *strategic planning* and *detailed execution* of marketing programs to support business growth and organizational goals.

Key Strengths: Analysis and planning... tailored marketing solutions... effective communications... collaborative relationship-building... priority setting... management of multiple simultaneous projects.

PROFESSIONAL EXPERIENCE

Computerkids, Round Rock, Texas, 2004–Present
Director of Marketing (2006–Present) ♦ **Marketing Coordinator** (2004–2006)

Direct all marketing initiatives for national 87-location children's computer training business, focusing on delivering a consistent message to highly targeted audiences to maintain company identity and attract business. Participate on management team, providing marketing expertise to support aggressive growth plans. Manage $650K marketing budget. Supervise Marketing Coordinator and Marketing Assistant.

- Create and execute strategic marketing plans for all segments of target audience: parents, staff, and potential investors. Work collaboratively with corporate departments and center managers for successful implementation.

- Develop integrated marketing/advertising campaigns: direct mail, multimedia advertising, print materials, signage, Internet presence. Coordinate work of freelancers, vendors, and agencies.

- Tailor campaigns for different markets, effectively managing marketing budget and developing strategic approaches that address location-specific concerns.

- Conduct market research to provide data for expansion and current business analysis.

- Serve as the company's public relations representative, developing media opportunities and responding to media requests.

- Conduct internal marketing and communications—newsletters, staff recruiting campaigns, benefits announcements. Train corporate departments and site managers on marketing and public relations skills.

Key Accomplishments

- Spearheaded effective marketing campaigns that facilitated company growth from **$10M, 1-state** organization to current **$88M, 11-state** status.

- Achieved significant and sustained increases in enrollment; current company average is consistently at **85% of capacity**—5%–10% above comparable program averages.

- Analyzed operations and developed marketing campaigns that turned around struggling locations, improved enrollments, and addressed unique challenges. **Improved enrollment 30%** at Knoxville center, to consistent 90% rate, through analysis, identification of a key parent concern, and subsequent marketing of a highly effective solution.

- Expanded marketing initiatives to increase visibility in the **corporate community.**

Central Texas University, Dallas, Texas, 2000–2004
Development Coordinator (2001–2004) ♦ **Employment Recruiter** (2000–2001)

EDUCATION

Bachelor of Arts in Psychology, 2000 ♦ Central Texas University, Dallas, Texas

With nearly all his relevant experience with one employer, we could devote quite a bit of space to the diverse activities of Daniel's position as well as his significant and measurable achievements.

Laura Millstone

8723 47th Avenue SW • Seattle, WA 98136 • (206) 555-8723 • lmills@gmail.com

Tourism Industry Marketing & Management Professional

Creative Leadership • Initiative • Project Management

- Collaborative relationship-builder who brings together diverse organizations to achieve goals.
- Strategic thinker expert in the development of marketing concepts and tactical plans.
- Cost- and profit-conscious project manager.
- Motivational team leader who can generate enthusiasm and commitment from diverse stakeholders.
- Effective communicator with strong writing skills, both business and sales.

Professional Experience

SEA-TAC VISITORS BUREAU, Seattle, Washington   2007–Present
Director of Tourism

Position and market Greater Seattle as a leisure destination for visitors/tourists. Manage $900K budget.
- Implemented an interactive reservation system that actively sells attractions and hotels. Solicited and coordinated participation among area properties. Achieved 7:1 ROI in year one.
- Designed and executed comprehensive multimedia marketing plan.
- Created and implemented collaborative marketing campaigns, working with and building consensus among 20 or more commercial and nonprofit partners.

PHOENIX ATTRACTIONS, INC., Phoenix, Arizona   2005–2007
Vice President, Marketing

Managed implementation of the Phoenix Retail Marketing Plan, developing marketing strategies and establishing collaborative working relationships with diverse downtown retailers. Created retail sales promotions and developed cooperative advertising.
- Managed Ho-I lo-Holidays, a highly successful annual event attracting more than a half-million visitors over the winter holiday season. Created theme, attracted sponsors, planned and coordinated events, developed marketing communications, managed volunteer staff, and handled media relations.
- Pioneered a unique collaboration among retailers, arts agencies, and tourism organizations, creating a regional marketing vehicle to promote Greater Phoenix as a visitor destination.

SUCCESS MARKETING, Scottsdale, Arizona   2001–2005
Marketing Consultant

Collaborated with clients to create, prepare, and direct the implementation of strategic marketing and business plans designed for immediate impact to the bottom line as well as contribution to long-range company goals and growth.
- Spearheaded the introduction of a retail product for an established food-service company and grew product revenues to $225K in 5 months.
- Wrote and executed start-up marketing plan for a new medical service and increased business more than 170% in its second year of operation.
- Prepared comprehensive financial business plan for corporate merger.

MOM'S COOKIES, Phoenix, Arizona   1998–2001
Southwest Regional Manager (1999–2001), **District Sales Manager** (1998–1999)

Directed a $22M retail and wholesale sales operation with 17 brokers. Surpassed sales quotas and increased new-item placement by 21% in total market. Achieved a company record district sales increase (573%) in first year as District Manager.

FRITO-LAY, Phoenix, Arizona   1996–1998
Area Sales Representative

Education

MBA, 2001 • SOUTHWEST UNIVERSITY, Phoenix, Arizona
BS Marketing, cum laude, 1996 • UNIVERSITY OF ARIZONA, Phoenix, Arizona

The tourism industry presents interesting marketing opportunities. With this resume, Laura moved to a Director of Marketing position for a regional tourism authority.

Brett Alexander

237 Chestnut St. #37B
Brooklyn, NY 11214

b_alexander@optonline.net

H: 718-349-4590
M: 718-890-3210

Business Development Executive

Marketing / Sales / Key & National Account Management

Clearly articulating value propositions and developing strategic, consultative, business-building solutions for client companies in diverse industries.

Repeatedly successful in capturing new business and establishing relationships with decision-makers at Fortune 500 firms. Expert in developing consultative business partnerships—assessing needs, learning marketing objectives, and devising creative strategies that deliver desired benefits. Demonstrated ability to introduce new concepts and nontraditional services at the highest corporate level. Background in management consulting / organizational performance; MBA.

- Strategic Marketing Planning
- Campaign Strategy & Execution
- Marketing Staff & Department Leadership
- Marketing Collateral / Corporate Identity

- Consultative Needs Assessment
- Executive-Level Presentations & Sales
- National Account Management & Retention
- Trade-Show Marketing & Lead Conversion

Experience and Achievements

MEDIA SERVICES, Flushing, NY   2003–Present

Advertising and information service company… provider of traffic, news, and weather content to the broadcast industry.

Business Development Director

Developed millions of dollars of new business with high-profile national accounts (Kraft, Blockbuster Video, Citibank, The Gap); overcame longstanding objections by developing executive-level relationships and creating marketing programs aligned with brand image and business objectives.

Develop strategic marketing plans for national accounts, successfully promoting a nontraditional marketing vehicle (drive-time program sponsorship) through needs-based analysis and custom proposal development. Combine heavy new-business development with ongoing management and growth of key accounts. Develop marketing plans and proposals; negotiate contracts; implement programs; follow through with a strong emphasis on service and development of client relationships.

Marketing, Sales, & New-Business Development:
- Achieved 100% or more of sales objectives every year—in 2008, performed at 130% of goal.
- More than 90% of sales represent new business.

Representative Accounts:
- Captured the firm's first contract with Citibank—a strategic target for 10 years. Built relationships with top decision makers and developed creative/consultative proposals that tied programs to specific brands. Grew the account from $13K first contract to more than $1M annually.
- Created innovative retailer-tagged sponsorship program for The Gap, a national account with a limited local-marketing budget. Aggressively promoted program tie-ins and carefully tracked results. Grew annual business from $500K to projected $1.5M by year-end 2008.
- Capitalized on program format (live reading of sponsorship announcements) to gain new business with Blockbuster Video—sold account based on proposal to customize the marketing message daily.
- Leveraged relationships and results with Kraft to capture additional business with multiple brands within the company.

Brett's success in landing major national accounts is a highlight of his resume because other companies seeking to break into these same markets will value his contacts and track record.

DREAM MEDIA, INC., New York, NY   1997–2003
Pioneer in the field of corporate special events

Marketing Director

Spearheaded marketing efforts that led to successful launch of a groundbreaking concept and growth of a multimillion-dollar business from the ground up.

Led all business-to-business marketing activities for innovative company providing multimedia event services for corporate events. Developed marketing strategy, message, corporate logo and identity, and marketing collateral; spearheaded PR, advertising, and trade-show marketing to build awareness in the corporate-meeting market.

Marketing, Sales, & New-Business Development:
- Drove business growth from start-up to profit performance 35% above projections in 2 years.
- Qualified all corporate leads, converting many into executive-level presentation opportunities by successfully communicating unique business benefits of new technology.
- Secured new business with key target accounts, including Budweiser, Coca-Cola, Sprint, GE, and Johnson & Johnson; effectively managed key account relationships and succeeded in gaining follow-on business.
- Designed innovative client programs that used technology to reinforce business themes, enhance training, and build consistent corporate image.

Corporate Strategy & Management:
- Developed 1-year, 5-year, and 10-year marketing plans; monitored and revised in response to actual business results.
- Established and managed formal marketing department as the company grew. Hired, trained, and supervised staff.

DRYDEN CONSULTING GROUP, New York, NY   1992–1997
Boutique management-consulting firm whose clients included GM, Chase Manhattan, Fruit of the Loom, and Delta Dental.

Management Consultant

Developed performance-improvement strategies for diverse businesses, participating in all phases of consulting projects from presentation and sale through assessment, analysis, recommendation and report development, and delivery of findings to executive management at client companies nationwide.
- Efficiently managed multiple consulting engagements and ongoing account relationships.
- Delivered client training programs to build business skills and foster goal achievement.
- Co-created a computer program that analyzed organizational climate by relating employee emotions to work attitudes.

EAST COAST CHEMICALS, Brooklyn, NY   1990–1992
Manufacturer and distributor of reagent-grade chemicals.

Product Manager

Brought on board to drive sales growth of bulk-chemicals business. Developed comprehensive marketing strategy and aggressively pursued new business while actively managing existing accounts. Developed proposals and negotiated sales.
- Increased sales 55% in less than 2 years.
- Introduced first catalogue for bulk sales—researched, designed, and launched.

Education

MBA in Marketing, 1992 ▪ **BSBA** in Marketing, 1989   Fordham University, Bronx, NY

Brett Alexander   H: 718-349-4590 ▪ M: 718-890-3210 ▪ b_alexander@optonline.net

Tania Montoya

5555 Cactus Lane, Taos, NM 87571
505-901-1234 • t.montoya@mac.com

MARKETING PROFESSIONAL with a record of *top performance* and the proven ability to design and deliver diversified, comprehensive, highly successful marketing initiatives... create demand for new products... identify and target niche markets... rapidly come up to speed in new environments and consistently deliver outstanding results.

Expertise:

- **Creative marketing planning and execution...** ability to envision innovative and effective sales and marketing programs and then develop strategies and follow through on all details to ensure successful implementation.
- **Strategic sales...** proficient in all stages of the sales process... talent for homing in on buyers' real motivations... proven ability to develop new business and to build and maintain positive customer relationships.
- **Business analysis...** accounting and business background provides foundation for solid analysis and the creation of meaningful financial projections.

PROFESSIONAL EXPERIENCE

Marketing Director—ENGLISH GARDEN LTD., Taos, New Mexico—2008–Present
Took on the challenge of penetrating the U.S. market for Canadian manufacturer of specialty gardening tools.

- Created catalog, developing focus and message from the ground up and supervising vendors in all aspects of production: design, photography, copywriting, and printing.
- Served as Sales Director for commission sales staff. Provided product training; developed and communicated effective sales strategies; maintained close communication to ensure a strong focus on our products among lines promoted by these multivendor representatives.
- Spearheaded total marketing strategy for the company's trade show activity. Designed booth and directed vendors in creation of display materials; oversaw booth setup and merchandise display; contributed to corporate decisions on specific target markets, including gardening retailers and gift/tool shows.

Marketing & Sales Associate—RE/MAX REAL ESTATE, Taos, New Mexico—1999–2007
Consistently achieved top-seller status among Taos-area RE/MAX agents. Developed highly effective strategies to market services through differentiation and personal identification.

- Envisioned and carried out large-scale marketing programs, including:
  — Total marketing services for several top builders in executive neighborhoods.
  — Comprehensive, multiyear marketing program for developer of 300-home subdivision, covering preconstruction through finished-home sales. Collaborated with developer to create vision for the neighborhood, amenities, and target clientele; prospected and selected 5 appropriate builders; represented the developer on all lot negotiations and sales.
- Averaged $5.8 million in annual sales. Achieved Million Dollar Club every year; "100% Club" for 6 years; New Mexico RE/MAX President's Award 3 years.
- Rapidly built revenue by identifying and penetrating an underserved market niche.
- Initiated collaborative alliances with developers and builders to market their properties.
- To market executive homes, held frequent broker tours/lunches; conducted neighborhood promotions; designed and created multipage information flyers for each property; produced videos to conveniently "show" properties to relocating clients.

— BS in Business Administration, Northern Kentucky University, Highland Heights, KY —
— Available to travel and relocate —

Tania's challenge was to continue focusing her career in marketing despite the fact that most of her background was in sales. The profile, strengths, and current position description do an effective job of de-emphasizing her previous real-estate sales position.

MARK W. MADDUX

43 Colonial Drive, Dumont, NJ 07628
201-249-6001 • mwmad@nj.rr.com

MARKETING / BUSINESS MANAGEMENT / SALES MANAGEMENT

▶ **EXPERTISE**

Domestic and international product positioning, marketing, and sales
Strategic marketing plan development and implementation
Technical knowledge base

▶ **STRENGTHS**

- Effective management/leadership style that encourages independent contributions and promotes collaborative working relationships across organizational boundaries.
- In tune with customer needs and requirements as a priority for successful marketing and profitable business operations.
- Able to create aura of excitement about products and services with customers and suppliers.
- Exceptional planning and organizational skills.
- Highly proficient in the use of computer applications as business productivity tools; continuously oriented toward increasing efficiency through the identification and use of innovative resources.
- Highly self-disciplined, extremely motivated, and always enthusiastic.

PROFESSIONAL EXPERIENCE

SEABOARD CHEMICALS, INC., Paramus, New Jersey   1999–Present

Marketing Manager (2007–Present)

Develop and execute strategic marketing plans for specialty petrochemical products with gross sales of $43 million and market penetration into highly fragmented markets and applications.

Provide marketing leadership to direct sales force and sales agents in Europe, Asia, and U.S. *First-year initiative:* implementing completely revamped European marketing strategy in a mature market. *Current focus:* developing the emerging Asian market (South Korea, Singapore, Taiwan, China, Japan).

Develop competitive marketing strategies for both mature and new products. Bring a highly focused, cohesive approach to marketing activities through effective communication with all arms of the company. Use effective leadership style and strong communications skills to gain support and cooperation of diverse contributors to the marketing function (communications, R&D, production, sales) without direct supervisory authority.

Create both long-range forecasts and short-range business and communications plans based on sound industry and product knowledge as well as personally developed forecasting tools. Represent Seaboard on the National Adhesives and Sealants Council.

▶ **PRIMARY RESPONSIBILITIES**

Product mix	*Market segment identification*
Pricing and profitability	*Product development stirring and prioritization*
Communication/advertising	*Strategic marketing plan development and execution*

▶ **KEY ACCOMPLISHMENTS**

- Reversed downward trend of a commodity- and price-driven product line through customer needs assessments and technical demonstrations (tours of sophisticated R&D facility and technical testing for customer problems). Continuing this initiative through advertising materials that promote the R&D operation.
- Piloted the company's first-ever trade show participation (Atlanta, 2007); extremely successful outcome led to participation in world's largest composite industry trade show (Paris, 2008). Seized opportunity to hold group meetings and training sessions with all European sales agents. Garnered inquiries from 67 countries.
- Driving force behind the company's development of a first-in-the-industry product group that positions Seaboard as an industry leader anticipating customer needs and industry trends. Prepared market analysis demonstrating low-risk, high-profit potential of products.

(continued)

In an already detailed resume, spelling out primary responsibilities in a simple list format is an effective way to communicate this information without adding dense text to the resume. It also serves as a break between paragraph-length responsibilities and accomplishments.

MARK W. MADDUX

PROFESSIONAL EXPERIENCE (CONTINUED)

Product Manager (2006–2007)

Scheduled production of 76M pounds annually of specialty polymers across 6 different product lines and 7 manufacturing locations. Managed the purchase of raw materials from more than a dozen suppliers and worked with many outside processors.

▶ **PRIMARY RESPONSIBILITIES**

Production planning	*Inventory management*
Raw-material planning	*Order exception management*

▶ **KEY ACCOMPLISHMENTS**

- Transformed operational vision from production orientation to customer focus. Successfully communicated customer orientation throughout the manufacturing operation.
- Created effective order exception management system by establishing priority rankings and developing complex spreadsheets that enabled precise comparison of production costs. Previously, exceptions had been considered using intuition, "best guess," and pencil-and-paper calculations that could not pinpoint the true costs of changes.

Market Development Manager (2003–2006)

Assigned the challenge of developing from scratch a comprehensive marketing plan upon company's decision to sever relationship with European distributor and market its own products on the continent.

▶ **PRIMARY MARKETING RESPONSIBILITIES**

Product mix	*Market segment identification*
Communications and advertising	*Strategic marketing plan development and execution*
Identification of product development needs	

▶ **KEY ACCOMPLISHMENTS**

- Identified 90% of accounts in a highly specialized market via industry market studies, use of consultants, and direct account contacts.
- Developed a sophisticated multi-table database that enabled detailed analysis of the European marketplace and facilitated timely decision-making.
- Completed comprehensive research, business analysis, and economic outlook. Created in-depth marketing plan that, when implemented, led to achievement of original corporate goal (increase market share from 3% to 10%) within 3 years.

Technical Sales Representative (1999–2003)

Called on existing and prospective customers in territory encompassing Northwestern U.S. and Western Canada. Lengthy sales cycle required effective relationship-building skills and demonstration of an understanding of the customer's business and technical needs.

▶ **KEY ACCOMPLISHMENTS**

- Played leadership role in sales automation program using notebook PCs by field representatives by proving new systems and demonstrating and obtaining distinct productivity advantages.
- Earned Seaboard Sales Achievement Award, 2000: one of 10 award winners nationwide.

EDUCATION

University of Washington, Seattle, Washington
Bachelor of Science degree: *Chemistry,* Science & Arts College
Certificate in Business Administration: *Marketing,* Business College

- Self-funded 100% of educational expenses.

Alana G. Kristoforo

14 Peter Road • North Reading, MA 01864
(508) 444-6767 • akristoforo12@earthlink.net

Marketing • Project Management • Promotional Events Planning • Trade Shows
Public Relations • Client Relations • Account Development

- **Accomplished, visible, and results-oriented Marketing/Special Events Management Professional** with track record reflecting ability to innovate and implement highly effective programs, optimize operations, ensure integrated marketing programs, and achieve performance objectives. Proven skill in maximizing results while motivating staff. Expert analytical and strategic planning abilities.

- Broad expertise managing all facets of trade shows and promotional events; creative strategist who can develop and execute targeted marketing programs and collateral materials that produce results consistently exceeding all expectations. Team player and consensus builder.

- Fluent in Spanish and Italian.

Professional Experience

QUEX MEDICAL SOLUTIONS, INC. • Bedford, MA   2004–Present

Project Manager (2007–Present)

Promoted to launch new transition support department and direct client services for QuexSys (Quex Medical Solutions' flagship medical software product) as pivotal member of implementation team. QuexSys Medical specializes in software for ambulatory surgery centers as well as doctors' offices. Manage staff of 4.

- Manage implementation process from onset of relationship with new client accounts; oversee implementation package execution, training by trainers, and 60-day transition period from clients' previous software to QuexSys. Highly proactive in anticipating client requirements and providing exemplary service and assuring focus through single-point staff account assignments.

- Successfully managed transition team throughout software implementation to relocate marketing activities from National HealthCare in Hartford, CT, to Quex Medical in Bedford, MA; proactively addressed all components of customer service to accomplish smooth transition.

- Developed standardized policies and procedures as well as implemented effective work-flow plans.

Marketing Manager (2006–2007)

Conceptualized and implemented fully integrated marketing program for National HealthCare (ultimately acquired by Quex Medical in 2007). Managed telemarketing team, developed strategic marketing and public relations plans, and launched multimedia campaigns.

- Substantially boosted brand through extensive participation in industry trade shows; managed and participated in up to 42 trade shows annually, including numerous multiday events.

- Staged innovative marketing programs that significantly increased trade show booth attendance and qualified lead generation (such as incentive trips and creative pre- and post-marketing contacts).

- Successfully managed development and execution of all marketing collateral; cultivated and oversaw vendor relationships (graphic designers, writers, printers); produced promotional materials, including flyers, feature-product documents, and company and client newsletters.

- Developed strategic content for website and intranet.

(continued)

Resume contributed by Jan Melnik, MRW
Packing keywords into the headline shows Alana's range of experience and capabilities within the broad field of marketing. Achievements support each of these capabilities.

Alana G. Kristoforo
(508) 444-6767

Page 2
akristoforo12@earthlink.net

QUEX MEDICAL SOLUTIONS, INC. *(continued)*
Product Manager / Client Manager (2004–2006)

Supported QuexSys, tracking client requirements and recommendations for enhancement; designed and implemented features for future upgrades. Directed support staff of 4 employees as Client Manager.

- Spearheaded efforts to consolidate and analyze software upgrade queries and contributed to steering committee; highly responsive to client concerns. Initiated client survey process.

- Developed and produced competitive analyses, product analyses, and win/loss reports.

EMBASSY HEALTH PLANS • Greenwich, CT   **2000–2004**
Supervisor, New-Business Development (2002–2004)

Promoted to manage new-business development for Embassy and build inside-sales team of 23. Implemented highly effective motivational and management strategies that boosted team loyalty, reduced turnover, and optimized training to enhance results.

- Team directly marketed Embassy health care products to company's largest strategic accounts (AT&T, Merrill Lynch, Smith Barney).

- Instrumental to doubling of membership from 1 million to 2 million members in just 1 year; it took Embassy 10 years to grow from 0 to 1 million members.

- Effectively managed organization fielding 70,000 calls in 4 most active months (plan conversion).

- Initiated strategic competitive analyses to identify distinctions between Embassy and other leading benefit providers.

- Earned highest team quality assurance scores in entire company; recognized by staff with "best manager award."

New-Business Development Representative (2000–2002)

Marketed Embassy's diverse benefit products (alternative medicine, wellness programs, and access to large network of physicians and pharmaceutical providers). Successfully developed large employer group accounts.

ARA FOOD SERVICE • Middletown, CT   **1999–2000**
Food Service Manager

Effectively managed cafeteria dining operations for such corporate clients as Wesleyan University, Middlesex Mutual Assurance, and Aetna; held full P&L responsibility for dining operations business unit.

- Directed all operational activities, from purchasing, inventory control, and menu selection to staffing/training, compliance with health codes, and supervision of kitchen staff and services.

Education   UNIVERSITY OF PENNSYLVANIA • Philadelphia, PA
- **Bachelor of Science Degree, Business Administration** (1999)

Continuing Professional Education Highlights include
- **Six Sigma Training** and work on **Greenbelt Projects**
- Training in **Health Insurance Portability and Accountability Act** (HIPAA)

GORDON ZACHAR

275 Mt. Auburn Place, Chicago, IL 60611
312-497-5566   gzachar@mac.com

PROFESSIONAL PROFILE

Marketing professional with a strong record of achievements in market development, new-product introduction, strategy creation and project management. Industry expertise in health care (products and services) and agricultural chemicals—Fortune 500 companies to entrepreneurial ventures. Keen ability to develop integrated marketing strategies to promote growth and support established business goals.

PROFESSIONAL EXPERIENCE

QUALITY HEALTH CORP., Evanston, IL—*Health care quality improvement organization*

Senior Associate for Marketing and Strategic Planning   **2007–Present**

Direct the company's marketing, marketing research, advertising, public relations, new-product development and strategic planning initiatives.

- Created business plans for 2 new lines of business, providing structure to enable sustained, long-term growth. Identified management information needs and processes. Developed strategy to strengthen relationships with primary clients, broaden points of contact and improve customer service. Outlined employee testing and development programs. Created blueprints for assessing customer satisfaction and developing new business.

    Results: — Consulting division achieving 10% growth per month.
    — More than doubled account base.
    — Reduced reliance on 2 primary accounts from 70% to 40% of the business while increasing sales in each of those key accounts.

- Initiated a public relations strategy to develop relationships with medical societies and hospital associations.

- Refined private-venture marketing communications and advertising to incorporate an external versus internal focus and increase reader appeal.

- Conceived a new business service that expanded business out of the primary hospital market.

- Led strategic planning workshops with health care coalitions to maximize event results.

- Strengthened relations with health care providers, associations and decision-makers.

AGRI-CHEM MARKETING, Chicago, IL—*Technical and marketing strategy consultants*

Senior Consultant   **2004–2007**

Designed, managed and delivered specialized marketing consulting services to clients in the agricultural chemicals industry. Responsible for case planning and management, data analysis, report writing, client presentations, survey design and testing, marketing interviews and data quality assurance. Projects included

- Customer satisfaction measurement through data gathering, analysis and approach model development.

- Distribution logistics analysis and development of a reengineered process for Fortune 50 client.

- Sales force optimization analysis and recommendations to improve effectiveness and efficiency of client's national sales force.

- Product pricing analysis.

(continued)

Looking forward to completing his MBA, Gordon updated his resume to look for a better-paying marketing job.

GORDON ZACHAR, Page 2   312-497-5566   gzachar@mac.com

PROFESSIONAL EXPERIENCE, continued

DURHAM LABORATORIES, Chicago, IL—*Educational Materials Division*

Marketing Analyst   (4-month contract assignment) **2003–2004**

Charged with analyzing the educational market and devising a market entry strategy. As a result, the company revamped its organizational structure and began implementing the recommended strategy.

MARKET / MANAGEMENT CONSULTANTS, Chicago, IL—*Market research and consulting firm*

Research Associate   **2000–2003**

Conducted market research studies and presented results to clients. Served as project manager, supervising information gathering and data analysis. Managed sales and promotional program: developed leads, made sales calls and prepared and tracked proposals. Projects included

- Customer satisfaction measurements.
- Analysis of acquisition candidates.
- Preparation of new-product introduction strategy.

MEDICAL SUPPLY OF CHICAGO, Chicago, IL

Sales Representative   **1998–2000**

- Increased customer base more than 35% in the first year.

HOSPITAL SUPPLY CORP., Milwaukee, WI

Sales Representative   **1996–1998**

- Created and implemented a marketing plan for the newly expanded Chicago territory.
- Developed a client base through extensive cold calling; generated break-even sales in the first year.

EDUCATION

NORTHWESTERN UNIVERSITY, Chicago, IL
M.S. Management, 2007–present—expected completion 2010

MARQUETTE UNIVERSITY, Milwaukee, WI
B.S. Business Administration, 1996
Specialization in Marketing and Human Resources Management

PROFESSIONAL AFFILIATIONS

Illinois Society for Healthcare Planning and Marketing
Illinois Association for Healthcare Quality

Curtis Kantu

645-558-5556 ● c_kantu@hotmail.com
85 Morgan Park Drive, Apt. 1112 ● Toronto, ON H2H2L2

Brand Management / Business Development / Strategic Sales

Marketing Strategy and Account Management

Innovative marketing professional and brand builder with 9+ years of business development experience conceiving and developing strategies that create unique brand experiences to differentiate products and generate revenue.

Proven track record as a take-charge leader whose account acquisition / management talents guarantee market growth and client loyalty. History of delivering winning solutions that achieve business goals in B2B and B2C sales and channel /retail account management for bottom-line results.

MBA, Strong School of Business, Toronto University (2008)

Industry Experience: **Petroleum Products ● Industrial Sales ● Retail Electronics ●
Logistics and Supply Chain ● Packaged Goods ● Durable Goods ●
Computer Hardware**

Areas of Expertise

World-Class Account Management

Strategic & Marketing Planning

Financial Accountability

Client Relationship Development & Management

Key Decision-Maker Networking

Consultative Value Selling

Market Analysis & Segmentation

Vendor Negotiations

Cross-Functional Teamwork

Professional Experience

▶ **UNITED PAPER SERVICES LTD.,** Toronto, 2007–2009

$125B Fortune 500, U.S.–based package delivery and supply-chain management company.

BUSINESS DEVELOPMENT MANAGER

Leveraged sales and marketing savvy to build market share in a territory with $500K in annual sales, evangelizing unique and powerful UPS tools that add value to North American businesses. Met with key decision-makers and logistics professionals in one-on-one consultations to win accounts while up-selling existing accounts to maximize sales and profitability. Demonstrated in-depth and personal understanding of client needs to offer solutions that capture business opportunities.

- Exceeded 100% performance to annual revenue goal in just 6 months.
- Revitalized relationships and turned around declining business with 12 customers by revamping shipping services to satisfy changing needs.
- Signed up 22 new customers by providing value-added solutions.

▶ **AFFINITY INDUSTRIES LTD.,** Mumbai, India, 2001–2006

Global Fortune 500, privately held petroleum products and refining company with annual revenues of $95B.

TERRITORY MARKETING MANAGER

Progressed through a series of fast-track, performance-based promotions—from Sales Manager to Retail Outlet Manager and Territory Marketing Manager—during a 5-year period of market share growth and profitability following the deregulation of the petroleum industry throughout India. Aggressively developed the Central Gujarat Market, researching retail locations and promising franchisees while overseeing all daily sales activities.

- Identified 32 retail outlet locations and presented the ROI-based franchise business model to potential franchisees for final selection.
- Hand-picked to lead pilot retail team of 52 employees that achieved sales of Cdn. $16M in the first year to become the second-largest revenue producer territory-wide.
- Developed and led intensive, customer-service-focused training program for employees.
- Designed and executed 2 promotional campaigns that increased diesel sales by 15%.

(continued)

Resume contributed by Majorie Sussman, MRW
With strong experience and accomplishments in both marketing and sales, Curtis gives them nearly equal weight in this resume to position himself for roles in which both skills will be of value.

Curtis Kantu   645-558-5556 ● c_kantu@hotmail.com

▶ **ATLANTIC INDIA LTD. (acquired by Seagram Micro),** Mumbai, India, 2000–2001
$7B top-tier IT distributor.

MARKETING MANAGER

Strategic marketing and project management roles, including P&L responsibility, for Acer and Hewlett-Packard product lines, leading initiatives that immediately optimized sales and profitability opportunities. Negotiated terms and conditions, rebate structures, and special deals with vendors.

- Led company to #1 position among HP distributors nationwide.
- Achieved highest quarterly sales of Acer products in company history: Cdn. $400K (up 12% from previous quarter).
- Launched regional HP brand promotion that triggered a 15% sales growth among resellers.

▶ **SIMON INDUSTRIES LTD.,** Mumbai, India, 1998–2000
$20M manufacturer of durable consumer goods.

SENIOR SALES EXECUTIVE

Oversaw network of 12 dealerships, managing accounts receivables, retail promotions, product displays, and demonstrations. Performance highlights included

- Grew dishwasher sales 13% while industry growth rate stagnated at 5% by resolving credit issues with key accounts and acquiring 2 new retailers.
- Reduced outstanding receivables by nearly 50% (60 days to 32 days) in 6 months.

▶ **BLOCK ELECTRONICS LTD.,** Mumbai, India, 1997–1998
$670M manufacturer of consumer electronic equipment.

MARKETING EXECUTIVE

Developed working knowledge of territory/channel management, generating a 60% boost in sales of one brand and developing an effective promotional strategy with a distributor to increase market awareness.

Profile

MASTER OF BUSINESS ADMINISTRATION, Strong School of Business, Ontario University, Toronto, ON (2008)
CERTIFICATE OF MERIT (MARKETING), Canadian Marketing Association Student Award (2007)
POST-GRADUATE DIPLOMA IN BUSINESS ADMINISTRATION, Mumbai, India
BACHELOR IN MECHANICAL ENGINEERING, Jawaharlal Nehru Engineering College, Maharashtra, India (1996)
SPIN SALES TRAINING, Toronto, ON (2008)

Marla Amanpour

860-347-7654   83 Winding Way, Broad Brook, CT 06016   marla@verizon.net

Expertise	**Product Management & Development / Marketing / Strategic Planning**
Key Strengths	• Leadership of teams, projects, and business units
	• Evolution of concepts into achievable business strategies
	• Product research, analysis, and justification for production
	• Negotiation and relationship building
	• Drive, creativity, and ability to reach objectives under demanding circumstances

Track Record

- Developing and implementing business strategies that increase market share and company profitability.

- Identifying and capitalizing on new growth opportunities through market analysis, product development expertise, and keen business instincts.

- Leading cross-functional teams that collaborate as a focused unit to achieve aggressive business goals.

- Developing sourcing relationships worldwide.

- Effectively managing product development/production process from concept through finished product, with close attention to budgets, timeframes, quality, and product specifications.

Professional Experience and Accomplishments

MEDI-PRODUCTS CORP., Stamford, Connecticut

Assistant Director of Product Management, 2008–Present

Brought on board for newly created position to formulate and implement marketing, product development, and merchandising strategies for product use within the health care industry.

Manage the development process for new and reengineered products: In 2009, 29 projects representing 6.5% of corporate sales.

- Lead a cross-functional coalition team representing Product Management, Material Services, Sourcing, Technical Lab, Regulatory, and Sales, providing team guidance to keep multiple projects moving toward specific objectives. Bridge communication between divisions and across functional areas.

- Focus on differentiating products through features, pricing, and promotion; and enhancing competitive advantage by developing cost-effective products.

- Established a 4-step Product Development Process that has been approved for implementation by cross-divisional VPs. Created a process to ensure efficient implementation of product timelines.

- Achieved growth in both sales *and* profits by driving team activity toward new sourcing and engineering solutions.

Coordinate product sourcing and development for the international marketplace.

- Selected to develop strategic plans to launch corporate initiative to grow international business to $100M annually within 2.5 years.

Spearhead new product tracking.

- Establish sales forecasts and track results by monitoring product conversions.

- Forecast inventory requirements and collaborate with production management. Monitor production levels during new-product ramp-up and replacement-product ramp-down.

Established a Design Control Process for medical devices.

- Collaborated with the Director of Regulatory/Medical Affairs to create a new process that ensures compliance with FDA requirements. As Project Manager for new South American surgical line, successfully implemented the new Design Control Process.

(continued)

Note the treatment of dates: To disguise a career in retail buying that started in the early 1970s, Marla's resume shows dates only back to 2003. Her recent experience is covered extensively because of her career target: She wants to remain in product management for a medical company.

Assistant Director of Product Management, continued

Gained expertise in the health care industry through sales and management activities.

- Provide direct selling assistance to the health care sales force through product consultation, resolution of product and quality issues, and assistance with product and sales presentations at hospitals and commercial laundries.
- Prepare monthly presentation to top management on product line sales, forecasts, and strategies. Participate in weekly Sales Analysis Report meetings with Regional VPs.
- Attend industry trade shows and professional meetings.
- Completed extensive high-level training on product classes and categories.

FINESTEIN DEPARTMENT STORES, New York, New York

Product Manager, 2003–2008

Identified private-label opportunities in multiple markets and led development teams through the design, merchandising, quality, sourcing, and sales evaluation process.

Traveled to Asia to evaluate and qualify factories for production, negotiate costs, develop manufacturing partnerships, and research opportunities. Gathered European and worldwide color and trend information; interpreted information into appropriate product mix for customer base. Communicated seasonal trend direction from corporate to store levels.

Instrumental in the evolution of the Private Brand Group.

- Selected as a key player at the inception of the product development area in early 2003; instrumental in formulation of mission, vision, organizational process, and conversion to focused brand status with cross-divisional marketing.
- Launched first Corporate Merchandising Maps to communicate seasonal private-brand assortments to store levels; format adopted for all divisions.

Managed private-brand development process in Intimate Apparel, growing volume from $1M to $20M.

- Devised business plan and oversaw the efficient implementation of product timelines.
- Implemented consistent quality standards and brand profile.
- Led Intimates Team to collaborate as a focused unit, blending individual team member strengths and fostering success, motivation, and mutual respect.

Quadrupled volume of Ladies' Outerwear through private-brand development.

- Formed manufacturing partnerships to achieve superior quality at below-market costs.

Built Juniors' and Children's private-brand penetration to $36.6M and $34M, respectively.

- Initiated an innovative "Shop Concept" for merchandising private-brand product.
- Effectively balanced style assortments and established successful relationship between quality and pricing.

Developed and implemented a business plan / sales strategy for private-brand Ladies' Suits that in first year represented 8% of department volume.

PRIOR EXPERIENCE, FINESTEIN DEPARTMENT STORES
Corporate Buyer, Children's Division—Corporate Assistant Buyer

---

Education

Professional Development
TOP Management—Completing 12 Management Certification Courses, 2008–Present
Dale Carnegie Course, 2005—Award Winner
Covey's First Things First Management, 2004
 Progressive Leadership, Conflict Resolution Management, Vendor Negotiations, Problem Solving
Connecticut College, New London, Connecticut—A.S. degree in Retailing and Advertising

CYNTHIA MOSCIEWICZ

829 West Marsh Road, Renton, WA 98058
Home 425-792-4250 • Mobile 425-209-1129 • mosciewicz@gmail.com

EXPERTISE   Marketing • Product Development • Business Development
Technical Program & Project Leadership

SUMMARY   Senior-level manager with proven ability to drive programs, projects, and products and to guide key corporate initiatives. Qualified for leadership positions that will benefit from

- **Marketing talent** to devise strategic and effective programs to deliver the company's message to prospects and customers.
- **Technical and analytical strengths** to provide a sound foundation for business decisions.
- **Management and communication skills** to lead teams, direct multiple complex programs, and effectively deliver technical information to diverse audiences.

PROFESSIONAL EXPERIENCE

INDUSTRIAL-TECHNICAL SOLUTIONS (ITS), Renton, Washington, 1995–Present

Major hardware, software, and service provider to the machinery information market. With acquisition of Technical Solutions in 2007, the company began a very aggressive 5-year growth strategy with the goal of becoming the dominant provider in the industry and growing from $48M to $200M by FY2012.

Strategic Project Manager, 2008–Present

As member of Strategic Development team, charged with evaluating opportunities and identifying the best new products and services to enable the company to meet its growth targets. Specific area of responsibility is software and follow-on service for monitoring industrial machinery.

Direct potential projects through 4 phases: initial review, in-depth analysis, development of integration plans, and, finally, for projects deemed viable, creation of a business plan and presentation of analysis and recommendations to senior management.

- Identified opportunity and provided technical evaluation that resulted in the acquisition of new Agribusiness division.
- Developed business plan and currently leading team in introduction of new service with projected revenue of $2M by FY2010.
- Leading multiple teams to identify market requirements, justify development, and create functional design specifications for next-generation hardware and software families.

As an unrelated, additional project, assumed key marketing responsibility for growing the company's business in South America. Responding to massive business opportunities that could not be addressed by the current business development team, prepared and began delivery of a series of informational seminars/marketing meetings with South American power plants (spring 2009). The identified market represents more than $2M in immediate business and offers strong potential for exponential growth.

Product Manager: Software Products, 2006–2008

In newly created, highly visible position, managed and provided future direction to the company's major product line—new and existing software products representing $17M in sales, as well as related hardware, training, and service.

Worked closely with Engineering, Marketing, and Sales to define requirements; create and execute engineering, marketing, and sales plans; coordinate launch programs; and develop sales opportunities with operations managers in the U.S., Australia, Europe, and South America.

- Managed obsolescence of duplicate software following merger with Technical Solutions.
- Introduced new software product and contributed to its first-year sales of $1.5M.

(continued)

Growing from a software engineer into marketing roles, Cynthia had significant product and project management experience.

CYNTHIA MOSCIEWICZ Page 2

PROFESSIONAL EXPERIENCE

INDUSTRIAL-TECHNICAL SOLUTIONS, continued

Technical Product Manager, 2003–2006

Provided technical direction, marketing leadership, and sales support for the company's new online system.

- Managed development, marketing, and launch program.
- Negotiated hardware supply contract with sources in the UK.

In addition, assumed unofficial position of "manager of lost causes," filling in at various sales, marketing, and service positions.

- A key interim project involved co-coordinating (with North American Marketing Manager) all marketing activities, brochure development, marketing alliances, and new product opportunities while the Director of Marketing and Marketing Communication Manager positions were vacant.
- Helped redefine new literature standards. Major contributor in design, layout, writing, and photographs for 7 full-color product brochures.
- Created theme for new magazine ad campaign and helped develop 3 ads.

Manager of Educational Services, 2000–2003

Directed education initiatives with the purpose of marketing the company's products through increased visibility and marketplace awareness.

- Designed and presented the first in a series of highly successful user seminars that were a major contributor to changing the company's image and enabling sustained growth through add-on products and support. Marketed seminars through targeted direct mail. Personally delivered 39 seminars to more than 900 attendees in first year. Trained sales force to present seminars (more than 200 presented to date).
- Started successful series of Regional User Group Meetings.

Application Engineer, 1997–2000

Implemented systems at customer sites; provided on-site training; performed in-field consulting.

Co-op/Part-time Development Engineer, 1995–1997

Contributed to various programming projects, including major upgrades of 3 of the company's primary software products.

RECENT PROFESSIONAL ACTIVITIES

PRESENTATIONS

Keynote Presentation: Systems Integration—New York Plant Maintenance Conference, 9/07

"Machine Maintenance"—Industrial Association Conference, Bologna, Italy, 6/06

Special Guest Speaker—Second International ITS User Conference, Hong Kong, 3/04

PUBLICATIONS

"Automated Maintenance," *Modern Manufacturing,* 3/09

"Solving the Maintenance Challenge," *MFG,* 11/07

EDUCATION

Bachelor of Science, Metallurgical Engineering, 1997: UNIVERSITY OF MICHIGAN, Ann Arbor, Michigan

SHERRY MILSTEIN

85 Gramercy Place #7-B
New York, NY 10023

sherrymilstein@aol.com

Home 212-492-6789
Mobile 212-505-8910

PROFESSIONAL PROFILE

Accomplished **Product Manager** with a 12-year track record of effective marketing and manufacturing leadership for Fortune 100 consumer goods company, consistently delivering process, volume, and market-share improvements. Experience and demonstrated abilities in

- Strategic Business Planning
- Brand Management
- Product Positioning

- Identification & Analysis of Market Opportunities
- New-Product Development and Rollout
- Team Leadership, Development, & Motivation

Key strength is ability to focus simultaneously on *vision* and *execution* —leading multiple functions and implementation teams to the detail level while retaining focus on long-term marketing goals and critical business objectives.

EDUCATION

Harvard Business School   MBA, 2005   GPA 3.7
California Institute of Technology   B.S. Mechanical Engineering, 1997   GPA 3.7

PROFESSIONAL EXPERIENCE

THE COSMIC COMPANY, New York, New York—1997–Present

Senior Assistant Brand Manager, Mane Attraction Brand—$90 million   2007–present

Direct all facets of U.S. and globally integrated marketing program: product development, positioning, pricing, marketing strategy, advertising. Accountable for performance against immediate and long-range corporate objectives.

- Grew Mane Attraction sales 25% to become national market leader in styling products.

- Achieved 40% increase in ManeStay hairspray sales by identifying and resolving strategic marketing message issues. Unified brand marketing message; developed new, hard-hitting copy; reallocated marketing support behind product leader to drive growth. U.S. plan adopted globally.

- Successfully introduced 10 new products nationally through effective leadership of multifunctional project teams and collaboration with R&D, Manufacturing, and Sales.

- Created vision to align ManeStay products with brand image, leveraging Mane Attraction equity to drive growth. Secured support of top management for rapid implementation. Worked with global counterparts for worldwide reapplication.

- Created and managed $100 million Mane Attraction media plan, the largest of all Cosmic brands. Identified and prioritized critical objectives and strategies to ensure efficient allocation.

- Designed $12 million sampling plan tested to deliver 21% conversion—3 times the average for hair care products.

Assistant Brand Manager, FaceFirst Brand—$28 million   2006–2007

- Grew sales of FaceFirst Wash to the #1 position among acne products by identifying top consumer needs, establishing aggressive, verifiable product claims targeted to those needs, and effectively incorporating claims in advertising and packaging.

continued…

(continued)

Sherry began a job search when family priorities dictated relocation to the Southeast. Note that her Harvard MBA is spotlighted on the first page of her resume.

SHERRY MILSTEIN   Page 2   sherrymilstein@aol.com

PROFESSIONAL EXPERIENCE

THE COSMIC COMPANY

Assistant Brand Manager, FaceFirst Brand—continued

- Spearheaded FaceFirst Cream restage, with resulting 30% growth in sales. Analyzed market dynamics and conducted consumer research to understand the product's lackluster performance. Led multifunctional team in development of new package, pricing, and advertising, taking project from concept to market in less than 5 months.

- Developed and tested winning marketing/advertising concept behind new acne technology, achieving 15% increase in forecasted sales. Created marketing plan and secured senior management support for national launch.

Operating Manager, Soap Category, Birmingham, Alabama   2003–2006

Held management responsibility and financial accountability for Cosmic Soap bulk production process. Established and efficiently managed operating budget of $6.4 million, including wages, equipment, and travel.

- Orchestrated the consolidation of Cosmic Soap's bulk production operations from 3 sites to 1. Massive construction / integration project completed on time and under budget.

- Quadrupled process efficiency to 85%, saved $1.2 million through 4-cent reduction in case cost, and led department through start-up of 10 new products.

- Created departmental vision and strategy based on category objectives. Consistently managed the department toward the vision by establishing stretch goals and incremental milestones.

- Managed, coached, and developed 60 technicians and 4 managers. Effectively managed tripling of staffing over a 2-year period.

Process Manager, Soap Category, Birmingham, Alabama   2001–2003

Led multifunctional Quality Improvement Team with representatives from 3 plants, R&D, and Engineering, charged with improving quality of production processes and soap products.

- Coordinated installation of real-time statistical software system in 3 plants.

- Reduced quality-related batch rejections 55% by implementing and managing statistical process control procedures.

- Served as Manufacturing liaison to the Marketing department for new-product introductions.

Team Manager, Mobile, Alabama   1997–2001

Managed, coached, and developed 13-member Packing team and 5-member Materials Management team.

- Improved team production throughput 30% by standardizing department productivity procedures.

- Developed and implemented control system that reduced raw material inventory by $2 million.

COMMUNITY LEADERSHIP

BOARD OF DIRECTORS
MANHATTAN CHILDREN'S FUND, New York, New York
PEOPLE'S HOUSING INITIATIVE, Birmingham, Alabama

Luke T. Mallette

257 93rd Street, Unit 7B
San Francisco, CA 94114

lukemallette@mac.com

Home 415-245-6655
Mobile 415-390-1115

PROFILE

Strategic marketing and management professional with a strong record of contributions in marketing, sales, promotions, and brand management of consumer goods. History of effective interaction and relationship management with consumers, field sales teams, creative agencies, and multifunctional project teams. Demonstrated ability to bring pioneering approaches to established marketing programs… innovative thinker with strong analytical and critical-thinking skills.

EDUCATION

MBA: The Wharton School, University of Pennsylvania—2008

University of Virginia Executive Education Program: Pricing Strategies and Tactics—2007

BA: Yale University—2002

PROFESSIONAL EXPERIENCE

CONSOLIDATED CONSUMER COMPANIES, INC., New York, New York, 2002–Present

Brand Manager: Deluxe Hair Care   July 2007–Present

Develop and execute $47 million consumer and trade promotional program for $600 million Deluxe brand, a global priority for Consolidated. Total brand sales increased 12%—versus 6% increase in total category sales.

- Conceived, researched, tested, and implemented an innovative, multiprogram consumer marketing concept that is the first of its kind for hair care products. Conducted extensive consumer research to assess need and develop rationale. Presented and sold concept to key retailers, achieving 10,000 installations—*double* the project goal.

- Invigorated and successfully launched a concept that had been in development for 3 years, an interactive touch-screen computer for consumer hair care assessments in retail stores. National implementation slated for January 2010; test sites have generated active consumer interest and stimulated sales (*more than 10% over control stores*).

- Supported major brand relaunch by leading the development of design and copy strategy for print materials, displays, and the company's first multimedia CD presentation for use by retail account executives. Succeeded in placing new displays in *60,000 stores*—75% of possible sites nationwide, about *twice* average penetration.

- Led a pricing strategy change and implementation that will deliver an incremental 20% in sales dollars with minimal volume decline.

- Created strategies to co-market Deluxe brand with key retailers. Developed and implemented $6 million marketing plan—direct mailers, TV, radio, print, sampling, product demonstrations.

- Spearheaded CCC's first co-marketing newspaper sampling program, involving collaboration with sample suppliers, packagers, and multiple retailers to execute the largest-ever drop of samples via newspaper in 1 day (*20 million samples*). Test sample achieved *21% conversion rate*.

- Collaborated with ad agency to develop strategies and plans for $5 million dedicated advertising fund for the Hispanic market, resulting in 1 print ad and 2 TV spots with *90% reach* (the highest of all brands in U.S. hair care industry). *Increased market share 15%.*

(continued)

This powerful resume is built on a strong and successful marketing career with a major consumer goods manufacturer. Luke's MBA is recent and from a top-10 business school, so it is featured on page 1. His cover letter to a specific company in his target state is sample 12-5.

Luke T. Mallette   Home 415-245-6655 • Mobile 415-390-1115 • lukemallette@mac.com

PROFESSIONAL EXPERIENCE

Senior Sales Technology Project Manager   February 2006–June 2007

Initiated and managed multifaceted projects to enhance the use of technology in CCC's sales operations.

- Led multifunctional project team in development of decision-support tool for use by sales force to enable effective planning and spending of $900 million in promotional funds. Created brand-name identity and generated demand on a "pull" basis. *Successfully deployed tool to 3,000 of 5,000 potential users, with subsequent high rate of use and positive feedback. Decreased cost per incremental promotion volume by 20%.*

- Conducted needs assessment and extensive research and then created and deployed an easy-to-use pricing analysis tool and computer-based training program for 3,000-member field sales force.

- Performed in-depth analysis of 1,600-person retail sales organization, assessing work process, roles, responsibilities, technology tools, and business-building value. Developed retail and account management vision, strategies, and tactics to be incorporated into 3-year retail sales execution plan that was endorsed by VP of Sales.

Account Executive: Food & Beverage   July 2004–January 2006

Managed a major retail account in the Houston area, providing business analysis, strategy development, category management, direct sales, and new-product support. Administered $900K merchandising fund and developed merchandising partnerships with key customer contacts.

- *Increased market share 20%* over prior year; generated *$32 million in sales.*

- Collaborated with customer and conducted extensive analysis to develop a category management plan; *increased category sales 20%.*

Operations Manager: Grocery   February–June 2004

Supervised and trained 7 sales reps who generated $15 million in sales at top food retailer in Texas.

- Initiated laundry category analysis for a key account to encourage total category management. As a result, account developed a concrete strategy for the category and achieved sustained improvement in brand sales (after 6 months, business was indexing at *145% versus prior year*).

Market Field Representative   December 2003–January 2004

Initiated and conducted technology training for 15 sales representatives. Training topics included software, general data analysis, and conceptual selling with data.

Sales Representative   August 2002–November 2003

Marketed, sold, and merchandised Consolidated grocery items in 40 stores in central Texas.

- Delivered *$3.2 million in incremental sales* via shelf improvements, merchandising displays, and new-item distribution.

- Created and implemented grocery manager training program that *improved in-store sales 2%.*

PERSONAL, PROFESSIONAL, AND COMMUNITY ACTIVITIES

CCC "Career Development Initiative" Mentor—2005–present

American Cancer Society fund-raiser—ongoing—personally raised $3,000 in 2008

Coordinated the activities of 10 CCC Sales Department summer interns—2005

Damian McMillan

1123 Adobe Street, San Diego, California 92138

Phone 619-555-7435 ▪ Fax 619-555-7436 ▪ damianmac@gmail.com

EXPERTISE Product / Brand Management and Marketing

PROFILE Creative marketing professional with complementary background in sales, marketing, and product development.

- Successfully launched 9 new product lines from concept through sales promotion.
- Balanced complex project details with constant focus on the big picture.
- Consistently contributed to business growth, profit, and the achievement of corporate goals.

> *"…his capabilities and work ethic are of the highest standard."* Jim Townsend, former VP Marketing / Acme Products
>
> *"Damian… is focused, innovative, a self-starter, assumes responsibilities, and can be trusted. A genuine pleasure to be associated with."* Ted Evans, Executive VP, Strathington Design, Inc.

PROFESSIONAL EXPERIENCE

2007–2009 BORDERLAND AUTO RENTALS, San Diego, California

22-location, $8.5 million business purchased by Dollar Rent-a-Car in 2004

Director, Sales and Marketing

Recruited to spur business growth through effective leadership of the company's marketing, sales, and public relations initiatives. Created and implemented promotional strategies. Oversaw the development of sales and marketing collateral.

- Increased sales 13% in highly competitive marketplace.
- Developed more than 200 new accounts through a successful marketing / sales campaign to insurance companies and agents.
- Established excellent relationships with corporate customers that yielded increased sales.
- Drove positive resolution of customer service issues as liaison between customers and district and branch managers.

1993–2007 ACME PRODUCTS (Division of Read Manufacturing, Inc.), San Diego, California

$35 million distributor of diversified product lines for the automotive aftermarket

Group Product Manager (2005–07) ▪ **Product Manager** (1998–05)

Held P&L accountability for product development, marketing, and sales of product lines that generated more than $32 million in annual revenue. Identified sources and negotiated prices. Developed budgets and sales forecasts. *Products included fasteners, brass fittings, studs, oil drain plugs, engine expansion plugs, body clips and fasteners, rivets, and various small parts.*

Conducted and maintained competitive analysis on all products. Designed planogram layouts for auto parts stores and mass merchandisers. Presented product lines at national and regional sales meetings and trade shows.

Directed marketing team in creation of catalog layout, application data, signage, and promotional materials. Developed company sales manuals and product support literature.

Trained marketing, sales, and customer service staff on new and existing product lines. Supervised marketing staff.

- Successfully sourced, negotiated pricing for, developed, and launched 9 retail product lines that generated sales in excess of $3.2 million—30% over plan.
- Maintained or revived 28 existing product lines with an emphasis on line growth. Reduced cost without reducing value and improved gross profit margins by 35%.
- Captured $90,000 in savings through effective negotiation with vendors.
- Instrumental in restructuring the company's entire wholesale / retail mix to promote profitability through more closely targeted marketing.
- Achieved $850,000 increase in sales through a new merchandising program that included researching and developing new packaging styles, dimensions, design, and graphics.
- Improved the capture of product ideas from customers and field sales force by implementing a new product / merchandising suggestion form and founding and steering a product review committee.
- Only member of 15-person marketing team retained after company buyout by Read Manufacturing (formerly our largest competitor) in 1999.

(continued)

After a brief detour into a sales and marketing leadership role, Damian wanted to return to pure product or brand management. His cover letter, in response to a want ad, is sample 12-6.

Damian McMillan
Page 2

Phone 619-555-7435 ▪ Fax 619-555-7436 ▪ damianmac@gmail.com

PROFESSIONAL EXPERIENCE

ACME PRODUCTS, continued

Marketing / Sales Coordinator (1996–98)

Served as liaison between Marketing, Sales, and field sales force. Provided internal support to National Accounts Sales Manager.

- Created the company's first field sales manual.
- Recognized as a product line resource for field sales force and customers.

District Sales Manager (1994–96)

Promoted to larger territory and challenged to reverse declining sales trend. Covered Southern California, Nevada, and New Mexico with minimal supervision.

- Increased sales 39% in 18 months.
- Revived dormant accounts, increased customer base, and captured new accounts.
- Awarded the company's first **"Soaring to Success" Award** for outstanding contributions toward new and innovative product, packaging, and merchandising plans.

Territory Sales Manager (1993–94)

Managed sales for Central and Northern California. Serviced established accounts and prospected for new business.

- Increased sales 17% in 4 months.

EDUCATION

BS Business Administration / Marketing, 1993
University of California at Los Angeles

Nina Costner

555-555-1410 Mobile • ncostner@emailme.com

Global Business Development and Expansion
Building and Leading World-Class Customer-Centric Organizations

Top-tier strategic Sales and Marketing Director, driving market penetration/expansion, elevating businesses to market leadership, and contributing multimillions of dollars to bottom-line profitability. Twenty-year track record meeting or surpassing corporate goals across diverse market sectors—Engineering, Construction, Telecommunications, Finance, and Real Estate. Valued advisor with unwavering integrity.

Wisdom and talent for creating golden business opportunities out of nothing.

Deep expertise negotiating and landing lucrative contracts, from $100,000 to more than $1 billion. Quickly connect with people, cement a bond of trust, and influence lasting, mutually beneficial relationships.

➤ Parker Telecom—Captured more than $25 million in contracts and increased capture rate 55% by winning 3 new clients within first 6 months of tenure.

Outstanding market analysis acumen with foresight to anticipate and profit from emerging market trends, leading businesses to build on success year over year, well into the future.

➤ Dallas Implementation—Doubled sales revenue to more than $360 million within 12 months, delivering the firm's highest-ever sales gain in its 57-year history. Increased sales commissions 27% per salesperson.

Articulate, consensus-building team leader. Engage and motivate teams to improve precision, think creatively on their feet, and devise solutions to generate increased sales revenue.

Business Development Management

PARKER TELECOM, INC., Houston, TX   2005 to 2009
Vice President
Envisioned and masterminded strategic/tactical planning and global market growth for new wireless implementation company specializing in equipment installation across 3G networks. Drove performance of global workforce across 2 parent companies.

Catapulted enterprise ranking to top 3 out of 100 preferred suppliers in the field.

➤ **Secured coveted installation contract with Siemens** (a German OEM) from short list of 6 firms pared down from 100 competitors.
Impact: **Built contract from $900,000 to $1.8 million in 11 months** and led Cingular (Siemens client) to add multiple markets.

➤ **Leveraged rapid-growth contracts with Nokia,** reducing Parker's dependence on single OEM client.
Impact: **Secured first U.S. contract and grew it from $1.8 million to $11 million in first 6 months.** Achieved global partner status with Nokia, becoming its preferred global supplier; **landed $1 million contract** as Nokia's preferred supplier in Latin America.

➤ **Captured savings of more than $2 million** after crafting Corrective Action Plan to accelerate completion of probation status with Ericsson and reinstate incentive compensation for Parker.

PARKER COMMUNICATIONS GROUP, INC.   2003 to 2005
Vice President, Business Development
Drove extensive industry analysis, developed profiles of target companies, and innovated contract, licensing, and business development strategies to achieve top profitability.

(continued)

Resume contributed by Meg Guiseppi
This resume is easy to skim because all of the information is presented in small "bites" rather than dense or wordy paragraphs. Notice the branding statement just below the summary paragraph.

Nina Costner

555-555-1410 Mobile • ncostner@emailme.com

➤ **Won $1 million contract** to study data centers on Alaska's North Slope. Uncovered and pursued this unsolicited opportunity after reading a newspaper article about the company.

DALLAS IMPLEMENTATION ASSOCIATIONS, INC., Dallas, TX   2001 to 2003
($360 million national design/build firm specializing in mission-critical infrastructure.)
Vice President, National Sales and Marketing
Focused market concentration on telecommunications, Internet technology, and financial and broadcasting industries. Clients included Bank of America, AT&T, Qwest, Wachovia, and Fox Network. Controlled $2 million annual budget and led nationally based sales team of 22, building new revenue streams.

➤ *Elevated 57-year-old firm to market leadership in the technology sector by innovating and launching high-visibility branding campaign.*

SUCCESS SOLUTIONS INC., Del Ray, FL   1999 to 2001
President
Established successful entrepreneurial venture—a business-development consulting firm to grow revenue and improve marketplace presence for client companies.

➤ **Increased sales 30%** for a dental practice.

➤ **Secured $30 million highway program** in Caribbean for Miami-based construction company.

SAMUEL T. HARRISON, INC., New York, NY   1996 to 1999
($100 million international civil engineering firm serving diverse market sectors.)
Vice President, Florida Operations (1998–1999)
Vice President, Business Development, New York (1996–1998)

➤ **Boosted revenues 25%,** fueling financial turnaround by innovating and integrating strategic program.

➤ **Slashed expenditures 20%** and enhanced program impact by consolidating job functions and streamlining processes.

EARLY SALES & MARKETING MANAGEMENT EXPERIENCE
Standout success building profitable relationships resulting in multimillion-dollar contracts for leading engineering/construction management firms:

VP / Director of Business Development, Parker & Stevenson, New York
Manager, Government Marketing, Foster Engineering Corporation, New York
Marketing Manager, Simon-Elgar Engineers, Inc., New York

Education

Bachelor of Arts, Journalism, Roosevelt University, Chicago, IL

SHANE WAINWRIGHT

15 Charming Street
Saratoga, CA 95070

Cell: 408-555-5555
Email: shanew@yahoo.com

SENIOR BUSINESS DEVELOPMENT MANAGER
GLOBAL TIER-1 VENDORS | TECHNOLOGY AND SOLUTIONS SALES
HIGH-VALUE TECHNOLOGY SOLUTIONS, SERVICES, AND OUTSOURCING

"Customers believe in him. He truly becomes the 'trusted advisor' to his clients."—State Manager

Senior Business Development Manager, acknowledged for well-defined understanding of the business-technology interface and capacity to identify and align clients' emerging technology needs with products and services. Successful and diverse background spanning technical, operational management, service delivery, project management, and business-development disciplines. Expertise in engaging decision makers and devising winning sales strategies and solutions.

VALUE OFFERED

- Business Drivers and Technology Alignment
- New Business Pipelines
- Executive Level Engagement
- Vendor Relationships
- Infrastructure Proposals
- Profit Maximization

- Systems Integration
- Technology and Business Solutions
- Tender, Proposal and Contract Development & Negotiation
- Business Value Propositions
- Consultative Selling

- Client Relationship Management
- Project Management
- Opportunity Analysis and Qualification
- Marketing Analysis and Campaigns
- Strategic Alliances

BENCHMARKS AND MILESTONES

- Developed qualified pipeline of $52M for a new line of business.

- Won the largest new outsource services contract in Volumable's history, later used as the managed-services flagship and reference company. The $5M three-year outsourcing contract surpassed offerings by prime competitor IBM and incumbent provider HP.

- Achieved 65% sales to budget from a zero base in just 12 months.

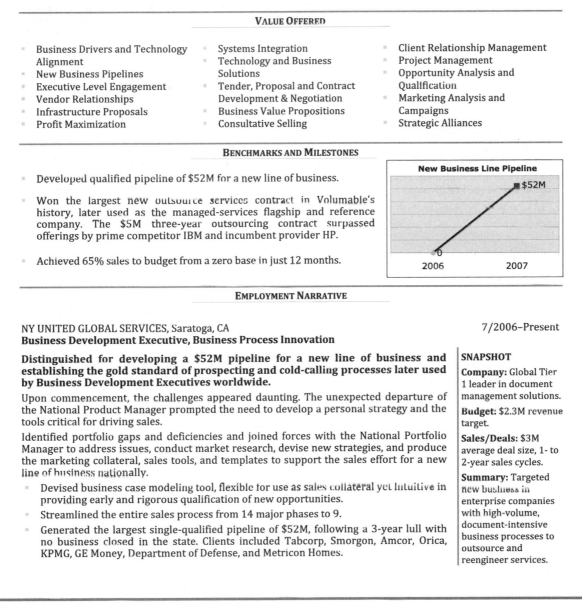

New Business Line Pipeline

$52M

0

2006   2007

EMPLOYMENT NARRATIVE

NY UNITED GLOBAL SERVICES, Saratoga, CA
Business Development Executive, Business Process Innovation

7/2006–Present

Distinguished for developing a $52M pipeline for a new line of business and establishing the gold standard of prospecting and cold-calling processes later used by Business Development Executives worldwide.

Upon commencement, the challenges appeared daunting. The unexpected departure of the National Product Manager prompted the need to develop a personal strategy and the tools critical for driving sales.

Identified portfolio gaps and deficiencies and joined forces with the National Portfolio Manager to address issues, conduct market research, devise new strategies, and produce the marketing collateral, sales tools, and templates to support the sales effort for a new line of business nationally.

- Devised business case modeling tool, flexible for use as sales collateral yet intuitive in providing early and rigorous qualification of new opportunities.

- Streamlined the entire sales process from 14 major phases to 9.

- Generated the largest single-qualified pipeline of $52M, following a 3-year lull with no business closed in the state. Clients included Tabcorp, Smorgon, Amcor, Orica, KPMG, GE Money, Department of Defense, and Metricon Homes.

SNAPSHOT

Company: Global Tier 1 leader in document management solutions.

Budget: $2.3M revenue target.

Sales/Deals: $3M average deal size, 1- to 2-year sales cycles.

Summary: Targeted new business in enterprise companies with high-volume, document-intensive business processes to outsource and reengineer services.

(continued)

Resume contributed by Gayle Howard, MRW
An eye-catching chart highlights Shane's most impressive achievements, which are described in more detail in the chronological Employment Narrative section.

(continued)

VOLUMABLE, Saratoga, CA

Business Development Manager

12/2004–6/2006

Won the largest new outsource services contract in the company's history, later used as the managed services flagship and reference company. The $5M three-year outsource service contract surpassed offerings by prime competitor IBM and incumbent provider HP.

Gained distinction as the first Business Development Manager to close deals across all seven lines of business within a single plan year—winning the highest number and value of new business for the company.

- Prevented damages claim and demand for refund from a failed Citrix implementation. Negotiated resolution of all outstanding issues without extra payment and persuaded customer to release additional funds to successfully complete the implementation.

- Assumed control of a customer dissatisfied with level of service and seeking to change suppliers at contract's end. Prevented loss of customer by building a convincing and credible case for a 12-month renewal with 1+1+1 options. Rebuilt trust through the effective sale and delivery of a major infrastructure upgrade and additional support services.

- Successfully closed $5M, three-year deal with DaimlerChrysler for desktop, help-desk, and network management outsourcing.

- Outshone competitors by closing $2M+ in new business with companies including NAB, Skilled Engineering, and Fosters Group.

- Delivered 250% to services revenue budget ($8M) and 113% to product GP budget ($712K).

SNAPSHOT

Company: Large systems integrator with $500M in revenues.

Reported to: Sales Manager

Sales/Deals: $1K to $5M, 1-week to 1-year sales cycle.

Summary: Targeted new business in SME and enterprise companies across all commercial verticals, with a full spectrum of technology offerings.

CORPORATE IT SOLUTIONS, San Francisco, CA

Business Development Manager

4/2003–7/2004

Gained distinction as a superior business-development performer, accomplishing 65% sales to budget from a zero base within the first 12 months. Later, handpicked to lead bid for the company's largest and most complex IT services proposal in its history that set a new benchmark for the ITS division.

In fewer than 12 months, provided leadership for many of the company's most prominent and strategic tenders and sales, in tandem with driving new innovations that enriched branding and reputation for quality of service delivery.

- Turned around long-term problematic yet strategic account. Beat aggressive competition in open tender to win back trust, securing the largest tender of its kind for a $1.5M national fleet refresh and network upgrade.

- Released "stranglehold" of several vendors with long relationships with Merrill Lynch. Within 6 months of establishing trust and optimizing service delivery on a small volume of sales, achieved preferred supplier status for all licensing, including MS Select agreements and hardware procurement.

- Selected to lead closed tender bid for major services and procurement contract for a leading bank—the company's first, largest, and most complex IT services proposal ever devised. Winning proposal was later acknowledged as having set a new national benchmark for excellence.

SNAPSHOT

Company: Largest supplier of a diverse range of business products to the corporate market revenues of $897M.

Budget: $650K GP ($5M revenue target).

Reported to: ITS Sales Manager.

Products/Solutions: technical services, managed services, procurement services, infrastructure products, software, and licensing.

EDUCATION

BA (Psychology) — University of California

Chapter 8

Advertising, Public Relations, and Marketing Communications Resumes

The functions of advertising, public relations, and marketing communications are integral to marketing and selling products and services. This chapter presents resumes that effectively communicate this area of specialization while showcasing overall contributions to marketing and sales success.

Tory Maguire

191-A Marlborough Street
Boston, MA 02116
617.555.8999
torymaguire@hotmail.com

FOCUS

STRENGTHS

Energetic, hardworking, and highly focused, with a passion for the business of advertising.

EXPERIENCE

Worked productively and energetically in a fast-paced environment with multiple ongoing activities.

Initiated planning meetings with sales team members to encourage delegation and stretch the parameters of my job.

Created innovative "Help Sheet" that provided structure for delegating assignments and collaborating on projects.

EDUCATION

Selected to co-direct the team's TV commercial. Placed third in region-wide competition.

Soaked up as much information as possible about the business of newspaper advertising.

ADDITIONAL INFORMATION

Advertising & Promotions

✓ Creative and observant, with a keen eye for the unique and unusual and the ability to translate these to marketing features.

✓ Talent for brainstorming, copywriting, and creative concept development.

✓ Complementary strengths in project management, organization, time management, and detail orientation. Proven ability to multitask and to juggle priorities to meet competing deadlines.

✓ Outstanding teamwork skills; energized by collaborative work environment.

BOSTON RADIO GROUP, Medford, Massachusetts
Promotions Assistant (2007–2009)

✓ Represented the company's radio stations (primarily KISS 108-FM, also WTAK 95-AM and WROC 85-FM) at a variety of promotional events, interacting heavily with the public and promoting both station and sponsor. On-air personality several times daily with live updates from promo locations.

✓ Managed details of a variety of promotional events. Contributed to brainstorming and concept and strategy development.

THE BOSTON HERALD, Boston and Quincy, Massachusetts
Sales Assistant (2006–2007)

✓ In newly created position, developed structure and activities that became a model for future sales assistants. Planned office organization following relocation from downtown to suburban sales office.

✓ On own initiative, took over the task of following up with clients on ad proofs. This enabled extensive client contact and the opportunity to advise on advertising strategies and copy improvements; concurrently, freed sales reps from daily proof calls and enabled graphic designer to better structure her time.

✓ Nominated for "Champion of Quality" award on several occasions.

UNIVERSITY OF MASSACHUSETTS, Amherst, Massachusetts
Bachelor of Arts in Advertising, 2006

✓ ADVERTISING COMPETITION TEAM: Participated in year-long competition sponsored by American Advertising Federation. With team members, developed and implemented creative concepts for assigned advertising client, including budget and comprehensive strategy (radio, print, TV).

✓ INTERNSHIP: Amherst Daily News, Amherst, Massachusetts, January–May 2006: Assisted retail advertising staff with diverse duties. Shadowed most of the staffers and maintained a daily journal.

✓ Strong computer skills: Word, Excel, PowerPoint, Quark, Dreamweaver.

✓ Portfolio gladly shared during interview.

The left margin is used effectively to call attention to qualities and experiences that will help Tory stand out from the competition.

Casey Strong

2759 Clifton Avenue • Cincinnati, OH 45217
513-209-1290 • casey_strong@mac.com

JOB TARGET

ADVERTISING — AGENCY-BASED CREATIVE & ACCOUNT MANAGEMENT

PROFILE

Versatile professional with creative streak, exceptional communication and teamwork skills, strong work ethic, and "just do it" (and do it right) attitude. Proven ability to thrive in fast-paced, demanding work environments that present diverse challenges. Background encompasses advertising, marketing, sales, promotions, TV, and radio.

EXPERIENCE SUMMARY

ADVERTISING—MARKETING—PUBLIC RELATIONS—PROMOTIONS
RADIO: Advertising Strategy & Campaigns, Copywriting, Voiceover, Production
TELEVISION BROADCASTING: Reporting (On-air & Scriptwriting), Production, Camera & Editing Work

ADVERTISING

Clear Communications (5-radio-station company), Dayton, OH   07–Present

ACCOUNT EXECUTIVE

Built client base from the ground up, using consultative selling skills and media knowledge to design radio advertising campaigns to fit the needs, budgets, and target audiences of each account. Manage all account activity, from sales (cold-calling, proposal development and presentation, negotiation) through service, promotions, radio schedules, and collections.

In a competitive market, starting from scratch, succeeded in gaining new business, penetrating "impossible"' accounts, and establishing partner relationships with key clients. Representative success stories:

- *Women's fitness centers:* Designed ad campaign and provided voiceover. Secured $2K monthly contract and doubled to $4K in second quarter. Ad was so well received, client sent it to national HQ as superior example of program marketing.

- *Dayton's largest Volkswagen dealer:* Built professional relationship and designed customer-appropriate ad campaigns that have the potential to deliver more than $20K in monthly ad revenue.

- *Xenia Toyota dealer:* Cold-called, built rapport, structured beneficial ad program tailored to client needs, and won $6K monthly ad revenue from largest competitor.

- *Retail jewelry store* (targeted unsuccessfully for 2 years by other reps and other radio stations): Zeroed in on target customer base and created convincing case for talk-radio advertising. Captured $5K initial sale.

- *Cincinnati financial institution:* Leveraged client relationships to earn introduction and then persuaded bank to expand its advertising into Dayton for the first time in its history.

- *Ice arena:* Landed 4-month, $6K campaign, ousting well-established competitor with dominant market presence. Developed innovative program concept and orchestrated Dayton Music Festival featuring local bands at ice arena—met client's goal of "cool" event that built attendance during previously slow periods. Generated $500 in co-marketing funds through outreach to record label.

(continued)

To support a career focus in advertising, we carefully presented diverse experience gained from several years of sales, marketing, and broadcasting positions. The success stories show creativity and a talent for advertising.

(continued)

Casey Strong

513-209-1290 • casey_strong@mac.com

| **MARKETING AND PROMOTIONS** | Pep Cola, Cincinnati and Dayton, OH | Mar 07–Aug 07 |

MARKETING MANAGER

Drove sales distribution of Pep-Pop energy drink in two markets, managing a team of subcontractors who promoted Pep-Pop at events every night of the week. Created promotional events and managed on-site implementation. Delivered weekly progress reports to Pep Cola executives in PowerPoint/Excel presentation format.

- Led the nation in sales and number of promotional events.
- Rapidly achieved sales penetration in 50% of target accounts.

| **BROADCASTING** | WTOL TV (CBS Affiliate), Toledo, OH | 05–07 |

TV NEWS REPORTER—PRODUCER—FILL-IN ANCHOR—OCCASIONAL ONE-MAN BAND

In fast-paced, demanding newsroom environment, performed every job, including on-set and in-field reporting, scriptwriting, editing, and camera work for 3 daily newscasts. Acted as producer for 3 weekend news shows.

| **BROADCASTING** | KDEN TV (ABC Affiliate), Denver, CO | 03–05 |

ASSISTANT PRODUCER (04–05), **REPORTER INTERN** (03–04)

Immediately hired for full-time role upon graduation. Wrote scripts from national newswire copy and information from reporters in field. Used beta equipment to edit segments to include VOs and teases.

| **PUBLIC RELATIONS** | Emerson College, Boston, MA | 01–03 |

PUBLIC RELATIONS/ACADEMIC COUNSELOR

Managed multiple programs designed to maintain academic performance of Emerson student-athletes, in compliance with stringent NCAA requirements. Prepared and presented study-skills seminars and provided personal academic counseling. Organized a professional media forum.

- Quickly advanced from part-time work-study position to full-time professional role (while attending school full time), filling in during Counselor's year-long leave.

| **EDUCATION** | Emerson College, Boston, MA | |

BACHELOR OF ARTS IN COMMUNICATION/MINOR IN JOURNALISM   03

- Dean's Scholarship—Dean's List
- Volleyball Scholarship—Volleyball Team Captain—NCAA Academic Award
- Senior Class Vice President

| **ACTIVITIES AND AFFILIATIONS** | |

- Dayton Advertising Club
- American Marketing Association
- Volunteer, Hamilton County Rape Crisis Center
- YMCA Volleyball Coach

Tamara Wilkins

81 Wild Meadow Lane
Durham, CT 06422

tamara_wilkins@aol.com

860-349-0090 Home
860-607-1218 Mobile

Goal

Public Relations — Marketing — Communications

Value Offered

- Creativity—in writing, page design, and approach to problem solving.
- Interviewing, writing, and reporting skills, honed through 3 years of experience writing front-page and feature articles for *Wesleyan Gazette.*
- Effective communication and presentation skills.
- Ability to work with diverse people, meet deadlines, perform under pressure, and rise to new challenges.
- Positive attitude and strong work ethic.

Education

Wesleyan University, Middletown, CT
BA Philosophy (2009)
- Strengthened critical-thinking skills through rigorous curriculum requiring extensive reading, research, writing, and analysis.

Truro Center for the Arts, Truro, MA
Biography Writing Class (Summer 2007)

Experience

Staff Reporter, *Wesleyan Gazette* (2005–2008)
- Reported and wrote news and feature stories covering campus events, activities, and organizations.
- Initiated publication of campus police reports.

Production Assistant, Middle Valley Photography (2007–2008)
- Provided on-site assistance during fashion photo shoots for corporate clients that included the Meriden Square Mall.
- Performed at a consistently high level in fast-paced, high-pressure, deadline-sensitive environment.

Marketing Assistant: Sandra Conway, RE/MAX Real Estate Agent (2007)
- Designed unique flyers to market individual homes for sale; managed projects from design and layout through proofreading and printing.
- Created organizational systems for files and paperwork; provided office assistance.

Senior Support Staff: Caché, Meriden Square Mall (2005–2008)
- Quickly promoted to senior position, supporting floor sales staff by closing sales and completing all cash-out functions.
- Selected to train all new support staff.
- Merchandised products and managed inventory.

Model: Manhattan View Modeling Agency (1999–2005)
- Modeled for fashion photo shoots.
- Quarterfinalist, *Elle* "It Girl" contest (regional competition, Boston), 2005.

Portfolio

Portfolio and writing samples gladly provided on request.

A script font, used judiciously, can help a resume stand out. Be careful not to use script for too much text, however; it can be hard to read.

Dana Forbes

75 Markerby Avenue, Reading, MA 01867
781-230-0716 • danaforbes@gmail.com

Creative Marketing Professional
Graphic Design — Photography — Print Coordination

Track record of building visibility, recognition, and positive market presence for diverse products and services through strong creative skills and proven ability to manage projects from concept to completion. Practical professional experience in all phases of marketing/communications project management. Effective problem-solving abilities and close attention to details and deadlines. Ability to communicate well with clients, vendors, fellow employees, and all levels of management.

- **Recommendations:** "Her creativity abounds… no matter what the job, she gives 110%." "I would strongly recommend her as a powerful asset to any company." "I was most impressed with her attitude, perseverance, and goal-driven attitude." "Not only does she work hard, but also she works smart. She completes projects on time and keeps peers updated on her progress. She would be an asset to any company."

Professional Experience

MARKETING DIRECTOR: Salem State University
2008–Present

Stabilized and unified brand image across regional campus and its 15 different units.

- Developed and executed comprehensive marketing plan and numerous campaigns to build awareness, image, and enrollments. Managed all facets from concept through creative design, photography, layout, and production; served as art director and worked with printing vendors on production. Updated photo files with current campus people and events. Developed new, brand-cohesive Viewbook (primary marketing vehicle for prospective students); built relationships campus-wide. **RESULTS:** Drove enrollments up 9% (previously averaging 5%) and achieved record turnout for important marketing events such as campus visit day and nursing program open houses.

- Directed multichannel advertising campaign. Wrote brand-cohesive TV and radio commercials and oversaw their production; handled media planning and buying; negotiated contracts and fees, seeking and gaining significant discounts. **RESULTS:** Secured $15,000 in print and web advertising for only $8,000. For spring radio campaign, earned Arbitron frequency scale of 5—a full point above average.

PHOTOGRAPHER: Corporate & Freelance
1998–Present

- Launched successful eBay business marketing limited-edition photographic images, 2005.

- For American Cancer Society (Danvers, MA), built event participation and contributions by creating effective marketing posters, flyers, and mailing materials. Acknowledged for putting "more 'feeling' into what was mundane paperwork." Requested to photograph regional events.

- Photographed business clientele and individuals: Smith Bros. Studios, Boston, 2003–2005; FotoFX, Hartford, 2000–2002; Marks Brothers Marketing, Hartford, 1998–2000.

A sharp design is part of the overall communications strategy for this resume. In the summary, the recommendations are a powerful endorsement.

Dana Forbes • Page 2   781-230-0716 • danaforbes@gmail.com

DESIGN ENGINEER: Elite Packaging   Attleboro, MA, 2007–2008

- Designed and managed production of bags for flexible-packaging firm. Created original artwork and adapted existing graphics; collaborated with R&D to create samples for unique customer needs; worked with production unit to ensure quality and timeliness of finished product. **HIGHLIGHT:** Creative lead on project that resulted in new printing process that provided a competitive advantage to our firm.

MARKETING MANAGER: South Shore Corporate Packaging   Weymouth, MA, 2005–2007

- Managed production of printed materials for packaging, point-of-purchase, advertising, publicity, trade shows, and product support; contributed to design of corporate web site. Effectively managed time, resources, and project details—never missed a deadline. **HIGHLIGHTS:** Completed 7 packaging projects in one year, versus one per year for prior Marketing Manager… brought innovative graphic designs and concepts to static marketing campaign… introduced use of photography for the first time in products' history… developed strong relationships with advertising account executives that resulted in beneficial treatment.

PROMOTIONS COORDINATOR: Pinstripes Productions   Hartford, CT, 2003–2005

- Gained radio airplay for band in the Hartford area, primarily through effective album design/overall visual presentation and persistent follow-up with radio stations.

ASSISTANT MARKETING COORDINATOR: YMCA   Hartford, CT, 2002–2003

- Revamped entire member recruiting package; produced effective, high-quality product on extremely tight budget. Managed project from concept through completion. **HIGHLIGHT:** As a result of campaign success, was chosen to develop and present program on low-cost marketing methods for 2003 National Assembly of YMCAs of U.S.

Professional Profile

- **EDUCATION**
  BA, 2002—Major: Studio Art; Emphasis: Graphics & Design   University of Hartford
  AS Design, 2000—Majors: Photography & Multimedia   Hartford Art School
  BS, 1998—Major: Marketing; Minor: Photography   University of Connecticut
  Dale Carnegie communications training (12-week course), 2008

- **HONORS & AWARDS:** Featured Artist at Gables Gallery, Salem, MA, 2005—record turnout and sales. Chosen as photographer for national advertising for L'Oreal and Bacardi, 1999. Selected to be part of National Portfolio for the Hartford Art School.

- **AFFILIATIONS:** American Marketing Association (AMA), National Council for Marketing and Public Relations (NCMPR), and University & College Designers Association (UCDA).

- **TECHNICAL PROFILE**
  Software: Photoshop, Illustrator, Dreamweaver, QuarkXPress, PowerPoint
  Photography: 35mm, 2¼, 4x5, studio and on-location lighting, custom color and B&W printing
  Audiovisual: dissolve units, external mike video mix units, video cameras, multiple slide projectors

Portfolio and complete references gladly shared on request.

Meredith Gray

513-869-0943   6841 Kenwood Road, Cincinnati, OH 45236   mgray@fuse.net

Marketing • Public Relations • Promotions
Advertising • Media Communications • Event Management

Strategic and action-oriented leader of effective marketing programs that generate revenue, boost attendance, attract sponsors, build advertiser participation, and create positive community image. Strong advocate of community groups; 16 years of experience in advertising, marketing, event management, and community relations, developing programs for schools, nonprofit organizations, and community fund-raising events. Expert in envisioning and negotiating win-win outcomes for sponsors, advertisers, and organizations. Effective team leader and project manager able to focus team and individual efforts toward common goals.

- Strategic Marketing Planning
- Media Kits, Media Buys, Media Relations
- Vendor & Sponsor Negotiations
- Market Research & Competitive Analysis

- Innovative Marketing Programs
- Creative Cost Reduction
- Schedule & Deadline Focus
- Multiple-Project Management

Experience and Achievements

The Cincinnati Journal,   Cincinnati, Ohio   2003–Present

Event Marketing Manager (2006–Present)

Promoted to lead strategic planning, marketing, and management of company-sponsored events—a diverse blend of community-relations programs, fund-raising events, co-sponsored activities, and education-related initiatives.

Create and execute comprehensive marketing plans. Plan, negotiate, and track print, billboard, radio, direct-mail, and television marketing messages. Develop and maintain profit-and-loss statements; analyze revenue and budget information to generate maximum impact for corporate and sponsor dollars. Conceive, negotiate, and manage corporate sponsorships and trade agreements.

Summary	Invigorated program planning and delivered measurable improvements in revenue, attendance, cost control, and residual benefits for all of the organization's major annual events. Sold event sponsorships totaling $965,000 in 4 years.
Print Run Road Race	• Increased participation 21% through highly targeted event promotions. • Cut 50% from T-shirt costs by buying in bulk for all of the newspaper's annual events.
Journal Soccer Tournament	• Doubled revenue and increased number of teams participating by 28%. • Transformed marketing focus from sports event to family program, providing an outstanding vehicle for local businesses to advertise at event that brings 12,000 people and $30,000 in revenue to the Cincinnati area. • Conceived new promotional-page layout and directed sales strategy that increased advertising pages from 1 to 12. • Secured hotel sponsorship that cut $700 from program costs, produced hotel sell-out, and created a competitive-bidding situation for next year's sponsorship.
Women's Expo	• Increased attendance 46% and program revenues 12% to 15% yearly. • Revitalized program and boosted company image by securing high-profile speakers at low cost. • Discontinued fee-based promotional services (saving $8,000 annually) and worked vigorously to secure new and higher-quality exhibitors. • Reduced costly services of outside consultant, saving $10,000 annually; took over vendor relations and persuaded 5 previous vendors to return as expo exhibitors. • Dramatically boosted visibility of nonprofit exhibitors by rerouting traffic flow; as a result, nonprofit participation increased 30% the following year.
Newspaper in Education (NIE) Program	• Spearheaded an aggressive sales campaign that increased orders from 1,200 to 28,000. • Secured third-party sponsor to share costs and further drive circulation growth. • Initiated follow-up contact with new subscribers to boost retention. • Researched grant-funding possibilities and grant-writing strategies; currently in process of writing grant proposals to secure program funding for 2009 and beyond.

Sidebar headings guide the reader and help organize a detailed resume.

Spelling Bee	• Conceived innovative sponsorship idea that resulted in increased advertising and community awareness while dramatically boosting quality and quantity of contestant prizes.
Additional Contributions	• Tracked sales and circulation trend data, creating reports for advertising staff that enabled them to increase revenues by selling demographically targeted advertising. • Motivated staff to surpass sales goals by focusing on customer service, interdepartmental communications, and quick, efficient responses to inquiries. • Initiated and led seminars to help nonprofit organizations improve the effectiveness of their advertising, fund-raising appeals, and corporate-sponsorship requests.

Marketing Specialist (2005–2006)

Transitioned to multifaceted marketing role and rapidly assumed leadership of special community programs as well as coordinating marketing activities and supporting a department of 11 individuals. Developed and maintained media kits and sales-presentation data.

Marketing Operations	• Slashed department operating costs 18% in first year by establishing a budget, streamlining the supply-ordering process, and reducing waste. • Attracted new advertisers and increased revenue by creating "bundled" advertising packages that allowed advertisers to increase and target coverage while earning volume discounts. • Eliminated mailing costs for several programs by collaborating with school districts for low-cost distribution directly to target audiences. • Developed marketing database that improved usability of marketing-department resources.
Community Relations	• Improved image and built visibility in the community by organizing employee volunteer opportunities, recruiting volunteers, and coordinating/managing events. • Initiated, organized, and moderated focus-group sessions with members of the community—resulting in changes/improvements to the paper, such as the introduction of a Friday "weekend entertainment" section. • Increased marketing power of various community and nonprofit organizations by devising marketing and advertising campaigns that maximized resources and reached target audiences.

Graphic Designer / Marketing Coordinator (2003–2005)

Working on-site at the paper's #1 account (a regional grocery-store chain representing nearly $4M in annual advertising revenue), planned and implemented comprehensive marketing and advertising strategies; developed themes, produced layouts, and managed production of print, billboard, radio, direct-mail, and television advertising.

Contributions	• Supported client's rapid growth from 6 to 23 stores, managing increased volume every year without adding staff. • Given free rein to develop and execute both innovative and traditional campaigns. • Improved store image by developing community programs and community-focused slogans and taglines. • Initiated weekly signage program that was effective in increasing sales.

Professional Profile

Education	Bachelor of Arts in Business Administration / Finance — GPA 3.7 — Miami University, Oxford, OH
Community Involvement	American Youth Soccer Organization • Board of Directors: Finance Director, 2006–Present; Publicity Director, 2003–2006 — Eliminated postage and production costs by initiating ad sales for organization newsletter. • Soccer Coach, 2005–Present Special Olympics volunteer
Computer Skills	• Microsoft Word, Excel, Access, PowerPoint • Adobe Illustrator; QuarkXPress; Multi Ad Creator; QuickBooks; TurboTax; Claritas market-analysis software; Map Info; other industry-specific software • Macintosh and Windows operating systems

Marcy Allen

250 Tammy Court, Nashville, Tennessee 37215

615-245-8090 marcyallen@aol.com

Profile

— **Public relations/communications professional** with an effective combination of *marketing, business,* and *creative* abilities and experience. Team-oriented, creative manager of people and ideas. Demonstrated ability to envision, develop, and market educational and entertaining presentations, programs, and events. Strong organizational and implementation skills; proven leadership ability. Experienced writer and skilled page designer.

Professional Experience

— GARDEN OF EDEN NURSERY, Nashville, Tennessee 2005–2009

Sales Manager (2007–2009)

Recruited, trained, and managed a top-notch sales team. Developed innovative training and sales tools that supported a resourceful staff and resulted in high levels of customer satisfaction. Created effective displays and signage. Played a significant role in planning, organizing, and managing entire nursery operation.

> **RESULTS:** Successfully instilled a customer-service focus and encouraged education and independent decision-making by staff. As a result, increased staff *and* customer satisfaction and reduced turnover (in a typically high-turnover industry).

Marketing Manager (2005–2007)

Designed and implemented marketing strategies for retail and wholesale business:

> Initiated and coordinated numerous large-scale public events both on- and off-site; engaged horticultural speakers, fine artists, craftsmen, musicians, caterers, and volunteers.

> Developed extensive mailing list and conducted market surveys.

> Created successful program of catered garden tours, lectures, and hands-on horticultural workshops that presented cutting-edge trends and information.

> Researched, photographed, and presented entertaining and informative lectures/slide presentations.

Responsible for development, maintenance, and profitability of extensive display gardens. As giftware/gardening merchandise buyer, coordinated selection and ordering of products for 2 garden centers, including selection of goods for start-up location.

— SPRINGFIELD VILLAGE HISTORICAL SOCIETY, Nashville, Tennessee 2003–Present

Major-Events Chair (volunteer, 2003–2006)

Conceived and organized successful community event/fund-raiser for 3 years. Recruited and coordinated communications for 6 co-sponsoring organizations, working committee, and over 200 volunteers. Currently involved as Committee Co-Chair, overseeing programming, fund-raising, and renovation of historic building.

> **RESULTS:** Attracted more people than any other event in the village's history; increased attendance, funds raised, and volunteer participation every year.

This resume includes volunteer experience because it was directly relevant to Marcy's career target of a PR/communications/event-management position.

Marcy Allen

615-245-8090
marcyallen@aol.com

Professional Experience, continued

— SPRINGFIELD, ROYCE VALLEY, and NASHVILLE SCHOOL SYSTEMS,
Nashville, Tennessee   2001–2004
Creative Drama Instructor (self-employed)

Independently developed and marketed successful extracurricular drama program for students in grades K–8 in 6 schools within 3 districts. Produced and directed full-length plays and original student performances using improvisation, puppetry, masks, storytelling, and mime.

> **RESULTS:** Increased number of programs each year through successful marketing and sales campaigns within individual schools and at the district level. Attracted new students through word-of-mouth marketing from satisfied students and parents.

— OUT-OF-TOWN PRODUCTIONS, Knoxville, Tennessee   1999–2001
Concessions Manager/Office Manager

Managed daily operations of theater concession business for Broadway, national, and international touring shows. Coordinated marketing materials for prospective investors. Oversaw construction/renovation of new office space. Redesigned office filing, invoicing, and inventory systems.

> **HIGHLIGHT:** Demonstrated valuable communication skill and discretion in contact with producers, talent, attorneys, and business partners during frequent absences of business owner.

— ALPHA OMEGA PUBLISHING COMPANY, Knoxville, Tennessee   1998–1999
Editorial Assistant

— KNOXVILLE COLLEGE, Knoxville, Tennessee   1995–1998
Drama Instructor

Education

— BELMONT UNIVERSITY, Nashville, Tennessee
  MA Communication Arts (in progress; anticipated spring 2010)

— UNIVERSITY OF TENNESSEE, Knoxville, Tennessee
  BA English

ALEX ANDREWS

75 Winding Trail, Boise ID 83713
Home 208-792-2309 ▪ Office 208-765-0921 ▪ alexandrews@gmail.com

COMMUNICATIONS / PUBLIC RELATIONS / MARKETING EXECUTIVE
EXPERTISE: Northwest Region Housing Finance Programs

Developed communications, marketing, and PR plans, programs, and initiatives that drove 400% growth in mortgage origination within the Idaho Housing Development Fund. Spearheaded market-expansion programs, including aggressive outreach to underserved Northwest communities, innovative/multistate programs, and national visibility for Idaho initiatives. Leveraged agency resources through extensive relationship-building and program coordination with nonprofit organizations, financing entities, federal and state representatives, and government agencies.

Proven ability to

- craft clear and compelling messages for multifaceted home ownership programs
- build relationships at all levels—federal and state legislators, lobbyists, financial institutions, professional associations, public-service agencies, consumers
- establish name recognition, brand identity, and positive image within multiple audiences
- tackle complex organizational challenges with creativity, practicality, and zest
- effectively communicate the dignity, potential, and promise of home ownership programs

PROFESSIONAL EXPERIENCE

Communications Manager, 1998–Present
Idaho Housing Development Fund, Boise, ID

In newly created position, shaped the role of Communications Manager—initiating programs to touch every one of the state's 44 counties, growing budget responsibility 30 times, and partnering with diverse agencies and organizations to increase the power, value, and effectiveness of statewide communications efforts. **Results:** 400% growth in number of mortgage originations; increased visibility and positive perception of the agency.

Perform full range of communications activities, from planning through detailed execution and follow-up. Build internal and external relationships to gain support and assistance for communications programs. Manage $300K communications budget. Member of executive staff developing IHDF policies and programs, including a variety of home ownership products to meet identified consumer needs.

Highlights of programs and achievements:

- **Built nonprofit relationships** through relentless outreach, joint program development, and shared mission.
  - Teamed with nonprofit agencies to identify home ownership success stories. Created publicity programs spotlighting agencies, availability of funding, and successful homeowners.
  - Partnered with Fannie Mae on successful joint programs (home ownership press event; Northwest Housing Summit sponsorship and participation).

Scope of responsibilities:

PROMOTIONAL MATERIALS
- Educational brochures and video
- Advertising
- News articles and press releases
- Annual report—website content

PRINT & ELECTRONIC MEDIA RELATIONS
- Primary media contact
- Press conferences and events
- Interviews—news stories
- Program information

PROGRAMS & SPECIAL EVENTS
- Event planning and management
- Team leadership
- Vendor selection and oversight
- Trade show displays

CONSTITUENT RELATIONSHIPS
- Citizens
- Legislators and lobbyist groups
- Affiliate agencies (federal, state, local)
- Board of Directors

HOUSING INDUSTRY RELATIONSHIPS
- Builders—Realtors—Bankers
- Nonprofit housing agencies
- Trade associations

PR AND PRESENTATIONS
- Panel presentations
- Industry and community speeches
- Internal training in public speaking

Blending PR, communications, and marketing communications experience in one job description, Alex's resume includes some strong, quantified achievements. Note the right-column box that allows detailed listing of responsibilities without detracting from the focus on accomplishments.

ALEX ANDREWS   Home 208-792-2309 ▪ Office 208-765-0921 ▪ alexandrews@gmail.com

Communications Manager, continued   Idaho Housing Development Fund

- **Pioneered television advertising.** Conceived, communicated, and coordinated a collaborative effort among the Housing Finance Agencies of Idaho, Washington, Montana, and Utah. Combined budgets and messages to promote affordable housing initiatives.

- **Staged successful media events** showcasing IHDF "success stories," with participation by Senators, members of Congress, Governor, Realtors, Fannie Mae, and other financing entities. Built strong legislative ties and earned significant publicity that consistently led to surge in inquiries.

- **Coordinated and hosted Northwest Housing Summit** (2008), an annual event in which 90 participants from state housing finance and nonprofit housing agencies in 5 regional states share programs, ideas, and strategies to better serve this niche market. Enlisted Fannie Mae as a sponsor.

- **Shared best practices and established national visibility for Idaho programs.** Frequent panelist and speaker for the National Council of State Housing Agencies communications sessions. Shared marketing experiences and successes with marketing peers at the national level.

- **Spearheaded educational programs.** Maintained in-depth understanding of 12 single-family and multifamily mortgage programs administered by the IHDF. Effectively communicated program details, facets, and benefits in layman's terms as well as to industry audiences.

Consumer Protection Director, 1997–1998   City of Boise, Boise, ID

Introduced groundbreaking programs and campaigns while representing consumers' rights. Performed extensive public speaking, community outreach, lobbying, and relationship-building in the business community and with diverse agencies and organizations.

- Initiated, coordinated, and hosted a weekly TV news segment providing education about fraudulent schemes, safety precautions, and other consumer protection news.
- Initiated Idaho's first legislation to prevent telemarketing abuse.

Sales / Marketing / PR, 1991–1997   Gem State Communications, Boise, ID

- Developed new business and managed existing accounts—consistently in top 20% in sales results.
- Built relationships that rescued a $100K account and captured long-sought business with Simplot.

PROFESSIONAL PROFILE

Education   Bachelor of Arts, 1988: University of Washington, Seattle, WA
          Master of Communications Studies, 2007: Boise State University, Boise, ID

Affiliations   Board of Directors / Past President / Volunteer (1993–2003): Idaho Good Neighbor Fund
          Member: Public Relations Society of America

Teresa Gomez

239 Cardinal Trail, Reston, VA 20193
703-309-2390 ▪ gomez@hotmail.com

MARKETING DIRECTOR ▪ ART DIRECTOR ▪ MARKETING PROJECT MANAGER

Developing and executing powerful, strategic, cost-effective marketing programs that build brand image, spur revenue and profit growth, and achieve strategic business goals.

- Strategic Marketing Plans
- Project Management
- Customer Loyalty Programs
- Creative Problem-Solving
- Team Leadership

- Brand Image Development & Management
- High-ROI Marketing Solutions
- Multimedia Marketing & Advertising—Print, Broadcast, Web
- Visual Design—Copywriting—Print Production
- Cost Control—Financial Oversight

EXPERIENCE AND ACHIEVEMENTS

Art / Marketing Director   **CLASSIC HOMES, INC.,** Reston, VA, 2004–2009

Unified and promoted powerful brand identity for a fragmented construction firm—spearheaded national sales and marketing programs that boosted sales, heightened visibility, and attracted acquisition interest.

Built and managed full-service in-house art and advertising department; directed local, regional, and national marketing and advertising programs; coordinated efforts of staff, freelancers, and agencies to achieve goals and meet deadlines.

- **Created and leveraged national brand identity.** Resolved a year-long stalemate and gained consensus from senior executives in multiple regions on use of logos and brochure materials. Initiated an aggressive brand-management and publicity program that garnered significant national attention, including a cover story in *Builder* magazine.
- **Slashed cost of marketing materials by 70%**—without diminishing quality or image—through expert knowledge of print production.
- **Overhauled website, extending the brand image,** and improved Internet marketing activities. Continuously added functionality and information in direct response to consumer comments.
- **Improved quality of photography to award-winning status,** including Gold at "The Nationals" and Silver at the Aurora Awards.

Art Director   **FREELANCE MARKETING PROJECTS,** 1995–2004

Delivered effective marketing solutions to diverse clients in multiple industries. Designed and produced newsletters, graphics, and advertising flyers; photographed products for use in advertising; managed projects start to finish and maintained exceptional client satisfaction.

- **Created a promotion for the Baltimore Orioles** baseball team and crafted a press release that resulted in a feature presentation in the *Washington Post.*
- **Built an art department from the ground up** for a new advertising-specialty division of a sports marketing company—managed design, layout, copywriting, and placement of print advertising.
- **Co-designed very successful trade-show booth and presentations.**

EDUCATION AND PROFESSIONAL DEVELOPMENT

- 2009—**Web Marketing and Design Certificate,** University of Phoenix
- 2008—**Certificates in Adobe Photoshop, Illustrator,** and **Acrobat**
- 1995—**Bachelor of Arts in Art History,** Villanova University

PROFESSIONAL AFFILIATIONS

- National Association of Photoshop Professionals
- National Association of Women in Construction

- National Home Builders Association
- Capital Area Builders Association

After a decade as a freelance art director, Teresa had taken a corporate position where she gained additional experience and delivered measurable results. Her concise one-page resume makes the most of this recent experience while also showcasing her freelance work.

Chris Brady

27 Village View Drive
North Branford, CT 06471

203-484-0943
brady@verizon.net

MARKETING / COMMUNICATIONS

Expertise in Health Care & Insurance Industries

Motivated, proactive marketing professional with a track record of initiative and results. Launched marketing department for a financial/benefits company; strategized, designed, and led multiple marketing, communications, advertising, and PR programs to build visibility and market presence.

- ▶ Efficiently managed multiple projects, adapting flexibly to changing priorities and varied tasks.
- ▶ Established pre- and post-program planning and analysis to ensure marketing efforts were aligned with business goals and delivering results.
- ▶ Improved business visibility, created beneficial strategic partnerships, and contributed to record business growth.

EXPERIENCE AND ACHIEVEMENTS

FINANCIAL BENEFITS COMPANY, Orange, CT   2004–Present
Privately held investment, insurance, and consulting firm with niche expertise in health care and not-for-profit industries.

Marketing Communications Director, 2005–Present

Promoted to newly created position—which I designed and proposed as a solution to an identified business need to build visibility and awareness within the Greater New Haven marketplace. Independently developed initiatives and overall direction for the position, steadily increasing activities and areas of influence while building knowledge of communications and marketing programs effective within our target markets.

- ▶ **Marketing efforts tied directly to business growth:** The company grew 15% annually in 2006, 2007, and 2008; in the previous 5 years, growth averaged 8%–10% annually.

Marketing Communications ────────────────────────────────

- ▶ **Newsletters:** Launched newsletters and oversee concept, design, writing/editing, and production.
  - — Employee newsletter (distributed to 45 employees)
  - — Group benefits newsletter (distributed quarterly to 3,000 New Haven–area employers)
  - — Securities/investment newsletter (sent quarterly to 7,000 investment professionals)
- ▶ **Advertising:** Develop all concepts and write copy for ongoing image advertising. Successful in increasing awareness, as reported by the sales team.
- ▶ **Brochures / Marketing Materials:** Produce 90% of marketing materials in-house. Write all copy; design layout; oversee production.
- ▶ **Web Site:** Managed all facets of creating company web presence. Created concept, wrote copy, and directed outside firm in design and development.

Public & Media Relations / Sponsorships & Alliances / Event Management ──────────

- ▶ Identify and approach potential partners for joint sponsorship of educational and community events. Manage partnerships and event details.
  - — Representative alliances: *New Haven Business Courier* (co-sponsor the annual "Health Care Awards" lunch); Greater New Haven Health Council (sponsor its annual business meeting and trade show).
- ▶ Boost business retention through trade-show sponsorships and events; manage all details of events, including pre- and post-marketing.
  - — Contributed to 95% retention of school-group business through participation in trade shows for school business and finance officials.
- ▶ Manage media relations and PR for quarterly "Benefits University" programs for area employers.
  - — Leveraged *Business Courier* relationship to gain program participation and media coverage.

(continued)

Within a broad marketing role, Chris really enjoyed the marketing communications aspects, so he decided to focus his job search in this area. The resume describes the broad scope of his activities but makes marketing communications most prominent.

continued

Process Analysis & Improvement

▶ Evaluated a variety of corporate business processes and identified opportunities for improvement and standardization.

▶ Created evaluation system to ensure the firm's charitable contributions and activities are aligned with niche markets and business objectives.

▶ Developed post-event analysis process to identify measurable results and opportunities for continuous improvement.

Training / Human Resources Development / Employee & Customer Surveys

▶ Implemented internal training programs to build employee skills in diverse areas, including e-mail etiquette and business writing. Located speakers and oversaw training events.

▶ Manage annual customer and employer surveys, including writing and administering the survey instrument.
— Consistently generate excellent response rate—40% for the most recent employer survey.
— Survey results are used to identify customer needs and business opportunities.

Account Manager, 2004–2005

Managed block of 85 small-business accounts for the firm's employee-benefits practice. As primary customer contact, resolved problems and provided information to ensure customer satisfaction and account retention.

▶ Exceeded the company's impressive 90% retention rate, losing just 2 accounts in 2 years.

▶ Recognized for ability to deliver personal and attentive customer service while managing a heavy case load.

EDUCATION

MBA, 2005
BA Political Science, 2001

Quinnipiac University, Hamden, CT
University of Connecticut, Storrs, CT

Michael Annunziata

2529 Ananas Boulevard, San Jose, CA 95135

mannunziata@usa.com ▪ 408-555-4444

Marketing Communications Professional

Expertise
- Creating comprehensive marketing communications strategies; executing print, audio, PowerPoint, trade-show, and web-site presentations to achieve marketing objectives.
- Translating technical information into compelling business-to-business marketing messages.
- Relating marketing messages to customers' needs and technical competencies.

Professional Experience

TECH SYSTEMS, INC., San Jose, California   2007–Present
Producer of Enterprise Resource Planning (ERP) software applications

Senior Marketing Communications Specialist

Contribute to the company's sales and marketing efforts through a variety of communications services:

- Interact with customers—MIS managers, PR officials, and manufacturing managers at Fortune 1000 manufacturing operations in North America and Europe. Visit customer sites and help pre-sales, sales, and post-sales staff identify key business issues.
- Edit quarterly magazine, *TECH TIMES,* targeted at both internal and customer audiences. Generate article ideas, interview key customers, write copy, and collaborate with designers and printers.
- Write customer histories and place in company web site and in trade magazines.
- Represent the company at trade shows, promoting products and services to sales prospects and the media.
- Research target industries and provide leads directly to the sales force.
- Introduce new processes internally to increase efficiency in the marketing operation.

Highlight
TECH TIMES named **"Best Magazine in the ERP business"** by Santoro Technical Research Institute. Competitors for this recognition were magazines from Oracle, SAP, Computer Associates, Baan, and other ERP vendors. (May 2008)

TECHNO-GRAPHICS, INC., Seattle, Washington   2005–2007
Producer of computer-controlled graphics tools

Marketing Communications Manager—*telecommuted from San Jose*

Directed the overall marketing communications strategy and provided a variety of creative services:

- Created concepts for print advertising; collaborated with designers on layouts for print ads and product brochures; wrote ad copy, news releases, and customer newsletter.
- Helped Japanese headquarters staff produce new-product materials for worldwide distribution.
- Recruited tech writers, designers, and industry leaders for marketing projects.
- Planned new-product campaigns and trade-show presentations.
- Interviewed press, dealers, and end users at 10–12 annual trade shows.
- Wrote and placed articles in magazines.

Key Accomplishments

Increased trade-show leads and customer traffic by more than 33%, achieved by recruiting respected industry professionals to demonstrate company products in an entertaining format. This trade-show presence was cited when company won 2006 "**Marketer of the Year**" award for its industry.

Enhanced status of the company's flagship product line by conceiving and producing a 12-page ad/brochure to upgrade our customer profile by showing the creative work of talented graphics pros who used the company's equipment. This initiative **contributed to a 30% U.S. sales increase** in 2006.

(continued)

Michael wanted to convey the level of responsibility at which he worked—not merely executing marketing strategy, but developing the strategy and programs for the company to communicate its marketing messages. Formatting enhancements call attention to notable highlights and key accomplishments.

Michael Annunziata mannunziata@usa.com ▪ 408-555-4444

TECHNO-GRAPHICS, INC.

Key Accomplishments, continued

Saved thousands of dollars by producing a 4-page advertisement/brochure internally. This piece, published in trade magazines, fueled the successful introduction of the company's first color-printing machine. Following introduction, the company rapidly reached and sustained monthly sales goals of $500K for this high-margin product.

Highlights Twice named Techno-Graphics **"Digital Employee of the Month."**

PACKAGE TRADE NEWSLINE, Los Gatos, California 2001–2005
Trade magazine for the packaging industry
Technical Editor

Investigated new products and technology trends in the custom-packaging industry. Wrote monthly column and 8–10 major articles each year and recruited industry leaders to write additional articles. Represented company at 4–5 trade shows yearly.

Highlights Developed the **3 most popular columns** in the magazine, according to a survey conducted by an independent marketing research firm.

Presenter, International Packaging new-product conference on digital imaging, Munich, Germany, March 2004.

TELECOM INFORMATION SYSTEMS, San Jose, California 1999–2001
Technical Writer for telecommunications software company.

TECHNO-DRAW CORPORATION, Dallas, Texas 1997–1999
Technical Writer for CAD/CAM software producer.

Education

RICE UNIVERSITY, Houston, Texas

Bachelor of Arts degree, English

TEXAS TECHNICAL SCHOOL, McAllen, Texas

Certificate, Computer Electronics

Joseph Markowitz

407-559-1245

8248-A Cypress Point Drive
Orlando, FL 32933
joemark@aol.com

MARKETING COMMUNICATIONS EXECUTIVE

Creative, results-focused leader, expert in devising and executing marketing strategies, campaigns, and communications programs that build corporate image and drive sales growth.

Accomplished professional with a consistent track record of results in both corporate and agency environments. Developed substantial new business with major accounts. Devised innovative consumer and business marketing, sales, advertising, and PR programs for clients that included Fortune 500 corporations. Consistently exceeded performance goals and delivered substantial business growth. Areas of expertise include

- Marketing Strategy & Execution
- New-Business Development
- Key-Account Management
- Staff Management & Motivation

- Marketing Communications
- Sales Promotions / Sales Campaigns
- Advertising & Public Relations
- Team & Project Leadership

PROFESSIONAL EXPERIENCE

DREAMLAND COMMUNICATIONS, Orlando, FL   2007–2009
Full-service marketing communications firm

Vice President, Marketing
Recruited to join start-up design firm to build large corporate accounts, both CPG and business-to-business.

- Spearheaded business transformation from design firm to full-service marketing communications provider, better serving diverse client needs and increasing opportunities to capture major projects. Developed new company portfolio and selling materials.
- Successfully developed major corporate accounts, generating $500K in annualized business, all new.
- Positioned firm as expert in field by writing and placing articles in leading trade journals.
- Chosen by major pharmaceutical and consumer-goods manufacturers to develop marketing campaigns for new-product initiatives, including a blockbuster new drug.

FIDO FOODMARTS, INC., Orlando, FL   2004–2007
$140 million global operator and franchiser

Director of National Consumer Promotions
Directed national sales promotion and relationship marketing programs for franchise and company stores.

- Initiated frequent-user club package system that increased sales 20%, generating $1 million in incremental revenue.
- Spearheaded successful restage of national relationship-marketing program, achieving 10% increase in member retention and 30% rise in franchisee participation.
- Implemented sales-promotion programs with 100 million impressions at no cost to system.

(continued)

Although his expertise is clearly in marketing communications, Joe has also handled multiple facets of marketing and management. Beginning with the summary, we kept the focus on mar-com without diminishing his other achievements.

Joseph Markowitz   joemark@aol.com • 407-559-1245

RESORT MARKETING AGENCY, Orlando, FL   **2000–2004**
$12 million marketing services / direct marketing company
  Manager, Client Services

  • Managed the agency's largest category account at above-standard profitability level.
  • Directed launch and managed frequency marketing program for *Orlando Sentinel,* achieving 50% increase in long-term subscriptions and 20% improvement in subscriber retention.
  • Created strategic direct marketing plans for Gannett communications properties.

SMITH HALSEY FRANKFURTER, Orlando, FL   **1995–2000**
$35 million advertising / sales promotion agency
  Account Executive, 1997–2000
  • Developed and implemented Drake's national "Takes the Cake" promotion. Sold promotion to Sears, resulting in first-ever brand display support and manufacturer partnership with a mass-merchandiser account.
  • Captured additional billings of $6 million through new-business efforts for sales promotion accounts.

  Public Relations Specialist, 1995–1997
  Planned, coordinated, and executed public, consumer, and media relations campaigns for Busch Gardens and the City of Orlando. Designed and coordinated national sales force communications and sales meeting programs for Colgate-Palmolive.

EDUCATION

Bachelor of Arts in Journalism/Major in Public Relations, 1995   University of Miami, Coral Gables, FL

Maria San Angelo

msanangelo@aol.com

225 Captain's Drive
Chelsea, MA 02150
Home (617) 792-3456
Mobile (617) 638-7890

Expertise

Executive Marketing Communications Management
Health Care, Financial, and Business-to-Business Markets

Strategic Marketing Planning	Program Planning and Implementation
New-Business Development	Trade Show Program Development and Participation
Relationship Marketing	Database Establishment and Manipulation
Operations Management	Agency Collaboration

Profile

Creative, results-oriented professional with track record of designing successful solutions to diverse marketing / communications challenges. High-energy, focused dynamo who moves easily from vision and strategy to implementation, problem-solving, and follow-through. Able to generate enthusiasm, participation, and support from individuals and teams at all levels, both internal and external. Skilled at operations / P&L management and staff / team leadership.

Professional Experience

MEDICA LABORATORIES, INC., Lynn, Massachusetts — 2008–Present
Director of Sales and Marketing

Challenged to increase revenue and market share for DNA testing laboratory poised for growth. Develop strategic marketing plan; create and implement marketing, communications, and sales strategies; direct the sales team; and collaborate with customer-service team to ensure a cohesive communications approach.

Manage $100K advertising budget; work with outside creative agencies. Supervise inside sales force (recruiting / hiring / firing / training / evaluation).

- Created the company's first ever strategic marketing document, with strategy and action plan to reach goal of doubling sales in one year.
- Developed strategic alliances with complementary organizations nationwide to establish Medica as industry expert and generate high-volume referral business.
- Refocused the company's advertising tactics to reach new target audience with the potential for significantly higher business volume. Concurrently, recast the marketing message in brochures, print, broadcast media, and billboard advertising.
- Overhauled all print materials, unifying company image and vastly improving graphic standards and professional appearance.
- Aligned sales team by industry expertise; improved focus, effectiveness, and customer responsiveness.
- Increased revenues 54% YTD through cumulative efforts.

MEDIA WORKS, Boston, Massachusetts — 1997–2007
Advertising and marketing communications firm known for award-winning integrated programs. Active in business-to-business, health care, and financial industries.
Vice President / Account Manager / New-Business Development Director

Directed client services, human resources, MIS, facilities management, professional and trade relationships, and lease and contract negotiations.

- Led team in design and implementation of business development plan. Reached plan goals for contacts and appointments; increased market share in targeted health care segment to 80% of business.
- Acquired NYNEX / Bell Atlantic national trade show program account under management contract, increasing client billings more than 15%. Program earned "Best of Best" trade show exhibit award.
- Spearheaded design of award-winning trade show program for Boston Business Forms.
- Implemented year-long direct-mail campaign that resulted in 30% to 64% increase in client's diagnostic imaging services business and won New England Hospital Association's "Gold Medal" award.
- Earned 52 national and local awards for various campaigns, internal and external crisis / risk / public relations programs, collateral materials, new-product introductions, logos and corporate identity programs.

(continued)

The Expertise section at the top of this resume is a good way to describe both general and specific competencies.

Maria San Angelo   Page 2

Professional Experience

DYNAMIC ADVERTISING, Chelsea, Massachusetts — 1992–1997
Advertising and graphic design, serving such clients as John Hancock, Gillette, WBZ-TV and Radio, NYNEX.

Account Executive, advancing to Manager, New Account Acquisition

Wrote the company's business-development plan and directed its implementation.

- Increased billings 50+% through acquisition of new accounts.

REDDI-SHOW, INC., Nashua, New Hampshire — 1990–1992
Custom manufacturer of trade show exhibits

Account Executive, advancing to Vice President of Sales

Managed trade show programs for key clients including Digital Equipment Corporation, Spaulding & Slye Real Estate, H.P. Hood, Wilsonart, and Boston Scientific. Also directed all new account development initiatives.

- Co-developed product launch program to introduce new Wilsonart products to the interior design industry. Program and products written up in *House Beautiful* and the *Boston Globe*.
- Achieved national publicity in *Real Estate Professional* for Spaulding & Slye trade show program.

CUSTOM OFFICE INTERIORS, Manchester, New Hampshire — 1988–1990
Designer / Sales Representative

Education   AA Interior Design: Massachusetts College of Art & Architecture, Boston

Professional Highlights

- Guest Presenter, Greater Boston Hospital Consortium: Crisis Public Relations
- Guest Lecturer, Massachusetts College of Art & Architecture
- Associate Board Member, Newsletter Editor: Massachusetts Society of Hospital Public Relations
- Director of Public Relations (volunteer): Boston Chapter MSPCA
- Facilitator, Executive Roundtable: Southern New Hampshire Chamber of Commerce

Additional Information

- Widely traveled (U.S. and internationally); available to travel and relocate.
- Fluent in Italian. Conversational skills in French and Spanish.

Chapter 9

Retail Sales and Marketing Resumes

The experiences and skills used in retail sales and marketing are not unique to that industry, but those who want to stay in the retail realm should be sure to include the right industry buzzwords to communicate insider status.

Samiya Rahman

23 Pacific Street
Portland, Oregon 97219
503-294-5030   samiya@hotmail.com

RETAIL SALES / MANAGEMENT PROFESSIONAL

Successful track record in

- **Improving sales and profitability.**

- **Managing operations,** with comprehensive experience in budgeting, merchandising, customer service, purchasing, and inventory control... P&L responsibility... strong leadership skills.

- **Planning strategically... envisioning outcomes... developing and implementing effective strategies for goal achievement.**

- **Building, leading, and empowering high-performing teams...** focusing activities on core organizational goals... developing staff for advancement.

- **Energizing existing activities through innovative operations and sales programs...** effectively communicating enthusiasm, energy, and team spirit to ensure program success.

- **Improving merchandising** at all levels: store appearance, floor layout, departmental displays.

- **Leading highly customer–focused organizations...** communicating, promoting, and ensuring a high level of customer service.

SELECTED ACCOMPLISHMENTS

- **Delivered exceptional profitability performance.** As store manager, exceeded both sales and profit goals for 4 consecutive years; through 3/09, exceeded *profit* goal by 122% on 0.4% increase in sales.

- **Significantly increased sales for a key annual promotion** (back-to-school): In 2006 (first year of management at Bayside location), increased event sales by 244%; in 2007, grew again by 140%.

- **Expanded breadth and depth of a major sales event,** incorporating additional departments and adding events of public interest. Grew sales 170% first year and 160% second year.

- **Initiated successful "Support Team" program** that freed up management time for floor supervision and sales training rather than labor-intensive paperwork. This program has since been adopted by other Standish's stores. Later, expanded the role of the support team to allow sales associates to focus more on our store-wide goal of providing "dazzling customer service."

- As Buyer for the volatile Juniors category, **increased business from $8.8 million to $11 million** and achieved **#1 sales status** among 11 Conglomerated buying groups.

- **Developed an exceptional track record of training, developing, and mentoring staff for advancement.**

CAREER HISTORY

STANDISH'S (a Conglomerated department store), Portland, Oregon: 1988–Present

Advanced through progressive management positions. Recognized for ability to achieve results through innovative thinking, leadership, and effective communication at all levels of the organization.

2006–Present	**Store Manager, Bayside** ($36 million annual sales; 23 managers, 350 associates)
2005–2006	**Store Manager, Valleyview** ($28 million annual sales)
2003–2005	**Area Merchandise Manager**
1997–2003	**Junior Sportswear Buyer**
1992–1997	**Department Manager, Bayside**
1988–1992	**Sales Associate, Western Rim**

EDUCATION

BA Business / Economics, 1990: Lewis & Clark College, Portland, Oregon

This functional format enabled us to highlight Samiya's diverse accomplishments without getting bogged down in repetitive details about the similar duties of her retail management positions.

Bonita Tavares

257 Moana Lani Trail
Honolulu, Hawaii 96815

Residence (808) 345-2345
Cell (808) 891-6767

Retail Sales / Marketing / Merchandising

Summary of Qualifications

- Extensive experience in all aspects of **retail merchandising and marketing,** with proven strengths in strategy development, implementation, staff development, and executive leadership.
- **Successful sales experience** built on strong customer service and knowledge of sales and merchandising strategies.
- A track record of building **highly effective buying and merchandising teams** through efficient recruiting, training, and motivation of staff.

Professional Experience

Manufacturer's Representative • CHAMPAGNE ASSOCIATES, Atlanta, Georgia (Hawaii territory)   07–09

Marketed numerous lines of gift items to gift stores; florists; floral wholesalers; and craft, garden, and chain stores throughout the Hawaiian islands. Key company representative at West Coast trade shows.

- Increased territory volume **600%** through development of new and existing accounts.
- Opened **150+ new accounts** and significantly **increased volume** in existing accounts.
- Established and maintained high standards for customer service and follow-up.

Vice President / General Merchandising Manager • SPORTS TRADER, INC., Honolulu, Hawaii   94–07

Managed the sales, merchandising, marketing, and advertising functions for full-line regional sporting goods chain. Reported to CEO.

Sales / Merchandising

- Developed and implemented merchandise and promotional plans that grew company from $4 million / 3 stores in 1994 to **$18 million / 7 stores** in 2007.
- Strengthened merchandising clout in the marketplace by developing partnerships with key vendors.
- Created and implemented all forms of advertising—television, radio, newspaper, and billboards. Managed **$200K advertising budget.** Implemented and helped create "Hey, Trader" advertising campaign that became extremely well-known throughout the islands.
- Directed highly successful soccer classification that grew soccer revenue from **$300K** to **$750K.**

Management / Operations

- Participated in **total corporate reorganization** plan that resulted in the company's emerging from Chapter 11 bankruptcy as a profitable, go-forward company in 15 months.
- Formed advertising partnerships with vendors that generated **$200K** in additional funds.
- Managed inventory planning / control. Successfully maintained inventory turnover at a better-than-average rate for the industry.

Divisional Merchandise Manager • WHITE HOUSE STORES, Orange County, California   92–94

$13 million full-line department store.

- Supervised 26 employees; consistently recognized for training and development abilities.
- Ranked **#1 in sales and profit increase** for 1992 and 1993 in Associated Dry Goods.

Management Assistant • CASUAL CORNER SPECIALTY STORES, San Jose, California   91–92

Mall-based national women's specialty chain.

- Achieved **10% sales increase** (well above company average) at fifth-largest store in chain.

Education

Bachelor of Science, Marketing • UNIVERSITY OF HAWAII, Honolulu, Hawaii   1992

Bonnie's long career with a sporting-goods store ended when the store went out of business. She was successful in direct sales but decided to pursue another retail sales/management position after moving to the mainland with her new husband.

JENNA B. WHITE

5900 Witte Road ▸ Turney, Missouri 64493
Residence: 816-632-5555 ▸ Cell: 816-632-5556 ▸ jennawhite@centurytel.net

RETAIL SALES / MARKETING PROFESSIONAL

AGGRESSIVE AND RESULTS-DRIVEN RETAIL PROFESSIONAL with a consultative approach to customer service and a genuine commitment to customer satisfaction. Proven leader with an eye to the bottom line and record of double-digit percentage revenue growth. Combine confident communication skills with a contagious enthusiasm and demonstrated ease in conversing across diverse audiences. Strong influencing skills exhibited at all levels of customer, coworker, and colleague. Possess an unshakable determination when challenged with strong personalities and demanding deadlines.

▸ **Retail Merchandising & Marketing**	▸ **High-Impact Presentations**
▸ **Staff Training / Development**	▸ **Organizational / Planning Skills**
▸ **Competitive Market Intelligence**	▸ **Solutions-Building / Problem-Solving**
▸ **Time Management / Project Management**	▸ **Dedication to High-Quality Standards**

HIGHLIGHTS

▸ Cinched **year-over-year profits** after launching fitness-supply store from start-up planning—market research, identification of location, and introductory advertising—to full operation. (Workout Gear)

▸ Achieved **35% to 45% revenue increase** month-over-month in retail business. (Workout Gear)
  - Identified/responded to customer needs by performing a consultative needs assessment survey.
  - Pinpointed, recruited, and trained customer-focused talent, ensuring staff's passions and abilities.
  - Excelled at customer retention: Cultivated personal relationships and facilitated a reaffirming, companionship-oriented, fun, and nonthreatening environment; performed a consistent written and spoken customer appreciation program; and orchestrated special client events.
  - Developed client advocates who touted Workout Gear's value to potential customers.

▸ Championed and led **high-profile projects/fund-raising**—Halloween festival, homeless shelter event, MS150 rest stop coverage—to increase Chamber's visibility. (Junior Chamber)

▸ **Boosted membership 130%** during tenure. (Junior Chamber)

▸ Won state Public Speaking Award and spoke at National Convention. (Junior Chamber)

CAREER SUMMARY

Workout Gear, Kansas City, Missouri   2003 to 2009
$70M in system-wide sales generated for Workout Gear franchisees in 2007/2008. (www.dancersize.com)
OWNER / FRANCHISEE

▸ Built start-up fitness-supply franchise from the ground up, competing successfully in a crowded market.
▸ Instituted regular advertising and promotional programs, including customer newsletters, thank-you cards, and media press releases that boosted customer retention.
▸ Used creative merchandising strategies to draw walk-by attention and generate media publicity.
▸ Grew revenue 35% to 45% month-over-month.

Junior Chamber of Commerce (Jaycees), Dayton, Ohio   1998 to 2003
Provides tools to people to build bridges of success in business development and philanthropy. (www.usjaycees.org)
PRESIDENT / VICE PRESIDENT

▸ As vice president, achieved 130% membership increase via high-profile program orchestration.
▸ As president, managed staff; directed initiatives in membership, finances, fund-raising, and projects; performed officer training, and acted as liaison between state and local chapters.

EDUCATION
BA in Communications / Minor: Business Administration, 1992

Resume contributed by Jacqui D. Barrett-Poindexter, MRW
A strong Highlights section pulls together achievements from both positions listed. The keyword list included in the summary is an effective attention-getter.

Toni Grevard

3490 Ranchway Drive #39
Dallas, TX 75214
469-671-4641   tonigrevard@hotmail.com

Sales / Marketing Professional

Exceeding sales targets... improving profitability... building and leveraging key account relationships... taking initiative to manage the business and deliver results.

Sales Success

- ✓ Met or exceeded sales goals each of the past 9 years in challenging sales environments.
- ✓ Customized product selections, sales programs, and presentations for specific customer needs.
- ✓ Delivered effective educational and sales presentations at the executive level.

Relationship-Building

- ✓ Provided "bend-over-backward" customer service that resulted in significant increases in revenue, account penetration, and profitability.
- ✓ Teamed with key accounts and internal resources to develop successful programs with solid profit performance.

Creative Problem-Solving

- ✓ Used proactive and creative tactics to prevent revenue shortfalls and lost business.
- ✓ Overcame obstacles to consistently deliver results.

Experience and Accomplishments

Lee Apparel Company, Merriam, Kansas   2000–Present
Account Executive: Dallas, TX (2006–Present)
Promoted to manage $40 million JC Penney account, #4 in the company, and $6 million Stella's account.

- ✓ Built strong customer relationships with key account. Refocused product selection; developed effective programs for special product categories; worked diligently to resolve product issues and ensure customer satisfaction.
  Results: 2007—increased product turn 25%, profit 4%.
            2008—grew sales volume 14.7%.
- ✓ Developed an effective planning tool that clearly showed necessary activity to reach revenue targets; captured additional $350K in business.
- ✓ Proactively addressed potential revenue shortfall, working with product development team to create a promotional piece with attractive profitability. Secured up-front commitment for two-thirds of volume needed to make production worthwhile; then approached other account executives for the balance. Exceeded revenue target and captured $900K in new business.

Account Executive: Nashville, TN (2003–2006)
Accountable for sales, profit performance, and overall management of two key accounts—Kohl's and three May Company chains. Performed full range of account management and sales functions.

- ✓ **Delivered outstanding sales results:**
  — Built Kohl's to Lee's #1 volume-per-store account and grew overall sales to $15 million.
  — Increased Youthwear volume 20%.
  — Grew business 22% in Special Size departments.

(continued)

Toni is involved in selling apparel to the retail industry. Because she would consider roles outside the industry, her summary is broad rather than specific.

Account Executive: Nashville, TN (continued)

- ✓ Rescued May Company business after corporate decision to discontinue Lee's lines. Leveraged relationships with buyer and divisional manager to create an assortment of fast-turning and profitable items in key stores; success with this initiative led to reinstatement company-wide.
- ✓ Proactively assessed account opportunities and recommended new programs to increase both sales and profitability.
- ✓ Introduced new products and expanded into new product categories.
- ✓ Communicated merchandising/presentation objectives to sales and management teams at more than 150 locations. Presented trend reports and product purchase recommendations at the executive level.

Field Sales Representative: Kentucky and Tennessee (2001–2003)
Managed $4 million territory with more than 400 accounts from specialty stores to regional chains.

- ✓ Increased territory sales volume by 12%.
- ✓ Built strong relationships with store managers, salespeople, and executives at client accounts.
- ✓ Created query system that gave replenishment information in faster, simpler form; system was adopted throughout the entire sales organization.

Retail Marketer: Kentucky, Tennessee, Mississippi (2000–2001)
Communicated company marketing and product strategy to #1 retail partner, Sears. Traveled three states, visiting more than 40 stores; delivered educational product seminars to customer employees.

- ✓ Improved product placement in stores, increasing visibility and stimulating traffic and sales.

Petite Sophisticate, Lexington, KY   1999–2000
Store Manager
Responsible for sales and profit of $2 million business. Trained, managed, and motivated 15 employees.

- ✓ Developed innovative service for mall employees; raised visibility and built customer loyalty.
- ✓ Successfully developed associates for management positions; 2 promoted within 6 months.

Parisian Department Stores, Montgomery, AL; Cincinnati, OH; Columbia, SC   1996–1999
Department Sales Manager (1997–1999)
Executive Sales Trainee (1996-1997)
Chosen for select management team that opened three new stores in new markets; provided start-up and ongoing management to $2 million departments in each location. Trained, coached, and supervised 25 employees.

- ✓ Initiated special programs and promotions to build customer base.
- ✓ Increased sales volume of Special Size department 45% (Columbia).
- ✓ Promoted the greatest number of sales employees of all departments in the store (Columbia).

Education

BS Marketing, 1996   University of Kentucky, Lexington, KY

ANTOINE JONES

7525 Gatehouse Lane
Loveland, OH 45140

AntoineJones@gmail.com

Home 513-859-2387
Mobile 513-905-1114

RETAIL SALES / MANAGEMENT PROFESSIONAL

Driving profitable growth for regional, national, and international retail operations.

Innovative, hands-on, inspirational leader of retail operations with a record of profit, people, and process improvements during 10-plus years of fast-track advancement through challenging sales/marketing/management roles. Demonstrated ability to establish best practices and instill corporate vision; quickly delivered results in turnaround assignments and restructuring situations. Talent for designing and launching programs that drive profitable retail traffic and spur year-over-year sales growth. Abilities and accomplishments in:

- P&L Management
- Revenue & Profit Growth
- Strategic Planning & Development
- Operational Execution & Productivity
- Business Planning & Forecasting

- Team Building & Relationship Management
- HR Management / Succession Planning
- Sales Team Training & Leadership
- Store Openings & Renovations
- Problem Solving & Decision Making

EXPERIENCE AND ACHIEVEMENTS

COLD COMFORT, INC.   **1995–2009**
Leading international retailer of super-premium ice cream.

▶ **Interim Director: South American Retail,** Santiago, Chile   2008–2009

Recruited to invigorate and reorganize South American Retail operations—14 stores in 6 countries, 60 employees, $5.4M sales. Directly managed 3 district managers and administrative staff; accountable for P&L and achievement of strategic business objectives.

Delivered rapid results amid corporate restructuring and uncertainty; exceeded all performance objectives, successfully instilled strategic vision, and created an effective blueprint for business growth.

- Achieved 9.5% annual comp-store growth rate.
- Developed 3-year strategic plan and operating plan for South American Retail operations; presented to president and CFO of Cold Comfort Worldwide, earned approval, and began implementation.
- Analyzed, identified, and closed unprofitable business in Venezuela for $300K EBIT savings.

▶ **Regional Manager,** Dayton, OH   2002–2008

Led 35-store, 10-state region ($25M sales) to top performance. Began with 22 stores, 6 states, $6.7M sales, and in 2003 corporate restructuring assumed leadership role for new, larger region—double the number of stores and triple the sales volume. Instilled a culture of *performance, excellence,* and *teamwork* and successfully led the region through turnaround, restructuring, and a challenging retail environment to consistent peak results.

Built the #1 region for Cold Comfort North America.

- Earned prestigious "Chiller" award for the company's top-performing region in 2003, 2005, and 2006, delivering greatest sales over prior year of all Cold Comfort stores in North America.
- Achieved 11.7% annual comp-store growth rate and exceeded financial performance goals every year.

Instilled vision and transformed culture, creating winning teams, boosting morale, and maintaining exceptional retention rates.

- Quickly turned around underperforming 4-state Central region (inherited in corporate restructuring), achieving sales-over-goal for the first time in 4 years. Key factor in financial improvement was leadership of a total culture change that became deeply instilled and bottom-line effective within 6 months.

(continued)

Antoine's strong retail experience was capped by a challenging international assignment. Bold achievement statements are supported by details in the bullet points below.

ANTOINE JONES

Home 513-859-2387 AntoineJones@gmail.com Mobile 513-905-1114

▶ **Regional Manager,** Dayton, OH, continued

- Achieved the #1 manager retention rate in the company through a talent-development strategy.
- Developed and implemented motivational programs and incentives that boosted performance in corporate benchmark areas.
- Effectively communicated vision, strategies, and goals to create a region dedicated top-to-bottom to continuous improvement.

▶ **Area Manager,** Columbus, OH   1997–2002

- Led a team of 6 stores with 40 employees and $1.9M sales.
- One of 17 managers chosen to pilot a new retail training & development program; delivered sales, profit, and overall performance improvements that led to expansion of the program nationwide.
- National Retail Achievement Award, 2000 and 2002.
- Regional Customer Service Award, 1999.

▶ **Store Manager,** Akron, OH   1995–1997

- Promoted from Retail Salesperson to Assistant Manager to Store Manager in 6 months.

PROFESSIONAL PROFILE

Education	BA Business Administration, 1961: University of Akron, Akron, OH
Certification	Retail Management certifications (PSS, MTP, MSS, MSC)
Affiliation	Member NRF (National Retail Federation)

CARLA SANDERS

11624 W. 112th Terrace ▶ Overland Park, Kansas 66211
913.451.1313 ▶ carlasanders@kc.rr.com

RETAIL SALES MANAGER ▶ STORE MANAGER ▶ STORE TEAM LEADER

Dynamic management career has included planning, managing, and controlling the profitable operation of a $30M, high-volume retail store in a manner consistent with the company's values and business image. Clear history of professional advancement is based on performance via strategic management/analysis efforts. Combine general management, P&L, and operating management experience with core competencies in marketing, business development, and cross-division management. Expertise is in start-up, turnaround, and high-growth companies. Focus is instilling exceptional guest service while developing/retaining key staff and achieving bottom-line goals.

AREAS OF ABILITY & KNOWLEDGE

Operations Management ▶ Profit and Loss Strategy ▶ Development of Strategies/Objectives to Meet Corporate Goals ▶ Staff Recruiting/Training/Motivating/Coaching ▶ People Development & Retention ▶ Forecasting/Meeting Scheduling Needs ▶ Customer Relationship Management ▶ Product Merchandising ▶ Payroll Management ▶ Competitive Market Trends ▶ Compliance with Policies, Administrative Processing, and Reporting ▶ Planning to Budget ▶ Start-up Planning/Staffing/Merchandising/Training ▶ Performance Management ▶ Financial Analysis ▶ Conflict Management

EXECUTIVE CAREER PERFORMANCE

AIM CORPORATION   2000 TO PRESENT

$42B upscale discounter providing quality merchandise at attractive prices in guest-friendly stores. (www.aim.com)

Fast-tracked through a series of progressively responsible leadership positions based on consistently increasing revenue, maximizing profitability, enhancing merchandising, containing costs, and delivering exceptional customer service/satisfaction. Introduced multiple people-development and operating strategies, procedures, and programs that were subsequently adopted throughout the organization and that contributed to revenue improvement. Planned, staffed, and launched start-up of the first SuperAim (regular Aim plus full-line grocery) in the Johnson County market.

STORE TEAM LEADER, OVERLAND PARK, KS/ST. LOUIS, MO (2004 TO PRESENT)
Hold full P&L accountability and overall charge of customer service, safety, logistics, merchandising, payroll, and margin management. Overland Park, KS: $30M sales, $4M operating budget, 180,000 square-foot retail and grocery store. St. Louis, MO: $25M sales, $3M operating budget, 110,000-square-foot retail store.

Bottom Line
▶ Achieved 8% year-to-date sales increase, 2008 (highest in district). (Overland Park, KS)
▶ 135% of goal for Aim Visa Card. (Overland Park, KS)
▶ Rallied executive and backroom leaders to reverse worst-in-district backroom error rate. Originated plan, processes, certification program, and rewards system that slashed backroom error from more than 5% to 2.3% in 3 months, consistently earning store top rankings and reputation area-wide as store to emulate. (St. Louis, MO)

Leading / Developing People
▶ Led 200 team members (mentored 15 executives, 40 team leaders, and 7 specialists) in Overland Park, KS. Managed 150 team members (mentored 9 executives, 20 team leaders, and 6 specialists) in St. Louis, MO.
▶ Developed 3 store managers, 3 store-managers-in-training, and 22 team leaders and specialists. Keys to success: Garnered 100% up-front commitment from each individual, established action plan, and closely monitored people through development stages and goal attainment.
▶ Retooled individual development plan for team leaders, simplifying an 8-page form to create a 1-page device focused on strengths/opportunities/accomplishments. Coupled form with structured executive follow-up and ultimately secured buy-in. Implemented plan across 300 regional stores; forecasted for rollout corporation-wide.

-CONTINUED ON PAGE TWO-

(continued)

Resume contributed by Jacqui D. Barrett-Poindexter, MRW
This retail manager's resume emphasizes bottom-line achievements; however, it also includes operational and staff accomplishments. These are indicative of the multifaceted role that people in retail play.

913.451.1313 ▶ carlasanders@kc.rr.com

EXECUTIVE CAREER PERFORMANCE
-Continued-

Customer Relationship Management / Process Improvement

▸ #1 in group of 90 stores for scores on customer satisfaction survey. (Overland Park, KS)

▸ Catapulted guest service scores from #7 to #1 in district. (St. Louis, MO)

▸ Fostered buy-in by executives and team leaders to a revamped trailer unload process by taking a field trip to another store and demonstrating the "benefits in action." As a result of implementing the process, cut 200 hours/week in St. Louis store and 150 hours/week in Overland Park store and enhanced guest satisfaction.

▸ #1 in district (9 stores) in cashier speed/sales floor response speed. (Overland Park, KS)

AIM CORPORATION, CONTINUED …

MERCHANDISING MANAGER, ST. LOUIS, MO (2000 TO 2004)

▸ Created standard merchandising program, instituted in 1,000 stores nationwide.

EARLY CAREER

▸ Sales, merchandising, and department management positions with Kmart and Best Buy.

EDUCATION AND DEVELOPMENT

MBA in Operations Management / Marketing Focus, 1999
BS in Finance, 1991
University of Kansas, Lawrence, Kansas

Graduate, Business College, 2002
Aim Corporation, Minneapolis, Minnesota

Chapter 10

Executive Sales and Marketing Resumes

In addition to strong sales and marketing results, executive resumes typically include evidence of corporate-level strategic activities and achievements. In many of these resumes you will note how early career experience is summarized just briefly, to make room for more recent (and more relevant) highlights.

T. Paul Eames

(H) 413-555-2525   (C) 413-555-0202

75 Kent Street, Unit 17C
San Francisco, CA 94117
tpaul@gmail.com

Senior Sales and Business Development Executive

❏ **Advanced Communications/Networking Technologies**

Top-performing sales and management professional with proven ability to drive business growth through aggressive sales initiatives that deliver revenue growth, market share, and market penetration. Strategic thinker who can plan and implement sales, marketing, and business initiatives to support corporate objectives. Experienced in technology/product launch, market expansion, and restructuring of the sales organization following merger, acquisition, and spin-off.

Greatest strength is identifying, establishing, and managing strategic partnerships to leverage the strengths of both partners and generate significant business opportunity.

Talent for identifying high-potential products and markets.

Professional Experience

MICRO-MASTERS COMPUTERS, INC., San Jose, California

❏ **Vice President, Global Business Development**—2008–Present

Retained by Micro-Masters following acquisition of NetAccess and challenged to build and lead a national and worldwide sales organization for communications/networking technology: remote-access servers and broadband (ADSL and cable) modems.

Direct the sales initiatives in 3 distinct channels: OEM, VARS, and access providers. Create complementary marketing programs to support targeted sales efforts and product focus.

- Successfully launched Micro-Masters as OEM supplier of broadband and RAS products.
- On target to achieve OEM percentage of $200 million sales quota in first year.
- Exceeded all sales and business development objectives established at time of merger.

Coordinate and manage sales programs and project teams to support our pivotal sales strategy: the establishment, maintenance, and expansion of strategic relationships with telecommunications providers and other key technology accounts. Identify new corporate opportunities through merger and acquisition, product development, channel development, and partner relationships.

- During first 6 months, established strategic partnership programs with Globaltel, Cal-tel, Bay Router, Kansas Computers, Clear Technologies, and Premier Cable.
- Beginning expansion to global markets (primarily European) through initiatives with international telecommunications companies.

Train, manage, and motivate 17 direct reports: sales team, systems engineers, project managers. Collaborate with Marketing and Engineering teams on new-product development and rollout. Accountable for sales results and profit margins.

NETACCESS (merged with Micro-Masters 1/07)

❏ **Director of Strategic Business Development**—2006–2007

- Grew OEM business from zero to more than 35% of company revenue.
- Established strategic relationships with Worldspan, Micro-Masters, and Couplers.
- Identified product potential and initiated acquisition of the NT RAS product line—now in its third generation and the foundation of future business direction and growth.
- Instrumental in developing the relationship with Micro-Masters that led to merger.

Paul had survived and thrived through several mergers and takeovers in the competitive, frequently changing world of telecommunications technology. There is a lot of name dropping in his resume to highlight the key players in the industry he had worked with. His accomplishments are easy to pick up in a quick read-through.

T. Paul Eames   (H) 413-555-2525 ▪ (C) 413-555-0202 ▪ tpaul@gmail.com

Professional Experience, continued

NETWORK SOLUTIONS (spun off NetAccess as a separate company, 11/06)

❑ **Director OEM Sales**—2004–2006

- Consistently led company in quota performance and total revenue generated.
- Established relationships with numerous manufacturers of computers and peripherals as well as telecommunications providers.
- Directly responsible for the business relationship that resulted in acquisition of Network Solutions and subsequent spin-off of NetAccess.

BUSINESS SOFTWARE SYSTEMS (acquired by Network Solutions 5/03)

❑ **Director OEM Sales**—2001–2003
East Coast OEM Sales Manager—2000–2001

- Recognized as the company's sales leader in quota performance and total revenue.
- Grew OEM sales program from ground up to more than 40% of company revenue.
- Established strategic relationships with key technology partners.
- Developed relationship with Network Solutions that led to its acquisition of the company.

ZEBRA SYSTEMS, Cupertino, California

❑ **District Sales Manager**—1998–2000
Senior Sales Representative—1997–1998

- Exceeded all sales quotas.
- Established distribution channel with national and regional distributors.

CIRCLE ELECTRONICS, Cupertino, California

❑ **District Sales Manager**—1996–1997
Computer Products Sales Specialist—1993–1996

- Exceeded quota 11 consecutive quarters.
- Significantly increased revenue within major accounts.
- Tripled share of total branch revenue supplied by computer products segment.
- Earned Advanced Technical Specialist certification from Intel and Control Data.

Education

B.S. in Computer Engineering, 1993: University of California at Berkeley

Jack L. Pierce

501 FM 3405
Dallas, Texas 78628
Mobile (512) 555-6399
jlpierce@alltelnet.com

SALES, OPERATIONS, & BUSINESS DEVELOPMENT EXECUTIVE
Expert driving sales, expansion, and profitability for start-up, turnaround,
and high-growth operations worldwide.

Proven top performer with start-up and Fortune 100 experience. Unique blend of technical and managerial expertise with advanced skills in strategic and tactical planning, international contract negotiation, new-market penetration, product development and launch, and resource allocation and management. Particularly strong relationship management, team building, and general business acumen; verifiable track record of success driving unprecedented revenue and profitability gains within highly competitive organizations, industries, and markets.

Visionary Planning & Leadership	Strategic Business Development
Product Expansion & Diversification	Global Sales & Marketing Management
Artificial Intelligence Engineering	International Project Management
Multinational Contract Negotiation	Team Development & Leadership
Mergers & Acquisitions	Debt & Equity Financing Negotiation

— Available for relocation —

PROFESSIONAL EXPERIENCE

Senior Vice President, Sales & Marketing
BJM Technologies, Inc. Houston, Texas (2007–Present)
Self-funded start-up, global provider of engineering software for the refining, petrochemical, power, pharmaceutical, and pulp & paper industries.

Recruited to provide all-encompassing leadership, creating vision, strategy, and structure for the organization. Reporting to the President, challenged to develop, direct, and maintain financial and business plans, cash-flow projects, revenue projections, manpower planning/development, and annual budgets presently exceeding $2.6 million. Continuously liaise between technology ("artistic") and engineering ("pragmatic") professionals, ensuring that current, foundational development supports the long-term sales and marketing vision.

- Designed/defined the e-Tools suite of engineering-specific software products, a groundbreaking, "intelligent" system and an exclusive PTI product.
- Developed and implemented appropriate sales vehicles that can overcome the barriers associated with inadequate messaging. Result: Increased sales from launch to $5 million in two years.
- Recruit and train the global sales force required to support planned revenue growth. To date, representation secured in Mexico, Canada, Korea, UK, and the Netherlands. By the end of 2009, expect representation in Venezuela, Germany, and Brazil.
- Continuously coordinate product development and release schedules to match revenue projections. Result: First order from an EPC company worth more than $2 million.

Director, Business Development—Continuous Processes
Emerson Electric—Performance Solutions Division Austin, Texas (2003–2007)
U.S. Fortune 100 company that designs and manufactures plant automation and control equipment, electric motors, telecommunications components, HVAC equipment, tools, and appliances plus services and engineering. Annual revenues are $16.5 billion; 100,000 employees worldwide.

With full departmental P&L responsibility, challenged to reverse steadily eroding market share by developing engineering services to complement existing deliverables. Managed all sales and marketing initiatives. Directed multimillion-dollar budgets for new product development and the 120-person global sales force.

Resume contributed by Debbie Ellis, MRW

Technology expertise is supported by an impressive list of publications, presentations, and patents on page 3 of this detail-rich resume.

- In a collaborative effort, instrumental in growing the (former Fisher-Rosemount) division from 150 people, $25 million revenue into a 2,200-person, $450 million organization within three years of tenure.
- Led the development of four new product lines resulting in $3.5 million in new sales and 10% increase in segment market share in two years.
- Delivered multinational, multimillion-dollar contracts ($5 million to $37 million) representing 65% of total divisional goals during the first year.
- In a partnership between Emerson Electric and GE Capital, negotiated project financing structures ranging from $5 million to $100 million and representing 30% of divisional revenue goals.
- Commuted weekly between Qatar, Korea, Germany, England, U.S., China, and Canada to coordinate and secure the support of 15 Emerson Division Presidents to win, over the well-positioned industry leader LG/Honeywell, a refinery expansion project from the Government of Qatar worth more than $37 million—the largest single project in Emerson history.
- Successfully reversing impending default status, renegotiated a highly complex, multinational $15 million contract with the Russian-based refinery, LukOil-Perm. Project was ultimately completed, surpassing profit projections by more than $1.2 million.
- Selected as key participant in the formation of Emerson Global Finance, a new division to provide financing for large-scale, multinational projects.

Manager, Business Development—Solutions Group
Fisher-Rosemount Systems Austin, Texas (2000–2003)
Division of Emerson Electric and a leading global supplier of high-technology process control and automation equipment. Annual revenues $2.8 billion.

Joined the organization as an internal consultant. Almost immediately, promoted into the new Products & Services Group, managing P&L and an annual budget of $3.2 million and providing direction and management for 20 software engineers, 9 direct reports.

- Created, led, and delivered the training programs responsible for pioneering sales for the division's software and engineering products and services worldwide.
- Designed and created two new products contributing to $10 million in sales with $1.5 million budget during first year.
- A result of the new products' success, organizational revenue delivered a full 60% of the Group's $25 million P&L.
- Solely and individually created and introduced a completely new control model, "Predictive Decision-Based System." Sought and won corporate support for building and patenting the unique prototype by selling the model as a "customer-funded-project" for $7.2 million. Sold three more systems during the execution of the initial project, generating more than $15 million in new revenue with no actual cost to the organization.
- The basic functionality of the system was quickly incorporated as standard into every control system and remains one of the division's most profitable products.

President/Consultant
BYTe Marketing Group Houston, Texas (1994–2000)
Privately held start-up that grew into a premier global consulting organization serving major clients within the controls and automation sector of the hydrocarbon industry. 2000 revenues $60 million.

Challenged to bring organization and structure to the loose partnership of independents. Successfully designed and implemented a business model to create a tangible asset to which all partners could contribute. Formulated budgets and core competency groups, making possible the migration from billable hours to contract assignments. Key client accounts include Honeywell, CAE, Invensys (Foxboro), Yokogawa, Hewlett-Packard, SACDA.

- As President, provided the strategic direction, leadership, motivation, and support to grow revenue (BYTe and its customers) from $5 million to more than $60 million in five years.

(continued)

Jack L. Pierce — Mobile (512) 555-6399 — jlpierce@alltelnet.com

- As Consultant, rescued client company from the brink of bankruptcy by moving it into a new industry and securing a contract generating more than $10 million in new sales within one year.
- Utilizing company personnel and with a budget of $4.2 million, designed, marketed, and sold a new simulation system for the Hydrocarbon Process ("EverGreen") that became, and remains today, a dominant program within the Hyprotech family of products.

PUBLICATIONS, PRESENTATIONS, & PATENT AWARDS

"Selecting Simulation Technology"—*Control Magazine,* 2007
"Selecting a Simulation Vendor"—*Control Magazine,* 2006
"Dynamic Simulation's Evolving Technology"—*Control Magazine,* 2005
"Dynamic Simulation: An Evolution"—*Control Magazine,* 2004
"Using Dynamic Simulation for Pre-Start-Up of an FCCU"—*Entech,* 1997
Exploring Dynamic Simulators with Control Applications (Coauthor M. Spuhler, ARCO)—2006 Petrochem USA
Using Control Systems with Predictive Control Applications—2005 Petrochem USA
Exploiting Object-Oriented Technology in Dynamic Simulations—2004 ISA USA
Exploiting Object-Oriented Technology in Dynamic Simulations—2002 ISA India
Using Equation-Based Simulation Solutions in Well Packing (Coauthor H. Klein, JAYCOR)—2001 Latin American Petro-Exposition
Using Equation-Based Simulations Solutions in Reactor Modeling (Coauthor H. Klein, JAYCOR)—2000 Latin American Petro-Exposition
The Multi-Uses of Dynamic Simulation—1999 Chile Instrumentation Conference
Using Dynamic Simulation in FCCU Studies—1994 ISA Brazil
Using Dynamic Simulation as a Predictive Analysis Tool—1997 ISA Brazil

U.S. Patent #5,752,008, Use of a control system in time other than real. 2000
U.S. Patent #5,752,009, Use of a control system as a simulation apparatus. 2000
(Both patents assigned to Fisher-Rosemount, a division of Emerson Electric)

PROFESSIONAL AFFILIATIONS

Current Member, Instrument Society of America (1991–Present)
Current Member, National Petroleum Refiners Association (1996–Present)

EDUCATION

Ashington Polytechnic
Ashington, Northumberland, England
Diploma, HNC Mechanical Engineering (Equivalent to Bachelor of Science)

SANDY GOLDFARB

79 East 179th Street, Apt. 204, New York, NY 10023
212-704-1120   sandygoldfarb@verizon.net

INTERNATIONAL SALES/MARKETING/BUSINESS DEVELOPMENT EXECUTIVE

Track record of notable sales, business development, start-up, and turnaround management accomplishments during 11 years in software sales in U.S. and European markets.

Fluent in French and Spanish, with strong cross-cultural communication skills and an extensive business and personal network throughout Europe. Adept in business communication/presentation to the executive level.

Ambitious, aggressive, and intensely focused on bottom-line results.

CAPABILITIES

- Develop and execute global market entry strategy and comprehensive organizational business plans.
- Build and manage business partner sales and customer support channels.
- Define internal/channel/external sales and consulting support processes.
- Manage and motivate sales teams to maximize revenues.
- Employ and teach consultative and target-account selling to build, manage, and close pipelines.
- Coordinate/manage/negotiate global, multisite sales campaigns.
- Create annual budgets, define forecasting processes, manage actuals versus budget.
- Craft clear compensation plans, territory strategies, and revenue-sharing guidelines.
- Negotiate win-win solutions in difficult or critical situations with prospects, clients, employees, business partners, and vendors.

PROFESSIONAL EXPERIENCE

ERPware, New York and Brussels—2007–2009
Director of Sales & Business Development: Europe

- Managed 35 sales, consulting, business partnership management, and operations professionals with combined revenue targets of $46 million in software, service, and maintenance. Exceeded all revenue goals:

	2007	2008	2009 (projected)
Revenue-to-Goal	109%	117%	112%

- Aggressively built pipeline of new business leads; in 16 months, generated $2 million in software and $4 million in service revenues from accounts not previously targeted.
- Transformed customer satisfaction scores from the lowest in the entire global organization to a record 72% increase in 1 year.
- Through persistence and a highly consultative sales approach, succeeded in capturing large/key accounts, gaining "company standard" status, and expanding ERPware installations to sites worldwide.

SIGNAL SYSTEMS, INC., New York, Paris, and Madrid—2005–2007
Major Accounts Sales Representative

- Recruited to Signal and challenged to turn around the company's stagnant European sales organization. Invigorated the sales team, rebuilt key account relationships, developed new business, and outperformed revenue targets:

	2005	2006	2007
Revenue-to-Goal	111%	134%	107%

(continued)

Exceptional sales achievements are highlighted in a table format, and a Capabilities summary section helps avoid too much detail in the position descriptions.

SANDY GOLDFARB

212-704-1120   sandygoldfarb@verizon.net

PROFESSIONAL EXPERIENCE, CONTINUED

SIGNAL SYSTEMS, continued

- Subsequently returned to U.S. and targeted European-owned accounts across North America. Developed new business and provided high-level customer support for complex technology implementations. Maintained consistently strong customer relationships.

ENTERPRISE SOLUTIONS, INC. (ERPware partner), London—2002–2005
International Accounts Sales Manager, 2003–2005
Marketing Manager: ERPware Solutions, 2002–2003

- Created and managed training/orientation program for European consulting team to ensure complete understanding of both the ERPware product and its business practices.

- Developed European-entry sales & marketing plan, trained sales team, and launched cold-call sales campaign to build pipeline. Leading by example, propelled sales team to results as high as 300% above goal.

	2002	2003	2004
Revenue-to-Goal	227%	275%	301%

- Working within tight budget constraints, created and executed marketing plan, published all materials, prepared ad copy, and developed and delivered seminars and trade-show programs.

- In 3 years, consummated 13 sales transactions and sold $3 million in software. Oversaw growth of the division from start-up to staff of 45 with $8 million in sales revenue.

- Bridged cultural and communications gaps to promote successful resolution of diverse business issues. Instrumental in resolving a contract dispute and thus enabling 3-year extension of partnership agreement.

EDUCATION

THUNDERBIRD, Glendale, Arizona
Master of International Management (MIM): 2002

UNIVERSITY OF MICHIGAN, Ann Arbor, Michigan
Bachelor of Science in Political Science: 1997

DAVID WASHBURN

Marketing & Business Development Strategist
Market Development Pioneer

Senior marketing executive experienced in building and nurturing successful organizations, mission-critical initiatives, and pioneering programs. Track record of accelerating growth by revitalizing business models, orchestrating beneficial strategic alliances, and creating acceptance for original concepts, new product categories, and innovative partnerships.

Full complement of executive leadership competencies, from business strategy and tactical implementation through management of P&L and all operational areas of fast-paced, technology-intensive organizations. Talent for inspiring team and individual performance above expectations.

PROFESSIONAL EXPERIENCE

GoNet.com, Santa Clara, CA   **2006–2009**

Leading provider of Internet-based business services.

VICE PRESIDENT OF MARKETING / GENERAL MANAGER OF VERTICAL BUSINESS UNIT

Recruited to provide marketing and business leadership to start-up business unit focusing on industry verticals; delivered immediate impact ($5M sales in first 6 months) through successful strategic partnerships and vigorous market development. Guided business strategy, product direction and development, brand positioning, product marketing, advertising, online/offline direct marketing, and public relations. Developed sales targets and appropriate lead-generation vehicles. Managed a $9.4M budget. In a highly matrixed environment, worked effectively with other senior management to execute on the company's strategy.

- Chief architect of the business unit's Growth Management Plan—determined sales targets, forecasts, and strategy to reach ambitious revenue goal.
  — Drove rapid-penetration initiatives, concentrating efforts on high-volume industries (such as financial services).
  — Directed technology-enabled marketing programs for customer acquisition, loyalty, and retention.
- Built a talented, versatile, and nimble staff who were able to capitalize on new learning and rapid shifts in the market.
- Led strategy and execution of programs to gain ubiquity across corporate desktops for GoNews newsletter delivery service—subsequently acquired by Microsoft.

Semitech, Santa Clara, CA   **2003–2006**

GROUP MANAGER, MARKET DEVELOPMENT / SEMICONDUCTOR

Defined and built the Windows CE market development department. Assessed market opportunities, created strategy, and launched initiatives encompassing competitive positioning, key messages, channel partnership plans, and performance metrics. Directed all related aspects of marketing communications and market research. Recruited, hired, and managed team of 8 marketing and engineering professionals.

- Key contributor to several "skunk works" projects to position Semitech in the next wave of chip application—worked with Apple to support Microsoft NT and built PowerPC NT support within Semitech and Microsoft.
- As Business Development Manager covering Asian markets, achieved design wins with multinational corporations.

david_washburn@gmail.com
25 Vanderbilt Way, Los Gatos, CA 95032

Home 408.742.3776
Mobile 408.814.2094

(continued)

Powerful introductory statements lead off each position summary for this resume showcasing a career in high-tech marketing and sales.

DAVID WASHBURN
david_washburn@gmail.com

Home 408.742.3776
Mobile 408.814.2094

Software Designers, Inc., San Francisco, CA   **1991–2003**

SENIOR MARKETING MANAGER, DEVELOPER PROGRAM, 2001–2003
SENIOR PRODUCT MARKETING MANAGER, 1999–2001

Authored and executed add-on strategy to sustain and entrench SDI products in existing vertical markets, leverage creativity of independent developers, and overcome competitive disadvantage that was eroding sales. As program manager for SDI Plus product line, stimulated development and marketing of add-on modules to core product line; defined the worldwide third-party developer marketing program; developed new distribution channels.

- Spearheaded the SDI Developers Cooperative—an innovative independent cooperative geared to market and sell add-ons for the existing SDI product line.
- Evangelized developer programs to the press, end users, and ISVs via press tours, direct mail, developer training camps, advertising, and trade shows.

INTERNATIONAL MARKETING MANAGER, SDI SOUTH AMERICA, Caracas, Venezuela, 1996–1999

Independently built South American subsidiary from the ground up to the company's #2 global market. Vigorously launched products, promotions, advertising, PR, and marketing programs to build strong presence and capture market opportunity. Provided sound business leadership (staffing, budgets, pricing, partner and channel development) for growing operation.

- Developed and strengthened partnerships with distributors and channels while consistently overachieving sales targets—grew sales 37% during recession and successfully launched 7 new products across South America.

OEM / CORPORATE MARKETING / SALES TRAINING MANAGER, 1994–1996
THIRD-PARTY MARKETING MANAGER, 1992–1994
MARKETING MANAGER, 1991–1992

Recruited as first marketing person for SDI, played a pivotal role in establishing crucial business partnerships, evangelizing the product line and establishing SDI as the market leader in CAD design software. Involved in all facets of marketing, PR, trade shows/seminars/events, and partner development. Repeatedly took on new roles and increased responsibilities during astonishing global growth of the company and industry.

- Successfully positioned SDI as partner-of-choice—developed, leveraged, and managed industry-first alliances for global product launches and joint promotions.
- Initiated highly successful Corporate Advisory Board and Corporate Services Program.

EARLY CAREER: Marketing Communications positions with Southern California technology companies

EDUCATION

BA, English, 1986: University of California, Berkeley

Susan Smith

Mobile: 923-333-5353
Email: susan.smith@att.net
1612 Cliff Street, Delaware, MD 54321

Senior Executive: Marketing | Sales | Customer Relations

Marketing strategist, innovator, and tactical leader of initiatives that build brand value and result in sustainable growth and profitability.

Accomplished executive with a flawless record of guiding startup and expansion organizations to profitable growth. Driver and champion of transformational programs; able to build internal support at all levels and create cross-functional project teams that deliver exceptional results. Expert in aligning strategy with organization vision and goals, interpreting the voice of the customer through enhanced customer insight and knowledge management.

- **Grew startup's sales** from $4.5M to $18M in 3 years. *(Radcliffe Laboratories)*

- **Repositioned marketing** to trigger $28M in new revenue. *(Badner Benefits)*

- **Led joint venture** to launch new product that exceeded first-year sales goal by 12% and achieved peak forecast of $500M within 3 years. *(Venture Pharmaceuticals)*

Value Offered:
Brand Building
Strategic/Operational Marketing
New Product Launches
Web-Based/E-Commerce Solutions
Cross-Functional Team Building/Leadership
Product Commercialization
Market Segmentation
Advertising/Public Relations
Consultative Sales Approach to Direct Marketing Campaigns
Market Opportunity Analysis
Strategic Alliances

Experience & Accomplishments

RADCLIFFE LABORATORIES, Catesville, MD, 2006–2009
(Start-up clinical/research laboratory that provides molecular testing services for leading organ-transplant hospitals and pharmaceutical/biotechnology research organizations)

Vice President, Marketing, Sales & Customer Service (2008–2009) | **Director, Marketing & Customer Service** (2007–2008) | **Director, Marketing** (2006–2007)

Planned, managed, and staffed all commercial activities of the company, creating business plans and marketing strategies and identifying new business opportunities that successfully grew market share. Member of leadership team that set strategic goals and new business/strategic alliance tactics company-wide.

Vision & Leadership

- **Delivered 30% sales growth** by developing strategic marketing plans, branding elements, public relations programs, promotional materials, and sales training standards that repositioned the company in new markets.

- **Raised the standard in hiring account executives and improved product/sales training** to shorten the time to first account from 6 months to 3 months.

- **Managed design and launch of website** that facilitated customer interaction and access to services.

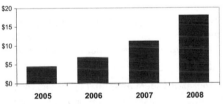

Sales ($ Millions)

- **Redesigned and expanded marketing platform and sales tools** to enhance brand image and ensure consistency of message across traditional and new media.

- **Implemented sales, unit, and financial forecasting models and a sales database** to allow analysis of company and individual performance.

- **Improved targeting, call effectiveness, and sell time** by implementing real-time reporting, sales performance expectations, and an integrated customer relationship management (CRM) tool for 3,000 clients and prospects.

Impact

- **Led commercial sales organization** to exceed goals year-over-year from **$4.5M in 2005 to $18M in 2008.**
- **Launched new division** that realized **$1.5M** in first-year revenues
- **Grew account base 36% and key accounts 32%** through segmentation and targeting initiatives.
- **Achieved 98.6% client retention rate** by monitoring customer needs and initiating new methods to ensure delivery on commitment to resolve client issues within 24 hours.
- **Automated the order-entry system by** using a web-based e-commerce solution.
- **Slashed error incidence 75%** by reengineering the data-processing system.

(continued)

Resume contributed by Marjorie Sussman, MRW
Susan's accomplishments are highlighted in bold type and with an eye-catching chart that visually demonstrates her sales success.

Susan Smith

Mobile: 923-333-5353
Email: susan.smith@att.net

BADNER BENEFITS, Kansas City, MD, 2002–2006
($1.2B non-medical employee benefits insurance provider)

Vice President, Segment Marketing (2004–2006)
Second VP, Market Planning & Analysis (2002–2004)

Generated $27.4M in new premiums over 2-year span through loyalty marketing program. Structured and led execution of marketing plan targeting preferred customer segments. Launched image campaign that realigned company and product line with $300M acquisition.

Vision & Leadership

- **Developed database marketing program** that targeted most responsive employer segments.
- **Implemented lead-generation program** that linked direct mail, print advertising, and website marketing efforts.
- **Introduced B2B promotional campaign** and a consultative selling approach as part of the direct marketing effort.
- **Expanded distribution** by adding direct and partnership channels to support existing revenue streams.

Impact

- **Triggered first-year market share growth of 25%** through branding and segmentation initiatives.
- **Catalyzed client retention 95%** through the implementation of new sales roles to reach end-users.

VENTURE PHARMACEUTICALS, Farnsworth, MD, 1990–2002
($7B U.S. division of $28B global pharmaceutical company)

Product Manager (1999–2002)
Manager, U.S. Commercial Development (1998–1999)
Manager, International Marketing (1995–1998)
Business Development Analyst, Global Business Information (1993–1995)
Account Manager (1990–1993)

Outstanding record of success and continuous performance-based promotion through progressive levels of responsibility to role of Product Manager tasked with planning and executing large-scale product promotions and new product launches in the U.S. market.

Vision & Leadership

- **Used psychographic profiling market research** methodologies to roll out a client loyalty/retention program based on long-term, high-potential, and repeat-purchasing habits.
- **Developed brand strategies,** collateral materials, and communication standards for 5 new products.

Impact

- **Generated $500M in annual revenues** as a direct result of launching a $30M promotional program.
- **Instituted $2.5M cost savings** through successful negotiations with advertising and public relations vendors.
- **Won *Fast Start Award*** for best product launch in 2002.

Education & Professional Development

EDUCATION:	**MBA** — UNIVERSITY OF FORT WORTH, Fort Worth, TX
	BS, Biology — UNIVERSITY OF TEXAS, Arlington, TX
EXECUTIVE PROGRAMS:	**Medical Marketing** — UCLA
	Accounting & Financial Management — Columbia University
	International Marketing — The Carl Düesburg Institute, Köln, Germany

Shelley Davis

3529 Slipperystone Lane
Cincinnati, Ohio 45208
Home 513-791-8345
Mobile 513-218-0921
shelleydavis@fuse.net

PROFILE

Senior executive with expertise in *strategic marketing planning* and *sales management* in the Technology/Telecommunications industry.

Track record of delivering strong results in sales growth, account penetration, and profitability. Key strengths include

- Developing and leading world-class marketing and sales teams.
- Analyzing markets; conceiving strategies; developing and executing action plans.
- Launching successful sales and marketing initiatives for new technical products.
- Building lasting relationships with new and existing clients.

Analytical and solution-oriented; customer focused; top-rank presenter and communicator.

PROFESSIONAL EXPERIENCE

GLOBAL TELECOM, Cincinnati, Ohio, 2005–Present
$15 billion worldwide telecommunications company

Director, Business Development (2007–Present)

Challenged to develop strategic market plans for the next generation of telecommunications systems technology. Additionally, continue to direct U.S. marketing strategies for digital wireless office systems following successful launch and penetration of vertical markets.

- Established joint marketing agreements with American Wireless, NationTel, and Bell Midwest, integrating capabilities to provide complete services to customers while expanding Global's outreach in rapidly growing digital wireless market.

Director of Sales, Enterprise Wireless Networks (2005–2007)

Led strategy development and implementation of sales/marketing program to launch Global's digital wireless technology in North America. Managed 3 sales managers and total sales and support organization of 25.

Conceived strategy of attacking vertical markets. Identified vertical markets with strong potential and directed the sales activities to capture those markets.

- From start-up in 2005, increased sales to $20 million and achieved the #2 market share in the U.S. for wireless systems.
- Established strategic partnerships with health care institutions. Became sole-source vendor for evolving wireless business that will represent millions of dollars per account over the next several years.

(continued)

The selected achievements are impressive and only briefly stated to avoid cluttering the resume. In a quick read, you can easily absorb key points of experience and accomplishments.

Shelley Davis   Home 513-791-8345 ▪ Mobile 513-218-0921 ▪ shelleydavis@fuse.net

TELE-SOLUTIONS, INC., Des Moines, Iowa, 2003–2005

Vice President of Sales

Guided Tele-Solutions from a small software supplier to a leading-edge, well-established provider of computer telecommunications integration (CTI) and call-center solutions. Recruited, trained, motivated, and directed national sales force.

- Increased sales from $750,000 to more than $5 million.
- Established distribution network of 5 regional Bell operating companies, 2 major independent operators, and several hundred small companies.
- Played a key role on Initial Public Offering team that structured $50 million IPO.

NATIONAL TELECOM, Chicago, Illinois, 1997–2003

Regional Sales Manager

Managed telecommunications region composed of 16 Midwest states.

- Established National in education vertical market with sales to 9 state university campuses.
- Successfully penetrated State and Local Government market niche.
- Grew sales to more than $20 million.

Director of Sales Support—Directed all engineering, proposal, and sales support activities for National in the Midwest.

Manager, Major Accounts—Successfully introduced new PBX system into Midwest region.

U.S. TELEPHONE, Evanston, Illinois, 1992–1997

Marketing Manager

Developed strategies and market action plans encompassing all traditional market management functions (price, place/channel, promotion, product).

- Initiated an innovative consultant liaison program.
- Formed financial marketing program that was the first to use outside sources to finance U.S. Telephone technologies.

EDUCATION

Bachelor of Arts and Sciences—University of Chicago, Chicago, Illinois

Professional Development
- Global Telecom Quality and Management Program
- U.S. Telephone Management Program
- Extensive education in telecommunications, computer technology, sales, and marketing

Gunther Mahre

77 Piccadilly Place
London W1 UK

Cell phone/voice mail: (44) 444-122-221
gmahre@telecom.com.uk

Profile

Senior Executive: Marketing • General Management • Project Leadership

Proven ability to create competitive value, identify and exploit business opportunities, establish and maintain market share, and devise and implement solutions to a wide range of business, technology, sales, and marketing challenges. Able to drive change, achieve objectives, and effectively manage projects in both corporate and institutional environments.

Skilled in strategic planning, budgeting and P&L management, team leadership, marketing, and delivery of technical products and services. Effective and experienced at leading teams and individuals in a matrix organization as well as traditional line/staff structure.

Widely experienced in global business initiatives, from market and technology studies through launching and running a business operation. Talented negotiator with keen cultural awareness.

A proven performer and leader who thrives on new challenges.

Professional Experience

EUROCOM—2004–Present

EUROCOM GREAT BRITAIN, London, UK

2009–Present   **Strategic Marketing Director**

Lead comprehensive marketing initiatives to extend and consolidate the company's 20% global market share:

- Design and establish the company's world price policy with dual focus on market share and margin. Continually evaluate and adjust policy to ensure competitive yet profitable pricing programs. Monitor and allow for multiple, constantly changing currency valuations. Direct 3 person pricing support team; also collaborate with other business units to develop and disseminate the price policy.

- To maintain long-term leadership in the market segment, research and propose new products, identify and develop new business alliances that leverage EuroCom's global service base and exploit partners' local service capabilities.

- Implement the market intelligence function for EuroCom's Wireless Capabilities Center, maintaining competitive knowledge of competitors, industry activities, and technological advances.

EUROCOM, Auckland, New Zealand

2007–2009   **Director—Southern Pacific**

Launched EuroCom's wireless solutions in the Australian/Southern Pacific market, directing the marketing function while concurrently managing business operations for rapid-growth start-up subsidiary with local and expatriate offices.

- Built this market from the ground up and gained leading market share status in 2 years.

- Participated in drafting (as liaison to legal department) and then independently negotiated and signed contracts that generated significant and sustained revenue: US$150 million in 2008.

EUROCOM, Mexico City, Mexico

2006–2007   **Corporate Product Line Representative—Central and South America**

Opened markets in Mexico, Belize, Argentina, and Chile. Provided general management and marketing leadership to establish and grow market share. Led collaborative team efforts among EuroCom personnel already on site in these locales.

- Led market research and analysis initiatives that identified and quantified these key business opportunities.

- Generated first-year business of US$40 million.

(continued)

Gunther had been using a traditional European CV but wanted a more dynamic U.S.-style resume to present his qualifications to U.S. and multinational companies.

Gunther Mahre Cell phone/voice mail: (44) 444-122-221 • gmahre@telecom.com.uk

Professional Experience, continued

EUROCOM MUNICH, Munich, Germany
2004–2006 **Senior Marketing Advisor**

- Performed the first global analysis and assessment for a billion-dollar niche market opportunity.

- Challenged to identify, analyze, and assess quality R&D problems and procedures affecting time-to-market. Collaborated with international consulting groups; developed and presented proposal that, if implemented, would have cut in half the company's time-to-market.

SCHMIDT INDUSTRIES, Munich, Germany—1995–2004
2001–2004 **Telecommunications Director**

- Directed the investment of US$200 million into telecommunications technologies, most of them new.

- Reduced operating expenses 20% yearly through organizational redesign, new technologies, and staffing reductions.

- Managed as many as 1,000 employees in line/staff organization.

1999–2001 **Project Director**

- Managed more than 20 telecommunications projects at the national level, many with ongoing operations.

1997–1999 **Advisor to Financial Director**

- Led reengineering initiatives for telecommunications installations.

1995–1997 **R&D Engineer**

Education

International Management in the Telecommunications Industry—London Business School, 2003

Executive MBA, 1999—University of Munich, Munich, Germany

Telecommunications Engineer Degree, 1994 —Technical School of Berlin, Berlin, Germany

Additional Information

Languages: Bilingual German/English; fluent French and Spanish.

Comfortable in multicultural environments. Business experience in 27 countries on 4 continents.

ELIZABETH E. WILLIAMS

lizwilliams@aol.com

3289 Wickham Avenue
Verona, NJ 07044

Residence: 908-635-5478
Cellular: 908-695-8874

SENIOR MARKETING EXECUTIVE
Accessories – Intimate Apparel – Luxury Brands – Beauty Products

SEALING THE PRODUCT'S BRAND INTO THE HEARTS OF CONSUMERS
Orchestrating integrated, multimedia marketing communication campaigns that propel brand awareness, accelerate customer traffic, secure customer loyalty, and increase bottom-line sales.

BRAND AWARENESS • CONSUMER PERCEPTION • SALES, REVENUE & PROFIT GROWTH

Pioneering, strategic-thinking executive with dynamic record of delivering marketing solutions that transform interested consumers into loyal customers. Consistently introduced new, "first-of-its-kind" marketing and advertising concepts that resulted in product differentiation and competitive advantage for leading retailers.

—MARKETING MANAGEMENT EXPERIENCE & PERFORMANCE HIGHLIGHTS—

SENIOR VICE PRESIDENT – MARKETING AND ADVERTISING, CLEARSOLES INTERNATIONAL, INC.   2006 to present

Brought on board to reposition and rebrand products suffering from declining sales due to increased industry competition. Restructured traditional advertising and direct marketing programs to support integrated marketing strategies that included direct mail, e-commerce, in-store visuals, and trade show exhibitions. Managed $12 million budget and staff of nine employees.

- **Public & Media Relations:** Attracted premium coverage in high-profile media outlets *USA Today, The Today Show, O The Oprah Magazine,* and *Lucky* magazine.

- **Online Product Promotions:** Drove significant surge in online product sales by directing the content development and relaunch of Clearsoles.com.

VICE PRESIDENT – MARKETING AND ADVERTISING, MAIDEN BRANDS, INC.   2003 to 2006

Recruited to develop and execute comprehensive marketing strategy for company's top-selling product during a period of accelerated growth. Charged with instituting advertising, branding, and communication initiatives to build product awareness, increase customer loyalty, and expand market share. Managed $10 million budget, nine employees, and contracts with advertising/public relations agencies.

- **Revenue Growth:** Championed the development of marketing and product promotion techniques that doubled annual revenues in just three years.

- **Corporate Branding:** Engineered a corporate-wide rebranding plan for product differentiation and identification. Revamped all corporate marketing materials and collateral, including company logo, building signs, business cards, and shopping bags.

- **Corporate Communications:** Garnered employee buy-in by introducing bimonthly corporate newsletter that celebrated employees' successes and increased peer-to-peer collaboration.

- **New Product Marketing:** Conceived the largest new product launch in 20 years by assembling fully integrated marketing program with department stores—direct mail, store displays, sales events, and special promotions. Organized international marketing campaigns in London, U.S., Canada, and Malaysia.

- **Public Relations:** Doubled product exposure in leading fashion magazines—including a featured editorial in the *New York Times* business section—by commencing highly targeted public relations events.

- **Product Brand Awareness:** Escalated product brand awareness to 97% by synchronizing marketing programs during events leading up to company's IPO on the New York Stock Exchange.

(continued)

Resume contributed by Abby Locke, MRW
Functional subheadings lead off each bullet point to draw attention to areas of expertise and results.

POLO RALPH LAUREN CORPORATION   1990 to 2002

Rapid career progression through increasingly challenging roles in brand and advertising campaign management, global product marketing, and multimedia marketing communications. Repeatedly instituted strategies that drove annual sales, promoted brand awareness, and increased product recognition. Career progression:

VICE PRESIDENT – MENSWEAR MARKETING, POLO BRANDS (2001 to 2002)

Selected to implement new marketing strategies and ignite sales growth for the Polo Ralph Lauren, Polo Sport, and Polo Golf brand in menswear department. Restored existing business relationships with national retailers to confer on cooperative advertising efforts, sales promotions, and special events. Managed $45 million budget and supervised up to 15 employees.

- **Multimedia Marketing Communications:** Drove sales on featured product 25% by pioneering a retail marketing program during the Father's Day shopping period for the first time in company history. Devised full scope of marketing, advertising, and branding initiatives encompassing direct mail, newspaper placements, in-store visuals, and charity special events.

- **Strategic Partnerships:** Delivered 40% increased sell-thru on featured product sales by forging media partnership between Polo Golf and *Golf Digest Magazine*.

VICE PRESIDENT – LICENSEE MARKETING (1997 to 2001)

Challenged to originate multifaceted luxury-brand marketing program for international affiliates in London, Paris, Hong Kong, Tokyo, Sydney, Santiago, and Buenos Aires. Tasked with creating marketing materials for in-store advertising, media, and public relations programs and identifying the right product mix for international consumers.

- **Global / International Marketing:** Spearheaded, coordinated, and hosted the company's first International Marketing Conference to educate global marketing executives on the Ralph Lauren brand, forge viable working relationships, and collaborate on standard marketing guidelines.

- **Strategic Market Plans:** Orchestrated store opening plans for seven freestanding locations and developed international marketing campaigns for 100 Polo shop-in-shop concepts.

- **Competitive Product Positioning:** Revitalized brand awareness and piqued consumer interest by developing shop-in-shop retail concepts, increasing media exposure opportunities, and coordinating high-profile special events.

DIRECTOR – RETAIL ADVERTISING (1993 to 1997)
MANAGER – RETAIL ADVERTISING (1990 to 1993)

Promoted to manage advertising and product branding programs for nationwide retail stores. Liaised between retail stores and corporate marketing department to ensure consistency in product promotions and advertisements.

- **Product Promotions:** Gave company access to $2 million in value-added programs by strategically negotiating magazine advertising.

- **Product Branding:** Increased product sales 25% and generated subsequent increases between 15% and 40% by launching Specialty Weeks with retail partners at flagship locations.

- **Public Relations:** Acquired more than $3 million in public service advertising incentives through financial support of a federally sponsored restoration program.

—EDUCATION—

BS, Marketing and Communications – Columbia University, New York, NY

S. J. McKenzie

540 Wishing Well Place, Mt. Prospect, IL 60056 ■ 847-294-7872 ■ sjmac@aol.com

Profile

Marketing / sales management professional with proven ability to build market presence—to create and execute integrated marketing and sales programs that improve visibility, sales, penetration, and account base while efficiently using marketing resources. Track record of developing products and building territories from the ground up to become substantial contributors to bottom-line success.

Proven management capabilities include strategic planning, P&L accountability, budgeting, and hiring/training/supervision. Strong interaction and relationship-building skills.

Consistent top performer eager for new challenges.

Professional Experience

General Manager / Sales Manager — <u>McKenzie Enterprises</u>, Mt. Prospect, IL, 2007–Present

Manage all business activities and sales functions for manufacturer representative firm marketing industrial equipment in 9 north-central states. Develop business growth strategies and operating procedures while performing direct sales and account service.

- Launched business and grew territory from negligible sales to $3.2 million annually.
- Achieved 57% sales increase for each of 2 primary product lines.
- Planned and executed successful integrated marketing and sales campaign to develop market presence in new territory—research and prospecting, direct mail, trade shows, cold calls, product demonstrations.
- Expanded territory from original 5 states after 18 months. Identified and contracted with independent agent in newly expanded region.

Vice President, Marketing and Sales — <u>Northern Industries</u>, Chicago, IL, 2005–2007

Industrial equipment manufacturing company — division of Acme Industrial Gear, Inc.

Held P&L accountability and management responsibility for all marketing and sales functions. Developed and executed strategies; managed staff of 22, including 7 regional sales managers. Developed ongoing corrective plans and cost-control measures to steer profit results to projected targets.

- Developed marketing plans that increased product demand by 150% without incremental investment.
- Generated a sales plan with pricing policies that added $650K to bottom line in 2006.
- Directed advertising, PR, direct mail, master list maintenance, trade show activity, and collateral material creation. Increased quality and output in all areas while reducing expense budgets by 10%.
- Co-invented and developed a revolutionary new product that launched to market in August 2006 and projected to add 6% to Northern Industries' overall sales in 2008.
- Forecast product sales by market to support the top-line goals.

(continued)

This resume shows an effective treatment of an entrepreneurial venture. Rather than use the "owner" title, we used job titles that reflect primary areas of activity that are relevant to current goals.

S. J. McKenzie

Page 2 ■ 847-294-7872 ■ sjmac@aol.com

Professional Experience

Marketing Manager — <u>Patco Engineering & Equipment Company</u>, Appleton, WI, 1997–2005

Created, directed, and implemented sales and marketing programs. Generated pricing policies, product line forecasts, promotional programs, advertising / trade show schedules, and service policies. Oversaw 9 direct reports and 18 independent sales representatives nationwide. Provided in-house product training, dealer training, and sales / service support.

- Contributed to five-fold growth of company from $3 million in 1997 to $15 million in 2005.
- Contributed numerous new product ideas and successfully expanded the company's single product offering to multiple integrated product lines.
- Steadily increased sales even during extended labor strike. Located and contracted with subcontractors to maintain production levels.
- Developed key account and national account networks with major retailers (such as Giant Industrial Supply) and catalog merchandisers. Successfully penetrated targeted accounts and grew business (in one instance, from minimal amount to $250K annually). Maintained close account relationships to protect catalog page placements.
- Guided creation of the company's first major / national marketing program.
- Researched and developed new target markets.

Promoted after one year performing customer service, equipment modification, and in-house training in **Technical Sales & Applications Department.**

Programmer — <u>Green Bay Systems Consultants</u>, Green Bay, WI, March–December 1996

Education

- Bachelor of Science in Industrial Science, 1996
  Marquette University, Milwaukee, WI
- Continuing education in Marketing and Programming
  Loyola University, Chicago, IL

Professional Affiliation

- MANA — Manufacturers Agencies National Association

FELICIA A. GARRISON

8223 Parlane Drive, Falls Church, VA 22041
Cell: 202-658-2540 ✦ Email: fgarrison@hotmail.com

SENIOR MARKETING EXECUTIVE
Director / Senior Vice President / Vice President

"I deliver growth for companies—every time." Accurately forecasting industry trends and consumer interests that allow companies to exceed revenue projections, maximize ROI performance, achieve strong profitability, and realize significant market growth.

Accomplished, passionate senior executive with proven record of delivering unprecedented revenues, profits, and market performance for startup, emerging, and growing companies operating in competitive, evolving industries. Forward-thinking strategist able to structure new program / service releases, finance investments, and joint ventures that increase business growth and minimize financial losses. Broad-based expertise with marketing to diverse cultural and ethnic groups in untapped domestic and international markets. MBA.

Core Marketing Management & Leadership Competencies

Strategic Market Planning & Direction	New Product / Program Development	Joint Ventures, Alliances & Partnerships
Market, Industry & Trend Analysis	Domestic & International Businesses	Revenue, Sales & Profit Growth
Cross-Cultural Marketing Strategies	New Business Development	Corporate Branding Initiatives
Staff Recruitment & Leadership	Project Management & Execution	Customer Relationship Management

CAREER PROGRESSION

Vice President of Sales & Marketing – North America, Middle East, and Eastern Europe
International World Television, Washington, DC (2003 to present)

Spearheaded company-wide initiatives that more than doubled revenues, tripled number of television channels, and strengthened oompany's position in the highly competitive broadcasting industry.

Scope: Implement innovative marketing strategies, advertising campaigns, and dealer incentives that spur business growth and service expansion. Oversee development of telemarketing plans, marketing brochures and letters, and cross-promotional programs. Collaborate closely with senior management to initiate programs and services that support long-term business growth objectives.

▸ **Business Growth:** Drove new operational, marketing, and business development strategies that impacted significant budget growth from $18 million to $40 million.

▸ **Sales & Revenue Expansion:** Generated more than $200 million in annual sales over five-year period through new satellite capabilities.

   – Achieved highest sales in company 2006, 2007, and 2008—consistently increased sales 25% each year.

▸ **New Program Development:** Played a pivotal role in influencing senior management to introduce Pay TV capabilities that helped company expand from 50 to 250 television channels.

   – Initiated 20 new "hot bird" television services in Europe and achieved $15 million in new revenues for five consecutive years.

▸ **Contract Negotiations & Agreements:** Negotiated and acquired lucrative agreement with LodgeNet, the largest company in the hospitality industry, and increased channel / service distribution to more than 6,000 motel / hotel outlets in North America.

   – Generated $10 million in new revenues by consulting and settling on two US government bids (for Hispasat satellite services) for DTH distribution in Latin America and the Middle East.

   – Landed 60 international IPTV contracts with major companies like Verizon, AT&T, MobiTV, and ConnecTV for additional channel distribution.

▸ **New Business Development:** Forged high-level business relationships with broadcasting companies including CNN, The Weather Channel, Encore Movie Channel, BBC World, The International Channel, Rogers Cable of Canada, and Comcast Cable.

(continued)

Resume contributed by Abby Locke, MRW
This distinctive resume leads with a personal branding statement that is supported by the many impressive achievements featured in the sections that follow.

Director of Sales & Marketing / Corporate Liaison
International Television Corporation, Washington, DC (1997 to 2003)

Launched aggressive sales strategy that propelled company growth from start-up phase to $10 million in annual revenues despite mounting industry competition and high-level financial risk.

Scope: Recruited by president to join new company that recently acquired the rights for two television channels. Assumed directive to grow business operations; lead marketing, promotional, and advertising campaigns targeted at ethnic and international customers; and build corporate brand. Managed vendor, dealer, and affiliate relations.

▸ **Business Growth:** Launched aggressive channel distribution, customer acquisition, and marketing strategies that attracted 200,000 new customers in record time.

▸ **Staff Training & Development:** Orchestrated comprehensive training and supervision of more than 300 customer service representatives serving a multi-cultural, multi-ethnic customer base.

  - Provided direction on wide scope of customer relation techniques including cultural differences, ethnic nuances, and customer opposition.

▸ **Marketing Direction & Planning:** Instituted standard procedures for marketing campaigns, employee operations, and dealer incentive programs.

▸ **Executive Advisement:** Partnered with vice president of sales and marketing and president to conceptualize sales, marketing, and business growth strategies.

▸ **Project Planning & Leadership:** Steered comprehensive project involving conversion of 130,000 international customers, supervision of 12 employees, and development of new marketing campaigns. Completed project in nine months versus normal 12- to 18-month timeline.

Sales & Marketing Manager
ABC International Marketing Division, Arlington, VA (1994 to 1997)

Exceeded sales and revenue projections by devising structured campaigns and leading strategic planning efforts for global sales in unpenetrated markets.

Scope: Directed myriad activities impacting new policies and procedures, new business opportunities, corporate goals and objectives, domestic / international dealer networks, contract negotiations, advertising, and budget administration. Reported to director of sales and marketing.

▸ **International Business:** Instituted new financial documents, business contracts, and letters of agreement that allowed company to conduct business internationally.

EDUCATION & AFFILIATIONS

BA in Marketing, University of Virginia, Charlottesville, VA (1994)
MBA in Marketing, Georgetown University, Washington, DC (2007)

STEPHEN P. MORRIS

83 Elm Street, Durham, CT 06422

860-555-8590 home • 860-555-8545 cell

stephen-morris@mac.com

QUALIFICATIONS SUMMARY

- Highly motivated and accomplished senior sales management professional with track record reflecting consistent advancement throughout career. Key industry and technical knowledge of instrumentation, controls, and valves across broad range of industries (pulp and paper, chemical, petrochemical, energy).

- Proven ability to develop strategic alliances, manage and close long-term projects, and master in-depth, highly technical knowledge and expertise.

- Strong technical sales ability combined with unwavering commitment to ethics, integrity, and honesty. Expert coaching skills with proven ability to elicit top performance from all levels of organization.

- Special expertise in developing and building sales channels and new distributor/ representative/reseller networks while aggressively penetrating new markets.

PROFESSIONAL EXPERIENCE

2007–Present   VALVE-PROS, INC. • Middletown, Connecticut

Vice President

As an original founding partner, dually manage sales and operations for key player in global high-performance valve industry with two international partners as well as an interest in the U.S. In start-up phase of establishing business, oversaw all components of infrastructure (from site selection/leasing to appointment of professional consultants, attorneys, and accountants). Established highly effective relationships with distributors, end users, and OEMs and developed protocol for training staff.

- Developed and implemented company's first comprehensive national sales and marketing campaign, elements of which include website design, development of all print marketing components, training of representative network, and creating new sales tools; directly manage staff of 4.

- Grew sales from $0 to nearly $160K in first year, $450K in second year, with potential pipeline representing in excess of $1.2 million at start of third year.

- Established importation logistics for all products, identifying optimal broker relationship. Mastered extensive knowledge of importation tariffs/duties and taxes as well as managing product launches stateside for global manufacturers.

- Collaborated with president to create highly effective national distributor network; mastery of technical product knowledge and logistics enabled seamless start-up.

- Pioneered well-designed inventory-control systems to monitor product and maximize profits while ensuring satisfaction of customer needs.

- Establish sales forecasts/budgets; track P&L; maintain AR to less than 33 days.

- Maintain up-to-date knowledge of all foreign currency exchange rates, adding significant value to cost accounting/pricing and AP policy decisions; assess implications of all financial decisions to maximize margins.

- Successful in securing industry approval from American Bureau of Shipping for Swiss line of imported products.

(continued)

Resume contributed by Jan Melnik, MRW

Leading off each accomplishment with a bold, black-square bullet helps make them easy to distinguish, which is important in a fairly lengthy list.

STEPHEN P. MORRIS   860-555-8590 home • 860-555-8545 cell • stephen-morris@mac.com   Page Two

---

PROFESSIONAL EXPERIENCE   (continued)

2004–2007   FOX INSTRUMENTS, INC. • Hartford, Connecticut
Outside Sales Representative
Fully oversaw all sales, marketing, and sales forecasting responsibilities for existing clientele while cultivating new business opportunities for industrial instrumentation distributor for the chemical, petrochemical, and pulp and paper industries.

- Orchestrated successful turnaround of sales operations through rejuvenation of existing accounts and highly effective account development across new niches; boosted sales by more than $.5 million in first year and consistently ranked among top two sales reps for entire company.
- Developed extensive industry knowledge and technical/applications expertise across 35 product lines; served in expert consultative capacity to clients.
- Achieved successful sale of first complete field bus installation in the U.S.
- Effectively managed through to successful closure projects across a broad range of sales cycle times; drew upon keen solutions-oriented approach to working with varied customers' applications and problems.

1998–2004   NORTHEAST INDUSTRIAL SUPPLY • Schenectady, New York
Branch Operations Manager, West Hartford
Direct responsibility for sales and operations management for branch facility of industrial supply house (gauges/fittings with instrumentation specialty). Extensive account development across territory comprising all of New England. Instrumental in developing annual sales revenues of $7 million branch operation.

- Successfully established instrumentation product line to rank in top third of all products from its previously negligible standing in bottom third for Northeast.
- Created extensive customer service communication program, impacting sales efforts across all channels (from customers and outside sales reps to branch and senior management); initiated redesigned quoting and proposal process.
- Effectively managed staff of 5 direct reports; oversaw all human resources activities, from recruiting and hiring industry experts to training and supervising; established key performance measurements and evaluated individual performance of all direct reports on an ongoing basis. Implemented highly effective motivational and incentive programs.
- Engineered JIT inventory management system to carefully balance most optimal inventory levels to ensure customers' needs were met while maximizing ROI.
- Developed state-of-the-art technical training for associates; authored quality manuals and collaborated extensively with senior management in designing and implementing key incentive programs targeting specific performance indicators.
- Involved in ISO 9000 and 9001 certification readiness audits and processes.

EDUCATION   WESLEYAN UNIVERSITY • Middletown, Connecticut
- **Bachelor of Science / Business Administration**

MEMBERSHIP   - Instrument Society of America (Member)   - Little League Baseball (Coach)

Barbara L. Mitty

25-B Travers Place, Wichita, KS 67213   316-794-3330 • BLMitty@aol.com

PROFILE

Sales/Marketing and Management Professional with broad skills in managing people, programs, and organizations. Proven abilities in

- Managing business growth.
- Planning, implementing, and overseeing effective sales and marketing programs.
- Selecting, training, and grooming staff members for increased levels of responsibility.
- Communicating effectively and persuasively: conducting sales training, making technical and sales presentations, working cross-culturally with diverse individuals.
- Accomplishing important business objectives by developing collaborative relationships within and outside the company.
- Managing business operations with a keen eye on effective utilization of resources.

PROFESSIONAL EXPERIENCE

1994–Present   VANGUARD CHEMICALS

Director, Plastics Additives 2006–Present   Wichita, Kansas

Direct worldwide sales and marketing of specialty chemicals. Create and implement marketing programs, lead and motivate sales teams, and represent the business to industry and trade groups.

- Develop sales, marketing, and management professionals, grooming them for increased levels of responsibility through effective supervision, training, and mentoring. Responsible for P&L; supervise 69 people worldwide in sales, marketing, technical service, and research.
- Justify new product development; oversee R&D staff and product development.
- Effectively deliver presentations to both inside and outside audiences (customers and industry groups)—sales presentations, sales training, business reporting presentations.

Representative Achievement: Grew European sales from $2M to $10M annually. Analyzed faltering operation and replaced ineffective distributor to improve penetration and drive sales growth.

- Supported manager and new distributor with resources and information.
- Oversaw implementation of highly successful customer seminars that improved product knowledge and developed relationships with direct product users.

Director of Sales & Marketing / The Americas 2006 Wichita, Kansas

Assumed marketing responsibility for the company's second-largest sales region (Canada, Central and South America). Formulated and implemented long-range strategic market plans using knowledge of markets, technology, and competition. Supervised 10-person sales staff and 2 marketing groups.

- Justified and managed new product development.
- Developed creative sales strategies to increase exposure to customers, including active participation in industry events to develop relationships within key accounts.
- Organized and trained sales/marketing staff.

(continued)

The Representative Achievement section under Barbara's current position allows detailed discussion of her most impressive career accomplishment.

245

Barbara L. Mitty

316-794-3330 • BLMitty@aol.com

PROFESSIONAL EXPERIENCE

VANGUARD CHEMICALS, continued

Senior International Market Manager 2003–2006   Louisville, Kentucky
International Market Manager 1999–2003   Louisville, Kentucky

Managed all export sales and marketing activity for specialty chemicals produced at Vanguard's Brown County plant. Led sales and marketing programs in Latin America, Asia, Japan, and Australia. Directed 5 international sales staff.

- Oversaw operations during start-up and through periods of significant sales growth. Grew total product sales to $21M from $12M base.
- Managed relationships with agents and distributors.
- Worked effectively in a matrix organization to achieve business results.

Senior Technical Sales Representative 1994–1999   Portland, Oregon

Doubled sales in Northwestern U.S. territory. Negotiated competitive pricing and annual contracts. Supervised customer technical evaluations in both laboratory and plant environments.

1993–1994   PHILLIPS EXETER ACADEMY, Exeter, New Hampshire
Science Faculty
Taught high school chemistry at prestigious New England boarding school.

EDUCATION

Bachelor of Science in Chemistry, 1992
    Williams College, Williamstown, Massachusetts

Additional coursework in Accounting and Economics, 2003–2004
    Bellarmine College, Louisville, Kentucky

Professional Training
    Strategic Planning, 2008 — University of Michigan
    Public Speaking and Presentations, 2008 — Communispond
    Personal Productivity, 2007 — LMI
    Strategic Sales and Marketing, 2001 — Sales Training Associates
    Account Development Strategy, 1997 — Learning International
    Deming's Theories of Quality, 1993 — Vanguard Chemicals

PROFESSIONAL AFFILIATIONS

Society of Plastics Engineers
Synthetic Organic Chemical Manufacturers Association (SOCMA) — Member, International Trade Committee
Toastmasters

Carole S. Adams

203-305-7904   73 Ocean View Lane, Stamford, CT 06902   c_adams@verizon.net

---

EXPERTISE   **Sales and Management—Business Development—Sales Force Leadership**
                Strategic Business, Sales, and Marketing Planning

Highlights
- Consistent track record of outperforming sales goals and building business in technology sales & service within a rapidly changing industry.
- Proven ability to build and leverage strategic relationships, such as key accounts and distributor sales organizations.
- Led successful sales initiatives and business planning to rebuild business following divestiture; quadrupled sales in 15 months.
- Key strengths are strategic planning, execution, leadership, and decision-making.

PROFESSIONAL EXPERIENCE

PRESS EXPRESS, INC., Stamford, CT, 2003–2009

Overview
- **Primary sales driver** for start-up company marketing prepress services and integrated systems and solutions.
- **Instrumental in successful business launch and expansion.** Aggressively promoted services to develop cash flow that supported expansion to capital equipment sales.
- **Advanced to corporate/sales leadership positions.** Played a key role in strategic sales planning, business-building, and corporate decision-making as company evolved from start-up to $6 million annual revenue and positioned itself for buyout.

Vice President Sales & Marketing, 2008–2009

Member of senior management team and senior sales/marketing executive for $6 million company, reporting directly to CEO. Managed 5 sales, customer service, and administrative staff, directed sales force of 3 Midwest and West Coast printing brokerages; personally managed key accounts and 9-employee, 3-shift production operation.

Highlights
- **Led sales organization in achieving 100% of sales goals** in a flat industry with rapidly evolving technology.
- **Achieved cash flow and profit performance** that were instrumental to company being acquired by its chief competitor in 2009.

National Sales Manager, 2006–2008

Promoted to lead the company's national sales organization following divestiture of computer systems division that left Press Express as a standalone service organization.

Highlights
- **Led company to exponential growth,** quickly replacing equipment sales and growing high-margin services revenue 300% ($2 million to $6 million) in 15 months.
- **Realigned the direct sales force** to provide more consistent coverage of key accounts and geographic territories. Created East and West Coast distribution channels.
- **Launched telesales unit** to increase customer base and allow direct sales force more time for key accounts.
- **Reorganized the Customer Service department,** brought that function under my supervision, and instilled a strong customer-satisfaction focus.
- **Personally managed major accounts,** achieving 8% growth through solution selling.
- **Installed Goldmine contact management system** linked to a database broadcasting system. Designed and implemented highly effective marketing and customer-communication campaigns using advanced features of the software.

(continued)

Using an Overview segment under the most recent company experience helped us tell a story of significant achievement going back to the very beginning of the company.

203-305-7904 **Carole S. Adams** c_adams@verizon.net

PRESS EXPRESS, INC., continued

Sales Representative, 2003–2006

- **Consistently led company sales,** selling an average of $1 million of system configurations and services annually.

LEXON SYSTEMS, Stamford, CT, 1999–2003

Regional Sales Manager

Managed a large U.S./Canadian territory in sales of proprietary client-server publishing system configurations. Planned and executed sales campaigns targeting large publishers. Identified specific client needs and configured systems to meet those needs.

- Working autonomously and without previous experience in system integration, maintained a constant $900K in annual sales.

A.B. DICK COMPANY, Bridgeport, CT, 1997–1999

Senior Account Manager

Sold both capital and consumer products for manufacturer of commercial-grade duplicators.

- #2 in the country in sales, 1998; consistently near top of 100-member sales force.

MERGENTHALER COMPANY, New York, NY, 1995–1997

Account Representative

Represented printing technology manufacturer throughout New England during product-line transition from digital to laser technology.

- Consistently among the company's top-performing sales representatives. Named to President's Circle (top 10 in U.S.), 1996; ranked #3 in Eastern Region, 1997.

EDUCATION

Bachelor of Science in Business Management, 1993: University of Connecticut, Storrs, CT

MATTHEW RILKE

2791 Heatherstone Lane, Cincinnati, OH 45241
513-792-0904 ▪ mattrilke@cinci.rr.com

▪ SALES & MARKETING EXECUTIVE ▪
Strong General Management Qualifications

Translating market trends to profitable products.

Consistently delivered revenue growth and record-setting profitability through effective leadership of sales and marketing organizations in consumer products/home decor and fashion industries. Led organizations through rapid growth, turnaround performance, acquisition integration, and other periods of significant change; successfully motivated sales and operations teams to set records in revenues, profits, and customer retention. Pioneered innovations in sales training and customer affiliation. Maintained exceptional front-line selling skills and industry awareness.

- Revenue & Profit Growth
- Multichannel Sales & Marketing Strategy
- P&L Management / Turnaround & Revitalization
- Direct & Distributor Sales Force Management

- Product Development & Introduction / Category Launch
- National Account Management—Major National Retailers
- Licensing—Brand Selection, Trend Identification
- Catalog / Trade Show / Promotional Products Marketing

▪ EXPERIENCE AND ACHIEVEMENTS ▪

MOUNTAIN FABRICS, Maysville, KY ($25M business unit of Textile Industries)   2005–Present

VP Sales & Marketing, 2007–Present ▪ **VP Sales,** 2005–2007

- **Sharpened and improved sales and marketing organization to achieve stellar performance in a challenging environment—grew sales revenue 20% in a down market, led smooth transition to new corporate ownership, and achieved 50% profit growth in the last 2 years alone.**

  Provide focused leadership to sales, marketing, and customer service organization for leading U.S. brand in woven textiles and home decor items. Create and execute sales and marketing strategy for $25M business unit; manage operating budget and up to 30 staff.

  Direct sales efforts to 20,000 customers through sales force of 250 manufacturer reps and as key account manager for major corporate clients (Macy's, Kohl's, Home Shopping Network). Lead product development and licensing initiatives; oversee catalog publication, corporate showrooms, and trade-show marketing.

Sales, Marketing, & Business Development
  - Consistently delivered profitability 10% above industry average.
  - Spearheaded the company's largest new-product introduction ever, generating $1.5M in first-year sales.
  - Launched new category with margins 65% above company average; grew from zero to $1.5M in 2 years.
  - Overhauled trade-show strategy and presentation and set a company record for sales results—$850K in new business—at the leading gift market for the industry.
  - Pioneered sales-training videos that resulted in 20% jump in new-product sales while dramatically reducing field-training costs. Planned, wrote, produced in-house, and deployed to nationwide sales force.

Strategic Business Initiatives
  - Conceived and successfully launched the company's first customer-loyalty program—and increased customer retention 15% to an industry-leading 95%.
  - Championed critical licensing program and grew to nearly 60% of revenue. Selected licensing partners and co-developed products strategically selected for "right place/right time" exploitation of industry trends.
  - Slashed 25% from production costs for full-color catalog by transitioning to digital photos.
  - Improved operational efficiencies by combining functions and cross-training staff.
  - Implemented company-wide ERP software package.

(continued)

Subheadings are used in the achievement section for the current position; this promotes quick scanning and breaks up a long list of bullet points. Note how each position is introduced with a summary statement of strong achievement.

MATTHEW RILKE   513-792-0904 ▪ mattrilke@cinci.rr.com

INTERNATIONAL DESIGN CONSORTIUM, Cincinnati, OH   2003–2005

National Sales Manager

▪ **Overhauled strategy, structure, and staffing of national sales program for home-goods importer.** Managed all sales and marketing activities for the company and its nationwide manufacturer-rep sales force. Personally handled all key account sales. Developed promotional plans and programs.

  ▪ Opened 2 new key accounts (Kohl's and Macy's) within months of coming on board.
  ▪ Created the company's first internal telemarketing program.
  ▪ Replaced 40% of rep force, ending relationships with underperformers and recruiting 4 new representative groups.

ANDIRONS AND MORE, Denver, CO   2001–2003

National Account Manager

▪ **Drove dramatic growth in targeted sales to national accounts.** Called on department stores, mail-order catalogs, furniture and chain accounts; handled national gift and furniture-buying offices of Dillard's, May Company, Federated, and Belk Stores. Developed merchandising and sales plans; administered cooperative advertising and merchandise-allowance programs; trained local sales representatives.

  ▪ Increased sales 76% in 2 years.
  ▪ Sold the company's largest order of limited-edition collectibles.
  ▪ Opened 7 new accounts, including Bed Bath & Beyond, QVC, and Saks.
  ▪ Contributed to product development and design.

EUREKA COMPANY, Bloomington, IL   1987–2001

Branch Manager: Central States, 1995–2001

▪ **Built the most profitable branch in the Midwest region and achieved branch sales in the top 15% nationwide.** Provided turnaround leadership for 5-state branch; held full responsibility for P&L, management of 30 sales and administrative staff, $700K advertising budget, and $1.5M operating budget.

  ▪ Grew sales revenue from $7.2M to $9.1M.
  ▪ Achieved #1 profit position among 14 branches in Midwest U.S.
  ▪ Personally managed relationships with key accounts.

Branch Manager: Akron, 1992–1995

▪ **Promoted and challenged to "fix" a struggling branch** with annual sales of $5.3M and staff of 14. Managed relationships with key accounts.

  ▪ Achieved rapid performance improvement: Only branch manager in the region to post a profit in 1994.

Sales Manager: Columbus, 1990–1992

▪ **Led sales team to #1 performance (20% above quota) and played a key role in branch's achieving the largest year-to-year increase in company history.** Managed 4 sales reps and 14 part-time demonstrators; concurrently maintained key account responsibilities for major department stores, appliance stores, and catalog retailers.

Early experience includes positions of increasing responsibility with Eureka, beginning in a part-time capacity while attending college.

▪ EDUCATION ▪

BS Political Science / Business Minor, 1989   The Ohio State University, Columbus, OH

Nadine P. Snow

630-240-7905   790 Trenton Circle, Naperville, IL 60566   nsnow@aol.com

---

Sales & Marketing Executive

Leading sales organizations to aggressive growth in the competitive health care industry.

✓ Strong management and leadership abilities; history of initiating successful sales, marketing, training, and goal-achievement programs.

✓ Highly profit-oriented; committed to increasing efficiency, improving business procedures, and maximizing the contributions of each employee.

✓ Proven ability to introduce new companies and services and quickly establish strong market position.

Experience and Accomplishments

GRAMBLIN HEALTHCARE CORPORATION, Chicago, IL   2003–Present

National Director of Market Development, 2008–Present

Advanced to national leadership role; took on the challenge of invigorating national training programs and improving the caliber and performance of sales managers across the country.

✓ Targeted market development in the hospice inpatient area and quickly captured new business in 2 major markets. Created marketing materials, developed presentations, and negotiated contracts.

✓ Spearheaded a curriculum-development initiative to improve training top-to-bottom for the sales-management force.

✓ Analyzed and restructured sales compensation to more closely align performance with strategic business objectives.

✓ Introduced and led quarterly selling-skills workshops.

Regional Sales Manager, Columbus, OH, 2005–2008

Promoted to 1 of 4 Regional Manager positions in the country, with accountability for P&L performance of $60 million Central Region. In addition, participated in corporate strategic planning and personally managed key national accounts. Recognized as company expert on sales process and sales training.

✓ Developed the fastest-growing region in the country: 12% growth in 2007.

✓ Turned around struggling Detroit area, reversing a negative profit situation by increasing profitability 7% in 6 months.

✓ Restaffed Milwaukee area from the ground up after inheriting management responsibility for an abandoned territory; built into a motivated, high-performing team.

✓ Created complete sales training curriculum and led corporate sales training programs.

Sales Director, 2003–2005

Trained, mentored, and guided 18-member sales force in effectively presenting and selling hospice services to physicians in the Greater Columbus area.

✓ Reorganized sales team, communicated innovative selling philosophies, and deployed new sales strategies. Delivered impressive gains in key performance measures:
  — 17% increase in days of care provided
  — 28% growth in admissions (industry average: 7%)
  — 14% growth in territory (from $14 million to $16 million) in one year

✓ Earned 2004 Chairman's Award and named "Director of the Year."

✓ Requested to expand sales and training methods nationwide. Assumed additional role of teaching sales strategies to all Directors and overseeing implementation of sales program in their territories.

(continued)

This resume format highlights steady advancement through sales and sales management positions to the current director-level role. Job titles really stand out.

Nadine P. Snow   630-240-7905   nsnow@aol.com

MERCY HEALTH SERVICES, Columbus, OH   1999–2003

Regional Director of Sales, Marketing, and Development (2001–2003)

Promoted to lead sales, marketing, and sales training for 20 staff in $10 million Midwest region.

✓ Developed and implemented sales training curriculum and Train-the-Trainer curriculum.

✓ Effectively led a geographically widespread sales operation with no on-site sales management.

General Manager (1999–2001)

Directed sales, marketing, operations, and P&L for multi-site 27-employee home health care provider. Initiated management development and sales training. Hired, trained, and supervised respiratory therapists, sales force, and office staff. Oversaw billing operations. Implemented compliance policies.

✓ Increased sales more than 500% in 3-year period, from $750K in 1999 to $4 million in 2001. Recorded commensurate increase in patient population.

✓ Achieved top-10 corporate ranking and maintained status over a 3-year period.

✓ Implemented new selling philosophy that dramatically increased referral business.

✓ Reduced employee turnover through progressive education and employee incentive programs.

✓ Led drive for JCAHO accreditation and restructured Respiratory Therapy department in preparation.

SANIBEL MEDICAL, Columbus, OH   1997–1999

Sales Manager

Instrumental in developing infusion services business in Columbus market from start-up to preferred provider status. Managed operations of local office, including hiring, staff management, and P&L responsibilities. Marketed company's services to physicians, managed care networks, and hospitals.

✓ Led preparation for JCAHO accreditation.

✓ Recruited more than 30 new prescribing physicians.

✓ Conceived and implemented sales training for nursing staff.

✓ Produced largest volume month in Columbus history, valued at $200K.

ORTHO PHARMACEUTICAL CORP. (a Johnson & Johnson Company), Raritan, NJ   1995–1997

Pharmaceutical Sales Representative

Completed 4-part Johnson & Johnson Management Developmental Program. Selected as Sales Trainer.

✓ Ranked #3 in company in total increase of key product.

✓ Developed physician target plan that resulted in a 4% increase in one quarter.

Professional Profile

Education	BS in Psychology, 1995: The Ohio State University, Columbus, Ohio
	Extensive professional development/continuing education includes Dale Carnegie, Wilson Learning, Professional Selling Skills, Consultative Selling.
Affiliation	American Society for Training and Development

SIDNEY MACK

1205 Ptarmigan Way, Ft. Collins, CO 80525
970-781-7775 sidney.mack@aol.com

EXPERTISE

SALES • MARKETING • MANAGEMENT

Eleven years of consistently successful sales experience in highly competitive markets. Proven ability to launch new businesses, develop new markets, establish market presence, and uncover new business opportunities.

Greatest strengths are a deep interest in people and a natural talent for creating and capitalizing on networks and business connections. Wholly focused on client satisfaction and able to use this as a competitive advantage.

Track record of effectively training, leading, and supervising staff (sales, marketing, and operational teams). Able to motivate staff and build enthusiastic and productive teams.

PROFESSIONAL EXPERIENCE

THE JONES COMPANIES, Denver, Colorado, 2003–Present

Career Profile / Highlights of Accomplishments

- Instrumental in the success and significantly increased visibility of The Jones Companies' managed care entities. Repeatedly tapped for challenging new roles/advanced responsibility; repeatedly delivered results above expectations. Successfully opened new offices, new markets, and new business lines.

- Recently promoted to revitalize sales for a separate entity, a national PPO co-owned by The Jones Companies' chairman.

Results

- Between 2004–2008, more than doubled in client enrollment in each PPO network.

- Increased business more than 235% each year for the company's two group health PPO networks.

- In two years, built Colorado Comp from the ground up into the largest worker's comp organization in the state, covering more than one million lives. In year 2, achieved 200% increase in enrollment with additional large-client business already contracted for 2009.

- Total assets and net income of The Jones Companies have increased more than 400% since 2004.

Career History

2009–Present **Regional Vice President of Sales**—American Health Care

Challenged to turn around 4-year-old national PPO that has steadily lost market share. Create and execute national sales, marketing, advertising, publicity, and communications strategies—most significantly, leverage positive relationships and excellent reputation in the industry to improve company visibility and sales.

2007–2009 **Assistant Vice President**

Led sales and business development activities for two of The Jones Companies' businesses: worker's compensation and managed care.

Worker's Compensation: Colorado Comp

- Instrumental in the launch of this business. Through sales and client services of the company's managed care services, identified strong business potential for worker's comp arm of the business. Developed business recommendation and secured contract guarantees to establish the business on a sound footing from day one.

(continued)

The Career Profile/Highlights of Accomplishments section gives a capsule view of a long and somewhat complex history with the company. Results are set off in their own section for maximum impact.

SIDNEY MACK

PROFESSIONAL EXPERIENCE, continued

- Launched intensive marketing campaign to develop and solidify the business.
- Worked closely with Operations and Information Services staff to ensure thorough product training and exceptional customer service.

Managed Care: YourHealth, Inc. (PPO), American Health, Inc. (PPO)

- Marketed group health products to all insured national carriers licensed in Colorado and in additional states as companies expanded regionally.
- Aggressively pursued national and regional TPAs and carriers that administered both worker's comp and group health products in order to achieve high levels of account penetration.
- Developed strong relationships with agents and brokers; developed carrier profiles to educate agents and brokers about carriers that were accessing The Jones Companies' managed care products.

2005–2007   **Director of Sales**

Challenged to develop the Southern Colorado market for the company.

- Hired, trained, and supervised Regional Managers; coordinated and assigned client base and regional territory alignments throughout Colorado and contiguous states.
- Developed weekly and monthly sales plans; assisted RSMs to utilize objective planning format. Identified and tracked all quotas and business activities weekly; coordinated commission structure.
- Educated RSMs on networking within the health care community. Assisted and supported RSMs in presentations to potential clients.
- Continued prospecting and relationship-building with potential clients while overseeing sales in Colorado.
- Participated in the development of new marketing materials and the company's web site.
- Coordinated national trade shows and exhibits in collaboration with VP of Advertising.

Assisted Chairman and President in the development and incorporation of 2 new Managed Care company subsidiaries. (Subsequently promoted to lead marketing and sales for these subsidiaries.)

2003–2005   **Regional Sales Manager**—Colorado and contiguous states

Charged with establishing the company's new service entity (PPO) and maintaining visibility in the health care community. Marketed PPO and Utilization Management services to large employers, brokers, health care consultants, Third-Party Administrators, and insurance carriers.

- As the company's sole sales representative, succeeded in establishing visibility and creating a strong sales foundation for the business.
- Consistently provided an exceptional level of customer service and responsiveness.
- Launched the company's Client Service department in response to significant growth of the business. Trained service representatives on product knowledge and customer service strategies.

SIDNEY MACK

PROFESSIONAL EXPERIENCE, continued

WESTERN HEALTH MANAGEMENT, Denver, Colorado, 2000–2003

2002–2003   **Sales Manager**

Trained, managed, and motivated account executives. Concurrently, marketed Utilization Review and Case Management business to large national Third-Party Administrators outside Colorado.

- Grew territory by 28%.

2000–2002   **Account Executive**

Marketed Utilization Review, Case Management, and Managed Care products to payors, carriers, and agents throughout Colorado.

- Developed new territory in central and southern Colorado.
- Within 3 days of coming on board, learned essential product knowledge and prepared 3 detailed service proposals, 2 of which were accepted and produced substantial new business.

MEDICAL STAFFERS, INC., Denver, Colorado, 1997–2000

Administrative-Operations Manager

Hired to start up and oversee new on-call medical staffing business. Focused on sales and marketing to create client base and establish a foundation for business growth. Created organizational procedures; selected and trained permanent and on-call staff; managed all financial and operational activities of the business.

- Achieved profitability within 2 months of start-up.
- Continued to increase sales consistently during tenure.

EDUCATION

Colorado College, Colorado Springs, Colorado: Bachelor of Arts, Psychology

LICENSURE

Colorado Division of Insurance: Life, Accident and Health, Variable Life

PROFESSIONAL AFFILIATIONS

National Association of Health Underwriters

Colorado Association of Health Underwriters

Denver Association of Health Underwriters

Sandy O'Brien

119 Beacon Street #4B, Boston, MA 02116   617.409.2390 ▪ s_obrien@boston.rr.com

SALES EXECUTIVE

- ▶ **STRATEGIC SALES MANAGEMENT**
- ▶ **KEY ACCOUNT MANAGEMENT**
- ▶ **MARKET ENTRY & RAPID GROWTH**

Ten years of documented, stellar success in sales, sales management, new-business development, and rapid market entry in highly competitive industries and uneven markets. Repeatedly rose to top performance in player/coach roles, concurrently managing individual territory, leading national sales team, and defining sales strategy for the company. Three times built first-class sales teams from the ground up—established disciplined sales methodology, motivated and guided individuals to success, and instilled a relentless focus on sales goals and strategic business objectives.

▶ **CORE COMPETENCIES**

Strategic Sales Planning—Competitive Market Positioning—Pricing—Product Development & Launch
Cold Calling—Prospecting—Pipeline Development & Management
Consultative Sales Process—Needs Assessment—High-Level Sales/Business Presentation—Closing
Key/National Account Development, Service, Management & Growth
Sales Team Recruiting, Management, Development & Retention—High-Performance Team Culture
Sales Analysis—Tracking—Tools—Measurement—Forecasting & Budgeting—Commission Structure

EXPERIENCE AND ACHIEVEMENTS

Athens Financial, Boston, MA   2006–Present
A leading provider of financial services and market intelligence for both businesses and consumers

▶ **VICE PRESIDENT, NATIONAL SALES—Revitalized dormant product line, achieving massive sales growth and dominant market position.** Brought on board to drive sales efforts for data products and services to the commercial market. Refined and improved the product line top to bottom. Recruited and hired top salespeople, set up sales territories, and created commission/incentive structures that motivated performance toward business objectives. Created sales strategy to capture new business from competitors, and served in dual sales/management role to achieve results that exceeded ambitious goals.

Sales & Sales Management
- Drove revenue from **$2M** (2006) to **$12M** (2008)—**600%** increase during economic downturn.
- Surpassed sales quotas by average **22%** annually.
- Built a competitive powerhouse, going from losing **75%** to gaining **66%** of prospects from competition.
- Grew market share from **20%** to **60%**.
- Motivated and led 12-person sales team, achieving **90%** retention in a high-performance culture.
- **#1** or **#2** in personal sales each month while concurrently managing team and overall group sales strategy.

Account Sales & Service
- Increased average contract size by **125%.**
- Achieved **93%** renewal rate at average **32%** contract increase.

Strategic & Organizational Leadership
- Created strong sales infrastructure: Implemented new lead prospecting methods, sales pipelines, and consistent sales presentations. Slashed time to sale from **90** days to **42** days in a 12-month period.
- Crafted a competitive product portfolio, developing **4** new products that now deliver **20%** of revenue.
- Introduced tracking and performance measurements for every area of sales, creating a central source of critical business information in demand company-wide.

With stellar sales achievements and rapid career advancement, Sandy is well positioned for an executive sales position. Sandy's cover letter is shown in e-mail format in sample 12-7.

Sandy O'Brien   617.409.2390 ▪ s_obrien@boston.rr.com

Data.com, Boston, MA   2003–2006
Comprehensive source of company intelligence/business information

▶ **CORPORATE SALES DIRECTOR—Spearheaded corporate sales initiatives for expanding/evolving online services organization. Set personal sales records while building and leading a top-notch sales and service team.** Recruited, hired, trained, reviewed, and managed team of 12 in 3 sales groups; created and executed sales strategies for 4 separate product offerings.

- Consistently surpassed sales goals, both individual and team:
  — **132%** of revenue stream forecast for 2006.
  — **$2.5M** total revenue for 2005, **20%** above goal.
  — Personal sales of more than **$1.4M** in 2004, **56%** of total group sales.
- Led group in securing **65** new clients in **15** months; delivered successful sales presentations to top executives at Fortune 500 corporations.

Specialty Window Company, Providence, RI   1998–2003
Canadian-owned manufacturer of residential and commercial window systems

▶ **NORTH AMERICAN SALES MANAGER—Spurred aggressive U.S. market growth for Canadian company; advanced rapidly from direct sales to leadership of 10-person sales team that generated more than $2M in revenues in its second year.** In first sales job, eclipsed all other sales performers through aggressive cold calling and territory building, generating sales approximately double the company average. Developed 180 accounts from the ground up to create a solid East Coast region; subsequently promoted to recruit, hire, manage, and motivate salespeople covering entire Eastern U.S.

- **#1** salesperson company-wide for **2** consecutive years before promotion to Sales Manager.
- Quickly learned and applied fundamental sales skills—prospecting and lead generation, cold calling, needs assessment, presentation, closing—and maintained consistently high call volume in a self paced rapid-growth environment.
- Aggressively targeted large chain accounts—developed strategy, built relationships, and closed business with **3** of **7** Lowe's regions nationwide (**$1M** initial contract, total **$3M** in new business).

EDUCATION ───

PROVIDENCE COLLEGE, Providence, RI
Bachelor of Arts—Sociology, 1998

Steven L. Taylor

415.721.3459   530 Nob Hill, San Francisco, CA 94130   steve@thetaylors.com

SALES & MARKETING EXECUTIVE

**Strategic Selling / Channel Marketing / Regional Management / National Account Management
Sales Turnaround / Revenue & Market Share Growth / New Product Development & Launch
Sales Training & Team Leadership / PFI Relationships**

Expert in building top-producing business relationships with target customers in the financial and real-estate industries. Repeatedly achieved strong and sustainable revenue, profit, and market-share increases, successfully positioning and differentiating products and services in crowded and competitive markets. Built, trained, managed, and motivated sales teams to top performance. Contributed to product development and led the company in strategic product sales.

Career Highlights

- Rapidly reversed declining sales, profits, and market share for real-estate services company. Differentiated services through strategic sales focus and positioning as ally/expert.
- Spearheaded development and launch of Internet banking product that quickly grew to 10% of company revenues and delivered positive ROI in just over 2 years.
- Built the #1 region in the country in sales of checks and related products to Western financial institutions.
- Led the company in sales of strategic products—high-margin, high-value differentiators that contributed to capturing 97% market share.

EXPERIENCE AND ACHIEVEMENTS

Home Check, Inc., San Francisco, CA   2006–Present
Regional home-inspection firm.

GENERAL MANAGER / VP SALES

Doubled sales revenue, doubled profits, and transformed poorly performing organization into a highly salable asset. Assumed leadership of organization struggling for success in a crowded market. Successfully rebuilt business by refocusing sales/marketing strategy on referral and channel relationships. Manage all aspects of business operations and personally lead all sales and marketing activities.

- In 3 years, increased annual sales 100% with corresponding surge in profitability.
- Identified and aggressively pursued new marketing methods to reach #1 target audience.
  - Built relationships with leading individuals in the real estate field—commercial brokers, builders, group realty offices, and individuals.
  - Designed and delivered CEU-accredited educational presentations on industry "hot buttons," attracting 500–1,000 attendees each quarter and firmly positioning expertise in target market.
- Zoomed to #3 in market share in fragmented and competitive market.

Secure Paper, Inc., San Francisco, CA   2000–2006
Provider of payment systems, marketing services, and technology solutions to financial institutions.

VICE PRESIDENT INTERNET BANKING, 2005–2006

Launched online banking product offering and grew from start-up to $13M revenue, more than 10% of total company sales. Created product strategy and spearheaded all facets of developing, positioning, pricing, and rolling out new service offering to customers and the sales force.

- Outperformed revenue and profit goals, earning ROI in 26 months—a standout performance in an industry where competitors remain unprofitable after more than 5 years.
- Identified needs and worked with development team to create product offering that met functionality, branding, pricing, and implementation needs of target financials.

A strong summary is enhanced by career highlights that showcase a career-long trend of top performance. Steven's companion cover letter is sample 12-8.

VICE PRESIDENT INTERNET BANKING, Secure Paper, continued

- Worked with customers during beta testing to refine product and ensure flawless functionality.
- Integrated strategic services such as online bill paying and push marketing to improve value/revenue generation for customers.
- Developed sales training, integrated into existing product portfolio, and trained entire company sales force on sales strategy.

WESTERN REGIONAL MANAGER, 2002–2005

Aggressively grew Western sales region—from $3.5M to $54M revenue in 3 years—and captured 97% market share of target financials. Led a team of 20 sales/service professionals in sales of check-printing services to commercial clients in 7-state Western region. Managed $3.5M budget.

- Led region to consistent top performance:
  - #1 in the country in every performance period but one over the course of 3 years.
  - 25% increase in market share (to 97%).
  - 100% growth in sales of strategic products (data processing, Internet banking and web hosting, ATM cards, custom debit and credit cards, on-demand MICR-coded checks)—key to revenue growth in a saturated market.
- Increased Western region's contribution to total business performance—from 25% of revenue in 2002 to 41% by 2005.
- Strategically focused sales efforts on financial institution relationships, partnering with target financials to jointly develop solutions.
  - Drove down product costs and created attractive product offerings to boost recommendations.
  - Became the dominant supplier even with accounts that had multiple vendor relationships—captured 90% of check sales at target financials.
  - Efforts were so successful, strategic focus became company directive.
- Built an accomplished sales team. Improved performance through sharp focus on presentation skills, solution sales, and strategic targets. Trained, motivated, and scheduled regular one-on-ones in the field.

DISTRICT SALES REPRESENTATIVE, 2000–2002

Built 2 new sales territories from the ground up. Played a key role in expanding the company's presence beyond its Bay Area hub. Methodically tackled new markets with focused sales strategies that emphasized brand-building and relationship sales. Hired and managed sales teams for each new territory.

- #1 in strategic product sales among more than 80 peers company-wide.
- Tapped to share successful sales strategies with other reps; developed audio and video training materials that were used throughout the company.

Great Western Title Insurance Company, Inc., San Mateo, CA   1998–2000

NATIONAL ACCOUNTS REPRESENTATIVE

Captured and managed business with Fortune 500 companies (Wendy's, BP, RE/MAX), selling one-stop title-insurance services to commercial clients nationwide.

EDUCATION

BS in Political Science, University of California, Berkeley, CA

Luke T. PEPPER

23 Princeton Street, Kalamazoo, MI 49006
616-349-1114 ▶ pepperpot@mac.com

Summary

Sales and management professional with specific expertise in the furniture industry and experience managing program implementation, retail and rental operations, and sales organizations.

Effective leader equally skilled at envisioning goals and then planning, implementing, and following through on the steps necessary to achieve them.

Professional Experience

HOME & AWAY, INC., Kalamazoo, Michigan   1995–2009
Office and residential furniture leasing company marketing services for temporary or short-term corporate needs and short-term housing rentals primarily for relocated employees.

SENIOR VICE PRESIDENT, 2006–2009 ▶ **VICE PRESIDENT,** 2001–2006

Sales, operational, and P&L responsibility for consistently profitable North Central region, with annual sales of $8.5 million and 70 direct and indirect reports (district managers, inside and outside sales staff). Managed operations of 2 warehouses and as many as 5 retail showrooms. Reported directly to owners.

- ▶ Selected and purchased residential and office furniture for all Home & Away operations nationwide (30 stores). Developed and maintained extensive contacts with furniture manufacturers. Priced merchandise for all retail and rental locations.
- ▶ Directly supervised outside sales staff in both the corporate and residential markets. Provided thorough training and ongoing supervision in basic sales skills, including leads generation and follow-up, effective listening, making sales calls, and completing reports.
- ▶ Managed site selection, staffing, and start-up operations for 4 new store locations.

Key Accomplishments

- ▶ Focused on customer service as a key distinguishing characteristic; instilled customer orientation into all inside and outside sales personnel and empowered them to take responsibility and make customer-focused decisions.
- ▶ Revitalized corporate recycling program, enabling company to reuse previously leased furniture. Implemented staff training on furniture reuse. Program revitalization resulted in significant savings in new furniture purchases.
- ▶ Instrumental in upgrading quality of furniture purchases.
- ▶ Centralized, expanded, and improved housewares program for rental properties, creating a significant profit center from what had been a casual operation.
- ▶ Oversaw production of residential brochure and catalog of furnished apartment layout options. Worked directly with photographers and advertising agencies. Pioneered the solicitation of vendor advertising allowances and achieved $60K, more than paying for catalog production.

DISTRICT MANAGER, MICHIGAN, 1999–2001 ▶ **STORE MANAGER, KALAMAZOO,** 1995–1999

CITY STYLE FURNITURE COMPANY, Kalamazoo, Michigan   1990–1995
SALES MANAGER, 1993–1995 ▶ **SALES REPRESENTATIVE,** 1990–1993

Education

B.A. History, 1984 ▶ University of Michigan, Ann Arbor, MI

Professional Affiliations

National Interim Housing Network ▶ Furniture Rental Association of America

This is another example of a rather extensive position description balanced by a strong section of key accomplishments with its own subheading.

JUDY GELMAN

805 Corryville Avenue, Cincinnati, OH 45207 • 513-205-7094 • jgelman@cinci.rr.com

SALES AND MARKETING EXECUTIVE

- Expert in developing and executing strategy for turnaround sales performance, successful market positioning, new-product introduction, and support of business mission and goals.
- Fifteen-year track record of delivering sales increases every year, in every position, in diverse industries and markets.
- Competitive, results-driven, and energized by new challenges and ever-higher goals.

Areas of Expertise

Strategic Sales and Marketing Planning	Strategic Alliance-Building
Product Development and Introduction	Sales Force Management
Customer Relationship Management	Rapid Sales Results

PROFESSIONAL EXPERIENCE

Director of Sales and Marketing

Southern Ohio Business Journal, Dayton, OH
2008–Present

Challenged to reverse declining sales for monthly business publication with distribution of 22,000. Reinvigorated sales through energetic leadership of campaigns and initiatives to build distribution and visibility as well as ad revenue.

- **Tripled ad revenue in 6 months.**
- **Built new business** with 35 new advertising accounts and attracted 15 former advertisers back to the publication.
- **Developed collaborative alliance** with 8 area Chambers of Commerce as a low-cost means to build database of target subscribers; increased distribution by 18%.
- **Initiated marketing partnerships** with regional radio station and Miami University.

VP Sales and Marketing

Creative Collectibles, Lebanon, OH
2003–2008

Developed and executed strategy to turn around deteriorating sales for manufacturer of handcrafted pottery to the collectibles/gift/tabletop industries.

- **Reversed decline and built business from $900K to $2 million.**
- **Increased sales an average of 18% annually** over 5 years.
- **Achieved 90% success rate** on new-product introductions.

Provided hands-on leadership and ongoing management for multifaceted sales and marketing initiatives:

- **Strategic Planning:** Developed strategic sales and marketing plans aligned to corporate goals. Conceived repositioning strategy that led to success at higher price points.
- **Sales:** Managed 65+ independent field sales representatives promoting products to retailers nationwide.
- **Customer Service:** Established "customer-first" culture and promoted a superb level of service.
- **Product Development:** Developed and merchandised 50+ new products annually. Sourced and developed ancillary products. Designed packaging, POP displays, and signage.
- **Marketing:** Established co-marketing programs with key accounts. Conceptualized and executed trade show and showroom displays. Provided art direction on catalogs.

(continued)

Note how sales results are presented first, followed by a summary of executive leadership activities, in the position description for Creative Collectibles.

Judy Gelman **page two**

Sales Manager
GlamRags, Middletown, OH
2001–2003

Managed inside sales for newly launched importer/wholesaler of women's apparel. Maintained and coordinated sales and communication with top 25 accounts. Served as key point of contact and information for outside sales force. Spearheaded product development, market trend research, and forecasting.

- Outperformed owner's sales projections by 20%.
- Accurate in forecasting design trends and directing designer toward targeted markets in the 30+ age bracket.

Territory Sales Manager
Global Gifts, Cincinnati, OH
1999–2001

Represented line of high-end collectibles and licensed products to independent card and gift stores in Ohio/Kentucky/Indiana territory.

- Named Salesperson of the Year, 2000; exceeded sales goals by more than 50%.
- Opened 250 new accounts and reactivated 33% of dormant accounts.

Special Account Sales Representative
Delhi Imports, Covington, KY
1994–1999

For importer/wholesaler of women's apparel, developed direct-order programs with major buyers and developed products for each program.

- Increased showroom sales by 125%.
- Reactivated 30% of former customers through telemarketing campaign.

EDUCATION

BA History, magna cum laude Ohio University, Athens, OH

PROFESSIONAL AFFILIATIONS

- Lebanon County Chamber of Commerce: Strategic Planning and Membership Committees
- The Taft Museum, Cincinnati, OH: Planning and Fundraising Committee

Charles G. Martin

432 Lakeview Park Drive
Chicago, Illinois 60616
312-608-6768 • cmartin@chicagonet.net

PROFESSIONAL PROFILE

Results-oriented sales and marketing manager with a track record of top performance in challenging assignments. Strategic thinker and planner equally adept at devising and executing tactics to support strategy. Strong customer service and account management skills.

Demonstrated achievements in

- **Strategic sales and market planning**
- **Key-account relationship management**
- **New-product introductions**

- **Sales growth and performance to plan**
- **Team leadership and motivation**
- **Staff development**

HIGHLIGHTS OF ACCOMPLISHMENTS

- Consistently exceeded performance benchmarks—P&L, KPI, sales versus quota.

- Chosen for steering committee that drove corporate reengineering and transformation.

- Led creation of innovative team-based business development strategy.

- Repeatedly developed staff to team, district, and corporate management positions.

- Selected to serve on President's "System Empowerment" program that achieved savings of more than $50 million in three years.

- Chosen to manage a cross-functional merchandising team whose efforts resulted in incremental merchandising support of 30% over prior year.

PROFESSIONAL EXPERIENCE

1996–Present   DIVERSIFIED CONSUMER PRODUCTS, Chicago, Illinois
2008–Present   **Director—Key Account Sales & Service**
17 direct reports; $172 million operation; diversified account base

Manage cross-functional sales/marketing team; hold full P&L responsibility for promotional strategy development, marketing and logistical execution, succession planning, and trade relations.

- Exceeded YTD profit and volume targets by 14%.

- Developed promotion evaluation/business scorecard template, allowing for consistent analysis of promotional tactics.

- Managed promotional activities for 5 new product introductions.

- Supervise subordinates' self-development programs and promote the improvement of core competencies to equip them for higher-level sales and management positions.

- Prepare and deliver marketing presentations that predict future direction of product lines to alert customers to trends and new promotional strategies.

(continued)

The Highlights of Accomplishments section is an effective way to showcase diverse areas of achievement—sales results, of course, but also leadership achievements and important corporate initiatives.

Charles G. Martin   312-608-6768 • cmartin@chicagonet.net

DIVERSIFIED CONSUMER PRODUCTS, continued

2006–2008   **Senior Sales Plans Development Manager**

Developed and managed corporate Laundry Products category (representing $600 million in revenue) trade marketing/promotion strategy and budget. Held P&L responsibility for trade promotion budget of $100 million, designed to achieve specific strategic metrics. Devised brand pricing strategies, distribution targets, trade/consumer promotion strategies, and merchandising objectives. Broad range of cross-functional responsibilities included interfacing with all corporate departments and leading or co-leading brand/customer-specific projects designed to deliver incremental volume and dollars while reducing costs.

- Developed category management portfolio strategy.

- Introduced new products to the market, designing trade and consumer promotion strategies and tactics within classes of trade.

- Achieved 53% increase in shipments for Clean-Up as a result of redesign of trade promotion strategy; 26% increase in shipments for Superclean following redesign of brand positioning platform.

2003–2006   **District Sales Manager**

Directed district sales team and led by example to meet specific volume targets by brand; included development of district/market brand sales strategies. Managed annual operating budget of $100 million. Recruited, trained, and evaluated staff: 5 Account Managers, 14 Sales Representatives, 4 office staff.

- Led district to #2 in sales nationally, 2005.

- Achieved top market-share positions for several products as well as strong sales performance for entire district.

- Established creative and highly successful "Goals Standards" program to motivate and reward performance.

2001–2003   **Field Sales Manager**
1999–2001   **Unit Sales Manager**—#1 nationally 2001, #3 nationally 1999
1996–1999   **District Sales Assistant; Senior Sales Representative; Sales Representative**

EDUCATION Syracuse University, Syracuse, New York

Bachelor of Science, Business Administration, 1996

Samantha Taylor-Massey

914-860-2222   23 Whiteoak Lane, White Plains, New York 10601   massey@optonline.net

Senior Sales / Marketing Management Executive

Effective combination of sales/marketing expertise and business management acumen.
- Thoroughly conversant with all aspects of the sales cycle; particularly proficient in developing customized, winning proposals.
- Equally skilled in business planning, financial analysis, goal-setting, and directing day-to-day operations to achieve objectives.
- Proven sales performer with both start-up and ongoing business operations; exceptional ability to develop new business through dogged persistence, thorough planning and research, and effective proposal presentation.
- A key strength is the ability to influence, motivate, and lead people—staff, prospects/customers, vendors—through effective communication and personal interaction skills.
- Highly goal-oriented; derive satisfaction from setting and achieving ambitious goals, both individually and through staff leadership.

Professional Experience

TAYLOR-MASSEY FOODS, Cincinnati, Ohio   2003–Present
President / Owner
Founded organization specializing in the packaging and distribution of candy, nuts, and assorted specialty items. Shepherded business through start-up phase to current level of success: a stable operation employing a staff of 12 with a developed customer base in the Northeast and South.

Manage all business operations: sales, marketing, product development, financing, employee training, budgeting, accounting, purchasing, and customer service.

Key Accomplishments: **SALES/MARKETING**
- Negotiated special promotions for national chain accounts representing 60% of total sales.
- Secured initial contract with the country's #4 food/drug store chain with an aggressive 3-month start-up period. Sold account based on quality of product, price/value, and professional presentation.
- Initiated and managed private-label program with the nation's #2 food/drug store chain. Pursued account for 2 years. Prepared detailed financial/sales projections; verified numbers through in-store test programs; successfully converted all stores chain-wide.

Key Accomplishments: **BUSINESS MANAGEMENT**
- Wrote business plan that led to initial company financing.
- Researched, introduced, and developed new private-label product lines.
- Prepared accounting budget, maximizing gross profit and existing business.
- Coordinated product development, including packaging, label design, and planograms.
- Implemented a cost-effective purchasing system to increase profitability.
- Solicit input from all employees during regular business meetings: brainstorm operations ideas, review income and expenses, and creatively address issues of cost control and resource utilization.

Key Accomplishments: **STAFF DEVELOPMENT**
- Motivate and manage staff of 12 employees in sales, operations management, and production. Personally recruit and hire all staff, drawing upon business contacts to attract ambitious and qualified candidates.
- Hold twice-weekly sales meetings to review sales data and objectives, introduce new products, and train on new sales strategies.
- Consistently develop and promote employees, encouraging their ability and drive through increased responsibility and opportunities for advancement.

(continued)

After running her own business for six years, Samantha was ready to return to a sales and marketing management role with another company. Her cover letter (sample 12-9) explains her decision.

Samantha Taylor-Massey

Professional Experience (continued)

NEW ENGLAND PACKAGING, Wilton, Connecticut   1999–2003
Premier manufacturer of high-quality packaging. Promoted rapidly due to sales initiative and proven management ability: increased sales 30% in first 2 years of employment.

Vice President / Sales (2000–2003)

- Developed sales and marketing strategy for U.S. and Canada representing sales volume of more than $7 million.
- Significantly increased business with existing high-volume accounts through successful negotiations.
- Prepared quarterly and annual budgets.
- Implemented quality control and customer service measurements.
- Managed communications network between operations, customer service, and sales, emphasizing goal attainment.
- Retained all responsibilities of Sales Manager while assuming additional planning and leadership role as Vice President.

Sales Manager (1999–2000)

- Developed training program for new sales representatives.
- Managed and advised 4 sales representatives on budgets, new accounts, existing business, and customer relations.
- Serviced a 5-state territory.

Sales Representative (May–November 1999)

- Demonstrated proven sales ability by increasing customer base and expanding existing business.
- Communicated with 2 manufacturing facilities, working closely with the production team.

NORTHERN WHOLESALERS, Albany, New York   1994–1999
Sales Manager (1998–1999)
Sales Representative (1996–1998)
Night-Shift Manager (1994–1996)

- Doubled sales during tenure as Sales Manager for regional tobacco and candy distributor.
- Developed training program for 8 sales representatives.
- Expanded existing accounts and set up distributor network.
- Managed 12 night-shift employees. Created and implemented successful order-fulfillment program.

Education

Bachelor of Science in Business Management: State University of New York, Albany, NY

S. Douglas Minor

2325 Shepherdscreek Court, Loveland, Ohio 45140
Phone / Fax 513-849-2389   dougminor@mac.com

Profile	**Results-oriented senior sales executive** with outstanding performance record recognized by rapid advancement through increasingly responsible sales and sales management levels (9 promotions in 16 years). Strategic thinker and planner with proven customer-service and business-development skills.

Expertise and achievements in

- Strategic Sales & Marketing Planning
- Key Account Relationship Management
- Team Leadership & Motivation

- Revenue Growth
- Profit Improvement
- New-Product Introduction

Professional Experience

1992–Present

PROCTER & GAMBLE, Cincinnati, OH

2006–Present

Director, Customer Management and Service—National Supermart Team

Hold full P&L accountability for P&G's largest grocery account ($120M operation encompassing 14 divisions and 2 central procurement warehouses). Develop promotional strategies, lead marketing and logistical efforts, manage trade relations, and plan for management succession.

Manage cross-functional team of 15 sales professionals. Develop and leverage ongoing relationships with top Supermart management in Logistics, Advertising, Grocery, and Reengineering.

- *Delivered outstanding business results:* Increased Fabric Liquid net sales value 12%, sales contribution 22%, shipments 16%; increased Soap net sales value 4%, sales contribution 14%, shipments 7%.
- *Reduced outstanding accounts* from 130 open deductions worth $1.5M to 21 open items worth less than $100K.
- *Developed 18-month strategic business vision* with Supermart, encompassing category management, logistics, marketing, and development of customer relationships.
- *Created spending and merchandising strategy* for key P&G Laundry brands that were losing share. Gained internal approval for funding and sold strategy to Supermart senior management. Implementation resulted in successful closing of all distribution gaps and a 20% distribution gain.
- *Co-developed new strategy for Laundry product lines,* working jointly with Supermart. Earned go-ahead for implementation corporate-wide across all Supermart divisions, 2008.
- *Conceived and began implementing strategy* to integrate marketing programs with grocery merchandisers to use consumer funding in micro-marketing events for 2009.

2004–2006

Director, Customer Management and Service—Northeast Team, Newton, MA

Held full P&L responsibility for $75M operation servicing major retailers such as Stop & Shop, Star Market, and Caldor. Managed, mentored, and developed staff of 10; recognized for effectiveness in guiding subordinate career development. Prepared and delivered marketing presentations predicting future product directions.

- *Achieved 110% of profit and volume targets* during all quarters.
- *Managed promotional activities for 12 new product introductions.* Created and implemented promotional evaluation scorecard.
- *Developed working 18-month vision* for the Northeast Team.
- *Spearheaded multiple "top to top" initiatives* with executive management.

(continued)

Doug planned to leverage his name-brand experience and strong sales record to find a new position in his home state of Florida.

S. Douglas Minor

2001–2004	**Senior Sales Plans Development Manager,** Cincinnati, OH

Developed and managed Liquid Detergent category trade marketing strategy and budget ($600M annual sales). Managed $130M promotional budget. Developed 12-month plan including input from marketing, forecasting, commercial and consumer promotion; fully accountable for results to plan.

- *Gained Executive Board agreement* to annual internal operating plan and field sales targets.
- *Spearheaded company's transition into Category Development Funding (CDF);* directed national launch and sales training.
- *Aggressively addressed threat of lost business* of largest liquid detergent brand in the club business by developing prototype packaging that gave P&G's product a competitive advantage. Prototype went to full-scale production and is currently in place in Costco stores.
- *Selected for key corporate initiative* to identify and develop cost-cutting initiatives. As member of brainstorming team, contributed to ideas that resulted in more than $25M in savings in 3 years.

1999–2001	**District Manager,** Ontario, CA

Led a team of 22 people covering 10 states and marketing to large retailers including Walmart, Ralph's, and Safeway. Met annual volume targets and managed operating budget of $50M. Hired and trained a significant number of new sales representatives.

- *Grew district from 20th to 2nd place nationally* (sales versus quota, 2001).
- *Rated #1 district in the division.*
- *Promoted 7 staff members* into management positions.

1992–1999	**Division Field Sales Manager,** Portland, OR — 1998–1999

Field Operations Analyst, Cincinnati, OH — 1997–1998

Sales Manager, Denver, CO — 1995–1997
- *Top 5 finish* in 1995 among 20 managers region-wide; Top 4 in 1996

District Field Sales Analyst, Orlando, FL — 1994–1995

Senior Sales Representative, Orlando, FL — 1993–1994

Sales Representative, Tallahassee, FL — 1992–1993
- *Rookie of the Year*

Education	FLORIDA A&M UNIVERSITY, Tallahassee, FL

BS in Business Administration / Marketing, cum laude, 1992
- Co-captain, Varsity Lacrosse

Committed to ongoing professional development. Participate in Procter & Gamble professional training covering sales, marketing, leadership, and management development, including several programs that require nomination by senior management.

Sawyer Monroe

sawyer.monroe@gmail.com
23 Strawberry Park Lane, New Rochelle, NY 10805
914-349-5550 (Home) ▪ 914-207-8243 (Mobile)

QUALIFICATIONS SUMMARY

- Highly motivated and accomplished senior management professional with entrepreneurial experience in all facets of sales, marketing, and operations.
- Proven ability to develop strategic alliances, successfully turn around declining operations, and significantly reenergize sales performance.
- Excellent analytical skills; able to rapidly assess competitive markets; implement effective strategic sales and marketing plans at national levels; and build, direct, and motivate highly successful sales organizations.
- Irreproachable professional ethics, integrity, and honesty.
- Expert relationship-building abilities and keen business acumen.

PROFESSIONAL EXPERIENCE

2006–Present   EUROSPORTS LTD. ▪ New York, NY
Director, National Sales

- Recruited as turnaround expert for this publicly held sporting-goods company to introduce revolutionary concept for repositioning European product and successfully launching it stateside; U.S. retail revenues now exceed $12 million.
- Engineered highly effective product design/development effort resulting in premier product.
- Established and successfully introduced a new brand and technology to the sporting goods marketplace without the benefit of an established "mother company."
- Report directly to president; design and implement strategic plans to ensure that sales objectives are achieved.
- Personally responsible for bringing in $1.5 million in sales during the past year.
- Created strong market interest for Eurosports products with more than 100 sports retailers; negotiated and successfully sold into such retail groups as Specialty Retailers (Sports Authority), Mass Merchants (Kmart), Price Clubs (BJs), Catalogs (Sears), Resorts (Disney).
- Directly manage sales force (staff of 36); developed strong organization of representatives; establish aggressive sales quotas and manage all sales forecasting.
- Implemented operational policies in areas of customer service and program pricing.
- Defined corporate mission statement; worked directly with New York's investment banking community in its successful drive to take Eurosports public.

2005–2006   PREMIER PRINTING ▪ Albany, NY
Account Executive/Sales

- Recruited to build significant market presence in new sales territory of Metro New York City for company specializing in high-quality waterless printing.
- Produced sales volume increase of $750,000 in first year and brought in 28 new clients; supported sales effort through development of strategic alliances through consortium of complementary companies.
- Provided creative oversight on marketing programs for such clients as ABC, American Airlines, and New York City Tourism Authority.

(continued)

Resume contributed by Jan Melnik, MRW
This resume highlights Sawyer's entrepreneurial bent to make him attractive to a company seeking aggressive growth. His cover letter is shown in sample 12-10.

Sawyer Monroe

PROFESSIONAL EXPERIENCE *(continued)*

2002–2005   ABC PRESS PROFESSIONALS ▪ New York, NY
Director of Sales

- Recruited to rejuvenate sales for regional lithographer that had no strategic plan, lost 25% of its first-time customers, and developed only 10 new clients annually.
- Brought in 30+ clients in first year. Persuaded 50% of Fortune 500 companies to top advertising agencies to hear presentations—closed record sales of 60%.
- Achieved additional 20% increase in sales volume through redesign of sales force procedures, boosting revenues from $1.5 million to $2.5 million in first year.
- Introduced highly effective bull's-eye strategic marketing approach.
- Helped position company for acquisition by major lithographer.

1994–2002   SAWYER SPORTS, INC. ▪ New Rochelle, NY
President/Founder

- Founded Sawyer Sports and purchased 20-year-old sporting goods company for zero dollars; bought inventory and fixtures at 25 cents on the dollar.
- Positioned company as high-end retail chain (3 stores) characterized by specialty service, top-quality merchandise, and innovative event advertising; voted #1 New York sports company 3rd year in business by leading consumer magazine.
- Grew sales 30% annually, building volume from $400,000 in 1994 to $2.5 million in 2002.
- Mastered event advertising, increasing business by 50% during off-peak season.
- Created advertising agency ($200,000 budget); reduced advertising costs by 15%.
- Introduced travel division; successfully negotiated to be first company to sell lift tickets away from ski areas. Achieved sales in excess of $100,000 in first season.
- Pioneered concept of establishing a "store within a store," now widespread.
- Negotiated with 150 new companies for license to distribute products in highly competitive environment; purchased $1+ million in merchandise annually for 10 departments; extensive U.S. and European travel.
- Conceived and implemented area's first consumer sport and travel trade show, a 3-day event generating $250,000+ in revenues; negotiated with national companies to rent space at show, which became an annual event.
- Poised business for successful sale at most propitious time.

1987–1994   ALBANY SKI 'N SPORT ▪ Albany, NY
Manager/Buyer

- Successfully managed high-profile, established ski shop over 7-year period.
- Increased sales by 46%, with company achieving #1 status in the East.

EDUCATION   STATE UNIVERSITY OF NEW YORK AT STONY BROOK ▪ BS Business, 1987

Sara L. McGuire

2902 Jordan Drive
Las Vegas, NV 89154

saramac@aol.com

Home (702) 239-0525
Mobile (702) 505-0526

EXPERTISE **Sales and Sales Management**
Relationship Management
Market and Business Development

Proven performer with a consistent record of building business by

- Identifying and capitalizing on niche markets
- Leading sales teams to high levels of performance
- Developing and communicating market-specific sales tactics
- Working with accounts on strategic sales, marketing, and business planning for mutual success

Experience includes **directing regional operations**—developing marketing strategies, conducting market and customer analyses with full P&L responsibility for regional business activity.

Key strength is **devising creative solutions** to overcome obstacles, adapt to changing circumstances, and achieve business goals.

PROFESSIONAL EXPERIENCE

Vice President of Sales   Tyler Global Products, New York, NY   2000–Present

Provide strategic direction, sales leadership, and operational management for 23-state region covering western half of U.S., selling promotional, novelty, and seasonal merchandise to supermarket and drug chains, mass merchants, specialty stores, and mail order. Build strong business partnerships with customers, sales agents, and East Coast corporate office, generating a team atmosphere and consistently contributing to business growth and profitability.

Recruit, motivate, and supervise independent sales agents—currently 27 productive sales organizations covering all major markets in western U.S. Work closely with sales agents to analyze market, customer, and business opportunities and develop business plans. Train sales force on effective sales strategies for each key account, market, and product.

- Spearheaded region growth from zero to $5.7 million.
- Identified and developed a lucrative niche market that now represents 80% of business company-wide.
- Created merchandising program that has become the company's trademark.
- Personally generated significant new business; developed the company's largest account from cold-call to annual sales volume of $300K–$500K.
- Targeted and captured a new market opportunity that has generated several hundred thousand dollars in sales in first year of implementation.
- Identified opportunities and recommended new products that exceeded sales expectations.
- Opened new markets by differentiating product lines through customized packaging.

Sales Consultant   McGuire Enterprises, Las Vegas, NV   1997–2000

Sold and consulted for Premier Glass, housewares division of U.S. Glass Works.

- Traveled extensively throughout northern Italy, researching glassware and dinnerware manufacturers and arranging exclusive agent relationships.
- Negotiated proposals for represented products that became multimillion-dollar product lines for the housewares division.

(continued)

The summary for this resume is a neat package of highly pertinent information. It quickly and clearly conveys the key points of Sara's background.

10-25

(continued)

Sara L. McGuire   saramac@aol.com   Page 2

PROFESSIONAL EXPERIENCE, continued

President   Desert Imports, Las Vegas, NV   1993–1997

Launched import business and secured relationship as exclusive U.S. distributor for Italian glassware and dinnerware factories. Negotiated contracts with ocean vessel lines and worked with custom brokers. Maintained corporate offices, downtown showroom, and inventory in public warehousing facilities.

- Established a network of successful national sales representatives promoting our products to department stores, mass merchants, catalog showrooms, and specialty stores.

Sales Representative   Paramount Sales, Denver, CO   1990–1993

Sold glassware, ceramics, and other product lines to department stores and independent retailers in metropolitan Denver.

EDUCATION

Master of Arts in Physical Education: University of Nevada, Las Vegas

Bachelor of Arts in Public Administration: University of Nevada, Reno

ADDITIONAL INFORMATION

Proficient in Microsoft Office (Word, Excel, Outlook, Access, PowerPoint).

National finalist, Club Golf Classic (husband/wife team); finals played at Pebble Beach, 2001.

Stuart R. Moore

srmoore@aol.com

Moscow, Russia
Tel.: (095) 123-45-67
Fax: (095) 456-78-90

Senior Sales Executive—Global Agribusiness
Building Presence for U.S. Corporations in Global Markets

- Strategic Planning and Executive Decision-Making
- Product Positioning, Packaging, Launch
- Sales and Marketing Strategy and Execution
- Market Penetration—New-Business Development

- Multicultural Business Operations
- Strategic Alliances and Partnerships
- Customer Service and Relationship-Building
- Team Leadership/Motivation/Development

Career Highlights

- Achieved rapid speed-to-market in successful product introduction in Russian market through hands-on leadership of strategic planning, product development, packaging, marketing, and distribution.

- Established substantial market presence for U.S. corporation in Russia—increased sales exponentially to multimillion-dollar level in first year of aggressive launch of new sales operation.

- Consistently delivered strong sales results, innovative sales programs, and creative team/partnership initiatives.

- Demonstrated ability to rapidly acclimate and develop strong business relationships in multicultural settings.

Experience & Achievements

URAL FOOD CORP., Moscow, Russia, 2007–Present
Distributor of branded food products through marketing affiliations with cartoon character licensees

—Vice President Sales and Marketing (2008–Present)
 Sales Director/National Sales Manager (2007–2008)

Advanced rapidly from Sales Director to VP; assumed responsibility for organization in transition and struggling to gain market share.

Successfully introduced in Russian market a line of 5 flavored milks and 2 white milks, all branded with cartoon characters through license agreements. Quickly led the organization from concept through packaging, distribution, and successful launch, in an invigorating environment of teamwork, joint problem-solving, and common commitment to goal achievement.

- Instrumental in strategic planning and crisis management to resolve differences with Russian joint venture partner. Took a leadership role in dismantling the joint venture relationship (through extensive government red tape) and reengineering the company for independent operations. Recruited a talented cross-functional management team for the new organization.

- Initiated the development of a B2B e-commerce platform to interface between U.S. companies and Russian retailers. This platform was a critical component of demonstrating a viable marketing strategy and retaining our investment funding.

- Investigated co-packing partners and established relationship with Eastern European branch of Tetra-Pak, one of the world's largest packaging companies. Directed product packaging redesign involving native Russian designer and extensive consumer test-marketing, resulting in packaging that was preferred by children 4 to 1 over original U.S.–created design. Identified and contracted with local distribution partner.

- Launched flavored milk products and spearheaded sales and marketing initiatives within a dynamic retail environment. Secured distribution with large multinationals and local supermarket chains.

- Managed all facets of product launch and marketing on extremely tight budget through effective negotiation and creative partnerships with packaging and distribution companies.

(continued)

The Career Highlights section brings strong accomplishments front and center and helps break up what would be an overlong profile. Stuart's cover letter is sample 12-11.

Stuart R. Moore

Experience & Achievements, continued

WORLDWIDE GRAIN PRODUCTS, Kansas City, MO, 1997–2007
Corn and wheat processor and distributor; worldwide sales US$8 BILLION
—**Director of Sales and Marketing**—Moscow, Russia, 2005–2007

Developed business strategy and directed all sales activities in Russia for global grain processor. Prepared budgets and forecasts; managed staff and operations; coordinated sales activities with U.S.-based support functions. Negotiated pricing, shipping, delivery, and other critical details of supply of perishable goods.

- Recruited to launch the company's Moscow office to increase market presence, capture market share, and develop business opportunities in emerging Russian market. Built operation from start-up: located, renovated, and equipped office; recruited, hired, and trained multinational staff; created and implemented business policies and procedures.

- Delivered immediate and impressive sales results: **2000%** increase over prior year in 2006; **400%** in 2007.

- Secured preferred position for the company's top-quality grain products in the best hotels in Moscow and St. Petersburg by identifying and supporting key distributors.

- Captured 20 new accounts for whole-wheat and wheat-germ products.

—**Manager, Unprocessed Grain Sales** (2000–2005)

Managed international and domestic sales, positioning, and pricing for 1.25 million tons of unprocessed grain products with annual sales of US$320 million

Developed corporate strategies and marketing programs with complete P&L accountability. Oversaw new-product development and marketing. Personally managed all international customers and sales initiatives.

- Built internal alliances to ensure integrated and coordinated sales and delivery efforts.

- Trained and mentored sales associates; successfully developed a high percentage for advancement.

- Developed long-term supplier arrangements with Procter & Gamble, Colgate Palmolive, and Lever Bros.

—**Senior Sales Representative** (1999–2000) / **Sales Representative** (1997–1999)

- Delivered significant cost efficiencies at two bulk terminals exporting product to the Far East and Europe.

- Created and successfully implemented innovative program to increase profitability by eliminating middleman.

Education and Professional Development

B.S. Agronomy, Agribusiness emphasis: University of Missouri—Columbia
Zenger-Miller and Frontline Management Training

Kathryn L. Turner

2575 Ebony Circle, Cincinnati, Ohio 45202

Home: 513-792-1234   Mobile: 513-608-8766   E-mail: kturner@fuse.net

SENIOR MARKETING EXECUTIVE: CONSUMER PACKAGED GOODS

PROFESSIONAL EXPERIENCE

THE PROCTER & GAMBLE COMPANY, Cincinnati, Ohio   1999–Present

Brand Manager, Young & Fresh Deodorant/Fragrance, Cincinnati, Ohio (2008–Present)

Selected by Vice President to return to Cincinnati to lead entire $120M Young & Fresh deodorant and fragrance businesses. Increased sales on both businesses (+10% Deodorants, +6% Fragrances) for the first time in 6 years.

- Led national launch of broad-scale sampling, new TV and print ads, stronger merchandising program, and web site development behind Young & Fresh Teen Deodorant. As a result, it is the fastest-growing deodorant in the category, with share up 35% and sales up 37% for the past 6 months.

- Led development and qualification of Young & Fresh Women strategic vision, projecting to increase sales 55% behind 2 new initiatives. One initiative—incorporating new package, revamped pricing structure, and breakthrough television advertising—has recently been qualified and exceeded pre-launch objectives. Introductory TV spot achieved the strongest test scores of any Y&F commercial ever tested.

- Focused Young & Fresh fragrance spending around holiday period behind new gift-set program, in-store scent demonstrations (14,000 sites), and new image-based TV/print campaign. As a result, Y&F increased its share leadership and grew sales for the first time in 6 years while profits increased 14%.

- Spearheading development of a new Y&F fragrance line extension targeted to young women as well as a new hair care product, which has the potential to deliver more than $30M in sales.

Brand Manager, BeautyBar Cosmetics, Hunt Valley, Maryland (2006–2008)

Assumed single-point leadership for entire $160M BeautyBar business, handling responsibilities previously shared by 4 brand managers. Managed 8 direct reports, 425 SKUs, and $61M marketing budget. Reported directly to General Manager.

- Led development and deployment of new worldwide marketing vision. As a result, sales increased by 13% and profits grew by $14M over previous year.

- Directed advertising agency in development of new campaign. Produced 5 national spots that increased business in the U.S. (+16%) and around the world (+9% in Germany, for example).

- Led creation of in-store merchandising system that grew share 13% in test and was expanded to more than 20,000 sites nationally at a cost of more than $17M.

- Launched 5 new products that delivered more than $20M in sales in 2007.

- Reduced non-value-added spending by leveraging P&G's other cosmetic brands, including Super-model package standardization, which will generate more than $7M annual savings by late 2009.

- Developed $1M public relations program into a competitive advantage, increasing placements by 37% in 2007 versus 2006. West Coast launch of "BeautyBar in Action" campaign has been cited as a corporate benchmark for success.

- Shifted promotion away from fashion trends/colors to product innovation, which increased promotion sell-in from 68% (2006) to 94% (2007), thus reducing returns by 20% and creating savings of $3M.

Assistant Brand Manager, Lemon Drop Shampoo, Cincinnati, Ohio (2003–2006)

In charge of product development, national TV and print advertising, packaging, media planning, and management of volume and spending for a brand with more than $150M in annual sales.

- Led 20-member multifunctional team in brand relaunch. Test market results exceeded objective; share grew by 25%, a $40M increase in sales nationally, while saving $5M per year in packaging costs.

- Provided overall leadership behind national product introductions. Developed package, advertising, promotional plan, sales presentation, and public relations program. Initiatives increased category share leadership and delivered $15M in new sales while growing share by 13% to a record high.

(continued)

This resume is rich in the language of marketing for large consumer-goods companies. Achievements include some details and lots of impressive numbers.

Kathryn L. Turner   Home: 513-792-1234   Mobile: 513-608-8766   E-mail: kturner@fuse.net

---

Assistant Brand Manager, Lemon Drop Shampoo, continued

- Developed and gained management agreement on overall strategic vision for Lemon Drop Styling Products and led/managed concept development process. Qualified concept that achieved a 43% "definitely would buy" score, or $20M in sales.

- Spearheaded agency/client development of new national TV and print advertising campaign (2 TV and 2 print ads). Advertising commercials received highest test score since 1989 Lemon Drop introduction.

Sales Intern, Health and Beauty Care, Cleveland, Ohio (Training Module, Fall 2003)

Completed 3-month field sales training, selling to 47 food, drug, and mass-merchandising stores.

- Sold Hair Europa introduction into 4 national accounts.

Assistant Brand Manager, Young & Fresh Deodorant, Cincinnati, Ohio (2000–2003)

Acquisition Team member for newly acquired brand. Responsibilities included promotion planning, pricing, budget management, business analysis, and entry-point marketing.

- Developed systems needed to start up business at P&G and completely overhauled promotion plan to maximize sales force strengths while reducing promotional spending by 25%.

- Created P&G's first comprehensive male teen marketing program, focusing on college sampling, junior high school education curriculum, and athletic event sponsorship. As a result, overall brand ratings among young men increased significantly from 2001 to 2002 and helped stop share decline.

- Developed and implemented brand's everyday value pricing strategy, which has played an instrumental role in its long-term growth.

- Led multifunctional team to develop and expand P&G's first trial-size antiperspirant since 1982, overcoming significant manufacturing obstacles.

Marketing Intern, Health & Personal Care Division, Cincinnati, Ohio (Summer 1999)

Developed marketing plan for BabyCare line extension and designed club store package for new developmental brand.

- Implemented direct-mail copy on $8M established baby products brand. Initiated and completed report that persuaded top management to change brand target to increase profits.

- Offered full-time position upon completion of MBA.

GENERAL ELECTRIC COMPANY, Evendale, Ohio   1994–1999

Specialist, Operations Budgets & Planning (1996–1999)
Financial Management Program (1994–1996)

One of 125 college graduates accepted into elite management training program from a candidate pool of more than 3,000.

EDUCATION

MBA, 2000: J.L. Kellogg Graduate School of Management, Northwestern University, Evanston, Illinois
BA Economics, 1994: Cornell University, Ithaca, New York

Chapter 11

Career Transition Resumes

When I work with clients who want to transition into sales or from one area of sales/marketing to another, I make sure they first do their homework: perform research, talk to people, and find out what's really involved in the type of sales job they're targeting. Then, together, we look at their background for evidence that they have the fundamental skills necessary for success in sales. The resumes in this chapter show how to make the most of this "evidence" to create a powerful resume.

Marissa L. Trenton

11 Rocky Road, Charleston, WV 25314
mltrenton@usa.net
304-341-0011

Goal: Pharmaceutical Sales

Opportunity to contribute to the growth and success of an industry leader through energetic application of strong persuasive, communication, organizational, and leadership skills.

- **Persuasive / Sales:** Proven ability to build consensus, generate donations, and motivate participation.
- **Effective Communications:** Listening, assessing needs, addressing both spoken and unspoken concerns, developing solutions.
- **Planning and Organization:** Record of identifying needs and effectively carrying out all stages of program planning and implementation.
- **Leadership:** Elected captain of 3 sports in high school; team leader of soccer team in college. Elected dorm representative in college. Currently chairing initiative to develop educational outreach programs.

Professional Experience

TEACHER — Sandridge Elementary School, Charleston, WV — 2007–Present

- **Improved parent conference participation from 30% to 95%** through an integrated campaign of parent communication and student involvement.
- Teamed with 3 other teaching professionals to **develop a persuasive proposal** for expanding grade levels within the classrooms. Conducted research and developed supportive documentation.
- Organized an after-school program as a **solution for an identified need.** Managed all stages of the program from planning through implementation.
- **Successfully met the challenge** of learning new teaching practices "on the fly" and integrating traditional and Montessori teaching methods.
- Constantly develop **creative and innovative methods** to motivate students and make learning meaningful.

▪ ▪ ▪

TEACHER — Robbins Montessori School, Lynchburg, VA — 2006–2007

- **Conducted successful sales campaign** to solicit donations from local restaurants for latchkey program. **Scheduled appointments, prepared and delivered effective presentation (including graphics), and achieved 100% participation.**
- **Conceived and implemented a successful program** to teach swimming to 52 kindergarten students.

▪ ▪ ▪

SWIM INSTRUCTOR — Lynchburg Country Club, Lynchburg, VA — Summers 2001–2006

- **Identified need** for an infant/preschool swimming program. Developed curriculum, trained instructors, communicated with parents, and managed scheduling.

Education

RANDOLPH-MACON WOMAN'S COLLEGE, Lynchburg, VA — Bachelor of Social Science, 2006
- **Personally financed entire education while maintaining 3.5 GPA.**

Additional Information

- Successful hostess noted for ability to plan and execute large dinner parties. Requested to manage food planning, preparation, and service for a wedding reception for 100 people in summer 2008.

How does teaching relate to pharmaceutical sales? The relevant elements from Marissa's background are highlighted in bold.

Maria Trujillo

29-A Primrose Court, Nashville, TN 37211
mariatee@hotmail.com • (615) 455-4555

EXPERTISE	**Sales and Marketing**
PROFILE	Energetic, persistent, and creative sales professional with a consistently successful track record of industrial/technical, business-to-business, and direct-to-consumer sales of tangible and intangible products and services.

Strengths
- Devising and implementing innovative sales and marketing strategies.
- Developing new business through persistent cold-calling to identified targets.
- Delivering effective sales presentations to diverse audiences.
- Negotiating prices, services, and contracts to ensure satisfaction for the customer and profitability for the business.
- Analyzing and identifying roadblocks… creatively solving problems to reach goals.
- Developing customer relationships through a strong customer focus and determination to find creative ways to meet their needs.

PROFESSIONAL EXPERIENCE

Primrose Path Residential Community, Nashville, Tennessee   2006–Present

MANAGER Focus on maintaining high occupancy rates through effective marketing and sales activities for residential apartment community for senior adults. In addition, manage day-to-day operations, supervise staff, and oversee facility maintenance.

Challenge *Maintain occupancy in a niche market with constant attrition.*

Actions
- Through aggressive cold-calling and relationship development, established active referral network with professionals in health care and elder services.
- Adapted sales presentation to focus on relevant features and benefits for individual audiences. Demonstrate strong customer orientation and excellent follow-through during lengthy, multistep sales cycle.
- Increased response to advertising through new classification in rental-property publication; persistently pursued this idea to successful conclusion.

Results **Reduced vacancy rate from 51% in 2006 to steadily maintained range of 1%–10% today. In first month on the job, conducted aggressive marketing campaigns that achieved occupancy for 90% of available units.**

OC Apartments, Nashville, Tennessee   2004–2006

MANAGER Oversaw all aspects of day-to-day operations of 128-unit apartment complex occupied by university students. Recruited, trained, supervised, and scheduled 4 full-time employees.

Challenge *Improve occupancy rate and stability of student-occupied complex; restore operating efficiency to poorly run facility.*

Actions
- Developed and implemented innovative marketing strategies to achieve goals for occupancy and stability. Created incentives for good grades and responsible occupancy; improved overall reputation of complex by increasing caliber of residents.
- Reorganized financial record-keeping, totally restructured the maintenance department, and tightly controlled and monitored expenses.

Results **Improved occupancy from 80% to 100% within 5 months; consistently maintained high rate during tenure. Increased profitability by significantly reducing operating expenses.**

(continued)

Maria's background showed a common thread of sales skills and accomplishments, although that hadn't always been her job title. Using the CAR approach, we presented her success stories. She received an excellent response from recruiters and hiring managers, and through persistent networking and follow-up she landed a job in office-furniture sales.

Maria Trujillo

PROFESSIONAL EXPERIENCE, continued

Mall Property Investors, Nashville, Tennessee   2002–2004
RETAIL LEASING SPECIALIST

Challenge	*Market new 24,000-square-foot shopping center from pre-construction to full occupancy.*
Actions	• Recruited new tenants through persistent cold-calling.
	• Maintained tenant satisfaction by serving as liaison and problem-solver between tenants, service contractors, and company.
	• Contributed to win-win negotiations with prospective tenants.
Results	**Secured and maintained 100% occupancy within time frame that exceeded the owner's expectations.**

Kountry Kraft Kabinets, Nashville, Tennessee   1999–2002
SALES REPRESENTATIVE

Challenge	*Sell residential and commercial cabinetry to contractors, builders, and homeowners.*
Actions	• Developed thorough knowledge of cabinetry and carpentry to enable effective problem-solving for unique challenges of each residence or business.
	• Provided consistently excellent customer service.
Results	**Recognized as one of the company's most successful sales representatives… frequently won sales contests even when working part-time and competing against full-time sales staff.**

EDUCATION

Vanderbilt University, Nashville, Tennessee   B.S., 1999
        Major: Communications — Minor: Management

Eduardo Torrez

edtorrez@aol.com

489 Champagne Court
Neenah, Wisconsin 54956
Cell (414) 549-5495

Sales/Management Professional with successful background in building and directing customer-driven organizations. Key contributor to business growth, organizational restructuring, and operating efficiency. Innovative and strategic thinker with strong understanding of business needs and the ability to put plans into action.

Strengths

- Assessing needs, building relationships, selling solutions.
- Identifying and capitalizing on market opportunities.
- Increasing sales and visibility through mutually beneficial business alliances.
- Leading and developing sales teams… building on the strengths and individual motivators of each team member.
- Rapidly learning new business environments and delivering both immediate and long-term results.

Professional Experience

TODAY'S SPORTS, Chicago, Illinois, 2000–present
Specialty sports retailer with a peak of 25 store locations; winner of "Best Mid-Size Retailer" award from National Association of Sporting Goods Merchandisers.

Sales & Marketing Consultant, 2008–present   Neenah, Wisconsin

Provide on-call consultation to Store Directors, assisting with sales, operations, and customer service issues.

Participate on the company's organizational development task force—the Job Redesign Team (2005–present), a continuous-improvement initiative with significant achievements to date:

- Eliminated several layers of middle management; trained retail sales staff in all operational areas; empowered front-line staff to make customer service and operations decisions.
- Improved performance and communication company-wide.

Communicate the team's efforts to sales staffs and store directors.

Store Director, 2000–2008   Neenah—Appleton—Green Bay

Contributed to the company's growth and success as Store Director in key markets and new locations. In last position, managed store with more than $1 million in annual sales.

Accomplishments: Sales and Sales Management

- **Increased profits 18% and unit sales 15%—reduced controllable expenses 3%— improved dollars-per-transaction 3%** during a period of competitive price reductions.
- Selected, trained, and developed staff, with a strong focus on product knowledge, customer service, and the individual motivators of each salesperson. **Sales teams consistently ranked 2nd to 4th in the company for weekly sales performance-to-goals.**
- **Led the company's expansion into the Wisconsin marketplace.** Developed local marketing strategies, launched start-up, and managed 3 highly successful stores.
- **Successfully positioned company name with primary target audiences** through affiliations with local sports teams and innovative radio station partnerships.
- With sales team, brainstormed sales strategies for used sporting equipment. Subsequently, implemented new pricing structure that **boosted margin over 50% for the first time.** Strategy was then adopted for use company-wide.

(continued)

Ed moved from retail management to direct sales after a lot of work on identifying his strengths and researching target markets.

Eduardo Torrez

Professional Experience

TODAY'S SPORTS

Store Director, continued

Accomplishments: Operations

- Directed ordering, merchandising, distribution, purchasing, and retailing of sports-related products, maintaining accurate inventory for more than 50,000 items.
- Improved accuracy and efficiency of ordering and thereby **increased in-stock percentages from 70% to 90%**… an essential component of maximizing sales opportunities for highly profitable impulse and trend-driven retail business.
- **Recognized for strong troubleshooting and problem-solving skills;** stepped in as interim manager or in a consulting role to resolve a wide range of sales and operational issues at several store locations.
- As **Total Quality Management facilitator,** championed the company's TQM initiatives and delivered training to peers, new hires, and newly promoted staff members.
- Participated on corporate Pay & Compensation Team; helped **determine and implement new company-wide pay structures** at all levels except senior management.

WISCONSIN GREENS, Neenah, Wisconsin, 1996–2000

Business Manager

Directed golf course operations. Oversaw accurate accounting, invoicing, and payroll; supervised golf cart fleet maintenance. Managed ordering, inventory control, and merchandising for pro shop sales of golf equipment and clothing.

Marketed the course and facilities to interested parties; negotiated reservation agreements; organized and scheduled corporate outings, tournaments, leagues, private and public tee times.

- **Improved efficiency and sales performance** through operational reorganization of the office, shop, and snack bar.

UNIVERSITY CENTER, UNIVERSITY OF WISCONSIN–GREEN BAY, 1994–1996

Manager

Managed food service and catering operations for multifacility sports and entertainment complex.

Education

B.A. in History, University of Wisconsin–Green Bay, 1994

Professional Training

Total Quality Management (facilitator)
Covey Leadership Training

Denise Powers, RN

489 Marlborough Street
Boston, Massachusetts 02116
(617) 221-2121   nursepowers@aol.com

Goal: Pharmaceutical Sales

Summary of Qualifications

- Nursing and Pharmacy education.
- Clinical care experience in hospital settings—understanding of medical and pharmaceutical terms, conditions, treatment, and protocols.
- Strong relationship skills and ability to interact effectively with physicians, nurses, and all members of the health care team.
- Experience negotiating and collaborating with home health agencies and DME companies.
- Proven ability to establish and achieve personal and team goals through leadership, persistence, follow-through, attention to detail, and focus on results.

Professional Experience

CHILDREN'S HOSPITAL, Boston, Massachusetts   2006–present

Registered Nurse—Critical Care Resource Team (2007–Present)

One of 2 nurses selected to participate on a coordinated health care team providing care to neonatal and pediatric ICU clients. Actively participate in treatment decisions. Develop patient care priorities through intricate assessment; evaluate client response and effectively troubleshoot to make beneficial changes in plan of care.

- Effectively and persistently communicate nursing viewpoint and recommendations to physicians while maintaining a positive teamwork environment.
- Maintain and evaluate quality-assurance measures. Follow through with post-discharge telephone calls to ensure client satisfaction.

Recruited as a member of the education council in the neonatal intensive care unit.

- Instruct weekly CPR classes for parents of newborns; educate on crisis intervention and physiological warning signs; coordinate outside resources for high-risk parents and children.
- Establish rapport and communicate effectively with diverse parent audiences. Consistently receive excellent post-presentation evaluations.

Patient Care Assistant—Pediatric Medical/Surgical Unit (2006–2007)

- Coordinated with physicians and nurses on interventions from admission through discharge.
- Negotiated and organized discharge needs through durable medical equipment companies and home health agencies.

NEWTON WELLESLEY HOSPITAL, Wellesley, Massachusetts   2005–2006

Patient Care Technician

- Delivered care to geriatric psychiatric clients. Collaborated with physicians and nurses in reality orientation and assessment of behavioral changes.
- Codirected family conferences and facilitated communication between family and physician.

CHILDREN'S HOSPITAL, Boston, Massachusetts   2005

Neonatal Intensive Care Unit Nursing Internship

- Chosen for internship following highly competitive selection process.

Education

NORTHEASTERN UNIVERSITY, Boston, Massachusetts

Bachelor of Science in Nursing, 2006
Pre-Pharmacy Major, 2001–2003

- Elected Treasurer of the Senior Class; held financial and record-keeping responsibility for student activities and philanthropies.
- Supervised and independently organized a Graduation Committee to plan and implement school commencement activities. Managed budget; delegated tasks; monitored team and individual progress.
- Delivered winning oral presentation for selection as 1 of 2 delegates from a class of 200 to represent the College of Nursing and Health at the National Student Nurses Association's Annual Convention. Prepared and presented convention summary to nursing school classes.
- One of 6 recipients (among 300 students) awarded the Nellie Franz Scholarship for Academic and Professional Excellence.

Although she had no sales experience, Denise captured the attention of sales managers and landed a job in pharmaceutical sales. Her strong nursing and pharmacy background were definitely important.

RHONDA MOTZ

503-769-1094   7943 Cherry Tree Lane, Salem, OR 97311   rhonda@motz.com

VALUE OFFERED TO WILLS COLLEGE AS DIRECTOR OF DEVELOPMENT

Sales/marketing and management professional with a career track record of driving organizational growth. Expert in developing new products that boost revenues and increase market share. Repeatedly built support for new programs and created cohesive teams within matrix management systems.

Delivered business results in competitive environments, demonstrating skills that will transfer to the challenging environment of gift support, sponsor development, and fund raising.

- Turned around a declining division in one year, achieving average 20% growth year after year.
- Created and led product-development organization that overhauled 50% of product line and contributed to business rank as #1 profit producer for parent company.
- Introduced more than 200 new products since 1995.
- Identified growth opportunities; developed strategic business plans; managed and motivated cross-functional organizations to surpass goals and achieve business objectives.

EXPERIENCE AND ACHIEVEMENTS

SENSIBEL PRODUCTS, INC., Salem, OR   2003–Present
Producer of storage solutions for the industrial/commercial, lawn & garden, and home & office products markets.

Product Development Manager

Recruited to launch and lead first formal product-development department for 48-year-old company. Led aggressive product commercialization and introduction program, taking 136 new products from concept to profitable market launch. New products were instrumental in reversing sliding market share and restoring competitive market position.

Lead marketing/product development for all of the company's consumer, industrial, and lawn & garden product lines. Manage department activities, cross-functional initiatives, and a broad range of outside vendors and consulting firms. Continuously strive to reduce costs, improve quality, and create product distinction.

Selected achievements include

- Built product-development department from the ground up. Recruited and hired a talented team; introduced a new computer system; instituted department policies and procedures.

- Galvanized the product-development process, successfully launching an average of 15 new products per year, representing annual investment of $3.2 million. Products introduced/updated since 2003 now represent 47%–60% of revenues in each of the 3 product lines.

- Spearheaded significant cost-reduction programs, leading product-development and manufacturing teams to identify and implement production savings opportunities. Notable results:
  - Annual product-line savings of $1.0 million with a one-time investment of $1.6 million.
  - 31% reduction in manufacturing cost for a core product; annual savings of $2 million.

- Developed the company's first strategic plan, creating a framework for profitable growth.

- Initiated monthly brainstorming/review meetings that ensure strategic focus and organization-wide support for new initiatives.

- Played a pivotal role in development of multichannel strategy to stabilize market share, accelerate growth, and capitalize on emerging channels.

This resume was adapted to help Rhonda transition from product management and marketing to director of development (fund-raising) at a private college.

503-769-1094   **RHONDA MOTZ**   rhonda@motz.com

GREAT GOODS, INC., Salem, OR   1995–2003
Manufacturer/marketer of indoor and outdoor organization, storage, and cleaning products.

Senior Product Manager / Specialty Products Division, 1999–2003

——**Drove successful turnaround of Lawn & Garden business—restoring sales growth, invigorating product line, and improving profitability through efficient product management.**

Led operating and strategic planning process, P&L, and all marketing functions for the Lawn & Garden business (3 product lines, $44.3 million annual sales volume). Within matrix management system, worked effectively with multiple departments at all management and manufacturing levels regarding daily operating issues, long-term strategic business directions, and new-product development.

- Reversed 3-year sales decline and steadily grew sales; led vigorous new product development effort; aggressively reduced SKUs to leverage core business sales and bolster profits.

	1999	2001	2002	2003
Growth	12%	17%	17%	34% (projected)
Number of new products		25	18	27
SKU reduction		29%	5%	13%

Manager of Forecasting, Inventory Planning, & Market Administration, 1997–1999

——**Selected to head up new department serving the recently realigned Specialty Products Division.**

Created and implemented integrated 30–60–90 day forecasts. Assisted in development of long-range forecast for division's Strategic Plan and annual Operating Plan.

Financial Analyst / Home Products Division, 1995–1997

——**Performed financial analyses, developed pricing projections, and assisted in preparing Strategic and Operating Plan financials.**

CREST HILLS CONDOMINIUMS, Salem, Ohio   1993–1995

Development Manager

——**Generated 47% (more than $700K) of $1.5 million sales volume achieved by 4-person sales team.**

Led marketing and sales efforts for new residential complex—special marketing events, direct-mail campaigns, advertising strategy, and implementation. Coordinated activities of sales team. Interviewed and selected real estate broker and homeowners' association management company. Assisted with preparation and analysis of cash-flow schedules and budgets.

EDUCATION

UNIVERSITY OF WASHINGTON, Seattle, WA   MBA Marketing & Finance, 1993
KENYON COLLEGE, Gambier, OH   BA Economics / Statistics & Accounting emphasis, 1991

Chapter 12

Effective Cover Letters

An essential partner to your resume, your cover letter is a complex document in a simple format. In just a few short paragraphs, you must introduce yourself, explain why you're writing, provide compelling reasons for the reader to want to speak with you, and ask for a meeting. While you're at it, don't forget to include specific information about the company and the opportunity—and, above all, be interesting!

Standard advice is that you should write each cover letter personally for the specific opportunity. Although this may be ideal, it is also a lot of work. I firmly believe that a good cover letter should be versatile enough to be used for many opportunities, with minor tweaking and personalization.

As with your resume and your entire approach during a job search, try to focus your letter more on the employer's needs than your interests. Because you need to do this while talking about yourself, it can get tricky. The sample cover letters that follow give you good ideas for opening and closing language, ways to present accomplishments, and formatting suggestions. The companion resume for each letter is identified so that you can see how both documents support a clear career target.

Cover Letter FAQs

Do I need to include a cover letter with every resume I send?

Yes, for professional and executive positions a cover letter is expected. And why not take advantage of another opportunity to sell yourself?

Many times you will be e-mailing your resume after a conversation with a recruiter, hiring manager, or network contact. In these instances, it is most appropriate to write a quick note rather than send a full, formal cover letter. This note might be brief, but be sure that it is professional in tone; uses correct grammar, spelling, and punctuation; and furthers the key messages in your resume.

Do hiring authorities really read cover letters?

My informal research over the years reveals that the hiring world is divided almost equally into three camps: those who peruse every letter, those who read them after a resume has caught their attention, and those who ignore them. Obviously, you must write your cover letters to the two-thirds of your readers who will or might read every word. And, just as important, don't omit important information from your resume on the assumption that you can include it in your cover letter, because this information will escape at least one-third of your target audience.

What if I don't know who I'm writing to? Should I use "Dear Sir or Madam"?

First, make every effort to identify an individual. But if that's not possible, I recommend eliminating the salutation altogether and beginning your letter with an "attention" or "regarding" line. Here are some examples:

Re: Marketing Management Opportunity
Attn: Human Resources

Re: Wall Street Journal Advertisement 10/15/09: Executive VP Sales

Re: Job Code XYZ-241, "Product Manager"

The "Dear Sir or Madam" salutation is dated, and the generic "Good morning" or "Good day" greetings some people use remind me of junk mail that tries to be personal (and fails).

How can I grab the reader's attention?

The primary way to capture a reader's interest is to show that you understand his or her needs and can offer a benefit. If you're responding to a posted position or writing directly to a company without a personal contact, try to make your first few sentences interesting enough that the reader will want to read on. In those instances when you're writing at the suggestion of a networking contact, use that person's name up front so that the reader feels obligated to continue reading and, further, to accept your follow-up phone call (see sample 12-1).

How long should my cover letter be?

It is very rare that you would write a cover letter longer than one page. In fact, "keep it short and snappy" is good advice. You don't want to bore your readers. You don't need to repeat all the information that is in your resume; just give them a few highlights that are relevant to the particular opportunity, company, or circumstance.

Should I indicate that I'll follow up?

Regardless of whether you say so or not, you should definitely follow up every resume and cover letter with a phone call if at all possible. If you say you will follow up, be doubly certain that you do so, or you'll risk destroying your credibility. If you can be precise, feel free to indicate that "I will call your office on Friday, October 1." Although it might not have a material effect on the disposition of your resume, such a promise just might prompt the recipient to let your letter hang around until Friday so that it's handy when you call.

The ad asks for salary requirements. What should I tell them?

In most cases, you're better off saying nothing. Companies asking for salary requirements are doing so only to screen out potential candidates. Remember, with a posted ad they'll be dealing with hundreds of applicants. Salary is a simple "in or out" benchmark. Formal surveys and informal conversations with hiring authorities reveal, time after time, that when they ask for salary and no information is provided, *they look at the resume anyway.* You'll improve your chances of being interviewed if you don't immediately disqualify yourself on the basis of salary. Your goal is to generate interviews—and who knows what they might lead to? So give yourself every opportunity to get in front of hiring authorities. However, as noted in chapter 13, you can share your salary goals or current salary with an executive recruiter. And if an ad says "resumes without salary information will not be considered," you must comply.

Should I explain my reason for looking for a job?

It's not necessary (nor always valuable) to share this information, but sometimes it makes sense to do so (see cover letter samples 12-1, 12-4, 12-5, 12-9, and 12-11). In general, present only positive information that will help sell your candidacy.

Finally, remember that although cover letters are important, you shouldn't let your job search get bogged down while you agonize over the perfect phrase. Develop a few good templates, adapt them as appropriate, be sure to follow up, and get down to the real work of your job search: meeting and talking with people.

Sample Cover Letters

Following are 11 sample cover letters.

Casey Stanton

7509 Laredo Avenue, Austin, Texas 78741
512-555-8755—casey@gmail.com

April 30, 2009

Mr. Eduardo Santayana
Vice President, Marketing
Mercedes-Benz of North America
275 Wall Street
New York, NY 10023

Dear Mr. Santayana:

At the recommendation of Phil Qualls, owner of Elite Motor Company, I am forwarding my resume for your consideration with regard to marketing/sales opportunities with Mercedes-Benz.

For the past four years I have had the opportunity to market and sell Mercedes-Benz automobiles. As a member of the professional and highly successful sales team at Elite Motor Company, I have been challenged and motivated to learn all details of the product line to compete against the best in the business.

Combined with strong sales performance in all my past positions in diverse industries, this recent experience has given me the knowledge and the confidence to pursue a marketing/sales opportunity with Mercedes-Benz of North America, following relocation to the New York area as a result of my husband's recent promotion to Exxon headquarters.

What do I have to offer?

- **Successful sales experience...** knowledge of all stages of the sales cycle... strong product marketing abilities.
- **A field sales background...** understanding of how marketing programs are applied at the dealerships.
- **A track record of relationship sales...** commitment to quality customer service.
- **A passion for automobiles...** enthusiasm for the industry... energy, commitment, and drive.

I would greatly appreciate the opportunity to discuss your marketing operation and explore how my skills, strengths, and experience can contribute to your continued success. I will follow up with a phone call to your office on Friday, May 8, and I hope to set up an appointment with you during my visit to New York the following week. Thank you.

Sincerely,

Casey Stanton

enclosure

Companion resume: 4-9

KATHLEEN STANSFIELD

257 Lakeview Drive, Apt. 15-B
Chicago, IL 60623
312-498 8888 ■ stansfield@aol.com

April 30, 2009

Robert Johnson
VP Sales
The Frith & Howe Company
2525 Michigan Avenue
Chicago, IL 60606

Dear Mr. Johnson:

A high-performing sales organization is essential to your company's continued growth and success. When adding to your sales and sales management team, you don't want to take chances: You want sales professionals whose track record and experience *prove* they have what it takes to be successful.

I think you'll agree that my accomplishments, highlighted in the enclosed resume, amply demonstrate sales, marketing, and management skills that can help your company grow.

In addition to strong sales results (performance-to-goal averaging 170% over the past seven years), my contributions have included innovative programs—some of which have been adapted company-wide—and numerous speaking engagements that have improved corporate visibility and enhanced my relationship with clients and prospects. My true strength lies in *consultative* sales. I know how to build relationships and develop sales recommendations that are true solutions for customer needs.

With a well-rounded background and a record of strong performance in each position, I am well-equipped and eager to handle diverse new challenges. I'd be very interested in speaking with you to explore how my skills, strengths, and experience can benefit your organization.

Thank you for your consideration.

Sincerely,

Kathleen Stansfield

enclosure

Companion resume: 5-15

Shaun L. Madden

781-639-9876 ▪ slmadden@aol.com

47 Mulberry Street
Wellesley, MA 02481

April 30, 2009

Brenda Cook, President
Innovative Software, Inc.
25 Meridian Boulevard
New Britain, CT 06050

Dear Ms. Cook:

With a record of leading sales organizations to the best records in their history, I have the expertise to deliver both *immediate* and *sustained* sales growth for your organization.

My track record reflects:

- An unbroken 11-year record of outperforming sales goals in both sales and sales management roles.
- Individual, team, and corporate-wide promulgation of *sales process* as the foundation for an effective sales organization.
- Leadership that results in outstanding contributions from *all* members of a sales team for predictable and consistent results and steady revenue streams.

In short, I am a leader both by example and through effective management of individuals and teams. I have contributed significantly to sales and profitability for companies in the advertising, marketing, and hardware/software/business solutions industries. Personally committed to continued growth and excellence, I have the drive, energy, vision, leadership, and implementation skills to make a positive difference to any sales organization.

Let's talk soon. I am confident that you will be interested in my track record and ability to help you achieve important business goals.

Sincerely,

Shaun L. Madden

enclosure

Companion resume: 6-1

IRINA PETROV

Permanent e-mail address: irinapetrov@hotmail.com

Through September 2009: Malaskaya 37/15, Moscow, Russia — Telephone (095) 555-23-45

April 30, 2009

Patricia Gelman
Director of Sales
Medianet Publishing Group
7229 Gardenia Boulevard
Los Angeles, CA 94023

Dear Ms. Gelman:

As the first advertising sales manager for *Trend* magazine in Russia, I played a key role in the successful launch and continuous growth of the publication.

The success of my efforts can be measured in advertising pages and performance to goals:

- For a special-edition *Trend 850,* I personally sold 200 pages of advertising and led my advertising team to set a record for number of pages of advertising in a single publication.

- As Advertising Director, I have consistently *exceeded* the publication's advertising goals by 20%–40% every issue. I am proud that we were able to maintain our performance even when Russia was experiencing economic difficulties.

If you have a need, I could deliver similar results for you.

With authorization to emigrate to the U.S. in late summer, I am excitedly looking forward to new professional challenges. I am confident that my fluency in English and exposure to international businesses will help me acclimate quickly and become a valued contributor. If your organization could benefit from my skills, strengths, and experience, we should schedule a time to discuss your needs. I am available by telephone in Russia until the end of the year, and in person in Los Angeles thereafter.

Thank you for your consideration. I look forward to hearing from you.

Sincerely,

Irina Petrov

enclosure

Companion resume: 6-18

Luke T. Mallette

257 93rd Street, Unit 7B
San Francisco, CA 94114

lukemallette@mac.com

Home 415-245-6655
Mobile 415-390-1115

April 30, 2009

Susan T. Phinney
Executive VP, Marketing
Southern Company
257 Robert E. Lee Boulevard
Richmond, VA 23173

Dear Ms. Phinney:

Success in marketing, sales, and strategic management can be measured by *results*. During my seven years with Consolidated Consumer Companies, I've delivered significant and measurable bottom-line benefits and have been continuously rewarded with new challenges and opportunities.

My career has been well-balanced among direct sales, project management, and brand management/marketing. As you'll observe from the enclosed resume, I have been an innovator, devising and executing new ideas, creative concepts, and original approaches that have led to new directions and positive results. Specific highlights include

- Conceiving and spearheading a new concept for in-store hair care product marketing that, on initial launch, was eagerly welcomed by retailers and successfully installed in twice the number of retail locations we had forecasted.

- Increasing market share 15% in a growing niche market through targeted advertising that reached 90% of available consumers within the market group.

- Developing effective and easy-to-use tools for promotion planning and pricing analysis to assist our global sales force in gaining maximum value from the $900 million the company spends annually on product promotions.

Continued advancement with CCC will mean remaining permanently in its New York City headquarters. Although my three years here have been rewarding, my strong desire to return to Virginia has prompted me to launch a search at this time.

My record shows my ability to contribute to a company's success and profitability. I'm confident I can deliver similar results for your organization. May we schedule a time to discuss our mutual interests?

Thank you for your consideration.

Sincerely,

Luke T. Mallette

enclosure

Companion resume: 7-15

Damian McMillan

1123 Adobe Street, San Diego, California 92138
Phone 619-555-7435 ▪ Fax 619-555-7436 ▪ damianmac@gmail.com

April 30, 2009

Sun-n-Sea Products Corp.
17 Ocean Boulevard
San Diego, CA 92138

Attn: Tracy, Human Resources

Your advertisement in Sunday's *San Diego Times* for a Brand Leader in your Marketing Department describes interesting challenges that seem to be an excellent fit for the experience and contributions detailed in the enclosed resume.

My 17-year career in progressively challenging sales and marketing positions has given me diverse opportunities to contribute to corporate growth and profitability, and I offer proven capabilities in product management and marketing that can benefit your organization.

Specific contributions relevant to your needs include the following:

- As a product manager, developed and launched 9 new retail product lines that outperformed sales expectations by 30%.

- Improved gross profit margins by 35% through effective expense management and a successful drive to spur sales across product lines.

- Significantly increased sales revenues through effective leadership of integrated marketing and sales strategies that delivered results in new business development, account penetration, niche marketing, and relationship sales.

- In direct sales, delivered consistently strong sales increases, including a territory turnaround that yielded a 39% improvement.

I'm confident that I can deliver similar results for Sun-n-Sea. May we meet to explore your needs and how my skills, strengths, and breadth of experience can help your company to achieve business goals?

Thank you for your consideration.

Sincerely,

Damian McMillan

enclosure

Companion resume: 7-16

```
TO:        Mark J. Russo [mjrusso@talentpartners.com]
SUBJECT:   National Sales Leader—Financial & Technical Products
```

Dear Mr. Russo:

For companies in 3 distinct B2B markets, I delivered superior sales
performance--double-digit annual sales growth, 300% market-share increase,
125% annual account increases--year after year, in dual roles as national
sales manager and top sales producer.

I would like to explore how I can achieve similar results for your client's
company. In brief, my qualifications include the following:

   == 11 years in sales, including 8 in sales management, always exceeding
   quotas, leading the company in sales, and delivering superior results in
   up and down markets.
   == Ability to sell complex products and services at the executive level.
   == Success launching innovative services and new products, penetrating
   new markets, and targeting and capturing strategic accounts.
   == Flair for recruiting talented salespeople and fostering top team
   performance.

In either a sales management or combined player/coach role, I can help your
client's company achieve (and exceed) its sales goals. I have the strategic
vision and organizational leadership skills to manage a regional, national, or
corporate sales organization.

My geographic preference is to remain in the Boston area, although for the
right opportunity, relocation is certainly an option. For the last several
years my compensation has topped $200K annually.

If you know of a company seeking a sales leader with my expertise and track
record, I would welcome your call.

Sincerely,

Sandy O'Brien

****
My resume is attached as a Word file.
****

Companion resume: 10-17
This cover letter is presented in e-mail format. For this type of letter, it's particularly important to use short paragraphs and capture the reader's interest immediately.

Steven L. Taylor

415.721.3459   530 Nob Hill, San Francisco, CA 94130   steve@thetaylors.com

April 30, 2009

Alison Edwards, President
Frontier Financial
450 Victory Parkway, Suite 7-A
San Francisco, CA 94144

Dear Ms. Edwards:

In nine years with Secure Paper, I delivered top-notch sales results and played a key role in strategic market focus, new-product development, and business expansion. Specifically:

- I led the company's expansion into Internet banking, developing and launching a product that precisely fit our target customers' needs, quickly generated 10% of total company revenue, and soon turned a profit.
- Under my leadership, Western region sales skyrocketed from $3.5 million to $54 million in just three years.
- In a district leadership role, I created successful new territories and led the company in sales of its high-margin strategic products.

Most recently, I turned around the sales performance of a real-estate services company, doubling sales and profits through a laser-like focus on strategic markets and relationship sales. This turnaround has prompted the owner to sell the business—thus my search for a new opportunity where I can again have an immediate impact on sales growth and profit performance.

Frontier Financial's products, customers, reputation, and market opportunities are exciting and an excellent fit for my background. I would like to meet with you to discuss the value I offer your company—my proven ability to build strategic relationships, dominate markets, drive sales growth, and deliver results in all areas of performance.

Thank you.

Sincerely,

Steven L. Taylor

enclosure: resume

Companion resume: 10-18

Samantha Taylor-Massey

914-860-2222   23 Whiteoak Lane, White Plains, New York 10601   massey@optonline.net

April 30, 2009

Edward Rivera
Executive Recruiter
Hudson / Smith Associates
257 Madison Avenue, Suite 11-B
New York, NY 10021

Dear Mr. Rivera:

Is one of your clients in need of a senior sales/marketing executive? If so, perhaps I can help.

During a career marked by rapid promotion and consistent success in increasing both sales volumes and new accounts, I have demonstrated strong skills in the following key areas that can benefit your client:

- **Sales:** personal achievements as well as success in leading and directing a sales team.
- **Account development:** persistent pursuit of key accounts; successful delivery of sales proposals.
- **Business planning/goal-setting:** for the sales operation as well as the business as a whole.
- **Staff leadership:** track record of successful staff development through maximizing abilities, training to improve skills, and encouraging input and autonomous decision-making.

Having taken my company from start-up to its current level, where, under the direction of managers I have groomed, it is functioning productively without my day-to-day involvement, I am eager to tackle a new opportunity. Frankly, I miss the stimulation of attacking a new challenge, building a sales and business operation, and achieving goals (both corporate and self-determined) through the implementation of well-planned strategies.

May we talk? I'm confident that my experience and accomplishments will be of interest to your client. I will follow up with a phone call to your office next week. I look forward to our conversation.

Sincerely,

Samantha Taylor-Massey

enclosure: resume

Companion resume: 10-22

Sawyer Monroe

sawyer.monroe@gmail.com
23 Strawberry Park Lane, New Rochelle, NY 10805
914-349-5550 (Home) ▪ 914-207-8243 (Mobile)

April 30, 2009

Evelyn Kirkpatrick
Executive Recruiter
Dewey & Hanson Professional Recruiters
283 Madison Avenue, Suite 17-B
New York, NY 10016

Dear Ms. Kirkpatrick:

If one of your clients could benefit through the addition of a senior-level marketing/sales professional with an outstanding record of turnaround success, I suggest it would be to our mutual advantage to meet.

As my enclosed resume demonstrates, my background reflects a continuum of progressively successful sales and marketing experience and a significant profit contribution for each company with which I have been associated. This experience is complemented by exceptional business acumen and proven success in establishing and exceeding strategic business initiatives. I have special expertise in defining business and organizational objectives and then staffing/directing/motivating people to achieve aggressive goals.

In my current post with Eurosports Ltd., I have utilized innovative and creative skills in developing a presence and building a U.S. business for this publicly held company in a highly competitive market. I have achieved rapid results through strong relationship-building techniques and a solid network of alliances throughout the industry. In some of my previous assignments, I demonstrated the ability to quickly turn around lagging operations and focus on premium service, cost-containment initiatives, and exemplary marketing/sales success.

I am equally confident of my ability to make a significant contribution to your client's organization. I look forward to speaking with you to explore how my background might represent an appropriate fit for one of your current or anticipated searches. Thank you for your consideration.

Sincerely,

Sawyer Monroe

Enclosure

Companion resume: 10-24

Stuart R. Moore

srmoore@aol.com

Moscow, Russia
Tel.: (095) 123-45-67
Fax: (095) 456-78-90

April 30, 2009

Philip Douglas, Executive VP—Sales
Breadbasket, Inc.
2525 Prairie Boulevard
Kansas City, MO 64114

Dear Mr. Douglas:

Expansion into international markets brings enormous rewards to companies that are well positioned for success: those that understand global cultures and economies, know how to position their products, and can count on experienced leadership for their international sales initiatives.

With 20 years of significant contributions in agribusiness sales and marketing—including remarkable success stories launching into international markets—I have much to offer your company. Representative achievements include the following:

- 2000% jump in business in year one, 400% increase in year two, for a newly launched sales operation in Russia.

- Successful introduction of branded products into the consumer market in Russia.

- Recovery of more than $20 million in an otherwise lost joint venture investment through astute analysis of import regulations and identification of business irregularities.

Living in Russia for the past 12 years, my family and I have gained a deep appreciation for its history, tradition, culture, and people. Family priorities dictate that we return to the U.S. for at least the next several years. For this reason I am seeking a U.S.–based opportunity where my broad experience and proven skills will be valuable to an organization's international sales and marketing operation.

Naturally, Breadbasket's agribusiness focus is a strong attraction. I am confident that I can help you initiate or expand your global sales activity. My consistent track record with Worldwide Grain Products and other agribusiness companies demonstrates my thorough understanding of the market focus and sales strategies that are successful for our industry, and I can develop both programs and people for successful achievement of sales goals.

May we schedule a time to explore mutual interests? I am readily available by phone (there is a 9-hour time difference between Moscow and Kansas City) or would welcome an initial dialogue via e-mail. As well, I travel frequently to the U.S. and can easily schedule an in-person meeting to coincide with my next visit.

Sincerely,

Stuart R. Moore

enclosure

Companion resume: 10-26

PART 3

Job Search Strategies for Sales and Marketing Professionals

Now that you've completed your resume, are you ready to launch your job search? Maybe, maybe not. Before you start, take the time to review this part of the book. It begins with chapter 13, an overview of a variety of job search strategies. I present the pros and cons of each method and give you a checklist for determining whether that strategy is right for you.

In chapter 14 I share some insight into how recruiters, HR professionals, and hiring managers view your resume and your candidacy. In chapter 15 I provide some practical information on how to manage and conduct your search in an efficient and effective way.

Chapter 13

Use Marketing and Sales Strategies for an Effective Job Search

As a sales and marketing professional, you have a giant job search advantage over people in other professions: You know the fundamentals of the sales process. Essentially, a job search is a sales campaign. For a successful search, apply your professional skills, and use the same process to market yourself as you would a product or service.

First, it's essential to know your product and to position yourself in the market-place. Start by applying fundamental marketing concepts to develop a clear picture of your marketability. Good sources of this information are the career target statement you developed in chapter 1 and the profile or summary on your resume.

The Four Elements of Your Sales Strategy

Product, place, promotion, and price are the four key components of classic marketing theory and practice. In this section we look at you, your resume, and your job search using these same four cornerstones.

Product

Your "product statement," a summary of your marketable skills, will be invaluable throughout your job search, particularly as a quick introductory summary for use in networking encounters or in response to the "So, tell me about yourself" request that starts off many interviews. Here's an example of a product statement for Stuart Moore, whose resume is sample 10-26:

I'm a senior sales manager with expertise in domestic and international agribusiness. Most recently I launched my company into the Russian market with a great deal of success—we actually increased sales 2,000% my first year in Moscow and another 400% my second year. In 10 years with Worldwide Grain Products I progressed through sales and sales management positions in the U.S. and gained considerable expertise in export sales and U.S. sales to Fortune 100 manufacturers. My key strengths are strategic sales planning, newbusiness development, and leadership of very productive teams.

Place

Continue your product statement by visualizing where you see yourself—at what level with your next employer, in what kind of environment, and geographically. Here's Stuart's "place" statement:

My experience at the director level in Russia has given me the opportunity to prove my leadership skills, and I feel very well equipped to take on a senior-level position where I can develop sales strategy and create programs at the corporate level. My family and I would prefer to return to the U.S. for the next few years, although we are very open to another global assignment in the future. I continue to find the agribusiness industry exciting and believe we're only beginning to realize global business opportunities. My international experience would be valuable to a company that already operates internationally or one that is contemplating this kind of expansion. My recent direct experience can help guide a new global initiative.

Promotion

What are the best channels for promoting your candidacy to potential employers? Later in this chapter I discuss a number of approaches and the rationale for using each, so you can develop your own unique promotional strategy. For best results, I recommend a broad, integrated strategy during a job search rather than a narrowly focused effort. In other words, you might feel confident that an executive recruiter is the best method for you—and you might be right—but you shouldn't limit yourself to that approach. The cliché about not putting all your eggs in one basket is very true in a job search. Because no single method works without fail every time, you're better off dividing your efforts among several channels to improve your chances of finding out about appropriate opportunities.

Price

What price will you command in the marketplace? While, of course, you're not a commodity with a firm purchase price, there are "going rates" for employees just as there are for products and services. Although it is never to your advantage to initiate a discussion of salary or to state salary requirements in your correspondence during a job search (with the exception of contact with executive recruiters, as described more fully later in this chapter), you do need to know the ballpark range for the positions you're considering.

You can glean salary information in a number of ways—among them, advertisements and Internet job postings, your knowledge of the salary ranges at your current and past employers, salary surveys (available through industry organizations and online research), informal networking, feedback from recruiters, and direct research into a specific company. Do your homework during your job search so that you feel confident that your salary expectations are reasonable for your target positions. And then wait to discuss salary until you're offered the job.

Craft a Sales Strategy: Identify Potential Buyers

Now that you've firmly established your marketability, you can develop a sales strategy to achieve your career goal. Determine which combination of methods you will use to find prospective employers—"buyers" for you and your skills.

The first step to finding an employer is finding *potential* employers. This means finding companies in your target industry or industries that hire people for the kind of job you want, or that have a demonstrated need for an individual with your capabilities. Furthermore, it's important to identify the names of individuals at those companies—people you can use as networking contacts, and the managers who make hiring decisions for your target position.

Some of the prospects you'll uncover will have immediate needs: an available job opening that matches your career target. Many others, of course, will need to be qualified and developed and may, given time and effort, yield valuable leads.

There are several generally accepted methods of finding out about job opportunities. Each has its benefits and drawbacks, but you should include all of them, to greater and lesser degrees, in an integrated search. The following sections discuss each method in detail.

Posted or Published Job Openings

This is the easy one: an announced opening for a job that suits your needs and matches your qualifications. Openings are still published in print (daily newspapers, business journals, and industry magazines and newsletters). Much more commonly, they also are published online, at general-purpose job sites (such as monster.com, careerbuilder.com, and craigslist.org), special-focus sites (such as the Web sites of professional associations), subscription sites (including execunet.com, netshare.com, and executiveregistry.com), and on the Web sites of many companies.

Benefits

◆ **Ease:** Ads are readily available and job requirements are clearly spelled out.

◆ **Convenience:** Contact information is given, making it a simple matter for you to throw your hat into the ring.

Drawbacks

◆ **Competition:** Thousands of competitors find out about these jobs just as easily as you do, meaning that no matter how closely your background fits the job requirements, there will be many, many others with equally good qualifications. In fact, applicants from all over the country and around the world have identical access to these posted openings.

◆ **Limited contact information:** Many help-wanted ads are published without the name of an individual for follow-up and may even be "blind" ads that don't identify so much as the company name. In most cases, both the position and the company are legitimate. Reasons for running blind ads include not wanting to be bothered by follow-up from job seekers and not wanting to alert the person presently holding that job that he or she is about to be replaced. In any event, quite often you'll be in the uncomfortable position of sending a resume to an unnamed person in response to an ad for a position with an unknown company. Before replying to these ads, try to obtain the name of the contact person (call the company if you can).

◆ **Fishing expeditions:** Occasionally a search firm will place a blind ad in hopes of attracting a field of good recruits for an assignment it anticipates receiving, or for an industry or field in which it is active. Companies have been known to place want ads to comply with corporate recruiting policies when in fact the position has been filled or there is a handpicked candidate in the wings. When you apply, you're sending in your resume for a position that does not exist.

◆ **Scarcity:** Particularly at higher levels of sales and marketing management, or in highly specialized industries, want ads for your target positions may be few and far between.

Conclusions

You shouldn't ignore published opportunities, but you should expend no more than 15 percent of your resources (time, energy, and money) pursuing this strategy during your job search. Approach these listings realistically, do what you can to develop contact names, and take the time to follow up each ad response with a phone call whenever possible. But don't be surprised if you receive no reply to ads for which you seem supremely qualified. Finally, consider using a job aggregator, such as indeed.com or simplyhired.com, which will compile all relevant listings from a vast array of online sources. This can help you be more efficient and waste less time surfing for long-shot opportunities.

CHECKPOINT ✔

I'll include posted openings in my job search strategy because I

❏ Want to become familiar with keywords and job requirements for my targeted positions.

❏ Work in a specialized field where one of the best sources of finding out about new positions is through an industry publication.

❏ Want to learn about companies and opportunities in a new city.

❏ Figure they're worth a shot.

Direct Application to Companies (with or Without a Posted Position)

Because many jobs are filled before there is a chance to advertise them, it makes sense to approach companies directly even if they have not advertised for someone with your qualifications. And, as mentioned in the preceding section, lots of companies post their open jobs on their corporate Web sites. An application can lead to an interview, or at the very least might yield some interesting information about the company and perhaps a new networking opportunity.

Companies receive unsolicited resumes all the time and rely on them as an in-house resource when they begin the task of filling a position. Resume databases and applicant-tracking systems have reduced the burden of storing and accessing thousands of resumes and made the phrase "We'll keep your resume on file" more than a polite form of rejection.

Benefits

♦ **Ease:** It's a relatively simple matter to identify companies that might need a sales and marketing professional with your background. Contact the research librarian at your local library for assistance with industry directories and other resources. Check the Yellow Pages, business-to-business directories, and other print and online resources. See if an annual business guide is published by the business journal in the cities and regions you're interested in. When sending a general-inquiry letter, send your resume to the head of the corporate sales and/or marketing department or the company CEO. In your correspondence, explain why you selected the company. What is it about this company that makes it an excellent match for your background?

♦ **Availability:** Another method of finding and contacting companies directly is through a direct-mail campaign. You can purchase a mailing list or work with a database provider to select criteria and develop a targeted mailing list of potential employers and then create and send mass-mail letters. A good resume service can point you in the direction of these database sources.

♦ **Ability to follow up:** Having uncovered a contact name at your target company, you can and should follow up all correspondence with a phone call and attempt to generate an in-person meeting. Remember, to get a job you need to interview with people who have hiring authority. Your initial get-acquainted meeting gets your foot in the door.

♦ **Development of the contact person:** Your letter, follow-up phone call, and initial interview can develop your contact person from a cold prospect to a warm lead. Even if your approach to this company is unproductive, your contact may be able to provide valuable information that can lead you to other companies and contacts. (See the "Networking" section later in this chapter.)

◆ **Being in the right place at the right time:** With the overload of resumes and applications most companies have to deal with, sometimes the person who's "on the spot" has a terrific advantage over others who are simply data in a database.

Drawbacks

◆ **No control over timing:** It's quite rare that you'll send your resume to a company just when an appropriate opportunity becomes available. Unless a need opens up during the time of your search, your overtures to this company will be unproductive.

◆ **Flood of applicants:** Because it's so easy to e-mail a resume or complete an online application, companies face an overwhelming number of applicants. Instead of sending your resume to every company you can think of, try to be certain that your qualifications are a good match for the company's products, services, and industry.

◆ **Expense:** Mass mailings can be expensive, and there's no guarantee that any of the companies you are cold-calling will yield strong job leads.

Conclusions

Direct contact with companies is a worthwhile investment of your job seeking resources, and your research can put you in touch with businesses you might never have thought to contact. Online applications can be a great time- and expense-saver, and a direct-mail campaign is a good way to broaden your search and reach hiring managers directly.

CHECKPOINT ✔

I'll include direct company contact in my job search strategy because I

❑ Am willing to do the research to locate target companies.

❑ Believe my background is well suited to specific industries.

❑ Believe company culture and growth plans are supremely important, and I will research and apply to companies that are a good match for my priorities.

❑ Can develop contacts at target companies through networking sources.

Executive Recruiters

Recruiters are in the business of filling jobs, so this approach seems like an obvious and easy choice. Bear in mind, however, that the recruiter works not for you but for the employer, who pays a retainer fee or commission for the recruiter's services. Recruiters have no vested interest in you as an individual, nor do they have any motivation to help you find a job, unless you closely match the requirements of a position they're trying to fill.

Many job seekers give recruiters poor marks for follow-up and future focus. After all, their reasoning goes, if these individuals frequently fill positions for people with my background, why wouldn't they want to keep my resume on file and spend some time getting to know me now, in anticipation of an upcoming assignment? There is logic to this thinking, and the occasional recruiter will make the effort to cultivate applicants for future consideration. However, the vast majority are simply too busy, and too focused on immediate needs, to take the time to do this. Recruiters also approach the search with a very specific set of "job specs" for the position they're trying to fill, and if you aren't an exact match, they will continue searching until they find candidates who are.

If you can keep in mind their motivating forces and priorities, you will not be disappointed when recruiters don't return your calls or fail to follow up on your response to an ad for which you are clearly qualified. Chances are, they have uncovered enough other candidates who are even more closely matched, or they have concluded that placement and moved on to the next assignment.

Because recruiters need to present a very close match to their clients, they don't want to waste your, their, or their client's time if there are any factors that will rule you out of contention. For this reason, it's acceptable to share salary information with recruiters so that they can place you in the ballpark of comparable positions. And because recruiter commissions are usually based on a percentage of your future salary, the recruiter has a strong incentive to help you negotiate a top salary.

Benefits

◆ **Excellent source of senior-level positions:** Many higher-level corporate positions are filled by executive recruiters.

◆ **Relative ease and availability:** There are print and electronic databases of executive recruiters. You can find them online or work with a resume writer or career coach to develop a targeted list of recruiters to contact. Send your resume by e-mail as a Word attachment. And don't be afraid to send it to many recruiters! If you wait for one recruiter to "find a job" for you, you'll be waiting an awfully long time (maybe forever).

◆ **Specialization:** Most recruiters specialize in functional areas or industries—or both. For instance, a recruiter might focus on the information technology industry, placing candidates for all levels and all kinds of positions, including sales and marketing. Another recruiter might place *only* sales and marketing people, but in a wide range of industries. Directories almost always provide the recruiter's area(s) of specialization, and databases make it easy to sort and classify the data into good matches for your functional and industry preferences.

◆ **Terrific source of "inside" information:** If a recruiter has recommended you to his client (the hiring company), you can be certain that the recruiter will do everything in his or her power to advance your candidacy. Listen carefully to interviewing suggestions, company information, hiring manager stories, or any other data the recruiter shares, and use it to your advantage during the interview process.

◆ **Ability to build relationships:** The best time to develop ongoing relationships with executive recruiters is when you're not looking for a job. When a recruiter calls you, take the time to chat for a few minutes and, when you can, refer a friend or colleague who might be a good fit for the currently available position (if you're not interested). Stay in touch from time to time with recruiters you like and respect, and call them first when you decide to launch a job search. You're then working from a warm relationship rather than a cold call.

Drawbacks

◆ **A recruiter's priorities may be different from yours:** Recruiters want to put together a perfectly qualified slate of candidates to present to their clients—and often they need to do so in a very short time frame. If you return a phone call a day or a few hours too late, their interest has evaporated. Remember, they're not really interested in you and your needs, but in how you fit the specifications of the job they're trying to fill.

◆ **Rigidity:** Recruiters have very little leeway in trying to persuade their clients to accept a square peg for a round hole. If you come to the job search from a different industry, or don't have a strong and progressive career in your field, you will have limited success with recruiters.

◆ **Investment:** Because it's evident that you shouldn't limit yourself to a handful of recruiters, the time and dollars needed to launch a wide recruiter contact campaign can add up.

Conclusions

Contact with executive recruiters should definitely be part of the self-marketing strategy for sales and marketing professionals seeking six-figure salaries. If you want to change industries or functions, invest less in this method and spend more time on networking activities (described later in this chapter), where you can develop personal introductions.

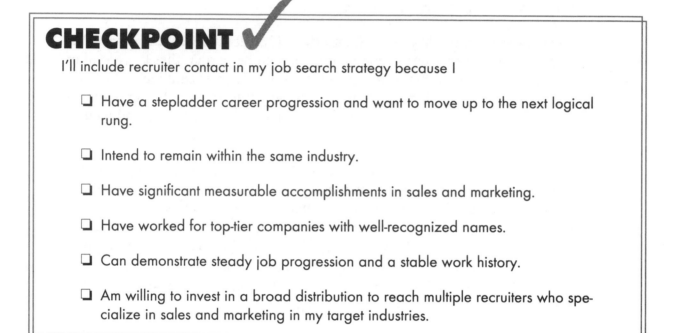

CHECKPOINT ✔

I'll include recruiter contact in my job search strategy because I

❏ Have a stepladder career progression and want to move up to the next logical rung.

❏ Intend to remain within the same industry.

❏ Have significant measurable accomplishments in sales and marketing.

❏ Have worked for top-tier companies with well-recognized names.

❏ Can demonstrate steady job progression and a stable work history.

❏ Am willing to invest in a broad distribution to reach multiple recruiters who specialize in sales and marketing in my target industries.

College or University

The alumni and/or career placement office at your college or university can be an excellent career marketing resource. This is particularly true if your school is prominent in the city you're targeting and has many graduates working and living in the area, if your school's alumni (or fraternity brothers or sorority sisters) form a tight network offering mutual support, or if your college major represents an industry or functional specialization that promotes feelings of camaraderie. From the alumni office or fraternity/sorority office, obtain lists of graduates indicating current employment. Then, either start a phone-call campaign or send a mass mailing or e-mailing to "fellow Tau Tau Taus from Saginaw Tech." At the career placement office, inquire about companies that frequently recruit your school's graduates and obtain the names of company contacts.

Benefits

◆ **Ease and convenience:** With a few phone calls, you should be able to develop a list of networking contacts and recruiting companies to integrate into your marketing strategy.

◆ **Networking connection:** Any cold contact is easier if you can start with a mutual frame of reference.

◆ **Broad scope of contacts:** Outreach to your college should yield a diverse group of contacts and an introduction to companies that you might not have learned about through other research methods.

Drawbacks

◆ **Tenuous connection:** Depending on the size of your college and the closeness it promotes among its graduates, you might feel uncomfortable trying to establish a connection with graduates you don't know.

◆ **Time and expense:** Your university research could generate a long list of contacts, and conducting an effective contact and follow-up campaign will require quite an investment of your resources.

Conclusions

If your college was small and your classmate and fraternity/sorority connections are close, this avenue will be more promising for you than for those who rather anonymously attended a large state university. But do take the time to make the initial phone calls to the alumni and career placement offices. You might find a warm welcome and lots of good suggestions, and you just might discover an entry to a company or industry you've been targeting.

CHECKPOINT ✔

I'll contact the alumni and career placement offices at my college because I

❏ Attended a school that is well recognized in my target cities.

❏ Belonged to a fraternity or sorority.

❏ Attended a small school with close-knit students and alumni.

❏ Have an MBA or other specialized graduate degree that is highly sought by recruiters, consulting firms, and prestigious organizations.

Internet Job Sites and Resume Posting Sites

Information and services available on the Internet form a central part of most job searches. There are literally thousands of job posting sites, resume and career services sites, career-related articles and blogs, and resume posting locations. But if you're not careful, the Internet can absorb enormous amounts of your time for small (if any) reward. It's easy to become engrossed in checking out job postings, reading articles, and following links to new locations, only to discover several hours later that you've made no measurable progress in your job search. But with good time management, you will find the Internet to be an invaluable tool and an amazing resource.

Do use the Internet to research companies and industries you're targeting or companies where you have scheduled interviews. Surf a few of the career information sites initially, and then select those that seem most promising and return periodically. A great place to start is www.job-hunt.org, a comprehensive source of career-related resources and sites.

Consider subscribing to one of the executive-level career sites. Unlike the free sites, these subscriber sites can be accessed beyond their introductory pages only by members. Mid- to upper-level professional and management positions are posted (minimum salary $100,000), and the sales and marketing field is well represented. The jobs listed are allegedly "unadvertised elsewhere." Most are posted by executive recruiters, who use these sites to attract a large number of high-caliber candidates. The sites I recommend to my clients are

www.execunet.com

www.netshare.com

www.executiveregistry.com

www.bluesteps.com

Job postings are not the only services available to members. You will also find such information as expert articles and industry reports, and such services as resume review and peer-to-peer networking.

Keep in mind that the competition for Internet-posted positions is fierce. Lots of people find out about them, and lots of people respond because it's so easy to simply e-mail a resume. Often you won't receive a response to ads for which you seem to be a perfect fit! A realistic approach is to view the Internet as one (small) part of your complete strategy.

On the Internet you also have the opportunity to post your resume on general sites such as Monster and CareerBuilder, industry-specific sites such as Dice.com for technology-related careers, and directly on the sites of executive recruiters and corporations. Again, as part of an integrated search, this can be a worthwhile activity, and in most cases it will not cost you anything but time. (You will need the ASCII-text version of your resume discussed in chapter 3.) Just don't assume that this is the only strategy you will need. Cover your bases, and then move on to other, more worthwhile activities that will put you in touch with network contacts or hiring managers.

Benefits

◆ **Speed, immediacy, ease, convenience, low cost, and wide availability of unlimited information:** The Internet is an excellent source of general job search guidance.

Drawbacks

◆ **Credibility:** Just because something is published on the Internet doesn't mean it's true. Apply the same healthy skepticism to any information you locate on the Internet as you would in real life. Before using an Internet service, investigate its credentials.

◆ **Time:** The Internet can consume an inordinate amount of your time if you let it. Set specific goals and time limits before signing on.

◆ **Passivity:** Remember, jobs are generated through interviews with people—not through resumes alone, and not by surfing career sites on the Internet.

◆ **Exposure:** It's not a good idea to post your resume on the Internet if your search is highly confidential.

Conclusions

The Internet has revolutionized how many of us conduct daily business and is a very large presence in the world of career transition. Use it wisely, and it can yield immensely valuable information and helpful connections, easily and at low cost.

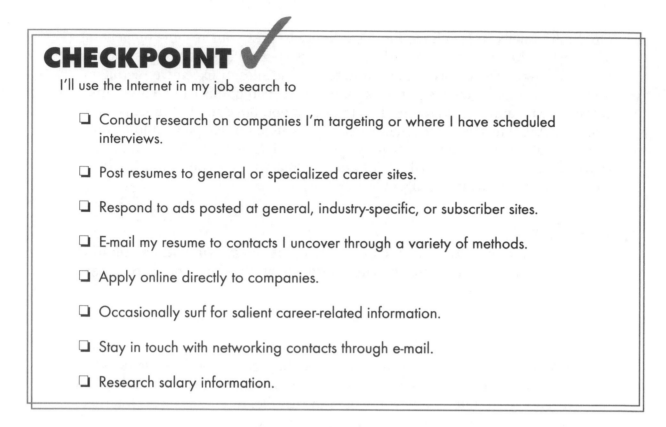

CHECKPOINT ✔

I'll use the Internet in my job search to

❏ Conduct research on companies I'm targeting or where I have scheduled interviews.

❏ Post resumes to general or specialized career sites.

❏ Respond to ads posted at general, industry-specific, or subscriber sites.

❏ E-mail my resume to contacts I uncover through a variety of methods.

❏ Apply online directly to companies.

❏ Occasionally surf for salient career-related information.

❏ Stay in touch with networking contacts through e-mail.

❏ Research salary information.

Professional Associations

Professional associations provide an instant network of people who can help you in your search. If you have been active in a professional association in sales and marketing, in your specific industry, or in a general business organization such as the Chamber of Commerce, you will have made excellent connections you can contact at the start of your search. If you haven't been active, it's not too late. Particularly if you are unemployed, it's helpful to become involved in your professional association: volunteer, take on a leadership position, and demonstrate your capabilities to people who can influence your job search. Many professional associations have membership beyond the immediate local chapter, and you can use membership directories to develop networking contacts just as you would use an alumni or fraternity/sorority list.

Conferences and meetings of professional associations also offer excellent networking opportunities and may allow you to connect with high-level individuals within your industry or people at the companies you're targeting.

Benefits

◆ **Natural networking opportunities.**

◆ **Ease and convenience** of identifying potential networking contacts through association directories.

Drawbacks

◆ **Time:** You need to build relationships and credibility within an organization before you can effectively network with fellow members.

◆ **Confidentiality and competition:** In the same field, you might feel reluctant to broadcast your job search for fear of alerting your current employer. And if you signed a noncompete clause, it might preclude you from seeking work with competing organizations. But you can certainly network with these people, regardless of your ability to accept a job with their organization.

Conclusions

Professional associations offer excellent opportunities and advantages for your job search. You'll be better positioned to capitalize on these if you have been an active member, but it's never too late to join and participate in association activities.

CHECKPOINT ✓

I'll include professional associations in my job search strategy because I

❏ Belong to one or more professional organizations whose members can be influential in my job search.

❏ Have a strong track record of active participation in association activities.

❏ Can attend seminars, conventions, or professional meetings to develop relationships and make connections with industry leaders.

❏ Can use association activities to demonstrate my leadership abilities and professional skills.

Your References

As part of your job search preparation, you should put together a list of four to six people who will give you a glowing reference when a prospective employer calls them.

But don't limit the assistance from your references to what they can do after you've uncovered an interviewing opportunity; let your references be part of your network. Once they've agreed to serve as references, send these contacts a copy of your resume and follow up with a phone call. Make sure they're clear about your career target, and ask whether they can offer any suggestions or referrals. Because your references are people who know you well and think highly of you and your professional abilities, they should be more than glad to assist you. They'll refer or introduce you to people who will be presold on you based on the flattering portrait your reference paints of you.

Benefits

◆ **Ease, convenience, and low cost.**

◆ **Personal and highly positive referrals.**

Drawbacks

◆ **Limited number:** Obviously, it doesn't make sense to rely on four, six, or ten references as your only source of personal referrals.

Conclusions

Mining your references for networking leads is a valuable and often overlooked job search tool. Your references should be glad to assist you; let them, and guide them in the best ways they can help. And, of course, be prepared to return the favor in the future.

CHECKPOINT ✔

I'll use my references as networking contacts in my job search because

❏ My references are well known and highly regarded in my field, industry, or target cities.

❏ My references know me well and have offered to assist me with my job search in any way they can.

❏ I value the expertise and wisdom of my references and will gratefully accept their suggestions.

Networking

It's trite but true: Most people find new jobs through people they know. This fact is borne out in survey after survey, year after year, and is as true today as it was 50 or 100 years ago.

Does that mean it's a waste of time to pursue any other activities? Of course not. There is no infallible formula for finding the best job for you at this point in your career. A job search is a journey with countless interconnecting paths, and it's to your advantage to incorporate many different strategies in your search.

However, it is important to spend most of your time during a job search in live conversation with real people. That's what networking means: talking to people, sharing your career goals, asking for their assistance, and soliciting their advice. Networking doesn't always mean a business-suited meeting with a corporate big cheese (although it can); it can be as casual as a conversation at a soccer game, a chat with your neighbor, or a comment to your dentist. The beauty of networking is that you never know how other people are connected—who they know, or who they're related to.

Nowadays, of course, online resources have sprung up to promote social networking, or the building and leveraging of relationships online rather than in person. Regardless of how you connect with a new contact—in person or online—the rules of networking remain the same. Be sure to follow them for the best results.

When you make networking connections, be sure to give your contacts something specific with which they can help you. Saying, "I'm looking for a sales management job; do you know of any?" will usually yield a negative reply and an end to the conversation. Instead, spend a few minutes sharing information about yourself (you can use your product statement, discussed at the beginning of this chapter) and—as specifically as possible—what you're looking for. "I've learned a lot about Acme Corporation, and it seems that their new product lines would be a great fit for my background. Do you know someone who works there?" Or simply ask for their advice, suggestions, and referrals.

Soliciting feedback on your resume can be a great starting point. One of my clients used this pretext to approach dozens of people she barely knew. Most were quite happy to give her their advice for improving her resume. She did this for a few months, always being extremely appreciative and taking care to impress the contacts with her professionalism and potential during their in-person meeting. She never changed a word on her resume, but she did garner great leads and, within a few months, a job offer with her number-one targeted company.

You can also find formal networking groups devoted to helping members find a job, land a piece of business, or otherwise succeed through personal introductions. In the job search field, the executive networking meetings offered by ExecuNet (www.execunet.com) are well established and are offered in many major cities.

Networking should be a central component of every job search, whatever your level, industry, or specific job target. As a sales and/or marketing pro, you are probably quite comfortable with the process of making connections, talking to people, and pursuing leads. If you feel uncertain about how to network, what to ask, and how to develop leads from your contacts, visit your local library or bookstore for one of the many excellent books devoted to the subject. Learn the process and follow it diligently, and you'll reap large rewards.

Benefits

◆ **Low cost and convenience.**

◆ **The most beneficial activity you can pursue.**

Drawbacks

◆ **Time-consuming and possibly unproductive:** Not all your networking contacts will be able to help you. And it will take a while to organize, contact, and chat with the many people you'll uncover during the job search process. Locating a job through word of mouth might be effective, but it's not systematic or particularly efficient; be prepared to go through a lot of contacts before you reach any solid job leads.

Conclusions

It would be foolish to neglect this strategy, the undisputed champion of helping people find jobs. Pull out that sales rep personality and go after leads, contacts, rumors, any scrap of information. Use the tiniest "in" to get in front of hiring authorities for jobs you want.

CHECKPOINT ✔

I'll incorporate significant networking activity in my job search strategy because I

❏ Realize it is the single most effective method of finding a new job.

Online Image Building

More and more recruiters and employers are routinely using the Internet to search out potential employees and investigate candidates during the selection process. If they google your name, will they find information that is consistent with the image you are portraying in your resume, during interviews, and at every stage of your job search?

Although you can't control every appearance of your name on the Internet, there is a lot you can do to reinforce your professional image. What's more, the more visible and active you become, the greater your chances of being found by a recruiter or employer, and the better your opportunities to make connections to your target companies through online networking.

Consider these sources and sites for establishing your online presence:

◆ **LinkedIn:** Currently the gold standard for professional online networking, LinkedIn offers free and paid services with increasing levels of interactivity. At the basic level, you can create an online profile, build a network, participate in forum discussions, and look for network connections.

◆ **ZoomInfo:** This site aggregates information that is available about you on the Internet. You should check it for accuracy, make any corrections, and insert a positive profile about yourself.

◆ **VisualCV:** At VisualCV.com you can create a stunning online portfolio to enhance your standard paper resume. The service is free to job seekers and offers some connections to employers who have signed up to view the VisualCVs. Multiple privacy settings allow you to control who sees your site.

◆ **Blogs:** You can create your own blog or simply read and comment on career-relevant blogs to make your name and opinions visible to other readers. Look for opportunities to express your expertise in your specific field of sales, marketing, or business development.

◆ **Twitter:** Build a following and follow others you admire. A key benefit of Twitter is its immediacy. You might just find out about the perfect opportunity and be able to connect with the decision-maker within seconds!

◆ **YouTube, Facebook, and MySpace:** Whatever you choose to put on your pages on these social sites, be 100 percent certain that it will not harm your career. It's perfectly acceptable to express your personality, but don't assume that hiring authorities will never see these sites because they are personal rather than professional. In fact, they will.

Online sites, services, trends, and capabilities continue to evolve at a lightning pace. Regardless of what innovations occur between the time I am writing this chapter and you are reading it, there is no doubt that the Internet will be an essential component of career management. Stay on top of what's new and use it to your advantage.

Benefits

◆ **Ease, convenience, and low cost:** All it takes is time and dedicated effort for you to establish a terrific online presence.

- ◆ **Longevity:** Whatever you put on the Net stays on the Net. (This can be a drawback, too!) It will be there tomorrow, next month, and years into the future.

- ◆ **Serendipity:** You increase your chances of being in the right place at the right time if your information is readily available, up to date, and easily accessed by anyone surfing the Internet.

Drawbacks

- ◆ **Permanence and lack of control:** As noted previously, anything that is negative or inconsistent about you that exists in cyberspace may be out of your control and impossible to eradicate.

- ◆ **Time:** You can spend a tremendous amount of time updating your online profile or Web portfolio; reading and writing blog posts; searching for network connections; and e-mailing, texting, or Twittering your existing and new contacts.

- ◆ **Poor connection to specific job opportunities:** For the most part, online sites and sources provide information and connections. They are not an automatic conduit to your next job.

Conclusions

It would be a mistake to ignore online resources or neglect your Web presence. If you become proficient at using the tools that have revolutionized traditional networking, you can take full advantage of their amazing power and reach and create the best possible online image for yourself.

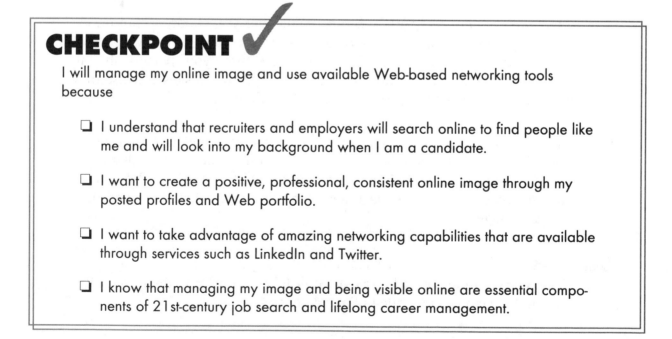

CHECKPOINT ✔

I will manage my online image and use available Web-based networking tools because

- ❏ I understand that recruiters and employers will search online to find people like me and will look into my background when I am a candidate.

- ❏ I want to create a positive, professional, consistent online image through my posted profiles and Web portfolio.

- ❏ I want to take advantage of amazing networking capabilities that are available through services such as LinkedIn and Twitter.

- ❏ I know that managing my image and being visible online are essential components of 21st-century job search and lifelong career management.

Integrate Your Strategies

Now that you've reviewed a number of sales channels for promoting your "product" (yourself), it's time to create an integrated job search campaign with a blend of activities that will lead you toward your goal.

Sample Strategy

As an illustration of how to combine many elements for an integrated search, the following is a sample job search strategy for Stuart, the agribusiness sales executive currently working in Russia whose product statement is shared at the beginning of this chapter:

◆ Identify **executive recruiters** who place high-level sales professionals in the agribusiness industry; send my resume and cover letter via an e-mail campaign.

◆ Develop a **list of target companies** in the industry. Use **networking sources** to develop as many contacts as possible within these companies; develop a personalized letter campaign. For companies where no contacts can be developed, create a **direct-mail campaign** to the company's top sales executive or CEO.

◆ Use my personal network to uncover hidden opportunities.

◆ Contact the **alumni office** at the University of Missouri. Try to develop a list of grads who are in agribusiness. See if the **business school** will share contacts or referrals.

◆ Scan **industry publications** for news that might indicate a need for sales leadership, particularly in new global initiatives. Write personalized, targeted letters for each of these possibilities.

◆ Exploit **active membership in American Agricultural Professionals.** Network with board members and fellow Nominating Committee members; visit the members-only Web site and review job postings; obtain an updated membership directory and contact selected members by e-mail or mail.

◆ Review and respond to **want ads** in industry publications.

◆ Subscribe to one or more of the **executive job posting sites.** Regularly check available positions and respond with an e-mailed letter and resume.

◆ Investigate my **online image** to be sure it is consistent with my current goals.

◆ Build my **online visibility.** Create profiles on LinkedIn and ZoomInfo. Build a VisualCV. Identify appropriate blogs, read them regularly, and comment whenever appropriate. Write an article on doing business in Russia and offer it to American Agricultural Professionals, American Marketing Association, and other sites.

◆ Schedule **interviews** for my next business trip to the U.S. Take a two-week vacation and fill it with prearranged visits and interviews.

◆ **Follow up on all contacts** with telephone calls whenever possible.

◆ Establish an **organizational system** to track contacts, sources, ideas, and opportunities, along with activities, follow-up dates, and outcomes. At the start of each week, establish goals and detailed action plans.

Be Active and Aggressive

One of the most important things to consider as you put together your campaign is whether your strategy is active or passive. Passive strategies involve an initial activity and then a "sit back and wait" approach; you're dependent on the actions of others to move your search forward. Responding to job ads or postings is a passive activity, as is waiting for networking contacts to call you back.

As much as possible, pursue active strategies: Keep the ball in your court and map out a well-organized plan to track your initial and follow-up activities so that you progress as quickly and efficiently as possible. Establish timelines and a schedule of daily and weekly activities, and put these at the top of your daily to-do list. It can be difficult to conduct an active job search if you're holding down a demanding job, raising a family, and involved in community activities. But your search will not be successful until you make it a priority.

DO IT NOW: Create your own self-marketing strategy.

Use a variety of channels, reviewing each "checkpoint" to develop a rationale for including that approach. (For a specific strategy to warrant a serious investment of your job search resources, you should have checked at least half the options in its Checkpoint section.) Concentrate heavily on active strategies and include significant networking activities. To promote action and accountability, break each strategy into specific action items with assigned deadlines for completion. Throughout your job search, review and update your plan at least weekly; establish activity goals for each day, and monitor your progress toward these goals. "Plan your work and work your plan" is just as effective in a job search as it is in daily business activities.

Chapter 14

Appealing to the People Who Can Hire You

From the very beginning of this book, I've talked about meeting the needs of three distinct audiences: executive recruiters, human resources representatives, and hiring managers. Let's examine the motivators and preferences of each of these authorities so that you'll understand and appeal to the needs of these people who are so influential in your job search.

Recruiters

Executive recruiters (sometimes called headhunters) are of two types, differentiated by how they are compensated by their clients:

◆ **Contingent recruiters:** As the name implies, the fees these placement professionals earn are contingent upon successfully placing a candidate with their client, the hiring company. Because there is no risk and some advantage to having more than one contingent recruiter working to fill a specific position, hiring companies sometimes assign a search to more than one search firm. The recruiter works quickly and aggressively to identify candidates, fill the position, earn the commission, and move on to the next assignment. Of course, the recruiter strives to generate repeat business by delivering good candidates and building positive relationships with HR people and hiring managers.

◆ **Retained recruiters:** These recruiters are paid a fee for their services regardless of whether they make a placement. For their fee, in addition to locating and recommending candidates, they might work with their client on additional services, such as writing job descriptions, evaluating internal candidates, and serving as a sounding board and expert resource for top management. Many retained recruiters build long-term relationships with client companies and have an excellent feel for the corporate culture.

Traditionally, retained recruiters have been used for upper-level searches (more than $100,000), but that is no longer strictly true. As the Internet has dramatically changed the business of recruiting, distinctions between recruiters have become less rigid, and these changes are predicted to continue. So don't assume that you should work only with retained recruiters if you're looking for a six-figure position. Instead, classify recruiters according to industry and specialization, and include both contingent and retained recruiters on your contact list.

Nor is it necessary to select recruiters by location. Although some search firms handle the majority of their placements in their immediate geographic area, many take on national and even international searches. There is very little rhyme or reason to a company's choice of search firm; it's often dependent on personal relationships, networking, and referrals, so a company in Atlanta could easily build an ongoing relationship with a search firm in Phoenix. What counts are relationships and results, not location.

Remember that to make headway with your target audiences, you need to appeal to their needs.

For a contingent recruiter, the primary need is to *fill a position* so that he or she can collect a placement fee. The road to filling the position begins with a strong slate of candidates to present to the client (the employer). Do you fit the requirements to a "t"? Are you an "easy sell," or will they have to press your case with their client? (Believe me, they will seldom make this effort.) Are your appearance and demeanor professional? Will you make a good impression on the client and, eventually, the client's customers? Do you have relevant industry experience? What expertise do you offer that will make the employer eager to meet you?

A retained recruiter's needs are similar, but usually with the added challenge of matching the candidate to the client organization's culture. The recruiter wants you to be an extremely good fit so that your presence at the company promotes the longevity of the client-recruiter relationship.

If you're marketing yourself through recruiters, you will be most successful if your career goal is closely related to your most recent position (preferably the next step on the career ladder), if you have a progressively responsible career background with measurable accomplishments in every position, and if you have relevant industry experience. If your career has "hop-scotched" or if you want to change industries, your best job search approach is probably not through recruiters.

With recruiters, your goal is to "pass" the interview process and get in front of the hiring manager. Without that access and interview, you will never get the job.

SURVEY COMMENTS: RECRUITERS

◆ "Search firms should not be used for candidates who want to change industries. Clients will be unwilling to pay our fees." —*contingent recruiter*

◆ "Our clients primarily look for success patterns rather than specific industry experience." —*retained recruiter*

◆ "No candidate with 10 years of experience should have a one-page resume."

◆ "Short tenures with sales and marketing are the kiss of death. Anyone who has... moved on, year after year, will [raise] suitability concerns within the culture of a company."

◆ "An objective or targeted profile is of paramount importance. Recruiters will not guess or take the time to care."

◆ "Candidates need to improve their ability to communicate their contributions, vision, and leadership."

Human Resources

In their role as corporate recruiters, human resources professionals function quite similarly to independent executive recruiters, although obviously for only one employer and without the reward of payment for placement. They should understand the organization's long-range needs and should be looking for someone who fits into that picture. They know the personality of your potential supervisor, the department as a whole, and the company's top executives. The very best HR people are valuable resources to the organization; most have responsibilities beyond recruiting and staffing and want the hiring process to proceed swiftly and smoothly.

When interviewing with human resources representatives, remember that these people do not make hiring decisions. Although your initial contact might be through HR, your goal is to get in front of the hiring manager. (One of my clients provided this pithy bit of advice following a six-month search for a sales position: "Avoid HR whenever possible.") As with executive recruiters, strive to show that you fit the requirements for the position and are worthy of being presented to the ultimate hiring authority: the department-level manager who will make the decision.

SURVEY COMMENTS: HUMAN RESOURCES

◆ "It's easy to get tired reading the same old stuff. Candidates should avoid clichés that amount to a bunch of fluff."

◆ "I look for good employment history with recognizable companies—i.e., Fortune 500, sales achievements, stability."

◆ "I'm impressed when a candidate can say why they want to work for us. I'm generally appalled by the lack of any real research and preparation."

◆ "Use a cover letter that speaks about your value to a corporation. Provide rich detail of the value provided at your current company and the industry segment in which you hope to work. Forget the hype."

◆ "It is always a good idea for job seekers to follow up."

Hiring Managers

The hiring manager—the person with the authority to offer you a job—is usually the head of the department where you'll be working. He or she knows precisely the business problems you'll be called on to solve. This person also is aware of such things as immediate and long-range sales goals; expansion plans; product development ideas; and the strengths, weaknesses, and personalities of the existing sales/marketing team.

With hiring managers, you must show that you understand the corporate culture, can help achieve business goals, are a good fit within the department, bring complementary skills, and fill a specific need. Interviews with hiring managers should be a process of mutual exploration: You find out more about the company, its quirks, and the position, and they determine whether you will fit on their team. Because these managers are intimately involved in the day-to-day business environment, they tend to be more lenient toward less-than-textbook career histories and might value some element of your background that a recruiter would ignore or denigrate.

SURVEY COMMENTS: HIRING MANAGERS

"I always review unsolicited resumes." —*president, advertising agency*

"I don't like receiving unsolicited resumes. I review them briefly, then file." —*sales VP, medical products company*

"[Candidates should] know their strengths as well as the products they sell."

"When interviewing, give specific examples."

"Candidates should find a way to show enthusiasm."

Hiring Survey Results

As a resume writer, I view the world primarily from the job seeker's perspective. Naturally, I try to maintain current information on career trends, hiring practices, and human resources issues. When I began writing this book, however, I decided to conduct a survey of hiring authorities to be certain the information I provided was consistent with the experiences, preferences, and expectations of those on the receiving end of job seekers' resumes.

Survey respondents were senior managers who hire sales and marketing people with salaries starting at $80,000, human resources managers, and contingent and retained executive recruiters who place senior sales and marketing people.

The quotes in the preceding sections were taken from the survey responses; specific data about resume preferences follows.

Preferred Method of Contact

The survey showed opinions all over the board about the best way to initiate contact. Just as firmly as one respondent stated "definitely e-mail" when asked about the preferred method of receiving resumes, another clearly favored faxed resumes, and a third said it doesn't make any difference. However, the preference for e-mailed resumes continues to accelerate, and in most cases you should e-mail your resume as a Word attachment, with your cover letter appearing as the body of your e-mail.

One preference was quite clear from my survey:

◆ For announced openings, 91 percent preferred that candidates forward a resume and then follow up with a phone call within a few days or a week at the most.

◆ Whether or not they liked receiving them, 80 percent agreed that unsolicited resumes should always be followed up with a phone call.

Reviewing Resumes

When asked to rate 11 factors in order of importance to them when reviewing a resume (using a scale of 1 to 11, with 1 being most important), the respondents answered as follows (listed here in order of importance, with averaged ratings):

Factor	Order of Importance
1. Relevant functional experience (sales and/or marketing)	2.8
2. Measurable accomplishments	3.0
3. Overall appearance	3.4
4. Industry experience	4.0
5. Education (bachelor's degree)	5.3
6. Targeted profile or summary	6.3
7. History of advancement	6.8
8. Can be skimmed in 30 seconds	7.0

9. Objective	7.4
10. Computer skills	7.9
11. One page	9.3

This response should certainly debunk the myth that it's essential to keep your resume to one page!

The findings do underscore the critical importance of demonstrating measurable accomplishments on your resume. By following the guidelines in chapters 1 through 3, you can create a resume that clearly meets the needs and preferences of all three of your target audiences.

Nearly as important is the overall appearance of your resume. When asked what factors would make them discard a resume immediately, 90 percent of the respondents mentioned quality and appearance factors (poor appearance, spelling and punctuation errors, sloppiness, typographical errors, low-quality paper, ripped or smudged resumes, failure to use a spell-checker).

You can tell from these survey findings that there is no absolutely tried-and-true method for writing and distributing your resume. Don't worry too much about doing it "just right"—meeting the precise needs of every audience and individual. Just follow the general guidelines I've provided, use common sense, and accept the fact that, to paraphrase Abraham Lincoln, you can't please all of the people all of the time.

Chapter 15

Managing Your Job Search and Your Career

Congratulations! You've identified your career target, written your resume and an initial cover letter or two, created a marketing strategy, and are all set to launch your job search.

Before you start, consider the following brief bits of advice that will help you run your job search more smoothly and productively.

Get Organized

Take the time to create an organizational system for your job search activities. Your system—whether you manage it with paper and pencil, with stacked piles of labeled folders, or with contact-management software—should enable you to

◆ Keep detailed records of people you contact, the gist of your conversation, and follow-up plans and timelines.

◆ Provide storage and ready access to information about positions you've applied for, such as a copy of the want ad or posting, a copy of your cover letter, and notes on your follow-up phone call.

◆ Track networking connections. For instance, if Uncle Joe suggests you contact his Army buddy Jim Kane, who's a purchasing manager at XYZ Corp., and Jim refers you to Anna Winston, the Sales VP at that company, and Anna forwards your resume to a friend who's in HR at Waco Widgets, who then sets you up with the Sales Manager, you need to be able to appropriately thank each link in the chain when you interview for a job selling widgets in Waco.

◆ Manage schedules, activities, and follow up to keep you on track, alert, and constantly aware of the progress of each element of your search.

Tip: Internet-based services have sprung up to meet the need for managing complex activities and connections during a job search. Two that I recommend are JibberJobber.com and CareerShift.com. Check them out and see if these subscription-based services will make your transition smoother and more efficient.

Just as you would for any major project, establish a plan of action to reach your career target. Set measurable goals and monitor your progress. Be as proactive and efficient as possible: Return phone calls promptly, send follow-up letters within a day of every interview, and concentrate your resources on the activities that will give you the greatest reward.

Follow Up

Follow-up letters are an often overlooked but potentially very valuable job search activity. Most people (about 90 percent, according to hiring authorities I contacted) do not send thank-you notes. You will make yourself memorable just by sending one! Not only that, a follow-up letter lets you reiterate key points of the interview, perhaps overcome an objection you didn't address in person, cement your candidacy in the mind of the hiring manager, and make a highly favorable after-interview impression.

Follow-up letters need not be in-depth or lengthy. They should always be positive, appreciative, and complimentary to the company and the person or people you met with.

The following pages show three sample follow-up letters.

Elizabeth D. Norton

23 Mehring Way #235, Cincinnati, OH 45202
513-891-1234   ednorton@fuse.net

October 15, 2009

Stanley Brown
Vice President, Sales
X-ACT Corp.
2357 Lakeview Boulevard
Evanston, IL 60204

Dear Mr. Brown:

Thank you for sharing your valuable time during my visit to Evanston last week. I was very impressed with your facilities and the obvious commitment to keep X-ACT head and shoulders above its competitors.

On a professional level, I am excited about the opportunity, aggressiveness, and technical excellence so evident at X-ACT. Your need for a regional sales manager who can penetrate new business markets seems to closely match my background and proven areas of strength.

During our conversation, we discussed my most recent employer, Cincinnati Software. I agree that the situation I described seems strange; however, it is quite true (though counter to the goals of a thriving business). To clarify any questions you may have on this matter, I urge you to call Sam Trout, Product Development Manager at Cincinnati Software (telephone 513-555-7777); he will be glad to answer your questions and verify my description of the situation.

Thank you for promoting such a friendly and relaxed environment for my visit. It was a pleasure to meet you and the other professionals at X-ACT. I look forward to continuing our dialogue.

Sincerely,

Elizabeth D. Norton

Maria Trujillo

29-A Primrose Court, Nashville, TN 37211
mariatee@hotmail.com • (615) 455-4555

October 19, 2009

Mr. John Allison
Executive Vice President, Sales and Marketing
Office Mates, Inc.
2529 Third Avenue
Nashville, TN 37211

Dear John:

Thank you for the leads you were good enough to pass along in our conversation last week. As I mentioned, my initial conversations and interviews with you sparked my interest in a career in office furniture sales. Since that time, I have done additional research and have been fortunate to make connections with other distributors. The result of all this research is great excitement about the industry and its opportunities, and a growing belief that I am extremely well suited to a sales career in this field.

You can be certain that I will follow up on the referrals you gave me as I am very eager to gain experience in the industry. I hope you'll consider me when your hiring needs change, as I'm certain that I'll be able to present even stronger qualifications than during our recent interviews.

John, thank you for your interest and help. I hope that I can return the favor sometime soon; feel free to call if I can be of assistance at any time. I wish you continued success—and, again, congratulations on your recent promotion!

Best regards,

Maria Trujillo

Corresponds to resume 11-2.

Matthew Adrian

341 Fairview Terrace
Cleveland, Ohio 44125

mattadrian@aol.com
Residence 216-439-7515
Mobile 216-704-1025

October 5, 2009

Ellen T. Wales
Vice President
Medi-Quip, Inc.
2323 Peachtree Plaza
Atlanta, GA 30319

Dear Ms. Wales:

Thank you for taking the time to speak with me on Thursday. I was very impressed with what I learned about your organization, and I remain extremely interested in the opportunity with Medi-Quip.

In particular, I was pleased to learn that Medi-Quip is investing resources in building an organization to serve the increasingly important national accounts market along with developing a program focused on managed healthcare services. These value-added programs can be a worthy negotiating tool and a competitive advantage in closing business important to the continued growth of your organization.

It seems that my background and expertise are a good match for your needs at this time. I look forward to continuing this dialogue.

Sincerely,

Matthew Adrian

Plan for the Future

Although it's impossible to predict just how many jobs you might hold in your lifetime, there is no doubt that the "job for life" mentality of a few decades ago is gone forever. What accounts for so much career transition?

◆ Companies grow, and opportunities for advancement arise. Top-performing employees are promoted into new responsibilities or new areas of the company.

◆ Jobs are eliminated when companies merge, consolidate, or downsize.

◆ Industries shrink and grow. Some even die out. Not too long ago, the job of typesetter required manually placing type to create the words, sentences, and paragraphs that make up books, newspapers, magazines, and countless other publications. That profession was made obsolete by computerized page layout.

◆ New professions are created.

◆ Individuals are fired—perhaps for poor performance, or maybe because of a poor fit with the job or the company.

◆ People change. They might decide to do something entirely different with their careers, and with the increasing availability of top-notch career coaches, they can find expert guidance to help them decide their next career path.

Those who benefit most from all this change, fluctuation, and opportunity are nimble, proactive employees who can respond rapidly when opportunity presents itself.

To make your next job change proceed more swiftly and smoothly, accept the need to constantly manage your career. Think about long-range goals, and take steps now to prepare yourself for your next career target. That might mean pursuing an MBA, improving your computer skills, seeking out a corporate-level project, maintaining networking contacts, or staying up to date on industry trends. By doing so, not only will you position yourself for a successful job change, but you'll become more valuable to your current employer as well.

A simple practice that will yield big benefits is to create and maintain a career portfolio. This can be nothing more than a file folder into which you toss notes, memos, project summaries, performance evaluations, and other evidence of your activities and accomplishments; or it can be as technologically sophisticated as an online portfolio like a VisualCV (see www.visualcv.com). The material in your portfolio will quantify and verify your contributions to your company and give you specific data for writing accomplishment statements for your resume. Periodically review your file and update your resume. Revisit your career target… spend some time thinking about your long-range goals… perhaps develop a mission statement that encompasses career and personal priorities. When it comes time to look for another position, you'll understand clearly where you've been, what you've done, and where you want to go. And you'll have a powerful resume that can help you get there.

May you enjoy the journey as much as the destination.

Index

Q–R